PHILOSOPHY AND YOGA OF SRI AUROBINDO
AND
OTHER ESSAYS

PHILOSOPHY AND YOGA OF SRI AUROBINDO
AND
OTHER ESSAYS

KIREET JOSHI

THE MOTHER'S INSTITUTE OF RESEARCH
in association with
MIRA ADITI, MYSORE

Philosophy And Yoga of Sri Aurobindo And Other Essays (First Edition) is co-published by The Mother's Institute of Research, A-9/24, Vasant Vihar, New Delhi – 110 057 in association with Mira Aditi, 62, Sriranga, 2nd Main, 1st Cross T.K. Layout, Saraswatipuram, Mysore – 570 009, India

© THE MOTHER'S INSTITUTE OF RESEARCH, 2003

All rights reserved. No part of this publication may be reproduced in any form, or by any means, without written permission of the Publisher.

The publication of this book was facilitated by a grant received by The Mother's Institute of Research from the Ministry of Human Resource Development, Department of Education, Government of India, which is gratefully acknowledged.

Cover Concept by Mukesh

First Edition 2003
ISBN 81-85137-94-3

Rs. 250
US $20

Printed at: GDMK Publishers Distributors
WZ-430, E/1, Naraina
New Delhi-110 028 (INDIA)
e-mail: sr_allbooks@vsnl.net

Contents

1. Sri Aurobindo: His Life and Work
   (A Brief Outline)   9

2. The Mother: Her Life and Work
   (A Brief Outline)   13

3. Philosophy and Yoga of Sri Aurobindo   19

4. Vedic Knowledge and Supermind
   in the Light of Sri Aurobindo   43

5. Sri Aurobindo's Philosophy of
   Indian Nationalism   71

6. Sri Aurobindo's Philosophy of
   Nationalism and Internationalism   91

7.	Sri Aurobindo's Philosophy of the Ideal of Human Unity	111
8.	Educational Philosophy of Sri Aurobindo	137
9.	Problem of Knowledge and Sri Aurobindo's Concept of the Supermind	159
10.	Causality, Change and Time Appendix	181
11.	Towards Applied Philosophy	195
12.	Yoga, Religion and Morality	229
13.	Spirituality, Science and Technology	237
14.	Yoga, Science, Religion and Philosophy	241
15.	Yoga and Knowledge	251
16.	Yoga, Consciousness and Human Fulfilment	261
17.	Bondage, Liberation and Perfection	287
18.	Philosophy of Indian Pedagogy	301

19.	Philosophy of Spiritual Education	329
20.	Yoga and Education	349
21.	Concept of Education in Ancient Indian Tradition and Culture: Its Contemporary Relevance	375
22.	Philosophy of Value-Oriented Education – I	401
23.	Philosophy of Value-Oriented Education – II	423
24.	Philosophy of Indianness	435
25.	Indian Identity and Cultural Continuity	449
26.	Indian Culture: Past, Present and Future	457
27.	Philosophy of Indian Art	473
28.	Towards Universal Fraternity	487

SRI AUROBINDO
HIS LIFE AND WORK
(A Brief Outline)

Sri Aurobindo was born on the 15th August 1872 at Calcutta. At an early age of seven, he was taken along with his elder brothers to England for education, since his father wanted him to have no Indian influence in the shaping of his outlook and personality. And yet, even though Sri Aurobindo assimilated in himself richly the best of the European culture, he returned to India in 1893 with a burning aspiration to work for the liberation of India from foreign rule. While in England, Sri Aurobindo passed the I.C.S. Examination, and yet he felt no call for it; so he got himself disqualified by remaining absent from the riding test. The Gaekwar of Baroda happened to be there at that time, and Sri Aurobindo accepted the proposal to be his Personal Secretary, and returned to India.

Soon thereafter, however, Sri Aurobindo switched over to the Baroda College as Professor of French and then of English, and when in 1906, he left for Bengal, he was the acting Principal of the College. It was during the Baroda period that Sri Aurobindo assimilated in himself the spirit and culture of India and prepared himself for his future political and spiritual work. Indeed, his political work had already begun in Baroda, but it was behind the scenes, largely of the nature of a preparation for an armed revolution for the liberation of India.

Sri Aurobindo was the first among the Indian leaders to declare and work for the aim of complete Independence of India. In 1905, Bengal was divided, and Sri Aurobindo left Baroda and, invited by the nationalistic leaders, he joined at Calcutta the newly started National College as its first Principal. It was here that Sri Aurobindo, while working secretly for the revolution, chalked out also a plan of outer action. This plan consisted of the programme of passive Resistance, Boycott and Swadeshi, which was later adopted as the policy of the struggle for freedom. It was here again that Sri Aurobindo wrote powerfully and boldly for *Bande Mataram*, and later for *Karma Yogin*; through his writings, he electrified the nation and surcharged the people with a new energy which ultimately led the nation to her freedom. It was, therefore, significant that when India attained her liberation in 1947, it was on the 15th August, the birthday of Sri Aurobindo.

The pioneering work that Sri Aurobindo did for the liberation of India was evidently a part of his larger work for the entire humanity and for the whole earth. For him, the liberation of India was an indispensable part of the new world-order. Moreover, the practice of Yoga, which he had started in 1902, led him, even while in the thick of intense political and literary activity, to major realisations of the Brahmic Silence, Nirvana, and also of the universal dynamic Presence of the Divine. And, in 1908, when he was in Alipore jail during his trial under the charge of sedition, he received through numerous experiences and realisations the assurance of the liberation of the country and also the knowledge of the initial lines on which his own future work was to proceed. For he saw that even in the field of Yoga something was still lacking, something radical that alone would help resolve the problems of the world and would lead mankind to its next evolutionary stage. And so, in 1910, soon after his acquittal from the jail, he withdrew to Pondicherry to concentrate upon this new research work, to hew a new path. It has been a most dynamic work with the entire earth as its central field. It was in the course of this work that Sri Aurobindo declared that the Suprpamental is the Truth and that its advent on the earth is inevitable. To bring down the supramental consciousness and power on the earth has been the central work of Sri Aurobindo.

Sri Aurobindo has explained the nature of this work, the nature of the Supermind, the necessity of its descent, the process of this descent and the dynamic consequences of this descent for the solutions of the problems of mankind, in his voluminous writings most of which were written serially in the philosophical monthly, *Arya*, which was started in 1914, immediately after the first arrival of The Mother from France to Pondicherry. Some of the most important of these and other writings are: *The Life Divine*, *The Synthesis of Yoga*, *The Ideal of Human Unity*, *The Human Cycle*, *The Foundations of Indian Culture*, *Essays on the Gita*, *On the Veda*, *The Upanishads*, *The Future Poetry*, *The Supramental Manifestation upon Earth*, and the epic *Savitri*.

When Sri Aurobindo withdrew in 1926 into his room for concentrating in the required way on the 'Supramental Yoga', Mother organised and developed his Ashram. In 1943, a school for the education of children was founded, and after the passing of Sri Aurobindo in 1950, Mother developed that school into an International University Centre, where numerous original and bold experiments of education were carried out under her guidance. This educational work was a part of Supramental Yoga, and we have rare insights into education and yoga in the volumes entitled *Questions and Answers*, which contain conversations of the Mother that took place in her classes. In

1958, Mother withdrew to her room in order to come to terms with the research in the problems related to the supramental transformation of the physical consciousness at the cellular level. In 1968, Mother founded Auroville, an International city as a collective field for the material and spiritual researches required for realising human unity as a part of the supramental action on the earth.

Mother's exploration into the body-consciousness and her discovery of a 'cellular mind' capable of restructuring the nature of the body is contained in a document of more than 6000 pages, published in 13 volumes. This is *L'Agenda de Mère* (*Mother's Agenda*), an account of her extraordinary exploration narrated by the Mother to Satprem[1] covering a period of more than twenty years, during which Mother slowly uncovered the 'Great Passage' to the next species by the supramental transformation of the physical consciousness and fulfilled the work that Sri Aurobindo had given to her.

---

[1] Satprem was born in Paris in 1923. After intense experiences in concentration camps and adventures in Guyana, Brazil and Africa, he came to India in 1953, became a Sanyasi and practised Tantrism. Then he left these paths to serve Mother and embarked upon the Integral Yoga of Sri Aurobindo. For 19 years, he lived near the Mother and became her confidant and her witness. He recorded innumerable personal conversations that form *Mother's Agenda*. He has written a biography of Sri Aurobindo under the title, *Sri Aurobindo or the Adventure of Consciousness*. He has also written a biography of the Mother in three volumes, under the titles: *Mother or the Divine Materialism; Mother or the New Species;* and, *Mother or the Mutation of Death*.

THE MOTHER: HER LIFE AND WORK
(A Brief Outline)

The Mother (Mirra Alfassa) was born in Paris on the 21st February, 1878. Her mother was Egyptian and her father was Turkish – both of them were perfect materialists. As a result, although she had inner experiences, including that of the divine presence, right from her childhood, she was in her external life an atheist until she entered into adulthood. In her early years, she had a good grounding in music (piano), painting and higher mathematics.

By the age of eighteen, she had begun to feel an intense need to KNOW, but all that she learnt and studied would explain nothing. Her need to know led here into two directions. The first was the world of painting. She mingled with the artists and widened her horizons. She married a pupil of Gustave Moreau, Henri Morisset, and she came to know Rodin and the great impressionists of that era. The second direction in which she turned was opened up when she heard of Max Theon and his teachings.

At this stage, she had a series of visions, and in several of these visions she saw Sri Aurobindo just as he looked physically, but glorified. She was to meet Sri Aurobindo ten years later in 1914 when she came to India from France, and it was then that she came to identify Sri

Aurobindo of the vision with Sri Aurobindo as she saw him then.

Around this time, she came into contact with Bhagavad-gita through an Indian who had come to Europe. He had told her, "Read it with THAT knowledge – with the knowledge that Lord Krishna represents the immanent God, the God within you." She not only studied the Gita, but within a month, she attained to the realization of the immanent Supreme.

Soon thereafter, she went to Tlemcen in Algeria to work with Max Theon and his wife Madame Theon. Theon was well versed in the Rigveda and he was the first to talk to the Mother of the idea that the earth is symbolic where universal action is concentrated allowing divine forces to incarnate and work concretely. Madame Theon was an extraordinary occultist, having incredible faculties. She could leave one body and enter the consciousness of the next plane, fully experiencing the surroundings and all that was there, describe it... twelve times. The Mother learned to do the same thing and, with great dexterity. In one of her experiences, while entering into the last stage before the Formless, she experienced total Unity. And she found herself in the presence of the "Principle" of the human form. It did not resemble man as we are used to seeing him, but it was an upright form, standing just on the border between the world of forms and the Formless, like a kind of standard or archetype. Afterwards, when Mother met Sri Aurobindo and talked to him about it, he said, "It is surely the prototype of the supramental form."

Soon after her return from Tlemcen in Algeria, there was in 1908 divorce from Henri Morisset. From 1910 to 1920 – these ten years were a period of intensive mental study for the Mother. This mental development in all its comprehensiveness led here to the conclusion that while all ideas are true, a synthesis has to be made, and that there is something luminous and true beyond the synthesis. In her philosophic studies, she was accompanied by Paul Richard who, in his visit to Pondicherry in 1910, had met Sri Aurobindo. In 1914, Mother accompanied Paul Richard to Pondicherry and met Sri Aurobindo on 29th March. In her very first meeting, both Sri Aurobindo and Mother, felt, at exactly the same moment, "now the Realisation will be accomplished." In one of his letters Sri Aurobindo wrote on the Mother as follows:

> Mother was doing Yoga before she knew or met Sri Aurobindo, but their lines of Sadhana independently followed the same course. When they met, they helped each other in perfecting the sadhana. What is known as Sri Aurobindo and the Mother?[1]

After the outbreak of the World War I in August, 1914, the Mother had to return to France along with Paul Richard and then she spent four years in Japan; but she returned for good to Pondicherry in 1920 in order to work with Sri Aurobindo.

On 24th November 1926, Sri Aurobindo attained to a decisive stage and the Overmind was brought down into Matter, and an overmental creation came into view. But the aim was to bring about the supramental creation. As Sri Aurobindo became too occupied with the descent of the supermind, he did not have the time to deal with people, and he put The Mother in charge of all the

---

[1] Sri Aurobindo on Himself, Centenary Library, Volume 26, page 459

disciples and external activities of the Sri Aurobindo Ashram. This was in 1926.

Sri Aurobindo has spoken of the four personalities of the Mother, namely, those of Wisdom (Maheshwari), Power (Mahakali), Harmony (Mahalakshmi) and Perfection in works (Mahasaraswati). In all her activities, these four personalities of the Mother could be seen at work. The work was microscopic; it was complex; it was both external and internal. It became clearer that the task of fixing the Supermind in the physical had to be done by opening up the physical cells. Just when the descent of the supermind reached a critical point, the Second World War broke out. This war was perceived by Sri Aurobindo and the Mother as a fierce resistance to the task of the Supramental descent. Hence, they put all their yogic force against Nazism and the war ended in 1945, with the victory for the Allies as Sri Aurobindo had willed. In early 1950, Sri Aurobindo told the Mother: "One of us must go. We cannot both remain upon earth." And when Mother said, "If one of us must go, I want that it should be me." "It cannot be you," he replied, "because you alone can do the material thing." He forbade the Mother to leave her body. "It is absolutely forbidden," he said, "you cannot, you must remain."

After Sri Aurobindo left his body on 5th December 1950, the Mother continued Sri Aurobindo's work. In 1951, she established the Sri Aurobindo International University Centre, which conducted extraordinary educational experiments to invent a new method of educating children from early childhood upwards so as to prepare them for the supramental work. On 29th February 1956, the Mother declared that the Supramental Light and Force and Consciousness rushed down upon earth in an uninterrupted flow. She wrote: "The manifestation of the

Supramental upon earth is no more a promise but a living fact, a reality."

In 1958, the Mother entered into a new phase of Yoga, which aimed at fixing the supramental consciousness in the cells of the body so as to establish in the world, the conditions of the emergence of the next species, the supramental species that would manifest the Supermind in the supramental body.

It was in the course of this "Yoga of the Cells" that the Mother discovered the "Mind of the Cells" which has the necessary capacity to reconstitute the physical body. This great yogic process has been described in thirteen volumes entitled "The Mother's Agenda", which consists of Mother's conversations with Satprem, one of her disciples, who had become her confidant.

In 1968, Mother founded "Auroville", an international township, a few kilometers away from Pondicherry, as a "laboratory of new evolution."

On 14th March, 1970, Mother declared that the work that Sri Aurobindo had given to her was accomplished. She said, "The physical is capable of receiving the Superior Light, the Truth, the True Consciousness and to manifest it."

Thereafter, she continued to accelerate the evolution of the new species, a task which is still continuing, even though she left her physical body on 17th November, 1973.

BIBLIOGRAPHY

Sri Aurobindo: The Mother, volume 25 of the Centenary edition, published by Sri Aurobindo Ashram, Pondicherry.

The Mother: 15 volumes of Collected Works of the Mother (published by Sri Aurobindo Ashram, Pondicherry).

13 volumes of Mother's Agenda (both in French and English, published by Institut de Rescherches Evolutives, Paris).

Satprem: Mother or the Divine Materialism (1980).
Mother or the New Species, 1982
Mother or the Mutation of Death, 1987.
Sri Aurobindo or the Adventure of Consciousness (1984).
On the Way to Supermanhood (1986).

Sujata Nahar: Mother's Chronicles, 7 volumes (published by MIRA Aditi Centre, Mysore).

Kireet Joshi: Sri Aurobindo and The Mother (published by Mother's Institute of Research and Motilal Banarsidass Pvt. Ltd.)

PHILOSOPHY AND YOGA OF SRI AUROBINDO

I

Sri Aurobindo has significantly been described as adventure of consciousness. Even in his quest of India's freedom, during the first decade of the last century, he departed courageously from the orthodox and conservative path of the Moderates and infused in the country a new electric force of Nationalism. He chalked out a new path of Swadeshi, boycott, passive resistance, and national education, -- the path that ultimately came to be adopted as the national programme during the subsequent period of the struggle. He even ventured to search for a spiritual force that could be applied to the political struggle so as to liberate the country from slavery to the British rule and attain freedom in its totality. In his search for this force, he turned to Yoga and initiated momentous experiments, as a result of which he arrived at the conclusion that Yoga was itself in need of breaking its boundaries so that whatever power it was capable of delivering to humanity would become irresistible in its impact and in the production of results which would secure, not only for India, but also for the entire earth, unshakeable foundations for a new world of freedom and unity.

The life and work of Sri Aurobindo are a living testimony of his victorious opening of the gates of a new power, and by means of summarising in himself the luminous results of all the best of the past systems of Yoga as also by developing a new Yoga, he came to build up new knowledge that humanity needs for its future development and fulfilment. It has, therefore, been rightly said that Sri Aurobindo does not belong to the past nor to history but to the future that is realising itself.

If we make a serious study of Sri Aurobindo, we shall find ourselves to be a participant of that adventure of consciousness which invites us to collaborate with that wide-ranging Yoga that can liberate us from the fetters of dogmas and preconceptions and inspire us to realise the highest and the best not only for ourselves but also for the entire humanity.

In 1908-9, Sri Aurobindo wrote a poem entitled 'Invitation', and it seems appropriate to read this poem and ask ourselves if we are ready to respond to it:

Invitation

> With wind and the weather beating round me
>   Up to the hill and the moorland I go.
> Who will come with me? Who will climb with me?
>   Wade through the brook and tramp through the snow?
>
> Not in the petty circle of cities
>   Cramped by your doors and your walls I dwell;
> Over me God is blue in the welkin,
>   Against me the wind and the storm rebel.
>
> I sport with solitude here in my regions,
>   Of misadventure have made me a friend.
> Who would live largely? Who would live freely?
>   Here to the wind-swept uplands ascend.

> I am the lord of tempest and mountain,
>   I am the Spirit of freedom and pride.
> Stark must he be and a kinsman to danger
>   Who shares my kingdom and walks at my side.[1]

II

There are many ways of approaching Sri Aurobindo, but the light that we can gain from him will depend upon the height and breadth of our own quest. It is only when we cease to be occupied with our egoistic interests, which oblige us to keep ourselves in the centre of the world, and ask most comprehensive questions in their profundity relating to the world and its future possibilities and the role that we are required to play as also how we should prepare ourselves to fulfil that role that we shall find the relevance of Sri Aurobindo. It is only then that we shall find ourselves truly equipped to study Sri Aurobindo and the supramental consciousness that he has discovered and brought down on the earth.

The journey to which Sri Aurobindo invites us involves a most difficult endeavour. Even when the goal becomes clearer, the paths will still require to be traversed which will impel revolutionary processes of progression; this effort will turn us increasingly and decisively into a process of Yoga that is as comprehensive as life and as integral as the totality of existence. This Yoga rises to the highest but also brings down the power of the highest into the lowest terms of consciousness. This Yoga aims at the conquest of the higher and higher pinnacles of consciousness and, crossing beyond mind and overmind, it lifts us

---

[1] Sri Aurobindo: Collected Poems, SABCL, Vol. 5, p. 39.

to the supermind. But this Yoga is not merely of the ascent but also of the descent, and it aims at the manifestation of the supramental light and power right into matter and even in the inconscient so as to transform them for purposes of the creation of divine life on the earth.

This Yoga has rightly been called the supramental Yoga; it rests on the discovery of the supermind and of special methods by which the supermind can be made to permeate Matter and the human body so as to awaken and transform the cells of the body, which might result in the evolutionary mutation and in the generation of the new supramental species that would change the mode of life of struggling humanity and mould it into new forms of increasing luminosity and unity. This Yoga is new as compared to the old systems of Yoga and Sri Aurobindo has brought out this novelty in the following words:

It is new as compared with the old yogas:

1. Because it aims not at a departure out of world and life into Heaven or Nirvana, but at a change of life and existence, not as something subordinate or incidental, but as a distinct and central object. If there is a descent in other yogas, yet it is only an incident on the way or resulting from the ascent – the ascent is the real thing. Here the ascent is the first step, but it is a means for the descent. It is the descent of the new consciousness attained by the ascent that is the stamp and seal of the sadhana. Even the Tantra and Vaishnavism end in the release from

life; here the object is the divine fulfilment of life.

2. Because the object sought after is not an individual achievement of divine realisation for the sake of the individual, but something to be gained for the earth-consciousness here, a cosmic, not solely a supra-cosmic achievement. The thing to be gained also is the bringing in of a Power of Consciousness (the supra-mental) not yet organised or active directly in earth-nature, even in the spiritual life, but yet to be organised and made directly active.

3. Because a method has been pre-cognised for achieving this purpose which is as total and integral as the aim set before it, viz., the total and integral change of the consciousness and nature, taking up old methods but only as a part action and present aid to others that are distinctive. I have not found this method (as a whole) or anything like it professed or realised in the old yogas. If I had, I should not have wasted my time in hewing out a road and in thirty years of search and inner creation when I could have hastened home safely to my goal in an easy canter over paths already blazed out, laid down, perfectly mapped, macadamised, made secure and public. Our

yoga is not a retreating of old walks, but a spiritual adventure.[2]

We must note, however, the contributions of the past systems of Yoga which have been assimilated in this new supramental or integral Yoga. The discovery of the supermind was already made by the Vedic Rishis, and even though Sri Aurobindo discovered the supermind without any previous knowledge of it, since he was at that time unacquainted with the Veda, he later found the confirmation of his discovery in the hymns of the Rigveda. This confirmation has thrown a new light on the Veda, and the Yoga of the Veda, as we now discover it, can be regarded as a most momentous system of the loftiest realisations which were attained by our ancient forefathers. It is for this reason that Sri Aurobindo wrote two volumes entitled *The Secret of the Veda* and *Hymns to the Mystic Fire*, and he declared that the recovery of the knowledge contained in the Veda is indispensable if the world has to find the solution to its present problems and arrive at the next step of its progress.

Sri Aurobindo points out that the Veda is not a closed book; for the Veda itself speaks of continuous development and declares that as one climbs from one peak to a higher peak, new fields of knowledge open before us. In elucidating this undogmatic and open attitude towards fresh experience and experimentation, Sri Aurobindo has provided us illuminating insights as to how Vedic Yoga has developed through the long history of India a number of systems of Yoga, as also how there have been periods of specialisation and also periods of synthesis. And his own synthesis of Yoga is an integration of

---

[2] Sri Aurobindo: Letters on Yoga, SABCL, Vol. 22, pp. 100-101.

the past systems and the new methods that he himself has discovered and perfected.

This new synthesis embraces within its wide embrace the truth of the Vedic synthesis of the psychological being of man in its highest flights and widest ranging of divine knowledge, power, joy and glory which had its crowning experience of the transcendental and blissful reality in whose unity the increasing soul of man and the eternal divine fullness of the cosmic can be made perfect and fulfil themselves. It includes also the high and profound synthesis of the Upanishadic spiritual knowledge. It places the Bhagavadgita's synthesis of the triple path of love, knowledge and works as something central in its processes. It also acknowledges the synthesis of the Tantra and utilises the methods of tantric Yoga for purposes of its new aims. It also acknowledges the Tantric idea of the divine perfectibility of man, which was possessed by the Vedic Rishis but was thrown into the background by the intermediate ages. It also includes the aims of the Hatha Yoga and the Raja Yoga although not their detailed processes. But the supramental Yoga does not limit itself within the limits of specialised systems of Yoga or even the previous systems of synthesis. Explaining the need to go beyond and to develop a new synthesis of Yoga, Sri Aurobindo states:

> We of the coming day stand at the head of a new age of development which must lead to such a new and larger synthesis. We are not called upon to be orthodox Vedantins of any of the three schools or Tantrics or to adhere to one of the theistic religions of the past or to entrench ourselves within the four corners of the teaching of the Gita. That would be to limit ourselves and to attempt to create our spirit-

ual life out of the being, knowledge and nature of others, of the men of the past, instead of building it out of our own being and potentialities. We do not belong to the past dawns, but to the noons of the future.³

In developing the new synthesis, Sri Aurobindo had also in his view the challenges of the contemporary times and the insuperable difficulties which they present to the human mind at its present critical stage. Sri Aurobindo had made a detailed study of human history as also of the evolutionary processes, and not only as we find them in the light of modern theories of Darwin, Bergson, Samuel Alexander, Whitehead, Teilhard de Chardin and others but more importantly in the light of Indian knowledge of spiritual forces working behind the external developments of forms that emerge through the evolutionary movement; and he had come to the conclusion that the present crisis of humanity is not an ordinary crisis, which can be explained in terms of social, political, economic or ideological developments. He pointed out that the present crisis is an *evolutionary* crisis and the human species cannot expect to be delivered except through radical means which can transmute the Mind, which is today the leader of human evolution, into the supermind which can thenceforth lead the future and develop divine life on the earth and can also solve the problems that humanity is struggling to solve but which it is incapable to do. The supramental Yoga has, therefore, been presented by Sri Aurobindo as a practical means by which humanity can be helped and lifted up on the path not only of its survival but also of its arrival and its fulfilment.

---

³ Sri Aurobindo: Essays on the Gita, SABCL, Vol. 13, p.8

III

The central theme in Sri Aurobindo is that of the contemporary evolutionary crisis of humanity, of the perception that man is a transitional being and that he is a *"thinking and living laboratory in whom and with whose conscious co-operation she (Nature) wills to work out the superman, the god."*[4] His *magnum opus*, *The Life Divine*, which has been regarded as the greatest philosophical work of our times, is not a mere intellectual building of an edifice of thought, actuated by intellectual curiosity or intellectual grappling with epistemological, cosmological, ontological, or axiological questions. Although it is entirely philosophical in rigour and method, it is an unprecedented presentation to the contemporary intellectuality of all the essential psychological and physical facts of existence and their relations to a discovered ultimate reality in order to arrive at the profoundest solution that can be successfully applied to heal the maladies of the contemporary crisis. Philosophy, according to Sri Aurobindo, *"can be conclusive only if the perception of things on which it rests is both a true and whole seeing."*[5] And the true and whole seeing that we find in Sri Aurobindo's philosophy was a result of his attainment of the integral supramental knowledge which, in turn, was inspired by deepest concern to find remedy of the quintessential problems that have been arising in the course of human history and which have now reached the critical point of their acme.

The philosophy of *The Life Divine* is the philosophy of complete affirmation; it perceives the truth behind each system of philosophy but rejects its exclusiveness; it is thus a denial of all denials. It denies the materialist denial

---

[4] Sri Aurobindo: The Life Divine, SABCL, Vol. 18, p. 4
[5] *Ibid.*, p. 493

of the Spirit, even while it affirms the reality of Matter; it denies the denial of the ascetic even while it affirms the reality of the Spirit; it reconciles the insistent demands of Matter, Life, Mind and Supermind in an integral harmony. In the affirmation of the Reality of the One without a second, it finds the origin of the many and all. In the One Existent, *sat*, it finds the sound basis for Conscious-Force (*Chit*) and also in their union the inalienable delight (*ananda*). If it finds the rational assurance that God exists not only on the basis of essential truths that lie behind the rationalistic, ontological, cosmological and teleological arguments, but also on other grounds that explain even such difficult phenomena as those of the ignorance, error, falsehood and evil, it also provides rational assurance that "*Life is neither an inexplicable dream nor an impossible evil that has yet become a dolorous fact, but a mighty pulsation of the divine All-Existence.*"[6] And these assurances are again confirmed in direct spiritual and supramental experiences.

All-comprehensive integrality is the basic characteristic of the philosophy of Sri Aurobindo. It is the philosophy of integral Monism that reconciles the supra-cosmic, supra-terrestrial and cosmic views of existence. In the history of Indian philosophy, the one system that comes closest to it is that of the Gita as expounded by Sri Aurobindo in his *Essays on the Gita*; and we must remember that the Gita is the digest of the Upanishads, which are themselves the culmination of the synthesis of knowledge contained in the Veda. The integral Monism of Sri Aurobindo is not pure Monism, although it sees in one unchanging, pure, eternal Self the foundation of all cosmic existence; nor is it qualified Monism although it places in the One his eternal supreme Prakriti manifested in the form of the

---

[6] Sri Aurobindo: *The Life Divine*, SABCL, Vol. 18, p. 231

Jiva and lays a great stress on dwelling in God rather than dissolution as the supreme state of spiritual consciousness. It avoids every rigid determinism as would injure its universal comprehensiveness.[7]

Sri Aurobindo, in a brief summary statement, describes the ultimate Reality as follows:

> There is then a supreme Reality eternal, absolute and infinite. Because it is absolute and infinite, it is in its essence indeterminable. It is indefinable and inconceivable by finite and defining Mind; it is ineffable by a mind-created speech; it is describable neither by our negations, neti neti, -- for we cannot limit it by saying it is not this, it is not that, -- nor by our affirmations, for we can not fix it by saying it is this, it is that, iti iti. And yet, though in this way unknowable to us, it is not altogether and in every way unknowable; it is self-evident to itself and, although inexpressible, yet self-evident to a knowledge by identity of which the spiritual being in us must be capable; for that spiritual being is in its essence and its original and intimate reality not other than this Supreme Existence.[8]

Sri Aurobindo's philosophy has been rightly described as a philosophy of the Real-Idea. It is idealism that is realistic, and it is realism that is idealistic. As Sri Aurobindo explains, the creative force that generates the world and its forms is not the fictional Idea, having no essential relation in real Truth of existence. This philosophy "*sees*

---

[7] See Essays on the Gita, SABCL, Vol. 13, p. 6
[8] Sri Aurobindo: The Life Divine, SABCL, Vol. 18, p. 322

the creative Idea as Real-Idea, that is to say, a power of Conscious-Force expressive of real being, born out of real being and partaking of its nature and neither a child of the Void nor a weaver of fictions. It is conscious Reality throwing itself into mutable forms of its own imperishable and immutable substance. The world is therefore not a figment of conception in the universal Mind, but a conscious birth of that which is beyond Mind into forms of itself."[9]

That which is beyond Mind is, according to Sri Aurobindo, Supermind, -- a supreme Truth-Consciousness, an expressive term, which Sri Aurobindo has taken from the Rigveda, which describes the Supermind as *ṛta-chit*, the consciousness of essential truth of being (*satyam*), of ordered truth of active being (*ṛtam*) and the vast self-awarness (*bṛhad*) in which alone this consciousness is possible. According to Sri Aurobindo, because the supermind is the basis of the manifestation of the world, we have rational assurance that supermind can manifest in the world and that the supramental whole seeing can come into the forefront and resolve the problems that the mind, the faculty of discursive reasoning and dividing consciousness, creates in the course of its development. For the world is not an illusion and a meaningless unreality but evolving manifestation of the self-existent and conscious being through the comprehensive determining supramental consciousness. This is the argument which Sri Aurobindo presents in the very first chapter of *The Life Divine*. Let us refer to this argument that he presents, since the rest of the book can, in a certain sense, be considered as an elucidation of this argument and its consequences for our life in the world at the present stage of evolution:

---

[9] Sri Aurobindo: The Life Divine, SABCL, Vol. 18, p. 117

For all problems of existence are essentially problems of harmony. They arise from the perception of an unsolved discord and the instinct of an undiscovered agreement or unity. To rest content with an unsolved discord is possible for the practical and more animal part of man, but impossible for his fully awakened mind, and usually even his practical parts only escape from the general necessity either by shutting out the problem or by accepting a rough, utilitarian and un-illumined compromise. For essentially, all Nature seeks a harmony, life and matter in their own sphere as much as mind in the arrangement of its perceptions. The greater the apparent disorder of the materials offered or the apparent disparateness, even to irreconcilable opposition, of the elements that have to be utilised, the stronger is the spur, and it drives towards a more subtle and puissant order than can normally be the result of a less difficult endeavour. The accordance of active Life with a material of form in which the condition of activity itself seems to be inertia, is one problem of opposites that Nature has solved and seeks always to solve better with greater complexities; for its perfect solution would be the material immortality of a fully organised mind-supporting animal body. The accordance of conscious mind and conscious will with a form and a life in themselves not overtly self-conscious and capable at best of a mechanical or sub-conscious will is another problem of opposites in which she has produced astonishing results and aims always at higher marvels; for there her ultimate miracle would be an animal consciousness no longer seeking but possessed of Truth and Light, with the practical omnipotence which would result from the possession of a direct and perfected knowledge. Not only, then, is the upward impulse of man towards the accordance of yet higher opposites rational in itself, but it is the only logical completion of a rule and an effort that seem to be a fundamental method of Nature and the very sense of her universal strivings.[10]

Sri Aurobindo's *magnum opus*, *The Life Divine* is companioned by another *magnum opus*, *The Synthesis of Yoga*. If *The Life Divine* is primarily philosophical, *The Synthesis of Yoga* is primarily scientific. What is established in *The Life Divine* as philosophically conclusive, is proposed to be realised in actual experience and realisation through the scientific methodology which is described in *The Synthesis of Yoga*. If the concern of *The Life Divine* is to prove to the intellect of modern humanity the possibility and inevitability of the supramental manifestation on the earth, *The Synthesis of Yoga* shows to the mind, heart and spirit of humanity those methods by which the individual and collectivity can arrive at that manifestation.

A significant message of *The Synthesis of Yoga* is that Yoga should be distinguished clearly from philosophy and religion with which it is likely to be confused. According to Sri Aurobindo, the age of philosophy and religion is over, and the new age will insist on the deepest, widest and highest realisations that can be attained by the methods of Yoga. For although philosophy aims at discovering the

---

[10] Sri Aurobindo: The Life Divine, SABCL, Vol. 18, pp. 2-3

highest reality, its methods are those of critical rational thought, which can only conceive but not realise; and although religion aims at connecting the individual with the highest reality, its methods are predominantly those of credal belief, rituals, ceremonies and prescribed acts embodied in various routines of life and social institutions, -- the methods that conflict with the modern insistence on undogmatic experiential demands of the search and realisation of realities. Both these, -- philosophy and religion, -- have now been found to be inadequate as means to the goal that contemporary humanity needs to arrive at. In contrast to these, Sri Aurobindo explains the meaning of Yoga in the following words:

> [Yoga is] a methodised effort towards self-perfection by the expression of the potentialities latent in the being and a union of the human individual with the universal and transcendent Existence we see partially expressed in man and in the Cosmos.[11]

According to Sri Aurobindo, what we need today is the practice of meticulous methods that can bring about radical change of consciousness by means of psychological transmutation of faculties and powers of our being.

The word Yoga is often confined merely to Hatha Yoga or Raja Yoga, but these are only two specialised systems, and what is proposed by Sri Aurobindo is to bring about synthesis not only of these two but all the other systems of Yoga. Since the crisis through which we are passing today is many-sided, the solution should be many-sided and nothing short of a synthesis of different systems of

---

[11] *The Synthesis of Yoga* (1970), p.2

Yoga would give the needed remedy. As Sri Aurobindo explains, an undiscriminating combination in block would not be a synthesis, but a confusion; nor would successive practice of each of them in turn be easy in the short span of our human life. Sri Aurobindo, therefore, effects synthesis by neglecting the forms and outsides of the Yogic disciplines and seizes rather on some central principle common to all which would include and utilise in the right place and proportion their particular principles. It also seizes on some central dynamic force, which is the common secret of their divergent methods and capable, therefore, of organising a natural selection and combination of their varied energies and different utilities. That one common principle and force is the principle and force of *concentration*, and Sri Aurobindo's *The Synthesis of Yoga* is based upon integral concentration of our entire conscious being on concentrated relation and contact with the Divine so that the Divine may transform our entire being into His. In psychological terms, this method translates itself into the progressive surrender of the ego with its whole field and all its apparatus to the Beyond-ego with its vast and incalculable but always inevitable workings.

Sri Aurobindo points out that there are three outstanding features of the action of the highest when it works integrally on the lower nature. In the first place, it does not act according to a fixed system and succession as in the specialised methods of Yoga, but with a sort of free, scattered and yet gradually intensive and purposeful working determined in such a way that, in a sense, each individual in this path has his or her own method of Yoga. And yet, there are certain broad lines of working common to all which can be used to construct, not indeed a routine system, but yet some kind of scientific method of the synthetic Yoga. Secondly, the process being integral, it accepts all life in order that all life is transformed. In this process, our nature such as it stands organised by our past evolution and without rejecting anything essential is brought under the force of *tapasya* so that all undergoes a divine change. Thirdly, the divine Power in us uses all life as the means of this integral Yoga. In this process, all life is perceived as Yoga of Nature, seeking to manifest God within itself, but the distinguishing mark of the integral Yoga is the self-awareness with which the movements which are loosely combined in our ordinary nature are gathered up and concentrated for purposes of integral transformation.

The integral method of the synthesis of Yoga produces integral results. There is, first, an integral realisation of Divine Being; and there is also an integral liberation, *mukti*, not only *sayujya mukti* in which the individual being attains unbroken contact in all its parts with the Divine, not only *salokya mukti* by which the whole conscious existence dwells in the state of *Sachchidananda*, but also *sadharmya mukti*, in which the divine nature is acquired by the transformation of the lower being.

Transformation is the keyword of the Integral Yoga of Sri Aurobindo. Sri Aurobindo explains this as follows:

> By transformation I do not mean some change of the nature – I do not mean, for instance, sainthood or ethical perfection or yogic siddhis (like the Tantric's) or a transcendental (cinmaya) body. I use transformation in a special sense, a change of consciousness radical and complete and of a certain specific kind which is so conceived as to bring about a strong and assured step forward in the spiritual evolution of the being of a greater and higher kind and

of a larger sweep and completeness than what took place when a mentalised being first appeared in a vital and material animal world. If anything short of that takes place or at least if a real beginning is not made on that basis, a fundamental progress towards this fulfilment, then my object is not accomplished. A partial realisation, something mixed and inconclusive, does not meet the demand I make on life and Yoga.[12]

The complete process of transformation is described by Sri Aurobindo as triple, -- psychic transformation, spiritual transformation, and supramental transformation. In the words of Sri Aurobindo:

... there must first be the psychic change, the conversion of our whole present nature into a soul-instrumentation; on that or along with that there must be the spiritual change, the descent of a higher Light, Knowledge, Power, Force, Bliss, Purity into the whole being, even into the lowest recesses of life and body, even into the darkness of our subconscience; last, there must supervene the supramental transmutation, -- there must take place as a crowning movement the ascent into the Supermind and the transforming descent of the Supramental Consciousness into our entire being and nature.[13]

For a fuller understanding of the synthesis of Yoga, we need to study three big volumes containing Sri

---

[12] Sri Aurobindo: Letters on Yoga, SABCL, Vol. 22, p.98
[13] Sri Aurobindo: The Life Divine, SABCL, Vol. 19, p.891

Aurobindo's letters on Yoga, which throw illumining light not only on the principles of the Integral Yoga but also on multitudes of difficulties that are encountered during the process of Yoga, as also on experiences and realisations. But, above all, we need to study *Savitri*, that great epic of the adventure of the Spirit, which accomplishes great conquest of death by the power of the light of the supermind. For it is through *Savitri* that one gains a ready access to the concreteness of psychic, spiritual and supramental experiences as also their impact on all parts and planes of the being through the magic of the rhythmic word and vision in their highest intensities. To study *Savitri* is to enter into the realm of experiences and into a veritable process of Yogic transformation.

IV

It is not expected that this great and difficult task of supramental transformation can be effected by the whole of humanity, although, according to Sri Aurobindo, the time has come for the generalisation of Yoga in humanity. The necessity of spiritual change is imperative, and the future of humanity will depend, according to Sri Aurobindo, upon the response that humanity will give to this necessity. In his book *The Human Cycle*, Sri Aurobindo has expounded the psychology of social development and shown how human society has not only crossed over the infra-rational age of human development but has also traversed a long path on the curve of the rational age and stands today at the end of the curve of the Reason. Speaking of the modern society, Sri Aurobindo points out that it has discovered a new principle of survival, the principle of progress, which aims at more knowledge, more equipment, convenience and comfort, more enjoyment, a greater complexity of the social economy, more and more cumbersomely opulent life.

He further points out that these things must, however, lead in the end to the increasing failure to find the secret of constant self-renewal. He, therefore, concludes: "*Only in its new turn inwards, towards a greater subjectivity now only beginning, is there a better hope; for by that turning it may discover that the real truth of man is to be found in his soul.*"[14]

Whether humanity will respond to the need of this new turn will depend upon its increasing perception of the necessity of spiritual transformation. Sri Aurobindo points out that a change from the vital and mental to the spiritual order of life must necessarily be accomplished in the individual and in a greater number of individuals before it can come to have an effective hold upon community. What is necessary is that the common human mind begins to admit the ideas proper to the higher order that is in the end to be, and the heart of man begins to be stirred by aspirations born of these ideas. Sri Aurobindo concludes that if this condition is fulfilled then there is hope of some advance in the not distant future.

In his book *The Ideal of Human Unity*, Sri Aurobindo refers to two important developments which indicate a prospect of the coming change in humanity. The first of these is internationalism, the idea of humanity as a single race of beings with a common life and a common general interest. Sri Aurobindo identifies those tendencies in human life at present which are favourable to the progress of the international idea. In his own words:

> The strongest of these favourable forces is the constant drawing closer of the knots of international life, the multiplication of points

---

[14] Sri Aurobindo: *The Human Cycle,* SABCL, Vol. 15, p.210

of contact and threads of communication and an increasing community in thought, in science and in knowledge. Science especially has been a great force in its direction; for science is a thing common to all men in its conclusions, open to all in its methods, available to all in its results: it is international in its very nature; ... Science also has created that closer contact of every part of the world with every other part, out of which some sort of international mind is growing... The growth of knowledge is interesting the peoples in each other's art, culture, religion, ideas and is breaking down at many points the prejudice, arrogance and exclusiveness of the old nationalistic sentiment... Religion... is beginning to realise, a little dimly and ineffectively as yet, that spirituality is after all its own chief business and true aim and that it is also the common element and the common bond of all religions. As these influences grow and come more and more consciously to cooperate with each other, it might be hoped that the necessary psychological modification will quietly, gradually, but still irresistibly and at last with an increasing force of rapidity, take place which can prepare a real and fundamental change in the life of humanity.[15]

But internationalism, according to Sri Aurobindo, is not enough; there is a need of a religion of humanity or an equivalent sentiment which recognises a single soul in humanity of which each human being and each people is

---

[15] Sri Aurobindo: The Ideal of Human Unity, SABCL, Vol. 15, pp. 527-28

an incarnation and soul form. This religion has already expressed itself in the philosophy of humanitarianism, which itself is a most prominent emotional result of the Age of Reason. Philanthropy, social service and other kindred activities have been its outward expressions; and democracy, socialism and pacifism are to a great extent its by-products or at least owe much of their vigour to its inner presence. But Sri Aurobindo points out that the purely intellectual and sentimental religion of humanity is not sufficient to bring about the needed great change in human psychology. For at its highest, it can only erect three great ideals of progress, -- liberty, equality and fraternity, but in application of these ideals, it would still be obliged to resort to the external machinery of society, and ego would act as the centre of this machinery. As a result, as Sri Aurobindo points out, when the ego attains liberty, it arrives at competitive individualism; when it asserts equality, it arrives first at strife and then at an attempt to ignore the variations of nature, and it constructs an artificial and machine-made society; when the ego asserts fraternity, it speaks of something contrary to its nature; all that the ego knows is association for the pursuit of common egoistic ends and the utmost that it can arrive at is a closer organisation for the equal distribution of labour, production, consumption and enjoyment. If, therefore, the gospel of the idea of humanism is to be fulfilled, we have to realise that brotherhood is the real key and that the brotherhood exists only in the soul and by the soul. Therefore, Sri Aurobindo concludes, the religion of humanity must be a spiritual religion of humanity, not an institutional religion, not an intellectual religion, not a sentimental religion. That humanity is pressing forward towards this spiritual religion of humanity is of great significance for all of us who are keen to find the solution to the contemporary crisis. And it is here that Sri Aurobindo's perception of the significance of the contemporary crisis and his philosophy and yoga of supramental transformation come to us as the needed light and guidance.

At the same time, we may note what Sri Aurobindo has stated about the first step towards the supramental manifestation. In this context, we may cite the following remarks that Sri Aurobindo had made in his *Letters on Yoga*:

> The whole of humanity cannot be changed at once. What has to be done is to bring the Higher Consciousness down into the earth-consciousness and establish it there as a constant realised force. Just as mind and life have been established and embodied in Matter, so to establish and embody the supramental Force.
>
> It would not be possible to change all that in a moment – we have always said that the whole of humanity will not change the moment there is the Descent. But what can be done is to establish the higher principle in the earth-consciousness in such a way that it will remain and go on strengthening and spreading itself in the earth-life. That is how a new principle in the evolution must necessarily work.
>
> It is first through the individuals that it [the supramental consciousness] becomes part of the earth-consciousness and afterwards it spreads from the first centres and takes up

more and more of the global consciousness till it becomes an established force there.[16]

---

[16] Sri Aurobindo: Letters on Yoga, SABCL, Vol.22, pp.13, 14, 15.

VEDIC KNOWLEDGE AND SUPERMIND
IN THE LIGHT OF SRI AUROBINDO

Sri Aurobindo made a very important statement in *The Foundations of Indian Culture*, in which he spoke of the immediate work of India. He said that there were three tasks that India had to accomplish.

The first task is to recover the ancient spiritual knowledge in its fullness, in its amplitude — this is the first task. And this means of course, basically, the recovery of the Veda, Upanishads, the Gita, the Puranas and Tantras. This is, one might say, the basic stuff of what can be called the ancient spiritual knowledge of India. I underline the word "knowledge" because, usually, though this knowledge is contained in what are called Scriptures, Scriptures are sometimes regarded as revelations which were made once for all and have to be accepted unquestioningly. Therefore, philosophers do not accept them as bodies of knowledge. The Vedas are Scriptures; the Upanishads, the Gita, Tantra, Puranas are Scriptures; but they must still be considered as books of knowledge, because India does not regard them as revelations made for all times which cannot be repeated or which cannot be verified. According to the Vedic tradition, the faculty of revelation can be so developed that one can have a constant stream of revelations. Therefore, it is not something which comes once and for all: one can have repeated revelations, and revelations can be verified by revelations, and they can be experimented upon. What is more, they can be enlarged as in scientific knowledge — you can enlarge upon the knowledge; you can even overpass; you can have a new revelation, a new knowledge. So Sri Aurobindo has deliberately used the word, "ancient Indian spiritual knowledge."

This has to be recovered. It has to be recovered because it has greatly been lost. Mother once wrote down a message for me in which She said: "India has or rather had the knowledge of the Spirit." She wanted to underline that India could not take pride in having today a living knowledge of the Spirit. India has deviated a long way from the possession of that knowledge and therefore it has to be recovered. This is the first task.

As for the second task, Sri Aurobindo said that India has to pour that knowledge and therefore it has to be recovered. This is the first task.

As for the second task, Sri Aurobindo said that India has to pour that knowledge into new modes of philosophical, scientific and critical knowledge. This is a very difficult task. In fact, it has been made easy because Sri Aurobindo himself wrote a huge philosophical work called *The Life Divine*, in which he has demonstrated how the ancient knowledge can be poured into philosophical modes of thinking, and how in modern times it can be presented in a modern fashion. He has even shown how we can advance from the past towards the new.

The third task, Sri Aurobindo has said, is to deal with the contemporary problems in a new manner, and to realise a spiritualised society. These are the three tasks, of which the last one, he said, is the most difficult task. And the proportion to which India can accomplish these three tasks — to that extent India will have fulfilled her mission. In fact Sri Aurobindo and the Mother have initiated the third task, and this great seat called Auroville is India's effort inviting the whole world to meet and attempt to create a spiritualised society.

But these last two tasks will depend very largely upon the recovery — the first task — the recovery of the ancient spiritual knowledge. It is a very difficult terrain. It is so complex, and it is buried under such a plethora of interpretations, that it is extremely difficult to penetrate into it; it is like a jungle. I, for instance, have been brought up in India right from childhood in the real India tradition; the Veda was my constant childhood friend — I had a home in which Veda was recited every day. And yet, in spite of this kind of upbringing, it was only when I came to Sri Aurobindo that I really entered into the real portals of Vedic knowledge. Till that time, all that I knew of the Veda and the Upanishads and the Gita and the Puranas was that they were a real dense forest, difficult to penetrate; it was difficult to walk, even one mile, into that big terrain. When we recited the mantras of the Veda, the hymns of the Veda, we understood a little, because sometimes the words were not so difficult and you could make out some meaning of them. But as far as penetrating into what we can call knowledge, it was a constant failure.

In fact, many of us who read the Western scholars interpreting the Veda found in their interpretations an echo of our own lack of understanding. The Western scholars came across this great body of Vedic knowledge in the early nineteenth century...

Perhaps many people may not know that vast corpus of the Veda itself. Apart from the interpretations of the Veda, which are also huge, the mere text of the Veda itself is very vast. What is called Veda consists of four huge books:

the first one is called Rig Veda; the second is called Yajur Veda; the third is called Sama Veda; and the fourth is called Atharva Veda. These are four huge volumes. Rig Veda is the biggest. It has ten chapters and totally it has ten thousand verses. Ten thousand verses! In a recent publication, the mere Sanskrit text along with the English translation has come to twelve volumes, the Rig Veda alone. The Atharva Veda is half of the Rig Veda, the Same Veda is the shortest and the Yajur Veda is more than one fourth of the Rig Veda. Basically, the Rig Veda is regarded as the Veda, and Sri Aurobindo made a study of this Rig Veda in depth.

But when this study was made by the Western scholars in the nineteenth century, they found after studying the Vedas that they seemed to be the compositions of barbarians, naïve in their imagination, superstitious, materialist, seeking for wealth, progeny, cows and horses. Not understanding the real depth and not understanding the connections of ideas, they felt that the entire Vedic corpus was imply a bundle of worthless material, which may be studied for historical reasons to show to people what barbaric people of ancient times thought and conceived and imagined, but for no other purpose. In fact, Max Mueller, after interpreting the whole of the Veda, wrote a letter to his wife: "I have now" — I do not quote exactly the words — "I have now accomplished the task of translating the whole of the Rig Veda. And when people, even in India, will read my translation and understand what the Veda contains, they will find that there is nothing in it, and then they will easily turn to Christianity and embrace it." This was the confidence with which he translated, and many others who came to translate and many of those who interpreted the Veda coincided in their interpretations. And many of the Indian scholars who read these Western scholars, also dared not depart from their interpretation. Even a philosopher like Radhakrishnan while writing on the Veda in his book called *Indian Philosophy*, says, "Sri Aurobindo sees a great light and psychological truth in the Veda," but he remarks: "But when we see that Western scholars do not agree with him, we also cannot agree with Sri Aurobindo." This is the remark of a man like Radhàkrishnan, who is supposed to be one of the foremost philosophers of India! You can see, therefore, how difficult it is for scholars to understand the Veda.

Now there is a history of the interpretation of the Veda, and this history has to be understood before we can appreciate how Sri Aurobindo penetrated through this great forest of the Vedic interpretations and brought out a great light out of the Vedic verses. This interpretation starts with the Upanishads. The Upanishads claimed that what was written in their compositions were nothing but reaffirmation of the Veda. Now, this is a very important point because the Upanishads are regarded by all scholars all over the world as being of tremendous importance and full of light. On this there is no dispute, neither in the East nor in the West. And the Upanishads themselves declare that they are nothing but affirmations of the Veda. Therefore, at least for the Upanishadic seers, the Vedas are books of knowledge.

When we come to the Bhagavad Gita, which is regarded to be the quintessence of the Veda, it also mentions that the Veda is a book of knowledge. The Puranas also claimed that Veda was a book of knowledge. Tantra also regards Veda as a book of knowledge. Indian schools of philosophy regard Veda as an authority, and it is a tradition in Indian philosophy that if your conclusions of philosophical thought do not coincide with what is in the Veda, then your conclusions are wrong, but what is in the Veda is true. Such is the tradition in Indian philosophy.

In spite of this great tradition of the authoritativeness of the Veda, there came a school of interpretation, and a long line of interpretation, starting with Yaska, one of the great interpreters of the Veda. And this line ended with a great scholar of the fourteenth century AD called Sayana. He was himself the Prime Minister of a state in south India and also a great Vedic scholar, and he had the possibility of employing a whole huge mass of scholars to assist him. And Sayana interpreted all the four Vedas — a huge task! To study them requires a long lifetime and therefore to differ from him would require a further time. Therefore, after a long period, Sayana's interpretation ultimately became the standard interpretation of the Veda in India. And if you read Sayana's interpretation, then it would seem that the Vedic Rishis and the greatness of the Vedic Rishis and the claim that Vedic texts contain knowledge is a colossal fiction. If you read Sayana, you would be obliged to conclude that his own claim that Veda contains knowledge, is a proposition that cannot be sustained. Sayana himself was a ritualist, who believed that the Vedas were written for ritualistic purposes. He revered the Veda; he was not like the Vedic interpreters of the modern time, the scholars of Western scholarship. He revered the Veda, he had respect for the Veda, but he believed that it was simply a book of rituals. Mantras have a magical effect, and if you recite these mantras properly they will give you certain rewards. In other words, these seemingly magical superstitions are not superstitions according to Sayana — these are magical mantras which can be recited, which can produce results in your life: results in terms of materialistic gains, progeny, wealth and so on. Such was the meaning of the Veda according to Sayana. It was on the basis of Sayana that Vedic scholars of the West made their interpretations. They went one step further, and whatever reverence there was in Sayana for the Veda was blotted out, and they tried to prove that the Vedas were important only from the point of view of primitive history, but of no further use of mankind in the future. It had no message.

Now Sri Aurobindo himself, when he came to study the Veda in the early stages of his life, without studying Veda properly, had felt that may be these modern interpretations were quite meaningful; may be they were quite valid. This was the climate of the modern Indians, and even now it is largely so. One of the last interpretations of the Veda was by a great scholar of the nineteenth century in India called Maharshi Dayananda Saraswati. He interpreted the Veda, criticising Sayana very severely and affirmed that the Veda is a book of knowledge. Sri Aurobindo himself has written a very illuminating article and essay on Dayananda. If one reads it, one can see what a great tribute Sri Aurobindo has paid to Dayananda.

And yet Sri Aurobindo does not coincide his own interpretation with the interpretation of Dayananda. When Sri Aurobindo turned to Veda seriously for the first time after coming to Pondicherry, he had already had three great realisations of his yoga. By that time, he had the realisation of the Brahmic nirvana, under the guidance of the Maharashtrian Yogi called Lele. He had a further realisation of the universal Vasudeva — Krishna — in the Alipore jail. And he had already in the Alipore jail, also heard the voice of Vivekananda for fifteen days uninterruptedly where Sri Aurobindo was given the knowledge of the planes between the mind and the supermind. It was after this background that Sri Aurobindo had numerous experiences to which he had not a clue, either in Western psychology, that is, modern psychology or ancient psychology or anywhere. But these experiences were rising in his consciousness; as he says himself, he had particularly the experiences of what the Veda calls Ila, Saraswati, Sarama, Daksha. These are four female energies described in the Veda and, without knowing this; Sri Aurobindo had already had the experience of these energies. What were these powers, which were rising in his own consciousness on their own? And then when he happened to read the Veda, with this background, he directly contacted and understood and found a confirmation of his own experiences in the Veda. This was the way in which the key of the Veda was found. It was found by his own personal experiences which *preceded* his understanding of the Veda. It is not as if these experiences came to him after reading the Veda and finding them in the Veda. It is not as if he found the confirmation later in his own experiences. It is the other way round. He already had the experiences of these highest powers of consciousness and he found a clue to them in the Rig Veda. It is said in the Veda that only the seer can understand the words of the seer. This is the Vedic expression itself, *ninya vachamsi*, that is, secret words, *kavaye nivachanani*, are revealed only to the *kavi*, to the poet, to the seer. And this is confirmed in the case of Sri Aurobindo: the secret meaning of the Veda was revealed only to the seer, to Sri Aurobindo. Sri Aurobindo studied the Veda in depth. In depth: to cover such a huge mass of Vedic knowledge, within two or three years, is really something like a Herculean labour! And he accomplished it within a short time, as if he dived into the Veda, collected all the treasures within a short time, brought the jewels and diamonds out and then began to express and put them before mankind. This was in 1914. That is to say, in 1910 he came to Pondicherry, and by 1914, within four years, he had attained such a mastery of the secret meaning of the Veda that he began to write a series of articles under the title *The Secret of the Veda*. If one reads *The Secret of the Veda*, one can see a masterly interpretation; it is a masterly interpretation because Sri Aurobindo found the proof of his own interpretation in the Veda itself. It is by internal evidence that he shows that the interpretation he has given follows clearly and obviously, luminously, from the Vedic verses themselves.

In the light of this, he says, the Upanishads also can be understood properly. In fact, although the Upanishads are famous for their knowledge, even today if one goes to scholars and ask them for an interpretation of the Upanishads, one will see that three fourth of the Upanishads, even now, is a closed door. Even today, even those who praise the Upanishads to the sky, whether in the East or in the West, if one asks them questions, one really finds that they are absolutely out of their depth. They cannot explain! And it is quite obvious, because unless you understand the Veda and the secret of the Veda, the Upanishads cannot truly be understood. Fortunately, Sri Aurobindo has also written for us at least two great commentaries on two important Upanishads: Isha Upanishad and Kena Upanishad, and he translated eight Upanishads in totality. That is tremendous help for understanding the Upanishads properly.

Similarly, if one does not understand the Veda properly, one cannot properly understand the Bhagavad-Gita. It is not a secret book like the Veda, it is not like the Upanishads, so pregnant with meaning. And yet the Bhagavad Gita, too, cannot be understood properly if the Veda is not understood. In other words, the recovery of the ancient knowledge — Vedas, Upanishads, Bhagvad Gita — cannot be achieved except in the light of what Sri Aurobindo has written on the Veda. That is why I consider Sri

Aurobindo's *The Secret of the Veda* to be of the highest importance.

Now I have spoken till now as if the Veda is important for India, for the recovery of India, but actually speaking, the Veda may be looked upon as the only document of ancient times available to the whole of humanity. That is to say, if you trace world history, and if you try to find out what was the earliest composition from the earliest stage of humanity, nothing is available to us today — except the Veda. This is the only document, the only composition that is available to humanity. There were of course many other traditions in ancient times, and there was certainly a great tradition of knowledge. There were traditions which you find in ancient Chaldea, in ancient Persia, in Egypt, in Greece, but all these traditions have been lost. There is hardly anything available in the form of any text. There are ideas; there are mythologies. Even Greek mythology which is available is a later statement of the earlier Ileusian tradition. But as far as texts and their secret knowledge are concerned, these are lost.

So, if one wants to know what was the earliest thought of mankind, and if one wants the proof of that earliest document of mankind, one has to turn to the Veda only, because it is the only document available for the whole of humanity. Thus, if one wants to reconstruct even human history, and the thought of human history, all the nations have to turn to the Veda to get the description of the earliest thoughts of mankind, for which one has proof. And what a proof! We must remember that right from the beginning this Vedic text was so much revered in India (obviously because at that time it was considered to be a book of knowledge. Whatever one may say about it in modern times, it was known to the Vedic seer that it contained the supreme secret knowledge), that a tradition had developed that this knowledge should never be allowed to be lost. And a system was evolved in India so that one section of people of India had the obligation to memorise either all the four Vedas or at least one Veda. This has been the tradition. And not memorising in a haphazard manner. A very special system of memorising, singing, chanting the mantras of the hymns was evolved, where every syllable was measured, and its place was fixed absolutely. Fortunately, even today, in spite of great losses of many kinds, there are at least two thousand chanters, singers, who can recite the Veda exactly as it was recited five thousand years ago. I have myself, in one of the capacities of my governmental work, made a survey in India, and we have a large number of singers of the Veda, in Andhra Pradesh particularly, and also in different parts of India, and I have tried tape-recording some of the chanting of these Vedic recitations. The speciality of this method of singing is that it is sung in seven different ways, and all the seven ways should coincide, so there is no mistake occurring anywhere.

Seven different methods! And the last method, which is called the *ganapatha,* the method in which you first pronounce the first syllable, then you pronounce the second syllable, then you go back to the first syllable, and pronounce again the second, and then pronounce the third, then you go back again to the second, and then pronounce the first, and then again you go back to the second, and third, and fourth, and go back to the third, and second, and first, until you come to the end of a verse, which takes nearly from ten to fifteen minutes, even to recite one mantra like: *Agnim ile purohitam yagnasya devamritvijam hotaram ratnadhatamam.* This is a simple verse, the very first verse of the Rig Veda. This recitation in this *ganapatha* takes at least fifteen minutes because of this method. And it is chanted, it is not only recited like prose, it is chanted. In fact, even the chanting is so wonderful. These repetitions are so beautiful and so marvellous that when you hear the chanting, you would like to go on hearing, hearing, hearing again and again... marvellous! And then the whole of Rig Veda, ten thousand verses! You can imagine what a tremendous feat that is to recite and memorise in this way! And these memorise remembering both ways, and every word, as they move forward and backward, they have complete memory of it. It is a part of the training: right from the childhood at the age of four or five they start memorising. This is a part of their work. The tradition is so revered that even till today we have at least two thousand people in India who can recite exactly in the way in which it was recited five thousand years ago. This is the reason why today we have an accurate text, about which there can be no question at all. If anybody has doubts about the text, you can just call a singer and ask him to recite in the *ganapatha:* every syllable is caught, even today, so that it is not left to the printer's mistakes. Printing came much later. In fact, throughout the history of India, it has been an oral tradition. That is why, as Sri Aurobindo says, today we have almost an accurate text of the Veda. Not only of the Veda, this is true also of the Brahmans, the Aranyakas and the Upanishads and many other scriptures. The same method was used. It is tremendous. What a prodigious memory these Brahmins developed!

In any case, there is no dispute about the fact that these Vedic texts are accurate. Whether we understand them or not is something else, but on this question there is no doubt that these are the most ancient texts available to mankind. So if human history has to be written correctly, if the thought of human mind has to be written historically, there is no recourse for mankind except to go back to the Veda. So the importance of the Veda is not only for India but also for the whole world. It is the world's earliest text available and therefore it tells us what the earliest man thought, what he conceived. If one wants to find out, one has got to go back to the Veda.

These texts may not be the most ancient of all because, as Sri Aurobindo says, it is very clear that the Vedas were preceded by a very great civilisation, a very powerful stage of civilisation. And it was only when that age was declining that the fragments of the knowledge of these Vedic seers were put together by a Rishi called Vyasa. In any case this is what the tradition says: there was a great Rishi called Vyasa, who knew the Vedas in their fullness and who made an anthology. So these four Vedas are not the full text of all that was available as the Veda in that civilisation. But this is only an anthology, these are only selections, it is a miscellany you may say. What we call Veda is therefore an imperfect statement of what was developed in that ancient time.

What must have been that civilisation at that time can only be imagined first when we understand the light that Sri Aurobindo had shed upon these texts, and secondly when we understand the poetic brilliance. One of the marks by which one can see whether poetry is barbaric or naive or primitive or very developed is the metrical perfection. As Sri Aurobindo remarks, if you read the Veda simply, the rhythms of the Veda are like the chariots of the Gods. They have a perfect symmetrical form - perfect. And this is a remark of Sri Aurobindo, who is one of the greatest poets. It is his tribute to the Vedic rhythms. What we find in the Veda are perfect symmetrical forms. So even if one does not understand the meaning of the Vedas, even if one thinks that they are barbaric, at least the poetical form is not barbaric, that is certain. Barbarians could not have produced that kind of symmetrical perfection of rhythms throughout the Veda. It is lyrical in its sublimity; both lyricism and epic character are present. If one recites the Vedic verses, - actually one should enjoy reciting the Vedic verses - if one knows the Sanskrit language, and even if one does not know and simply listens, one will experience that the rhythms, the symmetrical forms, the sounds, the ringing of these Vedic verses are perfect. As Sri Aurobindo says, as you sing these Vedic verses, you feel as if you were flying with your wings. This is the kind of power that the Vedic verses possess.

Sri Aurobindo said that Vedic poetry is mantric poetry. And this is a very important point to be underlined: Vedic poetry is mantric poetry. What does it mean? In fact Sri Aurobindo has explained the meaning of mantric poetry in his great book called *The Future Poetry*, and to understand the value of Vedic poetry, we must read this book. In short, Sri Aurobindo has said: To arrive at mantra - the word mantra cannot be translated into English, but, let us say, what Sri Aurobindo calls the highest expression, poetical in character is mantra. And in India, mantra is that rhythmic expression which, when recited, produces a physical effect. If you say *tathastu*, in a mantric form, "Let it be so", it will be so, physically. This is the Indian tradition: any mantric expression will produce physical effects. Sri Aurobindo's *Savitri* is entirely mantric in character. Sri Aurobindo had said in *The Future of Poetry* that future poetry will be mantric. The whole of *Savitri* is now available to us. It is mantric in character, and that is why *Savitri* is not merely poetry, it is effective force in action. And that is also true of the Vedic mantras. In brief, Sri Aurobindo said: The mantric poetry must satisfy three criteria: first, it must have the highest intensity of rhythm. In fact Sri Aurobindo has said that the one mark of poetry is rhythmic words. There is no poetry if there are no rhythmic words. Prose and poetry differ in this; in prose you may not have rhythmic words, but poetry is marked by rhythmic words. But merely rhythmic words are not enough; the mark of mantra is the highest intensity of rhythmic words. There are so many poems which are in rhythm, but that is not the highest poetry, that is not mantric. Mantric poetry must have the highest intensity of rhythmic expression. That is the first mark.

Second, highest intensity of style. What is style? It is the perfect correspondence between the mode of expression and the meaning of expression. What you want to say is conveyed exactly by the mode suitable to that meaning. The highest intensity of style is a second mark of mantric poetry.

And the third mark is the highest vision of the highest truth, the intensity of that vision. All poetry or all art is basically a perception. Where there is no perception, there is no poetry, no art, no sculpture. A deep perception. One goes on, deeply perceiving, until that perception produces an image. That is called a depth of perception. All art is nothing but a perception, perceived so deeply, so deeply, that what you are perceiving begins to take a form, an image. And if you can express that image, you are an artist. When the vision and experience of the highest truth, the widest truth, the most comprehensive truth not just anything like the experience of a beautiful moon or a sun - is captured in your poetry, that is mantra. And Sri Aurobindo has said that the entire corpus of the Veda is mantric poetry. So if the very poetic form of the Veda has got this much of power (apart from its meaning), how could it be termed as primitive or barbaric at all? This is the first point that we have to make with regard to what Sri Aurobindo has said about the Veda. Vedic poetry is mantric poetry.

The second point I want to make is that Sri Aurobindo discovered that the Vedas have been written in a secret way. Outwardly it has one meaning, inwardly it has another meaning, although there is a parallelism between the two. And there was a reason behind it. The reason was that a secret knowledge had to be communicated, and if that communication falls into the hands of an uninitiated, he can misuse it, both for himself and the others. Fortunately, in modern times, some of the secrets of knowledge are very difficult to find. Even if you start learning, it takes twenty, thirty years to find out the secret of that knowledge. But once it is known, like atomic energy, or any other, even with the telephone, and Internet and so on, you know how people can misuse all these instruments and what terrible effects it has already produced in our civilisation. Now this was known to the Vedic seers: if knowledge is given to an uninitiated, it can be very harmful to the people. Yet it had to be communicated. So they developed a secret code, and Sri Aurobindo calls it an algebraic code. If you do not know algebra and you read a book of algebra, what meaning can you make out of it ? Unless the meaning of the figures and symbols is known to you, you cannot make out anything. The Veda is therefore algebraic in character. This is a second point I want to make. The Veda is difficult to understand. The meaning of it is secret. It is written in an algebraic form. You use the word "cow". We all know what a cow is in the ordinary sense, but in the algebraic form, "cow" means "light". And if you read the Veda throughout, wherever the word cow comes, you put the word light, it will fit in very well. But if you don't put cow for light, it will look very bizarre. "The cow stands before a horse": what is the luminous meaning in it? Nothing! But if you say: The horse is for Power, Energy, Shakti; the cow is Light. So

Chit-Shakti. The cow and the horse together are a symbol for *Chit-Shakti*, which makes a tremendous meaning. Now wherever these words come, do not use cow and horse, simply use the words light and power. It will make a very simple, luminous, obvious meaning. But if one does not know this, then everything looks bizarre, and it may look very primitive, and barbaric. This is the reason why many people, not knowing the algebra of Veda, have come to the conclusion that the Veda is barbaric and primitive. It is Sri Aurobindo's tremendous insight (because of his own experiences) that he discovered this algebra of the Veda. His great book *The Secret of the Veda* gives you the algebraic meanings of various words and terms which have been used in the Veda.

The third point I want to make is that this Veda contains a very deep knowledge of reality, of the world, and of the self. A triple knowledge: god-knowledge, world-knowledge, and soul-knowledge (self-knowledge). Now, what is that knowledge, what is the content of that knowledge?

What is God? What is the ultimate reality? It is not the kind of god sitting in the seventh heaven with a long beard. In one of the first statements in the first chapter of the Rig Veda, we find a particular mantra which is very curious: *na nunamasti no shvah kastadveda yadadbhutam anyasya chittamabhi samcharenyamutadhitam vinashyati*. This Sanskrit couplet says: The ultimate reality is neither today nor tomorrow. Who knows that reality, which is wonderful? Why is it wonderful? It has motion - it is alone, there is no other but it has motion in another. Therefore it is *adbhutam*, wonderful. It has motion in another, and if you try to approach it through your intellectual thought, where you always distinguish between one and another, and divide the two, and don't understand the mystery of one itself being another, if you apply that intellect on it, it vanishes. In other words, if you try to understand it intellectually, you will never grasp it, because it is wonderful. It does not follow the logic of the finite; it follows the logic of the infinite. The one that is many. As. Sri Aurobindo says in *The Synthesis of Yoga*, the ultimate reality is simple complex. It is simple-complex at the same time. It is one that is many, it is static that is dynamic. It is the same thing which is said in the Upanishad. In the Isha Upanishad the same idea is expressed: *tadejati tannaijati*. It moves, it moves not." It is far, it is near. It is wonderful. Now this is the first starting point of the Vedic knowledge of reality, of God. And there are so many other verses to which I do not make reference here for the sake of brevity.

Then comes the world-knowledge. What is the world-knowledge of the Veda? They say that the physical world that we can see is only the outer fringe of the whole world. But even this world consists of three earths, not only one earth. Even the earth that we can see is not one earth. There are three earths. Then there is an intermediate world between earth and heaven. "Heaven" is a word which is used for "mind" in the algebraic language of the Veda. Wherever the word "heaven" comes in the Veda, one has to understand "mind". Wherever the word *prithivi*, earth, comes, one has to understand it to be the physical. The word *antariksha* is the algebraic term for intermediate world. So there are three worlds: the world of the physical, the world of the vital and the world of the mental. These are the first three, to which we have a normal access. But then it says: the Vedic seers took a long time in their search to find out *turiyam svid*. This is another word which is very important in Sanskrit, *turiyam svid*, "that fourth one". *Turiyam svid* is again an algebraic term, "that fourth one". There is a short story in the Rig Veda of a Rishi called Ayasya. The story is that there were nine

Angirasa Rishis (Angirasa is a name of a clan). Nine Rishis were in search of the highest possible. They were searching, and searching, and searching... At last in their quest they came across a great man called Ayasya. They got his help in this search. These nine Angirasa seers became ten with Ayasya, and then with his help they found *turiyam svid*, they found "the fourth one" - the fourth reality. The three were the earth, the intermediate world, and heaven: body, life and mind. But with what did they discover the fourth one? *Saptadhi* is again another algebraic term. *Saptadhi*, the seven headed-thought. A thought which has seven heads. That is, the mind has to be so wide as to become seven-headed. With the help of the seven-headed thought, Ayasya broke open the fourth world and with the opening of the fourth world he became universal: *vishvam ajanayat*. He manifested the whole universality. This fourth is regarded as the most important discovery of the Vedic seers.

Sri Aurobindo afterwards told us that "this fourth" is the Supermind. *Turiyam svid* is the Supermind. So the Vedic seers had discovered the Supermind. And beyond the Supermind, they discovered the triple reality which, in later times, came to be recognised as *Sat-Chit-Ananda*: Existence, Consciousness and Bliss. So, you now see that the world, as seen in Vedic times, consisted of these planes: the three highest Existence, Consciousness, Bliss. Then comes the supermind, and then come mind, life and matter. This was their world-knowledge. I must say that I am making a great injustice to the Veda by summarising so primitively and so briefly, so naively. But this is the basic formula, you might say, of the world-knowledge of the Veda.

What is soul-knowledge? According to the Rig Veda, this is one of the most secret knowledge. This soul is given an algebraic term in the Veda, it is called Agni. Agni is the mystic fire. Fire is that which you can see outside very easily but, inside, it is our inner self, our inner soul - that which we call "psychic being" in Sri Aurobindo's psychology. This psychic being is our real inner inmost soul. And this was discovered after a long, long search. If you read the Vedic verses, you will find how much is said on Agni. This is so important that Sri Aurobindo himself wrote a full book where he collected and translated all the hymns addressed to the mystic Fire in the Rig-Veda. And this is the most precious knowledge that we have now. Because Agni is the most profound secret of the Vedic knowledge, according to the Veda. In fact, the very first verse of the Veda starts with Agni. Without Agni, without fire, without the knowledge of the mystic Fire, you cannot enter into the portals of Vedic knowledge. You must know yourself very deeply, profoundly, to understand the world, and it is by rising from plane to plane that you rise to the Supreme and you discover this wonderful reality that has motion in the another. This mystic Fire has been described variously in the Veda. There are many Agni mantras in other Vedas also, but it is to the knowledge available in the Rig Veda about the mystic Fire that Sri Aurobindo makes a reference when he describes the psychic being in *The Life Divine*. And he says: It is the flame that burns in the heart, which is inextinguishable, it is the conscience deeper than the conscience of the moralist. It is the Daemon of Socrates, it is that which turns always towards the truth and beauty and goodness, that which detects the truth from falsehood, unmistakably. That is our true soul which is within ourselves. Without illumining this Fire, you cannot enter into the deeper knowledge contained in the Veda. That is the importance of the mystic Fire. What you are internally is this Fire. And this Fire itself has an origin.

Vedic Knowledge and Supermind in the Light of Sri Aurobindo

Sri Aurobindo speaks of the origin of the psychic being also. But in the Veda there is a very interesting story. Mother sometimes told that story. She said that a time came in the history of the world when the four emanations which had originated from the ultimate reality separated from the origin, and there came about a complete darkness. When that darkness came, the supreme Divine Mother went back to the Supreme Lord and said: An accident has occurred and there has come about a complete darkness. What is to be done? Then the Lord said: Create some other beings who will not separate themselves from the origin. And that was the origin of Gods. Gods were created. But when the gods saw darkness and when they were asked to go down into the darkness so that the light can come out of it, even they refused. They said: It is so dark, we shall not enter into it. It was then that the Gods saw in the Divine Mother, in Aditi (this is the Sanskrit name for Divine Mother) a special Light, something special, and they said: if that can be brought down, then it can bring back light into this darkness. That Light is the mystic Fire. That is the origin of Agni. His origin is in the Supreme Divine Mother. In one of her talks Mother has said that when the Supreme Divine Mother saw the darkness, a tremendous Love oozed out of Her, and when that Love crystallised and fell upon the darkness, the psychic element which entered into the darkness. And all the psychic beings are nothing but evolutionary developments of this original psychic element which is nothing but Love of the Divine Mother. And that is why the psychic being automatically turns to the Divine Mother in an experience of Love. This is the Vedic truth told in algebraic form.

There is a very important mantra in the Rigveda and it is said that if you recite this mantra, you will be free from all sins. This is the promise given. It is called *aghamarshana mantra*. *Agha* means "sin", *marshana* means "wiping out". A mantra which can wipe out all the sins. And that mantra is very simple: *ritam cha satyam chabhiddhat tapaso dhyajayata tato ratryajayata tatah samudro arnavah*. Why is it called the mantra that can wipe out the sins? Because if you know the origin of all this, what is all this darkness and how darkness can be removed by the power of the Divine Love and by the mystic Fire, if you know this, all sins can be wiped out. That is why it is called the mantra of wiping out the sins. It simply says: In the beginning there was *tapas*. (*Tapas* is nothing else but power of concentration, the power of concentration of the Supreme. There is first the Supreme which I have described earlier, that which is neither here nor there. That Supreme has a power of concentration.) From *tapas* comes out first, *ritam cha satyam*, -- Truth and Right. In other words, out of the *Sat-Chit-Ananda*, by the power of *tapas* comes out Supermind. (*satyam, ritam, brihat* is the formula of the Supermind. This is what Sri Aurobindo has revealed in *The Life Divine*. And also in his Secret of the Veda.) So from the power of *tapas*, comes out this great Supermind. Then, having brought out the Supermind, suddenly something happens: *tato ratryajayata*, from there arose the Night. A sudden jump — Supermind is the supreme Light, and suddenly there comes the night. In the night there is still some light because of the stars and the moon. But then it says: After the night, *tato samudro arnavah*, then came a complete ocean of darkness. Not only night but a complete darkness. This is what Sri Aurobindo calls the Inconscience. From the Supermind there was a descent, the separation from the origin. The night came and then came out a complete darkness. And then it says, *samudradarnavadadhi samvatsaro ajayata*, after this, out of this great darkness came *samvatsara; samvatsara* is an algebraic term for the mystic Fire. Agni was put here. And once Agni was put there, all the evolution came out. Then there is a description of Surya, Chandra, the sun, the moon, everything came out. It gives a description of the whole world thereafter. Now, this is the fundamental psychic knowledge, the knowledge of the soul. Again I am doing a great injustice to the Veda because I am speaking as if it is so simple and so brief as that, but it is not so. There are hundreds and thousands of verses on this knowledge in the Veda. It is this psychic being which is presided over by *hamsa; hamsa* is another algebraic term. *Hamsa* means swan. Over this mystic Fire is a swan which is tied up, according to the Veda, in hundreds nets, and cannot flutter its wings. It is in bondage. But, in this bondage, there is a tremendous battle going on. What is this battle?

In the Veda you find the great story of the forces of Light and the forces of Darkness. The forces of Light are called the Gods. The forces of Darkness are called *Dasyus, Panis, Pishachas, Rakshasas, Asuras*. There is a great battle between the two. If you want to fight the battle, this battle can be fought, and it can be fought systematically. This is the yoga of the Veda: the mystic discipline by which the psychic being and the soul, which are caught in this great battle, can be liberated. So the first step is the discovery of the mystic Fire within you. This is the first step in the mystic discipline of the Veda. Veda, Sri Aurobindo discovered, is a great book of Yoga. It is not any superstition or magic or any kind of barbaric mantras meant to get some gains here and there. It is a knowledge of the battle of Life. It is a revelation of the real nature of Life: suddenly, in harmony, disharmony comes about. Suddenly, when Rama is to be crowned, Kaikeyi happens to demand certain things overnight; Rama is thrown out and a great tragedy occurs; a battle takes place and only after the battle does the victory come. So, in human life, there are forces of Darkness and forces of Light which are described in detail in the Veda — what are the Gods; and the whole knowledge of the Gods, and how they can help. The Vedic seers found out the existence of the Gods, not as imaginations, or formations, or premonitions, but the real, objective existence of the Gods, and they found out the names of these Gods — the names, the meaning, the secret of each God — the function of each God. It is as if you are going to a Ministry, and you find out who is the minister and who is the secretary and who is the clerk and who is the cashier, what is the function of each one. Unless you know this, you can never succeed in a Ministry. Similarly, in the Ministry of the world, you cannot succeed unless you know who are the Gods, and what are their functions.

Very briefly I shall give only a few clues. As you rise up and kindle your mystic Fire, the first one that comes in answer is Indra. Indra is a name of a God whom Sri Aurobindo describes algebraically as the God of the illumined mind. You, first of all, come into contact with the illumined mind. He descends, that is his nature — Agni always ascends, the fire always rises up in aspiration. In answer there is a descent of the illumined mind. This is the first God that comes to your help. But he is very powerful and he is able to fight tremendously with the demons. But then, that is not enough. You gain a lot, but that is not the end of the story, you still have to rise higher. And higher than Indra is *swah*: this is a very special word in the Veda. It is present in the Gayatri mantra.

> *Om bhur bhuvah swah*
> *tat savitur varenyam bhargo devasya dhimahi*
> *dhiyo yo nah prachodayat*

Swah is constantly used in the Vedic lore. This *swah* is a light which has condensed itself by constant rising of the mystic Fire and the constant descent of Indra. It is a very beautiful world of Light. You come across this world of Light. But even that is not the Supreme Light. It is only the medium Light. There is a very famous proposition made in the Veda to distinguish between darkness, the intermediate light, and the Supreme Light. It is said in the Chhandogya Upanishad that Ghora speaks one word to Krishna and gives him the Supreme Knowledge. That mantra he gives is as follows:

> *udvayam tamasaspari svah pashyanta uttaram*
> *devam devatra suryamaganma jyotiruttamam*

This is the mantra: we went beyond darkness and saw the intermediate Light which is *swah*, but then we did not stop there; we went further; we went to the Gods; we went to Surya, Suryam, we went to the Supreme Light, *jyotiruttamam*, (it is a *jyoti* which is *uttamam*, Supreme). *Swah* is an intermediate Light. The Supreme Light is *uttamam*, it is Surya, the sun. The sun, Sri Aurobindo says, is the symbol of the Supermind in the Veda. But before you enter into the Supermind, there are four Gods who stand as sentries. They will not allow you to enter into the sun, into the Supreme realm. You have to be qualified. Who are these four Gods? Varuna — Varuna is the God of Vastness. Unless you become very vast, you cannot enter into it. The narrow-minded can never enter into it. That is why Sri Aurobindo constantly says: widen yourself. This is a Vedic knowledge: Unless you widen yourself fully, you cannot enter into the Supreme Supermind.

The second is Mitra. Varuna is always accompanied by Mitra. Mitra is the God of harmony. As long as you quarrel, you can never enter into that Light. That is certain. There must be harmony, a *tapasya* of harmony and vastness.

Then comes Aryaman. Aryaman is the Lord of austerity. Great *tapasya*, the fullness of *tapasya* you must do, greatest effort, you must master the effort itself.

And then Bhaga. Bhaga is the God of enjoyment. Unless you know how to enjoy truly, you cannot enter into the Supermind. But enjoy truly, that is to say. Usually a small joy is enough to make us dance and flutter and throw away all the energies. You should be able to contain the highest joy in yourself without shaking. In the Veda it is said that when the great soma, the great nectar, falls into the unbaked jar, this jar breaks down. It is only when you are purified, thoroughly purified that your jar becomes baked, and if the joy falls into it, you can hold it. This capacity to hold the joy allows you to enter into the Supermind. This is also called the attainment of Immortality. *Amritam.* This was the great achievement of the Vedic Rishis. The soul which is tied into hundred nets — the swan which wants to fly, which cannot fly and has to battle — goes beyond Indra into swah, and goes beyond swah to Varuna, Mitra, Aryaman and Bhaga, enters into Surya. And then comes soma. The highest is soma, the great delight. When that delight can be held in the body, that is Immortality. This was the greatest achievement of the Vedic Rishis. Sri Aurobindo has written about this in a chapter called, "The Victory of the Fathers". That was the Victory of the Vedic Rishis.

To hold the Supermind in the body was the highest achievement of the Vedic Rishis but Sri Aurobindo found that that was not enough. There is a distinction between the Veda and Sri Aurobindo's discovery. There is one step farther — not one step farther. Mother told me that Sri Aurobindo is not a logical continuity of the past. It is not as if you continue what they were doing and then you get Sri Aurobindo's path. No. It is something newly discovered. That is why Mother said: Sri Aurobindo does not belong to the past or to history. He is constantly fabricating the future. It was not known that apart from holding the Supreme Light in the body, there is also a possibility of the permeation of Light in the body. Now, this was the new knowledge that Sri Aurobindo gave in his yoga. It is a permeation, a penetration. It is only when there is a permeation of this light into the cells of the body that the human species can be turned into the supramental species. So one can see how much one needs to know the Vedic yoga to understand Sri Aurobindo's yoga, and how much certainty and confirmation you get by reading the Vedic yoga. One will get many clues in the Veda, in large amplitude; and if Auroville is to be the cradle of this Superman, in which the light of the Supermind has to permeate into the cells of the body, then the Vedic knowledge is indispensable.

SRI AUROBINDO'S PHILOSOPHY OF INDIAN NATIONALISM

I

A most luminous and revelatory exposition of philosophy of nationalism and of Indian nationalism is to be found in the writings of Sri Aurobindo. In fact, Sri Aurobindo's own life is a flaming example of Indian nationalism, not only in its uniqueness but also in its universality. If we study the history of Indian nationalism, we shall find that he stands out as the most heroic nationalist who formulated in the most inspiring terms the true aim of Indian nationalism, during the early period of nationalist struggle and accomplished the task of fixing it in the national consciousness within a short period of two years (1906-8) through blazing pages of the Bande Mataram. This miracle can be regarded as an unparalleled achievement in the entire world history of nationalism.

The greatest thing done in those years was the creation of a new spirit in the country, a new electric current that awakened the people to the true meaning of nationalism and filled them with enthusiasm that created waves after waves all over the country. Repression and depression could not silence the stir of this enthusiasm. After each wave of repression and depression, it renewed the thread of the life of movement for liberation and kept it recognisably one throughout nearly fifty years of its struggle. The cry of Bande Mataram rang on all sides, and people felt it glorious to be alive and dare and act together and hope. The old apathy and timidity was broken and a force was created which nothing could destroy, and it carried India to the beginning of a complete victory.

It must be remembered that the climate under which the message of the Bande Mataram had to combat with its adversary forces was entirely unfavourable. The British Government had detected in Sri Aurobindo *"the most dangerous man"* and had perceived the rising tide of nationalist movement with utmost severity and with harshest measures of repression. Within the country itself, there was the rising tide of the Moderate Party and its leaders who had belief in British justice and benefits from the foreign government in India, faith in British law courts and in the adequacy of the education given in schools and universities in India. They had assumed that the philosophy of nationalism was impracticable and they had stigmatised this philosophy as a philosophy of extremism. These leaders had an ambiguous attitude towards the demand of complete independence of India. Many of them preached the gospel of faith in the British and in the British rule. Even those among them whose heart rebelled against the servile doctrine were intellectually so much dominated by the British influence that they could not embrace the philosophy of nationalism with their whole heart and tried to arrive at a compromise between subjection and independence. They discovered an intermediate path in which the blessings of freedom could be harmoniously wedded with the blessings of subjection! They spoke, therefore, of colonial self-government. Some of these leaders were emotionally nationalists and yet intellectually loyalists. There was a view that disunion and weakness are ingrained characteristics of the Indian people and outside power was necessary in order to arbitrate, to keep the peace and to protect the country from the menace of the mightier nations. They also advocated that a healthy development was possible at the time only under foreign domination and that such development must be first effected before we could begin to dream of freedom or even of becoming a nation. In the view of the Moderate Party, the philosophy of Indian nationalism as advocated by nationalist leaders like Bal Gangadhar Tilak, Bepin Chandra Pal, Lala Lajpat Rai, Sri Aurobindo and others was untenable and was even an avoidable menace.

There was a view among journalists such as that of Mr. N.N. Ghose of the *Indian Nation* that because there is diversity of race in India, because there is diversity of religion in India, and because there is diversity of language in India, the essential conditions of a nationality were absent and there was no possibility of creating a nationality in our country. As this perilous contention is crucial to the understanding of the notion of nation, of nationality and of nationalism, it may be useful to refer to the article Sri Aurobindo wrote in Bande Mataram (August 17, 1907) in which he answered it effectively. He argued that every nationality has been formed in spite of diversity of race or religion or language, and not unoften in spite of the coexistence of all these diversities. He pointed out that the English nation has been built not only out of various races but keep to this day their distinct individuality and that each one of them clings to its language tenaciously. He referred to the striking example of Switzerland where distinct racial streams speaking three different languages and, later, professing different religions coalesced into and persists as one nation without sacrificing a single of those diversities. He referred to France where three different languages are spoken; he pointed that in America, the candidates for White House addressed the nation in fourteen languages; he referred to Austria, a congeries of races and languages, and he referred to acute divisions in Russia.

Sri Aurobindo maintained that the contention that unity in race, religion or language is essential to nationality will not bear examination. He acknowledged that such elements of unity are very helpful to the growth of nationality, but they are not essential and will not even of themselves assure its growth. Referring to the example of the Roman Empire, he pointed out that even though it created a common language, a common religion and life, and did its best to crush out racial diversities under the heavy weight of its uniform system, failed to make one great nation.

What, then, Sri Aurobindo asked, are the essential elements of nationality? And he answered:

> We answer that there are certain essential conditions, geographical unity, a common past, a powerful common interest impelling towards unity and certain favourable political conditions which enable the impulse to realise itself in an organised government expressing the nationality and perpetuating its single and united existence. This may be provided by a part of the nation, a race or community, uniting the others under its leadership or domination, or by an united resistance to a common pressure from outside or within. A common enthusiasm coalescing with a common interest is the most powerful fosterer of nationality. We believe that the necessary elements are present in India, we believe that the time has come and that by a common resistance to a common pressure in the shape of the boycott, inspired by a common enthusiasm and ideal, that united nationality for which the whole history of India has been a

preparation, will be speedily and mightily accomplished.[1]

In these brief but compelling lines we have a quintessential answer to the question as to what is a nation, what is nationality and what is nationalism. In the light of this affirmation it becomes clear that a nation or what may be called the soul of nation may exist and yet it may not be visible; it may take birth, but it may take long for it to create and develop; it may develop in many directions, but not yet integrally; it may be recognised by some or many in the country but not necessarily by masses of people; it may rest on a geographical unity, and yet it can become fragmented or disrupted or divided for short or long periods; it may attain even political unity as also geographical unity and yet its centrifugal and centripetal forces may not be in harmony with each other or in a balanced state of equilibrium. There may be rise and fall in the self-awareness of nationalism, new questions may arise that may disturb the manifestation of the soul of the nation. And yet, the seer of the soul of the nation will always recognise it and work for its manifestation.

II

Much has been written about the philosophy of nationalism and philosophy of Swaraj. Leaders of the Moderate Party, in order to belittle the importance of what they called extremists and their philosophy derided their opponents as votaries of violence and lawlessness and advocates of a blind or impulsive pursuit of the impracticable ideal of complete independence of India. Sri Aurobindo, in order to clarify the position of the philo-

---

[1] Sri Aurobindo: *Bande Mataram, Centenary Edition, Volume 1, page 507*

sophy of nationalism, wrote a brief but a powerful article on April 26, 1907, under the title *Nationalism Not Extremism.* He said that the new movement was not primarily a protest against bad Government but that it was a protest against the continuance of British control. He pointed that the new movement was born of a conviction that the time had come when India can, should and would become great, free and united again. He clarified that it was not a negative current of destruction, but a positive, constructive impulse towards the making of a modern India, that it was not a cry of revolt and despair, but a gospel of national faith and hope. He said that its true description was not Extremism but Nationalism.

Continuing his argument, Sri Aurobindo pointed out that there were not two parties in India but three, -- the Loyalists, the Moderates and the Nationalists, and he articulated clearly the philosophies of all the three parties so as to bring out clearly the philosophy of nationalists. This articulation is so succinct and brings out the philosophy of nationalism with such sharpness that we should read it in full. Sri Aurobindo wrote:

> The Loyalists would be satisfied with good Government by British rulers and a limited share in the administration; the Moderates desire self-government within the British Empire, but are willing to wait for it indefinitely; the Nationalists would be satisfied with nothing less than independence whether within the Empire, if that be possible, or outside it; they believe that the nation cannot and ought not to wait, but must bestir itself immediately, if it is not to perish as a nation. The Loyalists believe that Indians have not the

capacities and qualities necessary for freedom and even if they succeed in developing the necessary fitness, they would do better for themselves and mankind by remaining as a province of the British Empire; any attempt at freedom will, they think, be a revolt against Providence and can bring nothing but disaster on the country. The Loyalist view is that India cannot, should not and will not be a free, great and united nation. The Moderates believe the nation to be too weak and disunited to aim at freedom; they would welcome independence if it came, but they are not convinced that we have or shall have in the measurable future the means or strength to win it or keep it if won. They therefore put forward Colonial Self-Government as their aim and are unwilling to attempt any methods which presuppose strength and cohesion in the nation. The Moderate view is that India may eventually be united, self-governing within limits and prosperous, but not free and great. The Nationalists hold that Indians are as capable of freedom as any subject nation can be and their defects are the result of servitude and can only be removed by the struggle for freedom; that they have the strength, and, if they get the will, can create the means to win independence. They hold that the choice is not between autonomy and provincial Home Rule or between freedom and dependence, but between freedom and national decay and death. They hold, finally, that the past history of our country and present circumstances are of such a kind that the great unifying tendencies hitherto baffled by insuperable obstacles have at last found the right conditions for success. They believe that the fated hour for Indian unification and freedom has arrived. In brief, they are convinced that India should strive to be free, that she can be free and that she will, by the impulse of her past and present, be inevitably driven to the attempt and the attainment of national self-realisation. The Nationalist creed is a gospel of faith and hope.[2]

This statement is also a manifesto of the philosophy of Swaraj. This philosophy regarded Swaraj as not mere political freedom but a freedom vast and entire, freedom of the individual, freedom of the community, freedom of the nation, spiritual freedom, social freedom and political freedom. Sri Aurobindo, in a powerful article on Swaraj (February 18, 1908), argued that if political freedom is absent, the community has no great ends to follow and the individual is confined within a narrow circuit in which the superiority of caste, wealth or class is the only ambition he can cherish. He pointed out that if political freedom opens to him a wider horizon, he forgets the lesser ambitions. Moreover, he contended, a slave can never be noble and broad-minded. He could not forget himself in the service of his fellows; for he already is a slave and service is the badge of his degradation, not a willing self-devotion. When man is thus degraded, Sri Aurobindo observed, it is idle to think that society can be free.

Sri Aurobindo went farther and pointed out that not only social freedom but even spiritual freedom can never be the

---

[2] Sri Aurobindo: *Bande Mataram, Centenary Edition, Volume 1,* page 298-99.

lot of many in the land of slaves. He asked, "*If the mass of men around us is miserable, fallen, degraded how can the seeker after God be indifferent to the condition of his brothers?*"[3]

He stated further:

> Compassion to all creatures is the condition of sainthood, and the perfect Yogin is he who is <u>sarvabhūtahite ratah</u>, whose mind is full of the will to do good to all creatures. When a man shuts his heart to the cries of sufferings around him, when he is content that his fellow-men should be sorrowful, oppressed, sacrificed to the greed of others, he is making his own way to salvation full of difficulties and stumbling-blocks. He is forgetting that God is not only in himself but in all these millions. And for those who have not the strength, spiritual freedom in political servitude is a sheer impossibility. When India was free, thousands of men set their feet in the stairs of heaven, but as the night deepened and the sun of liberty withdrew its rays, the spiritual force inborn in every Indian heart became weaker and weaker until now it burns so faintly that aliens have taken upon themselves the role of spiritual teachers, and the people chosen by God have to sit at the feet of the men from whose ancestry the light was hidden. God has set apart India as the eternal fountainhead of holy spirituality, and He will never suffer that fountain to run dry.

---

[3] Sri Aurobindo: *Bande Mataram, Centenary Edition, Volume 1,* page 700

> Therefore Swaraj has been revealed to us. By our political freedom we shall once more recover our spiritual freedom. Once more in the land of the saints and sages will burn up the fire of the ancient Yoga and the hearts of her people will be lifted up into the neighbourhood of the Eternal.[4]

Swaraj without any limit or reservation came to be fixed as the aim of the philosophy of nationalism. Swaraj came to be seen as a life-belt, as the pilot, as the star of guidance. Sri Aurobindo also saw the necessity of Swaraj for the fulfilment of India's true role in the comity of nations. He wrote:

> India is the guru of the nations, the physician of the human soul in its profounder maladies; she is destined once more to new-mould the life of the world and restore the peace of the human spirit. But Swaraj is the necessary condition of her work and before she can do the work, she must fulfil the condition.[5]

The philosophy of Swaraj was accompanied by a programme of effective Boycott. Both Tilak and Sri Aurobindo were in favour of an effective Boycott of British goods. They wanted the Boycott to be a political weapon and not merely as an aid to Swadeshi. They both advocated national self-sufficiency in key industries and in the production of necessities of all manufactures in which India had the natural means. In addition, national

---

[4] Sri Aurobindo: Bande Mataram, Centenary Edition, Volume 1, page 700-1
[5] Sri Aurobindo: Bande Mataram, Centenary Edition, Volume 1, page 731

education was another item of the programme. The nationalist movement was also a movement of national education. This movement advocated the establishment of national schools and colleges so as to remedy the ills of education given by the British. Sri Aurobindo maintained that the British system tended to dull and impoverish and tie up the naturally quick and brilliant and supple Indian intelligence, to teach it bad intellectual habits and spoil by narrow information of mechanical instruction its rationality and productivity. Sri Aurobindo, in fact, wrote a full-fledged book entitled *National System of Education*, and another on *National Value of Art*. This entire programme, along with the programme of mass awakening and settlement of disputes by recourse to non-British tribunals, included a movement of passive resistance. This entire programme had a comprehensive aim of the attainment of all-sided and integral Swaraj.

III

Philosophy of nationalism was often described by the Moderate leaders as a philosophy of violence. In order to contradict this misleading contention, we must study a series of articles written by Sri Aurobindo in Bande Mataram on the doctrine of passive resistance between 11th April to 23rd April 1907. One of the main contentions of these articles was to point out that the problem that faced the country at that time was how to stave off imminent national death, how to put an end to the white peril, how to assert for the people of India their right to be themselves and to live. The only immediate answer, he said, was an organised national resistance to the state of things so as to achieve one goal, namely, freedom. He referred to three alternative courses open. The first alternative was that of an organised passive resistance. This was the kind of the course of action that was initiated by

Parnell when by the plan of campaign he prevented the payment of rents in Ireland and by persistent obstruction hampered the transaction of any but Irish business in Westminster. The second alternative course was the one illustrated by the first triumph of Russian liberty which involved a series of strikes on a gigantic scale that manifested widespread, desperate and unappeasable anarchy. The third course open to an oppressed nation, Sri Aurobindo contended, was of an armed revolt. Sri Aurobindo argued that the choice by subject nation of the means it will use for vindicating its liberty, is best determined by the circumstances of its servitude. On this point, Sri Aurobindo wrote:

> The present circumstances in India seem to point to passive resistance as our most natural and suitable weapon. We would not for a moment be understood to base this conclusion upon any condemnation of other methods as in all circumstances criminal and unjustifiable. It is the common habit of established Governments and especially those which are themselves oppressors, to brand all violent methods in subject peoples and communities as criminal and wicked. When you have disarmed your slaves and legalised the infliction of bonds, stripes and death on any one of them, man, woman or child, who may dare to speak or to act against you, it is natural and convenient to try and lay a moral as well as a legal band on any attempt to answer violence by violence, the knout by the revolver, the prison by riot or agrarian rising, the gallows by the dynamite bomb. But no nation yet has listened to the cant of the oppressor when itself put to the test, and the general con-

science of humanity approves the refusal. Under certain circumstances a civil struggle becomes in reality a battle and the morality of war is different from the morality of peace. ...But where the oppression is legal and subtle in its methods and respects life, liberty and property and there is still breathing time, the circumstances demand that we should make the experiment of a method of resolute but peaceful resistance which, while less bold and aggressive than other methods, calls for perhaps as much heroism of a kind and certainly more universal endurance and suffering. In other methods, a daring minority purchase with their blood the freedom of the millions; but for passive resistance it is necessary that all should share in the struggle and the privation.[6]

Sri Aurobindo also pointed out through the pages of Bande Mataram that the philosophy of nationalism is not the philosophy of unreasoning spirit of violence and preference of desperate methods, that nationalism does not advocate lawlessness as contended by the moderate leaders. He argued that the nationalists did not love the philosophy of suffering for its own sake. In positive terms, Sri Aurobindo clarified that nationalism has deeper respect for the essence of law than anyone else, because the building up of the nation is its object and because without a profound reverence for law the national life cannot persist and attain a sound and healthy development. At the same time, he argued that the philosophy of nationalism qualifies its respect for legality by the proviso that the law that the nationalist is called upon to obey is

---

[6] Sri Aurobindo: *Bande Mataram, Centenary Edition, Vol. 1, pp. 98-99*

the law of the nation, and not a law imposed from outside. The nationalist, he asserted, never loses sight of the truth that law was made for man and not man for law. Its chief function and reason for existence is to safeguard and foster the growth and happy flowering into strength and health of national life. He further stated that nationalism refuses to accept law as a fetish or peace and security as aims in themselves while it will not prefer violent or strenuous methods simply because they are violent or strenuous. The philosophy of nationalism, Sri Aurobindo elucidated, is to ask of the method whether it is effective for its purpose, whether it is worthy of a great people struggling to be, whether it is educative of national strength and activity.

It is true that philosophy of *ahimsa* which came to be advocated by Mahatma Gandhi later was not part of Indian nationalism as understood by the nationalist leaders like Tilak, Sri Aurobindo and others. On the subject of non-violence, there has remained a diversion of opinion, and if we study Sri Aurobindo and what he wrote on the subject of violence and non-violence, it is clear that a distinction should be made between acts of violence and acts of destruction. Violent act emerges from anger and hatred, but acts of destruction may not necessarily emerge from anger and hatred. A physician uses his knife for destruction of a disease; but in the motive there is no anger or hatred. Destruction advocated by Sri Krishna in the battlefield of Kurukshetra was to be carried out in consciousness of non-attachment and not in that of anger or hatred.

As this mater is very important, it will be useful to point out that while Mahatma Gandhi looked upon *ahimsa* as a matter of creed and a large number of his followers in the country also took it as such, many other leaders including

Jawahar Lal Nehru and others took it as a matter of policy under the-then prevailing circumstances in the country. A school of thought right through the freedom struggle continued to hold the view that the revolutionary movement using weapons of various kinds was indispensable. After India became independent, the National Policy considered Defence Services to be indispensable as a part of support to patriotism. Sri Aurobindo's views cannot be regarded as pacifist, since Sri Aurobindo had believed in the efficacy of revolutionary activities of destruction and he had joined the secret society whose purpose was to prepare a national insurgence. In his public activity, however, he took passive resistance as the means in the struggle, but not as the sole means. In fact, as long as he was in Bengal, he maintained a secret revolutionary activity as preparation for open revolt, in case the passive resistance proved insufficient for the purpose.

To get a fuller idea of Sri Aurobindo in regard to this matter, we should also add the following lines from his famous book, *Essays on Gita*:

> All this is not to say that strife and destruction are the alpha and omega of existence, that harmony is not greater than war, love is more manifest divine than death or that we must not move towards the replacement of physical force by soul-force, of war by peace, of strife by union, of devouring by love, of egoism by universality, of death by immortal life.[7]

---

[7] Sri Aurobindo: Essays on Gita, Centenary Editon, Vol. 13, page 42.

Sri Aurobindo regarded non-violence or peace as the part of the highest ideal, but contended it must be spiritual or at the very least psychological in its basis. He pointed out later in a letter that without a change in human nature it could not come with any finality. If it is admitted on any other basis (mental principle, gospel of *Ahimsa* or any other) it will fail and even leave things worse than before. Sri Aurobindo's position and practice in this matter was the same as Tilak's and that of other nationalist leaders. In any case, Sri Aurobindo insists that violence generated from anger or hatred or as an aggressive principle of action in the conditions of freedom and peace is entirely unjustifiable and it should not be resorted to any extent whatsoever.

IV

Philosophy of Indian nationalism is also the philosophy of patriotism. In view of this philosophy, patriotism is not limited to the love of the land of the country, *janmabhumi*, but it is also love for the people of the land. This philosophy goes even further and inspires love of the values of the culture that have been nourished and promoted through a long history of five thousand years and more. And beyond the values of this great culture, patriotism is in its heart-illumined worship of the smiling and beneficent and strong and powerful *Shakti*, which we call Mother India, *Bharat Mata*. As Sri Aurobindo wrote, a nation is not a piece of earth, nor a figure of spirit, nor a fiction of mind, it is a mighty Shakti composed of the Shaktis of all the millions of units that make up the nation. He further pointed out that the nation is veritably a soul, which is immortal and even when geographically fragmented or divided, it has the power to reunite itself as one unity in diversity.

Indian nationalism has been a source of a great recovery and reassertion of those qualities of Dharma which have been the force of upliftment of millions of peoples of this country. That philosophy inspired thousands of martyrs, great and gallant *Chidambarams*, brave *Padmanabhas*, intrepid *Shivas* who defied the threats of exile and imprisonment. The force of patriotism, of the value of self-sacrifice, of the value of worship of Mother India, -- this patriotism and its values live with us and we stand in the need to remember them, to collect them together and to pour them into a new system of education that we are striving today to construct. In an inspired article (March 11, 1908 of Bande Mataram) Sri Aurobindo gave expression to the voices of the martyrs from their cells which cry out to us and give us an imperishable message which we can incorporate in our studies that aim at value-oriented education:

> Work, but aspire, so that your work may be true to the call you have heard and which we have obeyed; labour for great things first and the small will come of themselves. Cherish the might of the spirit, the nobility of the ideal, the grandeur of the dream; the spirit will create the material it needs, the ideal will bring the real to its body and self-expression, the dream is the stuff out of which the waking world will be created. It was the strength of the spirit which stood with us before the alien tribunal, it was the force of the ideal which led us to the altar of sacrifice, it is the splendour of the dream which supports us through the dreary months and years of our martyrdom.

For these are the truth and the divinity within the movement.[8]

When we think today of value-oriented education and as we are planning to create among our students the immortal spirit of nationalism and patriotism, we are required to develop means by which the vision of the nation can stand out in the centre of their consciousness and they are able to feel and perceive the invisible but mighty soul of Mother India. At the same time, patriotism will also teach them to recognise the soul of other nations, the soul of entire humanity, in particular, the spirit of one united family of humanity. We need to ensure that students of today and tomorrow understand and work for those ideals for which leaders and youths, whether Hindus or Mohammedans, whether Christians or Sikhs, whether Jews or Parsis, irrespective of religion, language and race sacrificed their lives so that we may live in freedom and protect our freedom with courage and heroism.

Sri Aurobindo had conceived of a national system of education, which had three important elements. Firstly, he made it clear that national education did not mean that we have to exile Galileo and Newton and all that came after and teach only what was known to Bhaskara, Aryabhatta and Varahamihira. But it means that an adequate place should be provided for the study of the noble heritage of our country and, while we must keep abreast with the march of truth and knowledge, we must also fit ourselves for existence under actual circumstances. Our education, he suggested, must be up to date in form of substance and modern in life and spirit. Secondly, he pointed out that the major question is not merely what science we learn, but what we shall do with

---

[8] Sri Aurobindo: *Bande Mataram, Centenary Edition, Vol. 1, page 745*

our Indian science and how to acquire the scientific mind and recover the habit of scientific discovery, as also how we shall relate it to other powers of the human mind and scientific knowledge to other knowledge more intimate to other and not less light-giving and power-giving parts of our Indian intelligence and nature. The aim and principle of a true philosophy of national education, according to Sri Aurobindo, should not ignore modern truth and knowledge, but to take our foundation on our own being, our own mind and our own spirit. And thirdly, Sri Aurobindo pointed out that this philosophy of national education should underline the fact that the most advanced minds of the occident are beginning to turn in their red evening for the hope of a new and more spiritual civilisation to the genius of Asia, and at that moment, it would be strange if we can think of nothing better than to cast away our own self and potentialities and put our trust in the dissolving past of Europe.

The values of patriotism, the values of universal brotherhood and the values inherent in the philosophy of national education that demands the discovery of our national soul, -- these and their immense implications would constitute a new message that should guide the formulation of value-oriented education.

In that new system of education, in that new system of value-oriented education, the heritage of India, the heritage that has always inspired the higher aspirations and achievements in India must form an integral part. Philosophy of Indian nationalism, and philosophy of internationalism that respects mutuality of all the national souls and their unity, and the right understanding of the inspiring values of Indian heritage, -- this we need to put forward as the needed elements of India's reconstruction.

SRI AUROBINDO'S PHILOSOPHY OF NATIONALISM AND INTERNATIONALISM

I

There is a sense of something mysterious, invisible and intangible when we think of the concept and reality of the nation. For it is difficult to seize the essentiality of the truth of nationality and nationalism. A nation may exist, and yet it may not be recognisable; it may take birth and grow, and yet be overpowered or overshadowed by larger aggregates such as empires or leagues. The development of a nation may take long periods of centuries for its destructive formation as in the case of France, Germany and India. It may develop in many directions, but not yet integrally. A nation may be recognised as such by some leaders of the country, but not necessarily by the common mind in its self-consciousness. It rests on a geographical unity, and yet this unity can become fragmented or disrupted or divided for short or long periods. A nation may attain even political unity as also geographical unity, and yet its centrifugal and centripetal forces may not be in harmony with each other or in a balanced state of equilibrium. There may be rise and fall in the self-awareness of nationalism; new questions may arise in the course of tide and ebb of nationalism that may disturb the manifestation of what may be called the soul of the nation. And yet, the seer of the soul of the nation will always recognise it and work for its manifestation.

Political history, focussed on the development of human aggregates, particularly of empires and nations, can be variously interpreted for arriving at differing notions of nationality and nationalism. During the first decade of the 20th century, when nationalist philosophy came to preponderate in our country, there were conflicting notions as to what constituted a nation and whether India was really a nation or could become a nation and whether nationalist contentions in regard to nationalism could be justified. We find a brilliant exposition of these views as also their evaluation in the pages of *Bande Mataram* (1906-08) through which Sri Aurobindo provided not only a most luminous and revelatory philosophy of Indian nationalism but also an uplifting force of inspiration which created in the whole country a new spirit of awakening whereby the people were infused with enthusiasm, faith and hope. The cry of Bande Mataram was heard on all sides, and people felt it glorious to be alive and dare and act together. The philosophy of nationalism that was articulated was a philosophy of the truth of the Indian nation and its history, the philosophy of *Swaraj*, the philosophy of ends and means, the philosophy of patriotism, and the philosophy of education and national reconstruction. And the way and the speed with which this philosophy succeeded in a short period of two years in breaking the old apathy and timidity and in fixing in the national consciousness the idea and force of *Swaraj* and the programme through which *Swaraj* was sought to be attained has been rightly looked upon as a miracle and an unparalleled achievement in the entire world history of nationalism.

There were basically three important standpoints in regard to nationalism that were in conflict with each other during the momentous period during which the pages of *Bande Mataram* were being written. There was, first, the viewpoint of the Loyalists; there was, secondly, the view of the Moderates, and there was thirdly, the view of the

Nationalists who were also misleadingly labelled by the Moderates as extremists. According to Loyalists, Indians did not have the capacities and qualities necessary for freedom, and even if they succeeded in developing the necessary fitness, they would, it was argued, do better for themselves and mankind by remaining as a province of the British Empire. According to this view, India cannot, should not and will not be a free, great and united nation, and that India should remain satisfied with good governance by the British rulers and a limited share in the administration. The Moderates believed that India was too weak and disunited to aim at freedom; they welcomed independence if it came, but they were not convinced that India had in the measurable future the means or strength to win freedom or keep it if won. According to them, colonial self-government should be India's aim and they were unwilling to attempt any methods which presupposed strength and cohesion in the nation. The Moderate view was that India may eventually be united, self-governing within limits and prosperous, but not free and great. As against both these views, the Nationalists held that Indians were capable of freedom and that their defects were the results of servitude and could only be removed by the struggle for freedom. They maintained that the choice was not between freedom and dependence, between autonomy and provincial Home Rule, but between freedom and national decay and death. They held that the past history of our country and present circumstances are of such a kind that the great unifying tendencies hitherto baffled by insuperable obstacles had at last found the right condition for the success. They believed that the hour for national unification and freedom had arrived and India should strive to be free and that India could be free and that she would, by the impulse of her past and present, be inevitably driven to the attempt and the attainment of national self-realisation.

There was at the same time another line of thought, according to which diversity of race in India, diversity of religion in India, and diversity of language in India precluded India from becoming a nation and that there was no possibility of creating a nationality in our country. In answer to this perilous contention which was formulated by Mr. N.N. Ghose of the *Indian Nation*, Sri Aurobindo wrote:

> Rather we find that every nationality has been formed not because of, but in spite of, diversity of race or religion or language , and not unoften in spite of the co-existence of all these diversities. The Indian Nation has itself admitted that the English nation has been built out of various races, but he (N.N. Ghose) has not stated the full complexity of the British nation. He has not observed that to this day the races which came later into the British nationality keep their distinct individuality even now and that one of them clings to its language tenaciously. He has carefully omitted the striking example of Switzerland where distinct racial strains speaking three different languages and, later, professing different religions, coalesced into and persisted as one nation without sacrificing a single one of these diversities. In France three different languages are spoken; in America the candidates for White House address the nation in fourteen languages, Austria is a congeries of races and languages, the divisions in Russia are hardly less acute. That

unity in race, religion or languages is essential to nationality is an idea which will not bear examination. Such elements of unity are very helpful to the growth of a nationality, but they are not essential and will not even of themselves assure its growth. The Roman Empire though it created a common language, a common religion and life, and did its best to crush out racial diversities under the heavy weight of its uniform system failed to make one great nation.[1]

Sri Aurobindo also enumerated essential elements of nationality, namely, geographical unity, a common past, a powerful common interest impelling towards unity and certain favourable political conditions which enable the impulse to realise itself in an organised Government expressing nationality and perpetuating its single and united existence. He acknowledged that common interests may be provided by a part of the nation, a race or community, uniting the others under its leadership or domination, or by a united resistance to have a common pressure from outside or within. He underlined that a common enthusiasm coalescing with a common interest is the most powerful fosterer of nationality. He concluded:

> We believe that the necessary elements are present in India, we believe that the time has come and that by a common resistance to a common pressure in the shape of the boycott, inspired by a common enthusiasm and ideal, that united nationality for which the whole

---

[1] Sri Aurobindo: Bande Mataram, Centenary Edition, Vol. 1, pp.506-07.

history of India has been a preparation, will be speedily and mightily accomplished.[2]

II

The theme of Indian nationalism occupied Sri Aurobindo throughout his life, and he wrote on this subject even when he had left in 1910 active participation in the political activity on account of his total occupation with the future of India and the world and with the integral yoga that he was developing and perfecting as an aid to the solution of the evolutionary crisis of humanity. This theme was developed by him in four of his books that he wrote during 1914 and 1921, namely, *The Life Divine*, *The Foundations of Indian Culture*, *The Ideal of Human Unity* and *The Human Cycle*. In these books, we find illuminating analysis and exposition incomparable in depth and context with any other analysis and exposition of what may be called the philosophical foundations of nationalism and Indian nationalism. These foundations, as we discern them in Sri Aurobindo's writings, are those relating to the philosophy of the individual and the aggregate, philosophy of the national aggregate and national unity, philosophy of nationality and nation-state, and philosophy of nationalism, internationalism, and universality.

The philosophy of the individual and the aggregate underlines an inevitable interconnection between the human being and humanity, which is the largest aggregate for human beings. But this interconnection is mediated by the individual's membership of various groups of smaller or larger dimensions. And, at an import-

---

[2] Sri Aurobindo: Bande Mataram, Centenary Edition, Vol. 1, p.507.

ant stage of development, the formation of nations is initiated, and the resultant formation of national unity follows three stages. There is, first, some kind of looser yet sufficiently compelling order of society and common type of civilisation to serve as a framework within which the edifice of the nation can arise. The next stage is marked by a period of stringent organisation directed towards unity and centrality of control and perhaps a general levelling and uniformity under that central direction. Finally, there comes about a period of free internal development, which because of the gains of the second stage of development, would no longer bring with it the peril of disorder, disruption, arrest of the secure growth and formation of the organism. The first stage depends upon the past history and present conditions of the elements that have to be welded into a national unity. Although the spirit, form and equipoise worked out differently in different parts of the world, the motive force that everywhere was the necessity of a large effective form and common social life marked by fixity of status through which individual and common interests might be brought under the yoke of a sufficient religious, political and economic unity. The institution of a fixed social hierarchy seems to have been a necessary stage for the first tendencies of national formation. But in the second stage, there comes about the modification of the social structure so as to make room for a powerful and feasible centre of political and administrative unity. This stage is marked by a strong tendency towards the abrogation of liberties, and we can see here the historical importance of a powerful kingship in the evolution of the nation-type, as it actually developed in the medieval times. The monarchical state concentrated, in its own activities, the whole national life. But the powerful structure and closely-knit order of things were tolerated so long as the nation felt consciously or subconsciously its needs and justification. However, once when that need was fulfilled, conventions developed during the second stage came to be questioned with the growth of self-consciousness among the common masses of the people. This questioning could no longer be suppressed or permanently resisted. Hence, there came about the collapse of the old world and the birth of a new age.

As Sri Aurobindo points out, the nation-unit is not formed and does not exist merely for the sake of existing; its purpose is to provide a larger mould of human aggregation in which the race, and not only classes and individuals, may move towards its full human development. A stage must therefore come when in all directions, men and women have to come into their own, realise the dignity and freedom of humanhood within them and give play to their utmost capacity.

As a result, the ideals of liberty, equality and fraternity came to be formulated and the nation-unit is launched on a new path of maturity. Freedom of the nation and battle for freedom, equality and justice marks the third stage of development. Looking towards the future of this third stage, Sri Aurobindo states:

> Perhaps liberty and equality, liberty and authority, liberty and organised efficiency can never be quite satisfactorily reconciled so long as man individual and aggregate lives by egoism, so long as he cannot undergo a great spiritual and psychological change and rise beyond mere communal association to that third ideal which some vague inner sense made the revolutionary thinkers of France add to their watchwords of liberty and equality, -- the greatest of all the three, though till now

only an empty word on man's lips, the ideal of fraternity or, less sentimentally and more truly expressed, an inner oneness. That no mechanism social, political, religious has ever created or can create; it must take birth in the soul and rise from hidden and divine depths within.[3]

This is the stage which is marked by what Sri Aurobindo calls the discovery of the *nation-soul*, and with this discovery there arises the question of relationship among nation-souls and their relationship with the universal-soul. And this question is centrally related to the question of internationalism and universality.

III

It is against this background that we can profitably study the development of India as a nation and its nationalism. The evolution of India, according to Sri Aurobindo, gives evidence that the essential nation-unit was already existent presiding over the geographical boundaries ranging from the Himalayas up to the Southern Indian Ocean perceived as Rashtra even by the early Rishis of the Rigveda.[4] There was indissoluble national vitality

---

[3] Sri Aurobindo: Social and Political Thought, Centenary Edition, Vol. 15, page 360.
[4] See, for instance, Rigveda, X.121.4:
यस्येमे हिमवन्तो महित्वा यस्य समुद्रं रसया सहाहुः ।
यस्येमाः प्रदिशो यस्य बाहू कस्मै देवाय हविषा विधेम । ।
(Under whose greatness on the one side are the snow peaks of the Himalayas and on the other is the sea with the river-waters, whose both arms are these directions, whom else can we offer our oblations?)

necessitating the inevitable and ultimate emergence of the organised nation. Nation-unit is basically an expression of a natural psychological unity or of the nation-soul. In the striking example of India's development, what is remarkable to observe, however, is the operation of centrifugal forces, the character of which was strong, numerous, complex, and obstinate. And yet the centripetal tendency can also be seen right from the earliest times of which we have records and are typified in the ideal of *Samarat, Chakravarty Raja* and the military and political use of the *ashwvamedha* and *rajsuya* sacrifices. Ramayana and Mahabharata, the two great national epics, illustrate this theme. Mahabharata recounts the establishment of a unifying *dharmarajya* or imperial reign of justice. Ramayana starts with an idealised description of such a rule pictured as one existing in the ancient and sacred past of the country. Subsequent political history of India is marked by a succession of empires, indigenous and foreign, each of them destroyed by centrifugal forces, but each bringing the centripetal tendency nearer to its triumphant emergence. Sri Aurobindo points out that it is a significant circumstance that the more foreign the rule, the greater has been its force for the unification of the subject people. In the words of Sri Aurobindo:

> In this instance, we see that the conversion of the psychological unity on which nationhood is based into the external organised unity by which it is perfectly realised, has taken a period of more than two thousand years and is not yet complete. And yet, since the essentiality of the thing was there, not even the most formidable difficulties and delays, not even the most persistent incapacity for union in the people, not even the most disintegrating shocks from outside have prevailed against

the obstinate subconscious necessity. And this is only the extreme illustration of a general law.[5]

Commenting on the emergence of the nationalist movement in India in the early part of the twentieth century, Sri Aurobindo points out that it was a part of a world-wide movement where nations were seen feeling for their source, trying to find them, seriously endeavouring to act from the new sense and make it consciously operative in the common life and action. This tendency was most powerful in new nations or in those struggling to realise themselves in spite of political subjection or defeat. The reason that Sri Aurobindo assigns for this phenomenon is that it is these nations that needed more to feel the difference between themselves and others so that they could assert and justify their individuality as against the powerful super-life which tended to absorb or efface it. And, Sri Aurobindo continues, precisely because their objective life was feeble and it was difficult to affirm it by its own strength in the diverse circumstances, there was more chance of their seeking for their individuality and its forces of self-assertion in that which was subjective and psychological or at least in that which was of subjective or psychological significance. In the words of Sri Aurobindo:

> The movement of 1905 in Bengal pursued a quite new conception of the nation not merely as a country, but a soul, a psychological, almost a spiritual being and, even when acting from economical and political motives, it

---

[5] Sri Aurobindo: Social and Political Thought, Centenary Edition, Vol. 15, page 289.

sought to dynamise them by this subjective conception [6]

IV

The basic ontological foundation of the philosophy of the individual and the aggregate and of nationality and national unity is to be found in Sri Aurobindo's concept of the reality of the individual spirit and that of the cosmic spirit. According to Sri Aurobindo, the individual is not merely an ephemeral physical creature, a form of mind and body that aggregates and dissolves, but a being, a living power of eternal Truth, a self-manifesting spirit. It is for this reason that Sri Aurobindo points out that the primal law and purpose of the individual life is to seek its own self-development, to find itself, to discover within itself the law and power of its own being and to fulfil it.

In the same way, society, community or nation is also a being, a living power of the eternal Truth, a self-manifestation of the cosmic Spirit, and it is there to express and fulfil in its own way and to the degree of its capacities the special truth and power and meaning of the cosmic Spirit that is within it. It is for this reason, Sri Aurobindo observes, that the primal law and a purpose of the society, community or nation is to seek its own self-fulfilment; it strives rightly to find itself, to become aware within itself of the law and power of its own being and fulfil it as perfectly as possible, to realise all its potentialities, to live its own self-revealing life. The interrelationship between the individual and the nation can therefore be harmonised when there is a surge and discovery both of the individual and of the nation as also of the nations of their inner souls and the process of finding in these souls

---

[6] Sri Aurobindo: Social and Political Thought, Centenary Edition, Vol. 15, pp. 32-33.

the secret of their true development and their drift towards progressive perfection.

Sri Aurobindo sees in the heart of the nationalist movement of India and in the attainment of freedom for India a great possibility of opening a new age in which India can, because of its treasures of spiritual knowledge, discover further secrets whereby Spirit and Matter can be synthesised, and the luminous knowledge of the spirit can illumine and transform the physical life of the earth. India has also the possibility of becoming a pioneering partner in the task of formulating new forms of the largest aggregate in which each nation can relate itself with other nations and bring about a harmonious world-unity in which ideals of liberty, equality and fraternity can find their progressive harmony and fulfilment.

V

There is today much contest in respect of the concept of nation and nationalism, and it is even sometimes suggested that in the coming days of internationalism, globalisation and larger aggregation in the formation of a possible world union, nations and nationalities will be overpassed and the world will enter into post-national stage of existence. This debate and conclusion need to be considered seriously in the light of the real truth of the philosophical foundation of nationalism, Indian nationalism and its possible future.

Sri Aurobindo makes an important distinction between political unity and real unity, and pointing out the fact that the world history shows that there was in the ancient cycle of development a wide pre-national empire building, which is in contrast to modern cycle of nation-building. In other words, empires have been created in the past, indicating the tendency to overshoot nation-units even before they attain any maturity or stability, and that this shows that a nation is not a final unit of aggregation. But at the same time, Sri Aurobindo points out that although empires have exhibited political unity, they have not shown to have in them the force of real unity. He states:

> Empires exist, but they are as yet only political and not real units; they have no life from within and owe their continuance to a force imposed on their constituent elements or else to a political convenience felt or acquiesced in by the constituents and favoured by the world outside. ... If the political convenience of an empire of this kind ceases, if the constituent elements no longer acquiesce and are drawn more powerfully by a centrifugal force, if at the same time the world outside no longer favours the combination, then force alone remains as the one agent of an artificial unity.[7]

Empires are, according to Sri Aurobindo, perishable political unities, in contrast to the nation, a real unity, which is immortal and which will remain so until a greater living unit can be found into which nation idea can merge in obedience to a superior attraction.

Again, dwelling upon the distinction between political unity and real unity, Sri Aurobindo states that this distinction must be made because *"it is of the greatest utility to a true and profound political science and involves the most important consequences. When an empire like*

---

[7] Sri Aurobindo: Social and Political Thought, Centenary Edition, Vol. 15, pp. 285-86.

Austria, a non-national empire, is broken to pieces, it perishes for good; there is no innate tendency to recover the outward unity, because there is no real inner oneness; there is only a politically manufactured aggregate. On the other hand, a real national unity broken up by circumstances will always preserve a tendency to recover and reassert its oneness."[8]

Sri Aurobindo has given the example of the Greek Empire which has gone the way of all empires, but the Greek nation after many centuries of political non-existence, again possesses its separate body, because it has preserved its separate ego and therefore really existed under the covering rule of the Turk. Similar is the example of Italy and in the example of Germany. In all these cases, as was in many others, the unification of Saxon England, medieval France, the formation of the United States of America, Sri Aurobindo points out that there was a real unity, a psychological distinct unit which tended at first ignorantly by the subconscious necessity of its being and afterwards with a sudden or gradual awakening to the sense of political oneness, towards an inevitable external unification. It is, Sri Aurobindo concludes, a distinct group-soul which is driven by inward necessity and uses outward circumstances to constitute for itself an organised body.

Just as the individual is an ontological Spirit, and therefore it can never be reduced to become a mere cog in a machine, even so nation is a living spirit and soul, and therefore it can never permanently be reduced to a status of a mere province of larger and largest aggregates. At the same time, Sri Aurobindo underlines the fact that hu-

---

[8] Sri Aurobindo: Social and Political Thought, Centenary Edition, Vol. 15, pp.286.87.

manity is turning today towards world unity, and the central problem for the human endeavour in this connection will be as to how the nation will adjust itself to the pressure of the forces that are today creating phenomena which are global, world-wide and planetary in character.

In this connection, Sri Aurobindo makes a distinction between national ego and national soul, corresponding to the distinction in regard to the individual life where the superficial ego is seen to be distinct from the true individual soul. The mark of egoism, according to Sri Aurobindo, is its superficiality and its ignorant attempt to arrive at superficial unity whether that ego is individual or national. The mark of the ego is its sense of division from all the rest, its pretension to be entirely independent in a poise of superiority over all the others. Corresponding to this ego, Sri Aurobindo points out, there is no real reality. There is no ontological superficial reality, there is no independent divided entity which is superior to all the rest. The true individual, on the other hand, has indeed distinctiveness, but is not divided from the others. The true individual and the true nation-soul are characterised by mutuality, interdependence and inner oneness that manifests in diversity. Based upon this philosophical foundation, Sri Aurobindo perceives the future of nations as entities seeking and finding their inner souls by virtue of which they will remain free but mutually interdependent, and this, in turn, will provide the form of world unity that is supportive and not destructive of the nations. Sri Aurobindo speaks of a world union of free nations, each having status of equality, and all contributing through their distinctive capacities to the fund of richness and variety at the global level.

Sri Aurobindo formulates therefore an ideal law of social development in which the truths of the individual, of the nations and of humanity are all reconciled and synthesised. This is the law as he has formulated:

> Thus the law for the individual is to perfect his individuality by free development from within, but to respect and to aid and be aided by the same free development in others. His law is to harmonise his life with the life of the social aggregate and to pour himself out as a force for growth and perfection on humanity. The law for the community or nation is equally to perfect its corporate existence by a free development form within, aiding and taking full advantage of that of the individual, but to respect and to aid and be aided by the same free development of other communities and nations. Its law is to harmonise its life with that of the human aggregate and to pour itself out as a force for growth and perfection on humanity. The law for humanity is to pursue its upward evolution towards the finding and expression of the Divine in the type of mankind, taking full advantage of the free development and gains of all individuals and nations and groupings of men, to work towards the day when mankind may be really and not only ideally one divine family, but even then, when it has succeeded in unifying itself, to respect, aid and be aided by the free growth and activity of its individuals and constituent aggregates.[9]

---

[9] Sri Aurobindo: Social and Political Thought, Centenary Edition, Vol. 15, pp.63-64.

VI

It can be said that the fulfilment of this ideal law of social or national development is the task that still remains to be fulfilled. In this task, Indian nationalism can play a leading role. But before that task can be fulfilled, there are still some others which need to be initiated and developed. Sri Aurobindo has spoken of three aims that free India should concentrate upon. In the first place, a great effort must be made for the recovery of the old spiritual knowledge and experience in all its splendour, depths and fullness. Sri Aurobindo considers this to be the most essential work. Secondly, an endeavour must be made for the flowing of this spirituality into new forms of philosophy, literature, art, science and critical knowledge. The third aim that should be pursued should consist of an original dealing with modern problems in the light of Indian spirit, and the goal should be to formulate a greater synthesis of a spiritualised society. According to Sri Aurobindo, India's success on these three lines will be the measure of its help to the future of humanity.

We may also remember the following prophetic words of Sri Aurobindo, which give us a great inspiration and enthusiasm for the continuance of the work of Indian nationalism for today and tomorrow:

> India of the ages is not dead nor has she spoken her last creative word; she lives and has still something to do for herself and the human peoples. And that which must seek now to awake is not an anglicised oriental people, docile pupil of the West and doomed to repeat the cycle of the occident's success and failure, but still the ancient memorable Shakti recovering her deepest self, lifting her head

higher towards the supreme source of light and strength and turning to discover the complete meaning and a vaster form of her Dharma.[10]

---

[10] Sri Aurobindo: *The Foundations of Indian Culture, Centenary Edition, Vol. 14, pp.380-381*

SRI AUROBINDO'S PHILOSOPHY
OF THE
IDEAL OF HUMAN UNITY

I

Globalisation is an attractive word; for it evokes in us a noble sentiment of "one earth" and of humankind as one race born of one common Mother Earth; it raises in us a dream of the ideal of human unity and of universal fraternity. But when we examine the current phenomenon of globalisation, we find that it is a growing network spreading over the whole globe in which the old forces of competition and resultant asymmetrical relations constitute the central forum of action and reaction. Here globality is the globality of market forces that are free to develop hegemony of dominant and rich nations. We do not find here global relations of cooperation, even of friendliness. This is no manifestation of global consciousness in which unity and oneness predominate.

At its root, contemporary globalisation is a result of the material circumstances where scientific discoveries have made our earth so small that its vastest kingdoms seem now no more than the provinces of a single country. Considering also that the human intellect has at present been so mechanised that it is likely to push forward the tide of globalisation through mechanical means and through social and political adjustments. This is where we can foresee the perils of the coming day, unless the normative consciousness of humanity intervenes in a decisive way.

Globalisation can not be arrested; mechanical means for their operations and rapid advancements have been set to work, and there is no agency of wisdom which has yet come to the surface to control and to guide; and, in reality, wisdom can not become mechanical and can not translate itself into any artificial agency. If, therefore, perils of globalisation are to be avoided, efforts have to be made to effect a great change in the heart and mind of the human race; people have to awake to wisdom in time and accept the difficult process of inner change, even though external adjustments will also need to be effected. The truth behind globalisation is, indeed, that of the ideal unity of the human race, but to bring forth that truth and to make it operative, we seem to be in need of a deeper study of the issues and of a greater opening to profounder means and remedies.

At this juncture, we are impelled to think afresh of globality, global consciousness and the ideal of human unity. For globalisation can be turned into a favourable circumstance if we consciously strive at the concrete manifestation of unity of the human race, which has always been latent and secretly operative. It can even be said that the ideal of human unity seems to be making its way to the front of our consciousness because this is the opportune moment when that ideal can be actualised.

II

Four factors have combined together to generate the present phenomenon of globalisation. Firstly, there is the amazing triumph of science and technology which have been applied on a large scale to the production of services and goods and their transportation across the globe. Secondly, social, political, commercial and industrial institutions have tended towards standardisation, mechanisation and even dehumanisation in the processes of management, governance and even in human relationships. Thirdly, there has been a grim battle between the ideals of capitalism, socialism and communism which stand today at a point of disequilibrium that tilts heavily towards privatisation and capitalistic forces which favour the growth of multinationals and expansions of markets that promote multiplication of physical and vital wants, consumerism and motivations of economic security, competitive methods of enrichment, and profit-making. And, fourthly, science and philosophy, the two great magnets that uplift the powers of Reason towards greater heights of truth, beauty and goodness, have tended towards the denials that emerge from materialism resulting in refusals to inquire into claims of ethical and spiritual domains. The general climate that rules the globe today is that of the pull of humanity downward towards confinement to the demands of physical and vital life.

In terms of the history of civilisation, humankind is turning more and more decisively and globally, not only towards philistinism but even a kind of barbarism where the barbarian can roam about the world taking full advantages of the civilisation that has been created so far by the past achievements of culture, of reason, ethics, aesthetics and religious and spiritual pursuits. This is a kind of invasion of barbarism that aims at physical stability in what seems to be a hostile world. In the past, history has witnessed the floods of the overpowering invasions that have devastated the cultures that had reached some kind of climactic points of achievements. In the present stage of history, on account of the fact that science has reached such a triumph of knowledge and its application that the invasion of the barbarians from outside, except in terms of terrorism and allied forms, may become impossible. But the peril is that of the invasion of the barbarian from within, from the circle of the civilised world itself. And this peril, -- the peril of the monstrous barbarian controlling the civilised world on a global scale, -- needs to be combated if the future is to be saved from the suffocations and sufferings that afflict the inner spirit when it is denied its natural upward urge towards its highest cultural fulfilment.

Indeed, there are behind the contemporary globalisation higher and nobler motives at work, the most important of which is the drive towards the fulfilment of the dream of humanity to arrive at a form of organisation that would foster a united family of humanity in a state of perpetual progress, prosperity and multi-layered happiness that comes from constant ascension from height to greater heights. These nobler and higher motives that have inspired the ideal of human unity and brought about the birth of noble and momentous institutions such as those of the United Nations and its international agencies do not, however, seem to be strong enough to meet the present perilous situation that confronts us today. We need to study the reasons for this so that we may arrive at better propositions of solution than what have been offered to us so far. This study will lead us to the consideration of the problems of centralisation and decentralisation, of the relationship between the individual and the collectivity, the drift of history at the present juncture, and the possibilities of the future in the light of the nature of the human situation in its horizontal and vertical possibilities.

III

Human history may, in a sense, be perceived as a multi-layered and complex struggle to harmonise the claims of the individual and those of the collectivity. The development of this struggle seems to be cyclic or spiral rather than linear in character. This has also to be seen in terms of the evolution of the human species and the laws of that evolution. For these laws follow the curve of the development of the faculties of the body, life and mind in which the concern for the physical base and infusion of the developing and developed powers of life and mind in a very zigzag swinging curve of advance appears to be predominant. There are, what we may call, the laws of ascent and integration, as a result of which the relationships between the individual and the collectivity are being built up in such a way that as soon as lower elements of achievement reach a point of maturity they tend to higher grades of achievement in a gradual manner so as to interweave the lower and the higher in a complex series of harmony of conflicting claims. If we study these laws, we find that evolution is a continuous process and humanity is one of the crucial links in the process that seems to lead it to levels of progression that in turn lead the development of the mind to that which lies beyond the mind and even higher grades of consciousness which are appropriate to the spirit, and its wider, deeper and higher domains.

The evolutionary study of humanity has its origin in our times in the Darwinian theory, but it has found developments in the writings of philosophers like Bergson, Alexander, Smutts, Whitehead and Teillard de Chardin. But the most elaborate and comprehensive study is to be found in the writings of Sri Aurobindo, particularly, in his *The Life Divine, The Synthesis of Yoga, The Human Cycle* and *The Ideal of Human Unity*. In one of the important passages, Sri Aurobindo states:

> The animal is a living laboratory in which Nature has, it is said, worked out man. Man himself may well be a thinking and living laboratory in whom and with whose conscious cooperation she wills to work out the superman, the god. Or shall we not say, rather, to manifest God? For if evolution is the progressive manifestation by Nature of that which slept or worked in her, involved, it is also the overt realisation of that which she secretly is. We cannot, then, bid her pause at a given stage of her evolution, nor have we the right to condemn with the religionist as perverse and presumptuous or with the rationalist as a disease or hallucination any intention she may evince or effort she may make to go beyond. If it be true that Spirit is involved in Matter and apparent Nature is secret God, then the manifestation of the divine in himself and the realisation of God within and without are the highest and most legitimate aim possible to man upon earth.[1]

According to Sri Aurobindo, the evolution of the human being in regard to the development of human faculties and those that are beyond human limitations is conducted, firstly, by a conscious effort of the human mind, and it is not confined to an unconscious progression of Nature. Secondly, this evolution takes into account the sense of freedom that emerges along with the development of self-consciousness, and with the process of a rational and normative consciousness. The evolutionary process is, therefore, marked by alternative possibilities which can even be perilous, as in any great adventure. Evolution, as

---

[1] Sri Aurobindo, *The Life Divine*, American Edition, pp. 5-6

conceived by Sri Aurobindo, is a great adventure of consciousness, in which the operation of free will is a necessary component.

It is against this background that the conflict between the individual and the collectivity needs to be understood.

Human history may be considered as a long story of the sway of the developing consciousness between three preoccupations of human idealism, -- the complete single development of the human being himself, the perfectibility of the individual, a full development of the collective being, the perfectibility of the society, and, more pragmatically restricted, the perfect or best possible relation of individual with individual and society or of community with community. Hence, we find in history that sometimes an exclusive or dominant emphasis is laid on the individual, sometimes on the collectivity and society, sometimes on a right and balanced relations between the individual and the collective human whole. According to one ideal, freedom and growth of perfection of the individual is to be held up as a true objective of our existence. This ideal is sometimes conceived as that of a mere free self-expression of the personal being or as a self-governed whole of complete mind, fine and ample life and perfect body, or a spiritual perfection and liberation. In the perspective of this view, the society is conceived only as a field of activity and growth for the individual mind and serves best its function when it gives as far as possible a wide room, ample means, a sufficient freedom or guidance of development to his thought, his action, his growth, his possibility of fullness of being. The opposite ideal gives the collective life the first or sole importance; the existence, the growth of the race is of the highest value in this view; the individual is expected to live for the society or for mankind or even, he is considered only a cell of the society, and he has no other use or purpose of birth, no other meaning of his presence in Nature, no other foundation. Or, it is sometimes held that the nation, the society, the community is a collective being, revealing its soul in its culture, power of life, ideals, institutions, or its ways of self-expression. In this context, the individual life has to cast itself in the social mould, serving the power of its life, consent only to exist as an instrument for the maintenance and efficient existence of the society. In a third ideal, the perfection of man lies in his ethical and social relations with other human beings, his social being and his love for society, for others, for his utility to the race. In this view, society exists for the service of all, to give them their right framework of relations, education, training, economical opportunity, right frame of life.

Sri Aurobindo points out that in the ancient cultures, the greatest emphasis was laid on the community and a fitting of the individual into the community. Even then, however, there grew up an ideal of a perfect individual and it is found that the idea of the spiritual individual was dominant in ancient India, although the society was of extreme importance and the individual had to pass first to the social states of the physical, vital, mental being with satisfaction of interest, desire, pursuit of knowledge and right living – *kama, artha* and *dharma* – before he could reach fitness for the truer state of free spiritual existence (*moksha*). In contrast to this, Sri Aurobindo finds that in recent times the whole stress has fallen on the life of the race, to search for a perfect society, and the right organisation and scientific mechanisation of the life of mankind as a whole. Under this circumstance, the individual now tends to be regarded only as a member of the collectivity, a unit of the race whose existence must be subordinated to the common aims and total interest of the organised society, and much less or not at all as a mental or spiritual being with his own right and power of existence. Again, under the same circumstances, the modern State erects its godhead and demands his obedience, subjugation, and self-immolation. The individual is then required to affirm, against this exorbitant claim, the rights of his ideals, his ideas, his personality.

The conflict between the individual and the collectivity seems at this stage to have reached, according to Sri Aurobindo, the stage of an acute conflict of standards, which presses us towards a search for a unifying and harmonising knowledge, and even integrality of knowledge. The individual in Sri Aurobindo's view, is the key of the evolutionary movement; for it is the individual who finds himself and becomes conscious of the Reality and its relationship with the collectivity. According to this vision, the individual does not owe his allegiance, either to the State which is a machine or to the community which is part of life and not the whole of life; his allegiance to use Sri Aurobindo's own words, *"must be to the Truth, the Self, the Spirit, the Divine which is in him and in all; not to subordinate or lose himself in the mass, but to find and express that truth of being in himself and help the community and humanity in its seeking for its own truth and fullness of being must be his real object of existence."*[2]

Indeed, Sri Aurobindo acknowledges that so long as human being is undeveloped, he has to subordinate in many ways his undeveloped self to whatever is greater than it. As he develops, he moves towards a spiritual freedom, but this freedom is not something entirely separate from all existence. As he moves towards the

---

[2] Sri Aurobindo, *The Life Divine*, American Edition, page 930

spiritual freedom, he moves also towards spiritual oneness. In the words of Sri Aurobindo:

> The spiritually realised, the liberated man is preoccupied, says the Gita, with the good of all beings; Buddha discovering the way of Nirvana must turn back to open that way to those who are still under the delusion of their constructive instead of their real being – or non-being; Vivekananda, drawn by the Absolute also feels the call of the disguised Godhead in humanity and most the call of the fallen and the suffering, the call of the self to the self in the obscure body of the universe. For the awakened individual the realisation of his truth of being and his inner liberation and perfection must be his primary seeking, -- first, because that is the call of the Spirit within him, but also because it is only by liberation and perfection and realisation of the truth of being that man can arrive at truth of living. A perfected community also can exist only by the perfection of its individuals, and perfection can come only by the discovery and affirmation in life by each of his own spiritual being and the discovery by all of their spiritual unity and a resultant life of unity. There can be no real perfection for us except by our inner self and truth of spiritual existence taking up all truth of the instrumental existence into itself and giving to it oneness, integration, harmony. As our only real freedom is the discovery and disengagement of the spiritual Reality within us, so our only means of true perfection is the sovereignty

Sri Aurobindo's Philosophy of the Ideal of Human Unity

and self-effectuation of the spiritual Reality in all the elements of our nature.[3]

In the light of this larger vision, when Sri Aurobindo examines, in his book *The Ideal of Human Unity*, interesting periods of human life, he finds that the scenes in which life was most richly lived and has left behind it the most precious fruits are to be seen in those periods, and in those countries in which humanity was able to organise itself in small independent centres, but infused into a single unity. Sri Aurobindo marks out particularly three such moments in human history to which modern Europe owes two-third of its civilisation. The first of these moments is to be found in the religious life of tribes in Israel; the second moment was that of the many-sided life of the small Greek city states; and the third was the smaller, though more restricted artistic and intellectual life of medieval Italy. Similarly, as far as Asia is concerned, no age was so rich in energy, so well worth living in, so productive of the best and the most enduring fruits as the heroic period of India when she was divided into small kingdoms, many of them no larger than a modern district. The second best period of India, according to Sri Aurobindo, came afterwards in larger, but still comparatively small, nations and kingdoms like those of Pallavas, Chalukyas, Pandyas, Cholas and Cheras.

Again, Sri Aurobindo finds that even when there developed the organisation of nations, kingdoms and empires, it was groupments of smaller nations which have had the most intense life and not the huge States and colossal empires. His conclusion is that collective life, when it diffuses itself in very vast spaces, seems to lose intensity and productiveness. As illustrations, he points out that

---

[3] Sri Aurobindo, *The Life Divine*, American Edition, pp. 930-31

Europe has lived in England, France, Netherlands, Spain, Italy, the small states of Germany, -- not in the huge mass of the Holy Roman or the Russian Empire. He also notices that in the organisation of nations and kingdoms, those which have had the most vigorous life have gained it by a sort of artificial concentration of the vitality into some head, centre or capital, London, Paris, Rome. Sri Aurobindo sees in these examples the basic argument in favour of decentralisation and this favourable argument derives a special force from the fact that it is in the climate of decentralisation that the individual gains greater freedom from his subordination to the group or the community. On the other hand, in such examples as that of the Roman Empire, Sri Aurobindo finds that the individual freedom is greatly subordinated to the needs of the forces of centralisation which tend towards uniformity rather than towards freedom and diversity. Considering, however, that there is today a turn towards the formation of the larger human aggregate encompassing the whole world, Sri Aurobindo analyses the example of the Roman Empire from the point of view of the theme of freedom and the conditions under which the individual can attain through freedom his self-realisation and fullness. That Empire provides a historical illustration of advantages of organisation, peace, widespread security, order, and material well-being. But the disadvantages arose from its tendency to centralise, to impose union, and as a result the individual, the city, the region had to sacrifice their independent life and they became mechanical parts – a machine. As Sri Aurobindo remarks, the organisation was great and admirable, but the individual dwindled and life lost its colour, richness, variety, freedom, and victorious impulse towards creation. Eventually, therefore, the Roman Empire declined and failed; the huge mechanism of centralisation and union brought about smallness and feebleness of the individual; mechanisation prevailed and the Empire lost even its conservative vitality and died of an increasing stagnation.

The problems of the individual and the collectivity, of centralisation and decentralisation, of freedom and diversity and consequent richness and vigour of life without which the community cannot prolong its health and cohesion, -- these problems are extremely important, and Sri Aurobindo formulates an ideal law of social development that needs to be applied, if the world is to be united and which is yet to provide to the individual the needed freedom for his growth, self-discovery, self-realisation and self-perfection. Sri Aurobindo states this law in the following words:

> Thus the law for the individual is to perfect his individuality by free development from within, but to respect and to aid and be aided by the same free development in others. His law is to harmonise his life with the life of the social aggregate and to pour himself out as a force for growth and perfection on humanity. The law for the community or nation is equally to perfect its corporate existence by a free development from within, aiding and taking full advantage of that of the individual, but to respect and to aid and be aided by the same free development of other communities and nations. Its law is to harmonise its life with that of the human aggregate and to pour itself out as a force for growth and perfection on humanity. The law for humanity is to pursue its upward evolution towards the finding and expression of the Divine in the type of mankind, taking full advantage of the free develop-

ment and gains of all individuals and nations and groupings of men, to work towards the day when mankind may be really and not only ideally one divine family, but even then, when it has succeeded in unifying itself, to respect, aid and be aided by the free growth and activity of its individuals and constituent aggregates.[4]

Sri Aurobindo acknowledges that this ideal law has never become operative in the imperfect states through which humankind has so far travelled, and it may be very long before that law can be attained. But Sri Aurobindo maintains that the present is the stage of what he calls *the subjective age of humanity*, when knowledge is increasing and diffusing itself with an unprecedented rapidity, when individuals, societies and nations are attempting to discover their potentialities and their inner subjective states and selves, when capacity is generating itself, when men and nations are drawn close together, and this is the time when we can justifiably develop a conscious hope to arrive at a conscious discovery of that ideal law of social development and its conscious application. He finds that the present moment is opportune for an upward march, particularly when people of the entire globe are getting united, although partially and in an inextricable entanglement of chaotic unity. For this is the moment where we are being compelled to know each other and impelled to know more profoundly ourselves, humankind, and the world, and when the idea of self-realisation for ourselves and nations is coming consciously to the upper and outer surface. This is the time, according to Sri Aurobindo, for the human being in particular to know himself, to find the

---

[4] Sri Aurobindo: *The Human Cycle,* Centenary Edition, Volume 15, pp. 63-4

ideal law of his being and his development and to hold that law before him and to find out gradually the way by which it can become more and more the moulding principle of the individual and social existence.

IV

At the same time, Sri Aurobindo regards the present moment of human history as a moment of acute crisis. For the process of self-realisation, both for the individual and the collectivity is always difficult and it is marked by an acute struggle of groping in the darkness and in the welter of conflicts and uncertain alternatives. In Sri Aurobindo's analysis of the psychology of the process of maturation of self-finding, Sri Aurobindo examines the psychology of barbarism, philistinism, and of the rational, ethical and aesthetic culture, and examines also the means by which the society manages to arrive at some kind of cohesion at different stages of development, namely, through symbolism and later by typal thought, conventional thought and by subjective self-awakening both of the individual and collectivity. In the subjective age, which is marked by preponderance of Reason as also by a revolt against conventions, customs and traditions, Sri Aurobindo perceives the possibility of a true flowering of the inner spirit, which can harmonise the individual good, and the social good and in the context of which a form of world unity could be invented whereby human beings of the entire globe can live together in durable peace and progressive harmony as in one united family. In this context, Sri Aurobindo finds the three great ideals that were put forward explicitly and forcefully during the French Revolution to be most significant, namely the ideals of liberty, equality and fraternity. He finds that these three ideals served the purpose of motivating the great experiments that humankind conducted during the curve of the Rational Age, the Age which was ushered in by the Renaissance in Europe, the age through which humankind is at present passing, and which has now reached a kind of an end and which has the possibility of opening the gates of a beginning of a new age, which he calls the *Spiritual Age*. It is when Reason explores its possibilities and brings into operation its capabilities that the human race can arrive at a critical point of its self-realisation and self-perfection. For it is then, as it has now become clearer, that it is found that the role of Reason is not to govern but to become a medium and an intermediate power that can lift human life from the levels of blind impulse to the realms of light of the Spirit. For the real governor can be only that light and knowledge, which is integral and which unites the individual with the universal without requiring the individual to be abolished and which shows both to the individual and to the universal that their source is in the same transcendental that is the foundation of oneness and unity of existence.

The age of Reason, according to Sri Aurobindo, has shown that when the ideal of liberty is emphasised and sought to be implemented, the ideal of equality is required to be sacrificed; and when the ideal of equality is emphasised and sought to be implemented, the ideal of liberty is required to be strangulated. Towards the end of the Age of Reason, there emerges therefore the ideal of anarchism and the question arises whether anarchist thought can any more successfully find a satisfying social principle. Sri Aurobindo points out that the anarchist thought, although it is not yet formed in its assured form, cannot develop any appropriate basis or form of harmony as long as it relies on the powers of the intellect. He points out that a rational satisfaction cannot give to humanity safety from the pull from below nor deliver it from the attraction from above. It is true that the more the outer law is replaced by the inner law, the nearer will man be to his natural perfection, and the perfect State must be one in which governmental compulsion is abolished and man is able to live with his fellowmen by a free agreement and cooperation. But this can truly be secured by a power greater than that of reason. According to Sri Aurobindo, it is not intellectual anarchism but a spiritual or spiritualised anarchism that will bring us nearer to the solution or at least touch something of it from afar. In the words of Sri Aurobindo:

> It is a spiritual, an inner freedom that can alone create a perfect human order. It is a spiritual, a greater than the rational enlightenment that can alone illumine the vital nature of man and impose harmony on its self-seekings, antagonisms and discords. A deeper brotherhood, a yet unfound law of love is the only sure foundation possible for a perfect social evolution, no other can replace it. But this brotherhood and love will not proceed by the vital instincts or the reason where they can be met, baffled or deflected by opposite reasonings and other discordant instincts. Nor will it found itself in the natural heart of man where there are plenty of other passions to combat it. It is in the soul that it must find its roots; the love which is founded upon a deeper truth of our being, the brotherhood or, let us say, -- for this is another feeling than any vital or mental sense of brotherhood, a calmer more durable motive-force, -- the spiritual comradeship which is the expression of an inner realisation of oneness. For so only can egoism

disappear and the true individualism of the unique godhead in each man found itself on the true communism of the equal godhead in the race; for the Spirit, the inmost Self, the universal Godhead in every being is that whose very nature of diverse oneness it is to realise the perfection of its individual life and nature in the existence of all, in the universal life and nature.[5]

According to Sri Aurobindo, the present stage of human development can become a gate for the arrival of a spiritual age in which the ideal of brotherhood can come to be practised and it is only in that condition that a new form of human unity can be forged in which the individual and the collectivity, even on a global scale or organisation, can come to be harmonised. In the meantime, however, the transition from the end of the curve of Reason to the advent and progress of the spiritual age is a stage of crisis, which needs to be examined in a greater depth, since it is the crisis which has become accentuated today by the latest developments with which we are besieged today.

V

Sri Aurobindo considers the present stage of crisis as an evolutionary crisis in which the human will is called upon to make a free choice. This is the crisis where evolution of human Reason is required to make a choice under the pressure that impels the creation of a life of universalised rule of economic barbarism. At the same time, Reason is increasingly obliged also to exercise its role in lifting up

---

[5] Sri Aurobindo: *The Human Cycle*, Centenary Edition, Volume 15, pp.206-7

humanity to create a life of unity, mutuality and harmony born of a deeper and wider truth of our being. For there are three forces that work today upon humanity. On the one hand, there is a force that is striving to assert the barbarism within the civilised man. For it is possible to utilise the present scientific and technical knowledge to create an order of existence in which physical and vital wants of the human being can greatly, if not fully be satisfied, and this order of existence can be maintained by mechanical devices and application of the power of machines that can imprison the human spirit. There is also a second alternative in which human reason can continue to spin into larger or narrower circles propounding great dreams but never fulfilling them. And there is a third alternative in which the human being consents to rise to the higher levels than those of the Reason and consents to be spiritualised. The question, therefore, is whether the human being will choose to remain arrested in some kind of intermediary typal perfection like earlier animal kinds, or whether he will consent to rise to a higher level of evolution. The necessity to make the choice has created a state of a crisis, since the choice to pursue a higher level is not only difficult but appears at first sight to be almost impossible. Sri Aurobindo describes this crisis as follows:

> At present mankind is undergoing an evolutionary crisis in which is concealed a choice of its destiny; for a stage has been reached in which the human mind has achieved in certain directions an enormous development while in others it stands arrested and bewildered and can no longer find its way. A structure of the external life has been raised up by man's ever-active mind and life-will, a

structure of an unmanageable hugeness and complexity, for the service of his mental, vital, physical claims and urges, a complex political, social, administrative, economic, cultural machinery, an organised collective means for his intellectual, aesthetic and material satisfaction. Man has created a system of civilisation which has become too big for his limited mental capacity and understanding and his still more limited spiritual and moral capacity to utilise and manage, a too dangerous servant of his blundering ego and its appetites. ...A greater whole-being, whole-knowledge, whole-power is needed to weld all into a grater unity of whole-life.[6]

VI

As a part of this crisis, and as an aid to the higher choice that can be made by humanity, Sri Aurobindo perceives two important phenomena of the modern world which present a great sign of hope. These two phenomena are those of internationalism and of religion of humanity. But these two phenomena need to be understood in their inner implications. For internationalism seems to oppose the truth and force of nationalism, and this opposition can be fatal to a harmonious transition to a new world of harmony. There is today a sentiment helped and stimulated by the trend of forces that favours the creation of an international world organisation that may ultimately result in a possible form of unification. This sentiment is a cosmopolitan and international sentiment. At one stage, it came to be presented concretely in the conception of the League of Nations. As Sri Aurobindo points out, this

---

[6] Sri Aurobindo: *The Life Divine,* American Edition, pp.933-34

conception was not well inspired in its form or destined to have a considerable longevity or a supremely successful career. But the very fact that this idea was presented and even manifested in a concrete form, even though for a short term, was in itself an event of capital importance and meant the ushering in of a new era in world history. Sri Aurobindo points out that even though it failed, it could not be allowed to remain without a sequel. Accordingly, the League of Nations was replaced by the United Nations Organisation which now stands in the forefront of the world and struggles towards some kind of secure permanence and success in the great far reaching endeavour on which depends the world's future. Emphasising the importance of the United Nations Organisation, Sri Aurobindo wrote in 1949 (in a Postscript Chapter to his *The Ideal of Human Unity*) the following:

> This is the capital event, the crucial and decisive outcome of the world-wide tendencies which Nature has set in motion for her destined purpose. In spite of the constant shortcomings of human effort and its stumbling mentality, in spite of adverse possibilities that may baulk or delay for a time the success of this great adventure, it is in this event that lies the determination of what must be. All the catastrophes that have attended this course of events and seem to arise of purpose in order to prevent the working out of her intention have not prevented, and even further catastrophes will not prevent, the successful emergence and development of an enterprise which has be-

come a necessity for the progress and perhaps the very existence of the race.[7]

Following the idea of the United Nations Organisation, Sri Aurobindo foresees the development of a World-State without exclusions and on a principle of equality into which consideration of size and strength would not enter. Indeed, Sri Aurobindo raises the question of the freedom of the individual and of the nations in the context of the emergence of the World-State. And in this context, Sri Aurobindo considers it necessary that a profounder spiritual ideal of the individual and of the nation should emerge and vivify the world organisation in such a way that the spirit of the individual and the spirit of the nation, the freedom of the individual and the freedom of the nation are not only maintained but respected and perfected. Sri Aurobindo, therefore, speaks of a union of free people which could open the prospect of a sound and lasting order.

In this context, the emergence of a religion of humanity is of a greater significance, although he finds its present intellectual form hardly sufficient. Sri Aurobindo, therefore, advocates the emergence of a spiritual religion of humanity and explains that he does not mean by it what is called a universal religion, a system, a creed of intellectual principle and dogma and outward rite. For Sri Aurobindo emphasises the growth of the realisation that there is a secret spirit, a divine Reality, in which we are one, that humanity is its highest representation in the world, that the human being is the means by which it will progressively reveal itself here. There must be, according to Sri Aurobindo, the realisation by the individual that

---

[7] Sri Aurobindo: *The Ideal of Human Unity*, Centenary Edition, Volume 15, pp.556-57.

only in the life of his fellowmen is his own life complete. There must be, he adds, the realisation by the race that only on the free and fullness of the individual can its own perfection and happiness be founded. Finally, Sri Aurobindo points out the need of the discipline and the way by which each individual can be developed in accordance with his or her line of development towards integrality and an all-embracing perfection. In defining the spiritual religion of humanity in which the ideals of liberty, equality and fraternity can be harmonised, Sri Aurobindo states:

> Yet is brotherhood the real key to the triple gospel of the idea of humanity. The union of liberty and equality can only be achieved by the power of human brotherhood and it cannot be founded on anything else. But brotherhood exists only in the soul and by the soul; it can exist by nothing else. For this brotherhood is not a matter either of physical kinship or of vital association or of intellectual agreement. When the soul claims freedom, it is the freedom of its self-development, the self-development of the divine in man in all his being. When it claims equality, what it is claiming is that freedom equally for all and the recognition of the same soul, the same godhead in all human beings. When it strives for brotherhood, it is founding that equal freedom of self-development on a common aim, a common life, a unity of mind and feeling founded upon the recognition of this inner spiritual unity. These three things are in fact the nature of the soul; for freedom, equality, unity are the eternal attributes of the

Spirit. It is the practical recognition of this truth, it is the awakening of the soul in man and the attempt to get him to live from his soul and not from his ego which is the inner meaning of religion, and it is that to which the religion of humanity also must arrive before it can fulfil itself in the life of the race.[8]

In spite of the difficulties and critical trials through which humanity may be required to pass, Sri Aurobindo underlines the need of understanding the inevitability of the spiritual solution. Indeed, in presenting this solution, Sri Aurobindo is aware that it may be objected that it puts off the consummation of a better human society to a far off date in the future evolution of the race. But Sri Aurobindo affirms forcefully:

... if this is not the solution, then there is no solution; if this is not the way, then there is no way for the human kind. Then the terrestrial evolution must pass beyond man as it has passed beyond the animal and a greater race must come that will be capable of the spiritual change, a form of life must be born that is nearer to the divine. After all there is no logical necessity for the conclusion that the change cannot begin at all because its perfection is not immediately possible. A decisive turn of mankind to the spiritual ideal, the beginning of a constant ascent and guidance towards the heights may not be altogether impossible, even if the summits are attainable at first only by the pioneer few and far-off to the tread of the

---

[8] Sri Aurobindo: *The Ideal of Human Unity*, Centenary Edition, Volume 15, pp.546-7

race. And that beginning may mean the descent of an influence that will alter at once the whole life of mankind in its orientation and enlarge for ever as did the development of his reason and more than any development of the reason, its potentialities and all its structure.[9]

According to Sri Aurobindo, the world is a mutable world and uncertainties and dangers cannot be avoided. But he places before us a vision of the way in which a World-Union could come into being that would ensure the freedom and perfection of the individual and the freedom of nationalities could be ensured in a world federation. Perils are on the way, but Sri Aurobindo maintains that the ideal of human unity will no more remain an unfulfilled ideal but an accomplished fact and its preservation come into charge of the united human peoples. Much will depend, according to Sri Aurobindo, on the intellectual and moral capacity of humanity to carry out what is evidently the one thing needful, namely, a concentrated effort at the spiritual change that can sustain a global and united human family.

---

[9] *Ibid., page 207*

EDUCATIONAL PHILOSOPHY OF SRI AUROBINDO

Sri Aurobindo wrote a series of articles on education in the *Karma Yogin* during 1909-10 under the title "*A System of National Education*" and "*The National Value of Art*". He also wrote "*A Preface to National Education*" which appeared in the *Arya* in 1920 in two parts. His book, "*The Synthesis of Yoga*" in which we find extraordinary insights in regard to education, appeared serially in the *Arya* from August 1914 to January 1921 in four parts.

In "*A National System of Education*", Sri Aurobindo points out that the question is not between modernism and antiquity, but between an imported civilisation and the greater possibilities of the Indian mind and nature, not between the present and the past, but between the present and the future. He pointed out that *"the living spirit of the demand for national education no more requires a return to the astronomy and mathematics of Bhaskara or the forms of the system of Nalanda than the living spirit of Swadheshi, a return from railway and motor traction to the ancient chariot and the bullock-cart."*[1] He, therefore, spoke not of a return to the 5th century but an initiation of the centuries to come, not a reversion but a break forward away from a present artificial falsity to

---

[1] Sri Aurobindo: The Hour of God, A Preface on National Education, Centenary Edition, Volume 17, p. 194

India's own greater innate potentialities, which are demanded by the soul of India.

The major question, he pointed out, is not merely what science we learn, but what we shall do with our science and how too, acquiring the scientific mind and recovering the habit of scientific discovery, we shall relate it to other powers of the human mind and scientific knowledge to other knowledge more intimate to other and not less light-giving and power-giving parts of our intelligence and nature. Again, he pointed out the question is not what language, Sanskrit or another, should be acquired by whatever method is most natural, efficient and stimulating to the mind, but the vital question is how we are to learn and make use of Sanskrit and the indigenous languages so as to get the heart and intimate sense of our own culture and establish a vivid continuity between the still living power of our past and the yet uncreated power of our future, and how we are to learn and use English or any other foreign tongue so as to know helpfully the life, ideas and culture of other countries and establish our right relations with the world around us. He argued that the aim and principle of a true national education is not to ignore modern truth and knowledge, but to take our foundation on India's own being, own mind, and own spirit.

As against the idea that the modern European civilisation is a thing that we have to acquire and fit ourselves for, and so only can we live and prosper, and it is this that our education must do for us, he argued that the idea of national education challenges the sufficiency of that assumption. He pointed out that India would do better, taking over whatever new knowledge or just ideas Europe has to offer, to assimilate them to its own knowledge and culture, its own native temperament and spirit, mind and social genius and create there-from the civilisation of the future.

According to Sri Aurobindo, there is within the universal mind and soul of humanity the mind and soul of the individual with its infinite variation, its commonness and its uniqueness and between them there stands an intermediate power, the mind of a nation, the soul of the people. In his concept of a national system of education, Sri Aurobindo aimed at taking account of all these three elements so that national education would not be a machine-made fabric, but a true building or a living evocation of the powers of the mind and spirit of the human being.

Considering that India has seen always in the human being a soul, a portion of the divinity enwrapped in the mind and body, a conscious manifestation in Nature of the universal self and spirit, he concluded that the one central object of the national system of education should be the growth of the soul and its powers and possibilities as also the preservation, strengthening and enrichment of the nation-soul and the normative needs of its ascending movements. Not limited to these two, Sri Aurobindo put forth in its aim also the raising of both the individual soul and the national soul into the powers of the life and the ascending mind and the soul of humanity. He added *"at no time will it lose sight of man's highest object, the awakening and development of his spiritual being."*[2]

---

[2] Sri Aurobindo: *The Hour of God, A Preface to National Education, Centenary Edition*, Vol. 17, p. 200

II

Sri Aurobindo speaks of three principles of teaching, and when implemented, they provide a sound basis of a system of natural organisation of the highest processes and the movements of which the human nature is capable. They also form the basis of the theory and practice of integral education, which has been propounded in detail in Sri Aurobindo's book, "*The Synthesis of Yoga*" and the Mother's book "*On Education*".

In brief, the three principles of teaching are as follows in Sri Aurobindo's own words:

> The first principle of true teaching is that nothing can be taught. The teacher is not an instructor or task-master, he is a helper and a guide. His business is to suggest and not to impose. ...The second principle is that the mind has to be consulted in its own growth. The idea of hammering the child into the shape desired by the parent or teacher is a barbarous and ignorant superstition. It is he himself who must be induced to expand in accordance with his own nature. ... The chief aim of education should be to help the growing soul to draw out that in itself which is best and make it perfect for a noble use. ... The third principle of education is to work from the near to the far, from that which is to that which shall be. ... A free and natural growth is the condition of genuine development. ...[3]

---

[3] Sri Aurobindo: *The Hour of God, A Preface to National Education, Centenary Edition,* Vol. 17, pp.204-05

There are, according to Sri Aurobindo, three instruments of the teacher: instruction, example, and influence. The good teacher will seek to awaken much more than to instruct; he will aim at the growth of the faculties and the experiences by a natural process and free expansion. He will not impose his opinions on the passive acceptance of the receptive mind; he will throw in only what is productive and sure as a seed, which will grow under the benign fostering within. He will know that the example is more powerful than instruction. Actually, the example is not that of the outward acts but of the inner motivation of life and the inner states and inner activities. Finally, he will also acknowledge that influence is more important than example. For influence proceeds from the power or contact of the teacher with his pupil, from the nearness of his soul to the soul of another, infusing into the pupil, even though in silence, all that which the teacher himself is or possesses. The good teacher is himself a constant student. He is a child leading children, and a light kindling other lights, a vessel and a channel.

Sri Aurobindo's concept of integral education finds its full relevance in the context of what Sri Aurobindo has called the Evolutionary Crisis, a crisis that occurs in a species at a time when some kind of mutation is imminent.

According to Sri Aurobindo, one favourable factor, which is likely to help contemporary humanity, is the contemporary dissatisfaction that has arisen with materialism, on the one hand, and on the other hand, with asceticism, which has been negating the meaning and purposefulness of the material world. After centuries of experiments, materialism is gradually giving way to the pressures of new discoveries, which require exploration of the psychical and spiritual domains. Similarly, centuries of experiments in the spiritual fields have shown that the neglect of material life and neglect of collective welfare result in poverty or bankruptcy and even in economic and political slavery. As Sri Aurobindo pointed out:

> It is therefore of good augury that after many experiments and verbal solutions we should now find ourselves standing today in the presence of the two that have alone borne for long the most rigorous tests of experience, the two extremes. ... In Europe and in India, respectively, the negation of the materialist and the refusal of the ascetic have sought to assert themselves as the sole truth and to dominate the conception of Life. In India, if the result has been a great heaping up of the treasures of the Spirit, -- or of some of them, -- it has also been a great bankruptcy of Life; in Europe, the fullness of riches and the triumphant mastery of this world's powers and possessions have progressed towards an equal bankruptcy in the things of the Spirit. ... Therefore the time grows ripe and the tendency of the world moves towards a new and comprehensive affirmation in thought and in inner and outer experience and to its corollary, a new and rich self-fulfilment in an integral human existence for the individual and for the race.[4]

The knowledge of the secrets of the process of integral education is largely contained in the Veda and Upanishads, and what we find missing there has been the special subject of study and experimentation in Sri

---

[4] Sri Aurobindo: *The Life Divine, Centenary Edition,* Vol.18, pp.8-9

Aurobindo. It is in the light of all this that we can speak today with great assurance of the concept and practice of integral education and of the synthesis of the ancient secrets of the reign of Spirit over mind, life and the body and the modern secrets of utilisation of the life in perfecting the instrumentality of the body, life and mind.

Integral education would not only aim at the integral development of personality, but it would also embrace all knowledge in its scope. It would pursue physical and psychical sciences, not merely to know the world and Nature in her processes and to use them for material human needs, but to know through them the Spirit in the world and the ways of the Spirit in its appearances. It would study ethics in order, not only to search for the good as the mind sees it, but also to perceive the supra-ethical Good. Similarly, it would pursue Art not merely to present images of the subjective and the objective world, but to see them with significant and creative vision that goes behind their appearances and to reveal the supra-rational Truth and Beauty. It would encourage the study of humanities, not in order to foster a society as a background for a few luminous spiritual figures so that the many necessarily remain for ever on the lower ranges of life, but to inspire the regeneration of the total life of the earth and to encourage voluntary optimism for that regeneration in spite of all previous failures. Finally, it would encourage unity of knowledge and harmony of knowledge, and it would strive to foster the spirit of universality and oneness.

An important characteristic of integral education is its insistence on simultaneous development of Knowledge, Will, Harmony, and Skill as also various parts of the being to the extent possible from the earliest stages of education. And since each individual child is unique in the composition of its qualities and characteristics, its capacities and propensities, integral education in its practice tends to become increasingly individualised. Again, for this very reason, the methods of education become increaseingly dynamic, involving active participation of the child in its own growth.

III

An unprecedented kind of experiment in education was launched by Sri Aurobindo and the Mother, when in 1943, a school came to be established at the Sri Aurobindo Ashram at Pondicherry in South India. It was expanded into Sri Aurobindo International Centre of Education in due course, and the writings of Sri Aurobindo and the Mother on education have influenced greatly the innovative processes of education in the country, and they have also received wide attention from the world at large. Mention may be made of the Mother's small but great book on education as also to a series of *"Conversations"* and *"Questions and Answers"* which have been published by the Sri Aurobindo Ashram.[5]

---

[5] The Mother (Madame Mirra Alfassa) was born in Paris on February 21, 1878. In her early years, spontaneous experiences took on ranges out of her body, into the earth's past, and without her understanding, led her to the discovery of "past lives". She made thorough studies in piano, painting and higher mathematics. At the age of 26, she had several dreams of Sri Aurobindo – of whom she had never heard before. She later became acquainted with Max Theon, an enigmatic character with extraordinary occult powers, who for the first time gave a coherent explanation of her experiences and taught her occultism during her two long visits to his estate in Algeria. In 1914, she came from France to India, and met Sri Aurobindo for the first time on March 29. She realised that her work was identical with the work of Sri Aurobindo. She spent one year in Pondicherry and then four years in Japan and returned to Sri Aurobindo for good in 1920 via China. She organised and developed the Ashram as also its International Centre for Education. After Sri Aurobindo's passing in 1950, she guided experiments in education and invented new methods and new ways of education as also flexible structures in order to give a concrete shape to Sri Aurobindo's concept of integral education. In 1958, she entered upon the *"Yoga of the Cells"* which led her to the discovery of *"a cellular mind"* capable of reconstructing the nature of the body. From 1958 to 1973, she slowly uncovered the *"Great Passage"* to the next species and a new mode of life in Matter. An authentic and scientifically scrupulous account of this Passage is to be found in *"Mother's Agenda"* in 13 Volumes, which was published by Institut de Recherches Evolutives in France.

In 1968, she founded Auroville a few miles form Pondicherry, as a *"Laboratory of the New Evolution"*. Auroville has conducted various experiments in education, inspired and initiated by the Mother and published two important volumes of Educational research under the titles *"The Aim of Life"* and *"The Good Teacher and The Good Pupil"* which have received countrywide attention in India.

IV

Principles and methods of education advocated by Sri Aurobindo and the Mother have a profound bearing on psychic and spiritual education. These two domains bring into the picture all that is central to value-oriented education, and to higher and profounder elements of human psychology. Sri Aurobindo and the Mother have advocated new methods that are free from those of dogmas, rituals, ceremonies, prescribed acts. Spirituality, according to Sri Aurobindo and the Mother, is a vast domain of the inmost soul, of the immobile silence, of the higher objects of the higher psychological exploration. The justification for psychic and spiritual education rests upon three important considerations: (a) education should provide to the individual a steady exploration of something that is inmost in the psychological complexity of human consciousness; (b) the most important human question of human life is to consider the aim of human life and the aim of one's own life and one's own position and role in the society; and this question can best be answered only when the psychic and spiritual domains are explored and when one is enabled to develop psychic and spiritual faculties of knowledge; and (c) the contemporary crisis of humanity has arisen because of the disbalancement between the material advancement on the one hand and inadequate spiritual progression, on the other. If, therefore, this crisis has to be met, development of psychic and spiritual consciousness should be fostered. Unfortunately, spiritual consciousness is often conceived as a denial of material life and concerns of collective life. In Sri Aurobindo's and the Mother's view, however, there is no fundamental opposition between Matter and Spirit. True integrality, according to them, implies rejection of no element in human personality and no denial of anything that can contribute to the full flowering of faculties of personality.

Again, according to Sri Aurobindo and the Mother, psychic and spiritual development cannot be effected without effecting high level development of the body, life and mind, and that the perfection of the body, life and mind can be attained only when the powers of psychic and spiritual consciousness are bestowed upon the instruments of the body, life and mind.

At an important stage of experimentation, the Mother gave the message that while India has or rather had spiritual knowledge but neglected Matter, the West has knowledge of Matter but has neglected the Spirit, -- as a consequence of which both India and the West are suffering, and the solution would be to develop integral education, which would restore the development of matter under the guidance and authority of the Spirit.

V

There is a distinction between psychic consciousness and spiritual consciousness, as there is a distinction between spiritual consciousness and supramental consciousness. As the Mother pointed out:

> ...the psychic life is immortal life, endless time, limitless space, ever-progressive change, unbroken continuity in the universe of forms. The spiritual consciousness, on the other hand, means to live the infinite and the eternal; to be projected beyond all creation, beyond time and space. To become conscious of your psychic being and to live a psychic life you must abolish all egoism; but to live a spiritual life, you must no longer have an ego.[6]

As far as the supramental education is concerned, the Mother pointed out that:

> ...the supramental education will result no longer in a progressive formation of human nature and an increasing development of its latent faculties, but in a transformation of the nature itself, a transfiguration of the being in its entirety, a new ascent of the species above and beyond man towards superman, leading in the end to the appearance of a divine race upon earth.[7]

If these three aspects of higher education are to be conducted properly, one must take great care to ensure that methods of religion are not introduced. Religion implies normally the methods of belief or dogma, performance of rituals and ceremonies, and prescriptions of certain specific acts, which are considered to be religious as distinguished from profane.

---

[6] The Mother: *Education, Part I, p.38*
[7] *Ibid.*

VI

A constant insistence of Sri Aurobindo and the Mother has been on detailed perfection of the human mind, life and body. We may, therefore, turn to the three domains of mental education, vital education, and physical education as expounded and experimented upon at Sri Aurobindo Ashram at Pondicherry and subsequently at the Sri Aurobindo International Institute of Educational Research at Auroville.

Mental Education:

In regard to mental education, the processes and methods can best be determined by understanding the mind. Mind is concerned largely with the activities of understanding, and all understanding is a discovery of a centre around which the ideas or things in question are held together.

Mental education is a process of training the mind of students to arrive at such central conceptions around which the widest and most complex and subtle ideas can be assimilated and integrated.

It is again found that even these central conceptions point still to a beyond, to their own essential meaning, which can be glimpsed and conceived by the mind, but which cannot be held and possessed fully in experience by the mind. This point marks the climax of the mental development as also a clear sign of the limitations of the mind. Having reached there its office is to fall into contemplation of silence and to open to the higher realms of experience, to receive clearly and precisely the intuitions and inspirations from those higher realms, and to give creative expression to them.

To train the mind on these lines, there are five phases of the programme:

1. Development of the power of concentration and attention;

2. Development of the capacities of expansion, wideness, complexity and richness;

3. Organisation of ideas round a central or a higher ideal or a supremely luminous idea that will serve as a guide in life;

4. Thought control, rejection of undesirable thoughts so that one may, in the end, think only what one wants and when one wants; and

5. Development of mental silence, perfect calm and a more and more total receptivity to inspirations coming from the higher regions of the being.

Multiplicity of ideas, richness of ideas, totality of points of view – these should be made to grow by a developed power of observation and concentration and by a wideness of interest. Care should be taken to see that the central ideas are not imposed upon the growing mind – that would be the dogmatic method, which tends to atrophy the mind. The mind should grow towards central ideas which should come as a discovery of the mind made through rigorous exercise of the rational faculty.

Stress should fall not only on understanding but also on criticism and control of ideas; not only of comprehension, synthesis, creativity, judgement, imagination, memory and observation, but also on critical functions of comparison, reasoning, inference and conclusion. Both these aspects of human reason are essential to the completeness of the mental training.

One of the best methods is to create an atmosphere in which massive and powerful ideas are constantly thrown as a stimulation and challenge impelling the student's to arrive at them or strive to grasp and assimilate them.

Thinkers alone can produce thinkers; and unless teachers are constantly in the process of building up great thoughts and ideas, it is futile to expect a sound or vigorous mental education.

An atmosphere vibrant at once with ideation and silence, an atmosphere surcharged with synthetic thoughts and most integral aspirations and an atmosphere filled with the widest realisation and a harmonious unity – such an atmosphere is indispensable for perfect mental education.

A constant attempt should be made to present each topic to the student in a challenging way so as to stimulate him and create his interest in the topic. To find new and imaginative methods, to compile materials from various sources, to introduce new concepts and new interpretations in various subjects, to develop new subjects, and above all, to attend in detail to all the psychological faculties and their development in such a way that the mental education does not veil the soul – this, in brief, should be the endeavour and its spirit.

Vital Education:

Vital education aims at training the life-force (that normally vibrates in emotions, desires and impulses) in three directions: to discover its real function and to replace its egoistic and ignorant tendency so as to become the master by willingness and capacity to serve higher principles of the psychological constitution; to subtilise and sublimate its sensitivity which expresses itself through sensuous and aesthetic activities; and to resolve and transcend the dualities and contradictions in the character constituted by the vital seekings, and to achieve the transformation of the character.

The usual methods of dealing with the vital have been in the past those of coercion, suppression, abstinence and asceticism. But these methods do not give lasting results. Besides, they only help in drying up the drive and dynamism of the life-force; and thus the collaboration of the life-force in self-fulfilment is eliminated.

The right training of the vital then is much more subtle and much more difficult, needing endurance, endless persistence and an inflexible will. For what is to be aimed at is not the negation of life but the fulfilment of life by its transformation.

First, the powers of the senses have to be developed, subtilised and enriched. Next, there are inner and latent senses which are to be discovered and similarly developed. Third, the seekings of these senses have to be trained to reject grossness and coarseness and to enjoy the finer tastes and higher aesthetic experiences. Finally, there has to be a deeper and piercing observation of the desires, passions, ambitions, lusts, etc., their risings, revolts and contradictions, and an attempt by various methods to separate out in each movement the elements that contribute to the concord and harmony from those tending in the opposite direction, and to eliminate the latter from the very nature and fibre of our psychological constitution.

The effective methods of this last aspect are:

- To instil in the child, as soon as possible, the will towards progress and perfection;

- Rational arguments, sentiment and goodwill, or appeal to the sense of dignity and self-respect according to the nature of the child in question;

- To insist on the idea that the will can be developed, and that no defeat should be taken as final;

- To demand from the will the maximum effort, for the will is strengthened by effort;

- Above all, the example of the educator shown constantly and sincerely.

But still the direction in which the effort has to be made can be known only by the training of the mind and by the opening of the secret knowledge that is within our psychic being. To develop therefore in the vital the habit to open to this light and to act in that light would be to place the vital in its proper place as a will-force executing the inner and higher knowledge.

Vital education is greatly aided by stress on different kinds of fine arts and crafts. Sri Aurobindo has written at length on the contribution that Art can make to the integral education in his important book, "*The National Value of Art*". He has pointed out that the first and the lowest use of Art is purely aesthetic, the second is the intellectual and the third and the highest is the spiritual. He has even stated that music, art and poetry are a perfect education for the soul; they make and keep its movements purified, deep and harmonious. He has added:

These, therefore, are agents which cannot profitably be neglected by humanity on its onward march or degraded to the mere satisfaction of sensuous pleasure which will disintegrate rather than build the character. They are, when properly used, great educating, edifying and civilising forces.[8]

A great lesson in vital education is to develop the will of the individual and to encourage the exercise of the will in which what is valued most is not the result but application and doing one's best.

Physical Education:

On the subject of physical education, it must be mentioned that the physical is our base, and even the highest spiritual values are to be expressed through the life that is embodied here. *Sariram ādyam khalu dharma-sādhanam,* says the old Sanskrit adage, -- the body is the means of fulfilment of dharma, while dharma means every ideal which we can propose to ourselves and the law of its working out and its action.

Of all the domains of education, physical is the one most completely governed by method, order, discipline and procedure. All education of the body must be rigorous, detailed and methodical.

The education of the body has three principal aspects: control and discipline of functions of the body; a total methodical and harmonious development of all the parts

---

[8] Sri Aurobindo: *The Hour of God, A Preface to National Education,* Centenary Edition, Vol. 17, p.246

and movements of the body; rectification of defects and deformities, if there are any.

Physical education must be based upon knowledge of the human body, its structure and its functions. And the formation of the habits of the body must be in consonance with that knowledge.

The child should be taught right from the early stage the right positions, postures and movements.

A similar training should be with regard to the choice of food. The child should develop the taste that is simple and healthy, substantial and appetising. He must avoid all that merely stuffs and causes heaviness; particularly, he must be taught to eat according to his hunger and not make food a means to satisfy his greed and gluttony.

The child should also be taught the taste for cleanliness and hygienic habits. It is important to impress upon the child that he is not more interesting by being ill, rather the contrary. Children should be taught that to be ill is a sign of failing and inferiority, not of virtue and sacrifice.

VII

A very important problem in respect of integral education arises from its insistence on proper synthesis between freedom and discipline. Since education is a creative process, and since compulsion and creativity cannot go together, freedom has to be a very important instrument of education. The ideal condition is obtained when discipline becomes the child of freedom and discipline is transformed into self-discipline.

We have to recognise that different children react to various activities of education differently. There are children who feel a powerful attraction towards creative activities such as arts, music, dance, composition of poetry, drama, etc. They should, of course, be given freedom to pursue these valuable activities. But there are instances where children who do not have this natural inclination towards creative activities are also compelled to be engaged in these activities. This is entirely unacceptable.

We may also need to note that there are children who do not easily respond either to the activities of creativity or activities of production, but who are deeply reflective and to whom abstraction of thought and clarity and beauty of ideation constitute a fascinating project. We must recognise that a deep exercise in ideation and organisation of ideas is a very active engagement. It is a great activity of concentration.

At the same time, an exclusive pursuit of ideation without devoting any attention whatever to creative or productive activity may lead to a lopsided development of personality. The remedy is not to make things compulsory, but to counsel children, to motivate and suggest to them how gradually various kinds of activities can be blended together for a harmonious development. But while counselling, the teacher must realise and appreciate that there are periods where psychologically even an exclusive development of ideative activity or productive activity or creative activity has its legitimate claims. To what degree this claim has to be satisfied and in what way this claim has to be subordinated to the other claims of development will demand from the teacher a very deep insight into the inner psychological workings of the formation of the personality and his sympathetic understanding of the psychological differences among various children.

It may also be noted that there are children who are deeply interested in activities of self-sacrifice or of purifying their base emotions, or of the worship of the noblest ideals of life. Sometimes they may show no interest in studies or in arts or in crafts and often teachers complain of their dullness or their lack of concentration in studies. But a good teacher should ask himself if the child in question is not inwardly engaged in what may be called activities of *"purification"*.

There could also be children like Yuddhishthira who would not claim that they have learnt a lesson unless they have succeeded in practising it in their daily life. These are indeed noble children and the teacher should be able to appreciate their nobility and encourage it so as to lead it to its perfection.

During the course of educational process, students often come up with some very fundamental questions but they often remain unanswered. Why, for example, should one learn mathematics? What does really history teach us? What is the relationship between language and mathematics? What is the aim of life? There should be freedom to raise these questions and also enough time and readiness to answer them, even though they may not be a part of any prescribed syllabus.

Another important point that should be noted is that a great care should be taken to get the development of the child in such a way that in spite of the growth of knowledge, the student does not lose freshness and sense of wonder and mystery. This indeed is the most difficult part of the work of the teacher.

VIII

If we make a deep study of the experiments in education guided and conducted under the inspiration of Sri Aurobindo and the Mother, it may be said that there are three important features that come to the forefront and which may help us to define what may be called "*New Education*":

1. Learning by practice;

2. Search for meaning and unity of knowledge; and

3. Unending education and perpetual youth.

New education insists on the development of the mind, life and body, it aims at development of these instruments for the discovery of the inner psychic being; it proposes to utilise mental, vital, physical perfection as instruments of the perfect manifestation of the inner and higher realities. The effort is to make the body supple, strong, agile and beautiful; the vital is to be trained to become dynamic, disciplined, obedient and effective; the mind has to be cultivated to be intelligent, observant, concentrated, free, rich and complex. But at every stage the paramount importance is to be given to the needs of the psychic and spiritual growth. As the Mother writes:

> The will for the great discovery should be always there above you, above what you do and what you are, like a huge bird of light dominating all the movements of your being.[9]

---

[9] The Mother on Education, Collected Works, Vol. 12 (Centenary Edition), p.35.

PROBLEMS OF KNOWLEDGE
AND
SRI AUROBINDO'S CONCEPT OF THE SUPERMIND

> But our nature sees things through two eyes always, for it views them doubly as ideas and as fact and therefore every concept is incomplete for us and to a part of our nature almost unreal until it becomes an experience.
>
> SRI AUROBINDO, *The Life Divine.*

There is an ascending movement of knowledge which seeks to find its fulfilment in the attainment of the highest, completest and the most indubitable knowledge. In this search it rises higher and higher and on the way it stops at certain stations wondering at each whether it is not the terminus it wants to arrive at. The first such station at which it stops is the level of perception.

For a percept by itself is complete and of the facthood and of the immediate truth of which we have to refer to nothing outside it. That there are percepts and that what is perceived is really perceived are indubitable facts and whatever higher knowledge there may be and whatever correction it may make in the knowledge by perception, it cannot abolish these facts except by denying them with the help of the idea of a mysterious Maya or of the inexplicable; but then such abolishing knowledge would not be the highest knowledge.

However, very soon it is found that perception is only a station on the journey, not a destination; for the reason that compares one percept with another finds a certain opposition between them; it finds that two given percepts concerning the same object are so opposed to each other that if one is true the other must be false; and within the field of perception itself there are no means to determine the final truth of either. And this gives rise to the doubt regarding the whole realm of perception. May it not be that all percepts are false? But the idea of falsity presupposes the idea of truth which in turn presupposes for the reason at least an existence of the truth. But when the field of perception itself is held in question we cannot discover the existence of that truth while confined solely to that very field.

Or if we do not raise this extreme doubt we may arrive at an intermediary kind of doubt; for if we observe the percepts we find that they change according to the position that the subject takes with respect to the object of perception. And this gives rise to a doubt whether the percepts do not depend entirely upon the percipient. And this doubt is reiterated by the fact that in perception we perceive no necessity of the existence of the object so that of no object we can say it must therefore be existing even when perceptual contact is withdrawn. But as against this we also observe that we cannot perceive things at will, and if the objects depend upon the percipient the latter would not have to labour to understand the object; there would then be no questioning, no groping, no error with respect to the objects of perception.

It may be then that the objects exist independent of the percipient; and with respect to this hypothesis also two positions can be taken. According to the first position, objects are so independent of the perceptual-conceptual activity of the percipient that there is no correspondence between them and therefore what the percipient can know of the objects is not the objects as they are, the objects-in-themselves, but only his mental ideas about the objects, the mental categories which are *a priori* and underived from experience although elicited through sense-experience. These categories are purely mental and entirely inapplicable to objects-in-themselves and if an attempt is made to apply these categories to objects-in-themselves we are led to antinomy and opposition. But this view can hardly be substantiated by any perceptual evidence and therefore so long as we remain on the perceptual level we cannot decide upon this view.

The second alternative position returns to the primary certainty of sense-perception with which we began; it holds the reality of the objectivity of the object and its qualities and Space and Time and maintains that our knowledge of them is determined by them and not by the mental constitution of the percipient. But in view of the uncertainty of the knowledge by sense-perception it confesses that certainty of knowledge is not possible and that the highest that we can attain to is approximation and probability.

But if objectivity is real and can be so known by the percipient, the subject, then it is reasonable to suppose that objectivity and subjectivity are not opposed to each other; and since the object presents itself before the subject and can be known only by the subject, and since the subject can know, that is to say, enter into the object -- for how else can it be known? — the ultimate stuff of the two should be identical. For then only knowledge is possible. Nevertheless, if the differentiation of the subject and the object persists we may suppose that identity is not opposed to differentiation. The subject and the object then may be regarded as essentially identical and yet each as the same Identical presenting to the other for its self-revelation.

This indeed is a speculation and as of any other so of this there is no possibility of being certain on the perceptual-conceptual level. For here on this level we have no direct experience of this essential identity of the subject and the object, their revelation as the subjective and objective faces of the One. The object does not reveal itself to the subject: the subject has to grope and attempt a difficult and practically unsuccessful entry into the object; the subject also retains its separation from the object and uses indirect means which maintain that separation rather than unite the two. The subject and the object are thus divided from each other and so certainty of knowledge is not possible at this level.

Still we can note the conditions under which alone we can attain to the definite and indubitable knowledge of the objects which we as subjects attempt to know and yet fail to know. The first condition is that I, the subject, and the object should in some way be identical, that is to say, identical in the very stuff of being; for to know the object means to know the very essence of it, the object-in-itself; and if that essence of the object is fundamentally different from me, the subject, I shall never know the object. The second condition is that although this essential identity is indispensable, there should be real, that is to say, as opposed to illusory, differentiation of the subject and the object; for unless there is this differentiation I shall never know the object as object. And yet if, and this is the third condition, I am to know the essentiality, the peculiarity, the very differentia of this differentiation of the object from me, the subject, I should myself be capable of throwing myself into that object and becoming that object, and still at the same time not losing my subjectivity, the essentiality, the peculiarity, the very differentia of my differentiation from the object—for otherwise once again I would cease to be the subject and thus would not know the object as object.

Whether these conditions are capable of fulfilment or not is a separate question, but this much at least is clear that since these conditions are not fulfilled as yet, the present conflict between rationalism and empiricism, subjectivism and objectivism and idealism and realism adds only to the uncertainty of our knowledge and therefore no final solution is possible on any one of these conflicting lines of thought. And in this uncertain state of knowledge if we are so determined as to deny any higher possibility, we may deny it; but then it would be dogmatism.

As a matter of fact, as we rise higher new fields of knowledge open before us. For if the reason operating on sense-perception and sense-data disturbs the simple certainty of the percept, it also arrives by liberating itself from the occupation with sense-data at the metaphysical knowledge which gives us the certainty of the concepts of pure reason. These concepts are found to be the very stuff of the pure reason and therefore are undeniable for it; pure reason exists by them and to deny them would be to deny pure reason itself.

One such concept is that of the Infinite as the underlying Reality of the universe. To reason an absolute end or an absolute beginning is self-contradictory and therefore cannot be; there can be no limit which it can assign or fix in Space and Time before which there is nothing or after which there is nothing. Not only that, reason goes farther and looking at the Movement and finding there not the Stable and Permanent which alone can be the support of this Movement, it goes beyond the categories of Space and Time and comes to conceive an Existence-in-itself, timeless and spaceless, the Infinite, the Eternal, the Absolute to which the categories of quantity, quality, relation and modality do not apply.

This Reality, this Self-existence, says the pure reason, must be; and yet in positing this the reason points to something beyond itself; something of which it is certain and yet which it cannot and does not know. And reaching this utmost limit of its operation, it returns upon itself for a critical self-examination. And it finds that it fails to know the Whole, the Perfect, the Infinite because whereas the Infinite must be or rather is—for that which must be is for the pure reason — unitary, its own movement is piecemeal; it operates through cutting and dissecting the concrete into that and what and thus misses the unity. It applies the same method to all its concepts of Space, Time, Quantity, Quality, Relation and Modality and finds that these concepts also betray the same self-contradiction with which it is itself ridden. These therefore cannot be real; the Real is that which goes beyond all these, the One without the second.

And then the inevitable question arises as to how all this movement, these things of perception, these categories of thought, this division and differentiation, the entire mass of the discord and disharmony that we call our ordinary existence — how all these are reconciled with or contained by that Transcendental unitary self-existence that is the Infinite. Is it that they are not reconciled at all? For the world of our perception and thought by its inherent disharmony and discord appears to be fundamentally and essentially different from that other harmonious and unitary Absolute Reality. But this cannot be because if Reality is Infinite nothing can be outside it; all that is must be in it or must be That itself. Shall we then say that only That exists and all else is false, that is to say, an illusion, a false perception, an error of limited consciousness? But if That alone exists how did the false perception arise? And in whom did this false perception arise? It must be in That only for nothing else exists. But then we return to the original question still unsolved. The only answer that we are forced to give is that if the facts are what they are, all the discords of the world are somehow, inexplicably, contained in the Infinite, and when so contained and viewed as such from the point of view of the Infinite the present discord ceases; and then what we get is the all-harmonious, perfect, unitary and unrelational Whole, the Absolute.

But this last note of 'somehow' and 'inexplicable' shows that we have reached here the utmost limit of pure reason. For it becomes clear now that just as it cannot know the Infinite although it is compelled to posit It, even so it cannot know how to unite the universe and the Infinite although it is compelled to regard the universe to be somehow contained in the Infinite. But this ignorance is sufficient to raise certain doubts regarding the completeness of our premiss. We may be certain of our concept of the Infinite, but so long as we do not know what that Infinite is how are we to know whether the Infinite is opposed to the finite, the Indeterminate to the determinate? We do not have, on the other hand, true knowledge of the universe which has been declared to be ridden with self-contradiction. On the perceptual-conceptual level we do not have any certainty about the true nature of the universe of our perception; pure reason gives us certainty — but only the certainty about the Infinite in which the universe must be contained. It does not throw any further light on the nature of the universe; on the contrary, in returning to the universe it still takes the same perceptual-conceptual view of it. If so, we may suppose that the insuperable difficulty is not really in the problem but in the incompleteness of our premiss. And this opens out a fresh line of approach.

For it may now be argued that if in the vision of the Infinite or rather in the unitary concrete experience of the Absolute all discords cease to be, then is it not because there was in reality no discord, and all the discord that we were imposing was not in fact but only in idea relative to our finite mode of seeing and thinking? In fact it may be that the fundamental categories of world-existence are not self-contradictory and therefore not the elements of discord which have to be resolved. For if they were not essentially in harmony with the Infinite, they could not have any existence whatsoever, not even a false and perceptual existence.

But this is a speculation and as of any other which attempts to fathom into the mystery of the as yet unknown Infinite, so of this we cannot be certain. For Reason does not stand at the origin of the determination of the universe; it is itself a determination and as yet unable to see the primary relation between the Indeterminate and the determination; there is still a veil between it and its original source; and until the two aspects of knowledge — the knowledge of the Infinite and the knowledge of the universe — meet in a supreme act of knowledge, we would be encircling in vain to relate the two entities which are very largely to our Reason two words without precise meaning.

Still we can see and note down what could be the nature of that faculty or power, if there is any such, which alone could know with certainty what reason attempts to know and yet fails to know. Firstly, it must be identical with the

Infinite; for to know the Infinite is to know the essence of the Infinite, the Infinite-itself; and if that essence were different from the essence of this power or faculty which attempts to know the Infinite, it will never know the Infinite. Secondly, it must itself be identical with that principle of differentiation which is responsible for the categories of world-existence. Thirdly, the subject, the knower, himself should be identical with the Infinite and the power or faculty of perfect knowledge; for otherwise he would not know their uniqueness and the totality of the knowledge of the Infinite and the universe; and finally, the Infinite and that faculty of perfect knowledge should be the determinant and constitutor of the knower, the subject, for otherwise they would not know the determination of the subject and thus lack of completeness of knowledge which we demand of them.

Whether there is any such faculty or not or, if in existence, whether it is possible for us to have such a faculty is a separate question; but this much is certain that if we do not admit the possibility of such a suprarational or supramental faculty we shall never be able to be certain of the relation that this world holds with the Infinite. And in the absence of this certainty even whatever certainty that we have of the metaphysical knowledge would come to be seriously doubted and challenged. For there are always two ways of obtaining knowledge, through ideation and through experience; and unless we realise in experience what we idealise, our idealising will remain almost unreal to our need for experience. Therefore our need of experience also has a kind of reason which accepts not the reason of ideas but the reason of facts and experience: to it therefore anything which is unrealisable is a meaningless word, a non-sense. So it is possible always to question the concepts of pure reason until they are realised. Thus the rationalistic philosophy in the West which denies the possibility of our having the realisation of the Infinite has come to be challenged by Positivism according to which metaphysical concepts are meaningless and therefore metaphysics is a non-sense. Positivism therefore turns back upon pure reason and returns to the primacy of sense-experience.

This in fact represents the present and immediate crisis of the Western mind; for this reaction of the sense-mind against the higher and nobler faculties has come at a time when that high certainty which was felt with respect to physical sciences has itself come to be questioned and scientific knowledge is being gradually regarded as only probable. It is thus a movement towards uncertainty, as never before. The Western mind has therefore to decide if it wants to rise higher to new vistas of experience and knowledge or to deny or thwart the persistent instinct or intuition in man to realise the highest.

In fact the opposition between reason and experience is fallacious. For if we examine carefully, we find that just as sense-mind needs for its operation the presentation of sensible facts, even so pure reason also needs for its operation on them the presentation of its ideas. Thus the concept of the Infinite is not the product of reason, it is the very stuff of its being; and if we go still deeper we find that there is in us the faculty of intuition which gives its first intimations to reason of the existence of the Infinite. And the foundation of intuitional knowledge is conscious or effective identity between that which knows and that which is known. The possibility therefore of our having that intuitional knowledge is already implied in the very functioning of pure reason.

On the other hand, the positivist appeal to experience and verifiability is incomplete. For in the first place, sense-experience gives us no certain knowledge, and it can at the most arrive at tolerable probabilities; this would mean that not only metaphysical knowledge but in fact even the concepts of science are little more than non-sense. In the second place, the refusal to admit the truths of pure reason is arbitrary since it is based upon an unfounded assumption that reason and truth are entirely divorced from each other. And finally, if we are impartial enough, we have to take note of supraphysical experiences; for then it becomes possible for us to see that we can enter through the inner consciousness into subtler planes of existence and even to the highest and supreme experience of the Infinite.

Thus the movement of knowledge must rise higher into the field of spiritual experience to see if it gets there what it seeks. And indeed once again we find in the spiritual field the same kind of, though intenser and wider, certainty of the facthood and of the truth of the experience as we got in the field of sense-perception. As there, so here, the experience is complete by itself and for the facthood and truth of which we have to refer to nothing outside it; as there, so here, the fact that there are spiritual experiences and that whatever is experienced is really experienced is indubitable; and whatever higher knowledge there may be and whatever corrections it may make in the knowledge by spiritual experience, it cannot abolish the facthood or truth of spiritual experience except by ignoring them; but then such ignoring knowledge would not be the highest knowledge.

But unlike in sense-experience, in spiritual experience the subject finds its final rest and so of all search of knowledge. The experience is found to be so total and integral that the spirit and reason feel justified in regarding it as the ultimate and final destination of all knowledge. The spirit knows then that the Truth and reason supports it; and there is no possibility of moving anywhere farther.

But if we look here for the fulfilment of the conditions of integral knowledge we find that all of them are not fulfilled in any single spiritual experience; where we find the identity of the subject and the object the differentiation between the two is absent, and vice versa. And this leads to variation in knowledge and claims which conflict with each other.

There are three fundamental experiences in terms of which we can translate roughly all the multitudinous varieties of spiritual experience. The first is one in which the Subject finds itself as the inactive Witness Self or Purusha to which an entirely alien principle of active Nature or Prakriti presents its construction of the world as Object. The ultimate difference between Subject and Object or an ultimate dualism is a position which we have met before and reason has considered it to be untenable. But now in the light of this experience which has an inherent certainty and finality about itself, reason also comes to see that its reasonings were mere constructions, perhaps sufficient within themselves but having no relevance to the ultimate facts of existence; for experience shows that there is an ultimate dualism. And thus we get a dualistic philosophy armed with its own mental logic and its appeal to intuition and experience.

The second is the experience in which the Subject, the knower, merges himself completely into the pure and indeterminable eternal existence of the Infinite beside which there is nothing else, the experience of the Immutable and unqualified Absolute, the *Nirguna* Brahman. And then if we ask of the universe in relation to this experience we are told that that universe is a lie, an illusion, an existence which in fact never existed except to false vision. This again is the position which we have met before and reason has found it to be untenable. But in the light of this experience which has an inherent certainty and finality about itself, reason also comes to see that its reasonings were mere constructions and that reason being itself ridden with self-contradiction cannot really give us the truth; it finds now that its constructions have no relevance to the fact of supreme experience. And thus we get the philosophy of Illusionistic Monism which is armed with its own mental logic and appeal to intuition and experience.

And the third is the experience in which the Subject finds in the Object, the Infinite, the true Subject of himself as well as of the universe which in turn are found to be the objective self-determinations of the Infinite, the *Saguna Brahman*. In this experience we find a promise of greater knowledge of the Infinite as related to the universe, but here there is a lack of the experience of the identity of the terms of knowledge which prevents us from coming to any certain knowledge about the ultimate relation of these terms. But in the light of this experience, once again, reason comes to see that its demand for complete knowledge is presumptuous and has no relevance to the final fact of experience. And thus we get the philosophy of Qualified Monism armed with its own mental logic and appeal to intuition and experience.

Had we to meet the one and the single realisation at the end and summit of every spiritual endeavour our reason would be obliged to accept the final test and authority of that experience however much it may disappoint the expectations of reason. For then reason would recognise its limitations and submit to the supremacy of knowledge by experience. But here we find that different roads lead us to different goals, different summits, and the reason which compares these experiences remains undecided between them.

It has however been argued that essentially these spiritual experiences point to the same Reality and that so many different philosophies are only so many different ways of stating the same Truth. But this argument errs by over-simplifying and therefore explaining away the real problem. It is true that each of these philosophies speaks of the Being or the Infinite as the content of spiritual experience; but each gives a different and opposing account and this difference and opposition is clearly meant and upheld by the originators of these philosophies themselves.

Faced with this conflict, if we are to argue with each position that the other is invalid then we are led to three alternatives, namely, either that none is valid or that one of them or two of them are valid or that each one is valid. But none of these alternatives can be proved. For to prove we must be in possession of some such knowledge whose validity is not in question. This situation therefore pushes us to a greater and higher and more certain knowledge in the light of which this conflict could be resolved. For at this level we find as yet a limitation which prevents consciousness to look beyond its present occupying experience. It may be that the spiritual experience is not the plane of ultimate experience but of the penultimates. And the phenomenon of opposing spiritual experiences would point to a probability that the Infinite is so complex as to combine and harmonise apparently opposing principles. Indeed there is nothing inconceivable in the fact that that which is really Infinite should have various faces of Itself each of which can be variously experienced and yet should give in each experience the sense of perfection. For may it not be that the Infinite is the original Mystery of which what appears to the limited mind as contradictories are really its equal and complementary truths?

But this is a speculation and unless we find a substantiating experience we cannot be certain about it. For here there is still something that escapes us. We are in search of the knowledge of the Infinite and the mystery of the origin of the universe, the action of the determining power of the Infinite and the process of self-determination of the Infinite. But here on the spiritual plane when we attain to the Infinite and attain identity with it the world disappears, determinations are found to be substanceless name and forms having no reality, and the subject, the knower, also merges into the unqualified oneness of the Infinite, the *Nirguna* Brahman. On the other hand, when we approach the Infinite in His creative activity, the subject, the knower, can enter into a relation with Him, embrace Him, realise his truth as a portion of Him and realise also the truth of the universe as a determination of Him, but still the identity with Him which alone can give us the complete knowledge of Him, the subject and the universe, is still denied. There is still a veil between that *Nirguna* Brahman and this *Saguna* Brahman and we do not know as yet the principle which determines this differentiation and therefore in which we can hope to arrive at the ultimate all-comprehensive knowledge.

Still we can be certain that if these spiritual experiences are valid, they must be of an Infinite which is not a blank indeterminable but which by its own power of self-determination determines itself into various aspects of itself. If there is the Infinite, there cannot be anything alien to itself and therefore the power of determination

173

also must be its own power; not only that but that Power must be in essence identical with the Infinite for then only can it effect the real determinations of the Infinite. To the cognition of this Power then there would be no opposition or conflict between these various aspects of the Infinite but, on the contrary, harmony between them and even ultimate oneness. And yet, thirdly, we have to suppose that in each of these aspects there must be independent completeness; for otherwise we would be led to the illogical position that the perfection of the Infinite is broken in its determinations.

Whether there is such a power or not is a separate question; but if there is no such power we have no explanation of the conflict of spiritual experiences, no way to bridge and synthesise the truths of these spiritual experiences; if there is no such power we have no means to attain to the indubitable knowledge of the Infinite in its relation to the universe and the knower of this universe; and finally if there is no such power we shall not attain to the indubitable knowledge of the objects of this universe which our very physical senses demand of us to have. If there is no such power we shall have no certainty of any knowledge; we are left between conflicts without any hope of issue or solution.

But already in some of the ancient records of Knowledge such as the Veda and the Upanishad we find the description of the Supreme Reality which shows that the seers of those ages had ascended to a plane of knowledge where these opposing experiences meet and fuse so as to give a synthetic and integral knowledge. In fact in India this synthetic knowledge has always remained and even when afterwards in the Age of Reason different schools of philosophy came into existence each with its own exclusive truth, efforts were made from time to time to recombine the divided aspects into some image of the old catholicity and unity. But for the past several centuries after the age of the *Acharyas* there has come about a stagnancy both in spiritual as well as philosophical fields. The exclusive philosophies of the *Acharyas* gave rise to endless controversy and in the absence of any higher synthetic experience no further development could take place. This stagnancy represents the inner crisis of the spirit of India; for it shows that when a decisive stage was reached when different spiritual experiences coming in a direct conflict showed the necessity of rising to a still higher place of experience where the conflict could be resolved, no such effort came forth.

This crisis still continues to a large extent because although we find now developments in the spiritual and philosophical fields, the stagnancy of the past seems to have taken such deep roots that they have not been sufficiently understood or even noticed by the general philosophical and spiritual mind of the nation.

Nevertheless a leap has been taken and a higher ascent has been made. And the complete result of this supreme effort we find in Sri Aurobindo's revelation of the existence and effective operation of the Supermind. And if we study this concept of the Supermind we find in it the answer to all our questions that have arisen in the course of our enquiry.

In the first place, we find that on the supramental plane the different and opposing truths arrived at by different spiritual experiences are in fact not opposed to each other but are complementary aspects of the Supreme Infinite Being; they are not illusory but real determinations of the Infinite; in the supramental consciousness these aspects meet and fuse into each other. The supermind sees these truths of the Infinite, and for the creation and as a basis of creation puts them forth. But this determination does not involve the division of perfection: "An independent completeness of identity," says Sri Aurobindo, "with each of the primal aspects and powers—not narrowing as in the mind into a sole engrossing experience seeming to be final and integral, for that would be incompatible with the realisation of the unity of all aspects and powers of existence—is a capacity inherent in consciousness in the Infinite....But the Supermind keeps always and in every status or condition the spiritual realisation of the Unity of all."

This explains also why perfection is experienced in any given aspect of the Infinite. In fact we may suppose that all sense of perfection of any plane of experience is due to the indivisibility of the original Perfection of the Infinite. In all determinations the Infinite remains undivided. But at the same time it becomes clear that absorption in any single experience is a sign of limitation and has to be explained in terms of the operation of the dividing act of the Mind.

There are two aspects of the Supermind which render its knowledge of the Infinite and the universe infallible. The first is the fact of its being the self-awareness of the Infinite; the second is its being the power of self-determination which is inherent in that self-awareness. Now when we speak of the self-determining power of the Infinite it should be clear to us that the Reason which still borrows the contents of its ideas by analogy from the facts of sense-experience commits a fallacy when it puts the Infinite and determination in irreconcilable opposition to each other. To it determination is a division which breaks the whole and thus destroys the perfection of the whole; to it therefore determination of the whole is a self-contradictory idea and therefore something that cannot be; and if the facts of experience compel it to regard the fact of determination as something ultimate, it takes resort to 'somehow' and 'inexplicability'. To the Supermind, on the contrary, determination is not a division, but a self-manifestation of the Infinite; necessarily therefore determinations pre-exist in the Infinite and to create, that is to say, manifest them, the Infinite has not to be broken; determinations are the eternal truths of the Infinite and the Supermind brings them forth and arranges them. The determination of the Infinite therefore is not to the supramental consciousness a mystery or an inexplicable phenomenon but a fact of direct knowledge and execution. The phenomenon is not mysterious, it is the Reality itself which is to our limited mind a Mystery. It is this mystery which Reason has to accept, not the unaccountability of the phenomenon of the Infinite creating teeming finites ad *infinitum*. To the supramental consciousness the Supreme is not a rigid Indeterminable, an all-negating Absolute. And this the Supermind knows because it is itself the self-awareness of the Infinite and because it is itself the self-determining power of the Infinite.

This being so we can now be certain of what this universe is; we can be certain that the universe is not ultimately an illusion but a real self-determination of the Infinite; it is, in other words, an objective representation of Reality to itself effected by the instrumentality of the Supermind which mediates as what Sri Aurobindo calls the Real-Idea between the Infinite and the objective self-representation. For what is contained in the Infinite is simultaneously conceived, that is to say, idealised subjectively and realised, brought forth objectively by the Supermind. Therefore nothing in the universe is a mere idea without any substance behind it; so not only subjective idealism but also the theory which reduces our world-experience to certain universal mental categories which are regarded as having no correspondence with the objects, that is to say, the substance of the objects, is fallacious. For ultimately the subjective and the objective are only the two sides of a single vision, and there is therefore in the supramental cognition a complete correspondence between them. The conflict therefore between subjectivism and objectivism also is fallacious.

On the supramental plane we come to know with certainty the original relation of the three terms of existence, the Infinite, the universe and the individual. It becomes certain here that the individual is at once identical in essence with the Infinite and yet in manifestation a concentration of the Supreme Consciousness of the Infinite; it is thus from the point of knowledge a self-objectivisation of the Infinite so that the Infinite can look at itself from the point of view of the individual. In this relation we find the primary conditions of complete knowledge entirely fulfilled: here there is a complete mutuality and identity of the terms of knowledge. The individual can know the Infinite for it is in fact one with the Infinite, the Object-in-itself; but this identity does not abolish the differentiation of the individual so that the two terms can be known subjectively and objectively on the basis of identity. And the same relation holds true of the individual and the universe, the subject and the object. Here again the subject and the object are in essence identical with the infinite, and therefore the subject can know the essence of the object, the object-in-itself; moreover, the object is seen as an objective differentiation proceeding from the subject itself; and therefore it is possible for the subject to throw, to project itself into the object and know the essentiality, the peculiarity, the very differentia of the differentiation of the object from the subject and yet without losing its own subjectivity, the essentiality, the peculiarity, the very differentia of the subject's differentiation from the object.

This then is the possibility when the movement of knowledge reaches the summit of being and experience. And having reached this summit it is again possible to come down and convert our lower instruments of knowledge and to fulfil them by uniting them with their corresponding higher terms. Thus the spiritual knowledge can be heightened into the supramental; the reason can be converted into a form of the self-luminous intuitional knowledge; and our physical senses too can be so converted as to the physical means of supramental knowledge.

CAUSALITY, CHANGE AND TIME

The tree does not explain the seed, nor the seed the tree; cosmos explains both and God explains the cosmos.
SRI AUROBINDO

*I*f we are to mean by Causality the necessary, as opposed to contingent, relation between events, so as to explain the phenomenon of change, then indeed such relation is not evident to our perceptual cognition. For what we perceive is merely the succession of constantly changing events, but nowhere any necessity or power necessitating change. On the contrary, there is visible to us the phenomenon of infinite variation which cannot be explained by any law of necessity. It is true, however, that by close observation we do not perceive certain uniformities, that is to say, certain broad repetitions of sequences of events; but there again, they are not entirely uncontradicted, and since what we per-ceive belongs either to the present or to the past but never to the future, and since it is impossible to observe all the instances of uniformities, no causal law of necessity can be established.

It has, however, been argued that the proof of Causality has not to be sought for in our sense-experience or observation of the world. For it is contended that Causality is not an idea constructed or derived from experience but an innate or an *a priori* category of Pure Reason. Reason, it is thought, is so constituted that it cannot conceive of an event except in the framework of Causality, that is to say, except as related to another by which it is determined and therefore from which it necessarily follows. To Reason, therefore, it is held, Causality is an undeniable and self-evident concept.

And yet, pursuing this line of thought, it has been concluded that Causality, when reflected upon, turns out to be unintelligible, unreal and impossible. It has been argued that Causality is a rational attempt to show the necessity of the occurrence of an event or change; but since everything in the world which we may regard as a cause of another is itself an event, we are led to postulate a Cause or Determiner, transcendent, self-existent and free from any necessity. For if we do not postulate a Free Cause, it is argued, we are led to infinite regress resulting in failure to show the necessity of the event in question and thus proving the absurdity of the idea of Causality. But on the other hand, so the argument continues, if there is a Free Cause, there will be a beginning of the causal series to being which there will be a first act unpreceded by any previous act or necessity. And this, it is held, contradicts the idea of Causality according to which there is always a previous necessity to cause an event. It is concluded therefore that Causality is an antimony implying at once the necessity and impossibility of the beginning of the causal series, a self-contradiction, unintelligible and therefore something that cannot be.

Shall we then return to the primary perceptual certainty of the phenomenon of Change and Becoming? But it has been held that Change too is as much ridden with self-contradiction as Causality. It has been argued that the very conception of change implies the existence of a permanent to which change belongs; for if we do not postulate a Permanent Substance, it is argued, we would be obliged to say that there is nothing which changes and thus prove the absurdity of the idea of change. But, on the other hand, if there is a Permanent Substance, so the argument continues, change must belong to it since otherwise it would fall outside it and thus be unreal. But if it belongs to the Permanent Substance, the latter will be affected by change and thus cease to be permanent. It is concluded, therefore, that Change is an antinomy implying at once the necessity and impossibility of a Permanent Substance, a self-contradiction, unintelligible and therefore something that cannot be.

But then how are we to account for the phenomenon of change? For we have on the one hand, a Permanent Substance and on the other, the phenomenon of change which cannot be and yet which we perceive and experience. It has been declared that the problem is insoluble and therefore it is wise not to raise it.

But this insolubility does not satisfy the demand of our Reason for explanation and solution. Perhaps there is somewhere, we begin to think, some incompleteness of experience or fallacy in the argument which pronounces the phenomenon of change as self-contradictory or illusory. Perhaps there is some missing link between that Absolute and Infinite Permanent, on the one hand and this relative world of change, on the other. Perhaps there is no fundamental contradiction in the co-existence of the Infinite which is the Permanent and the Change. It may indeed be argued that the Permanent cannot be a fixed form which ceases to be when afflicted with change; it must, on the contrary, be some essence which remains what it is always and eternally without any form or in any number of forms, even as sweetness, for instance, remains the same in all the various forms of sweet things or even as clay is the same whether it assumes the form of a toy or a jar or any other form or none at all. If it is merely formless, no form could ever come into existence – for there is no other reality from which it could derive its existence; on the other hand, it is not impossible for the Infinite to have a power of self-formation in infinite names and forms –nay, on the contrary, it must have this power since the denial of this power would contradict the perfection of the Infinite. We arrive then at the idea of Reality as a permanent and perfect essence which is at the same time an omnipotent power of self-formation and realisation of infinite potentiality of inherent names and forms which it may or may not assume and yet remain what it is, -- a paradox, but is it a self-contradiction? For does potentiality not presuppose, not any incapacity or want, but instead a capacity or a power of realising what is already and essentially is? What is not there is merely the actualisation of essence in manifestation; but the perfection of the essence does not depend upon its manifestation; it is already there eternally and permanently. Manifestation is only a free exercise of the omnipotent power of realising in Time what is already and essentially is eternally and timelessly.

It is then by the recognition of the omnipotent Power, one with and inherent in the Infinite, as a link between the essence and the phenomenon of change that we are able to arrive at a solution of the problem. For then we see that change is a process of self-realisation of the infinite potentialities inherent in the essential Reality. It proceeds from Reality and effects real formations without affecting the eternal and permanent essence of the Being. It is thus not an illusory or a non-existent superimposition on the eternally inactive Absolute but an effective and real process effected by the inherent power of the Absolute itself.

In effect, we have arrived at the idea of Reality as at once a self-existent Being and a Free Causal Will or Power capable of projecting and realising its own potential names and forms. But can we, it may be asked, accord our acceptance to this idea which implies the reality of causality – causality which has been declared, as we have seen, to be an insoluble antinomy? But it may be that this antinomy arises not because of any inherent inadequacies in the idea of causality but because of some confusion or fallacy in the argument. It may indeed be admitted that the causal series does imply a Free Cause; but it may also be pointed out that if the existence of the Free Cause is taken to imply a temporal beginning of the causal series we have to declare that to be impossible. For since the idea of beginning is valid only in Time, the idea of the beginning of the temporal or causal series is unthinkable. But if the Free Cause is transcendental and therefore Timeless, is it not reasonable to suppose that its causal activity also is timeless? For that which causes the temporal and causal series cannot itself be a temporal event, having a beginning at some date or moment. It must be a Timeless act of the Infinite. This would mean that there is between the Timeless Eternal and the Time-Eternity an intervening Timeless Will causing timelessly a beginningless temporal and causal series. It is then the recognition of this intermediate Timeless Will which enables us to solve the antinomy of causality. For in that will and act we have the sufficient explanation of the necessity of the causal series without involving us into the impossible situation of supposing a beginning of the temporal or causal series. We can then be certain that the universal causal relations which our reason is obliged to suppose in the sequences of events are not imaginary constructions having no corresponding truth in the objective universe; for we see now that Causality is a fundamental character of the Truth of existence and that our mental category is a reflection of that objective Truth – the subjective idea corresponding to the objective fact. The causal laws are, we might say, that Timeless Will working in different conditions and circumstances, the manifestations of that original Law of creation.

But what about the phenomenon of infinite variation? Does this phenomenon, it may be asked, not contradict the operation of the causal law? Our reply is that this phenomenon does not contradict our position: for our supposition is that the Reality to which the Timeless Will belongs has infinite potentialities and therefore there is nothing impossible in its manifestation of infinite variety. For the omnipotent Will may bring forth and arrange potentialities in some order and uniformity but it may also permit infinite variation of the complex working of the Time-Eternity.

There is, however, still the question of the relation between the Timeless Will and the Time-Eternity which it causes; but we can be certain that since these two are not temporal events they cannot be related in terms of Time. The only way therefore by which we can relate them is by supposing a simultaneity of the two in the all-powerful Infinite. We have already seen how Reality is simultaneously a self-existent Being and the omnipotent Power; we may now say that the self-existent is the Timeless Eternal which becomes the Time-Eternity through the free exercise of its omnipotent and Timeless causal Will.

But it may be objected that the temporal series, that is to say, the Time-Eternity, which the causal will is shown here to be causing is so ridden with self-contradiction that it is unintelligible, unreal and impossible. For it has been argued that the temporal series is a succession of diverse elements needing a further reconciliation by a further relation, and so on *ad infinitum*. It is concluded therefore that Time is an antinomy implying at once the necessity and impossibility of succession, a self-contradiction, unintelligible and therefore something that cannot be.

Now it may be admitted that there is undoubtedly the successive movement implying a diversity of moments, for otherwise there would be no phenomenon of change and development. But just as all forms and names are potentially present in the Infinite and therefore reconciled with each other through their common basis in the Infinite, even so the diversity which succession implies may be regarded as inherent in the Infinite and therefore reconciled with each other through the same common basis.

This would mean that the Infinite is at once the basis of Time and Time itself, an infinite extension by self-projection and an eternal successive movement by self-observation; for if it is not an extension, it cannot be the basis serving as the common support of successive moments: and this extension presupposes a power of self-projection on the part of the omnipotent Infinite. Again, if it is not successive movements the latter would be alien and therefore unrelated to it; and this successive movement presupposes a power of successive self-observation. But there is no impossibility in the Infinite having this double power. For neither self-projection nor self-observation involves any unbridgeable division in the Infinite. For if there were such division we can arrive at it by analysis of the presented Time at irreducible and indivisible units of moment. But what we find on the contrary is that any given unit of Time is infinitely divisible; and this means that at the bottom of the presented Time, there is something which always remains undivided. In fact, we can even go farther and say that since there is infinite, divisibility there is in reality no such thing as a process of division which can break the given object into two unbridgeable units. What we call division is then merely demarcation which delimits but does not cut. We may then conclude that the infinite Time-Extension and successive Time-Eternity imply no impossible division in the Infinite but they are only a process of self-delimitation which can justifiably be attributed to the omnipotent power of the Infinite. Indeed, an omnipotent Will exercising freely its power of self-limitation is the secret of all creation and causality.

APPENDIX

TIMELESS AND SPACELESS REALITY
AND
SPACE AND TIME

An extract from Sri Aurobindo's *"The Life Divine"*.

The original status is that of the Reality timeless and spaceless; Space and Time would be the same Reality self-extended to contain the deployment of what was within it. The difference would be, as in all the other oppositions, the Spirit looking at itself in essence and principle of being and the same Spirit looking at itself in the dynamism of its essence and principle. Space and Time are our names for this self-extension of the one Reality. We are apt to see Space as a static extension in which all things stand or move together in a fixed order; we see Time as a mobile extension which is measured by movement and event: Space then would be Brahman in self-extended status; Time would be Brahman in self-extended movement. But this may be only a first view and inaccurate: Space may be really a constant mobile, the constancy and the persistent time-relation of things in it creating the sense of stability of Space, the mobility creating the sense of time-movement in stable Space. Or, again, Space would be Brahman extended for the holding together of forms and objects; Time would be Brahman self-extended for the deployment of the movement of self-power carrying forms and objects; the two would then be a dual aspect of one and the same self-extension of the cosmic Eternal.

A purely physical Space might be regarded as in itself a property of Matter; but Matter is a creation of Energy in movement. Space therefore in the material world could be either a fundamental self-extension of material Energy or its self-formed existence field, its representation of the Inconscient Infinity in which it is acting, a figure in which it accommodates the formulas and movements of its own action and self-creation. Time would be itself the course of that movement or else an impression created by it, an impression of something that presents itself to us a regularly successive in its appearance, -- a division or a continuum upholding the continuity of movement and yet marking off its successions, -- because the movement itself is regularly successive. Or else Time could be a dimension of Space necessary for the complete action of the Energy, but not understood by us as such because it is seen by our conscious subjectivity as something itself subjective, felt by our mind, not perceived by our senses, and therefore not recognised as a dimension of space which has to us the appearance of a sense-created or sense-perceived objective extension.

In any case, if Spirit is the fundamental reality, Time and Space must either be conceptive conditions under which the Spirit sees its own movement of energy or else they must be fundamental conditions of the Spirit itself which assume a different appearance or status according to the status of consciousness in which they manifest. In other words there is a different Time and Space for each status of our consciousness and even different movements of Time and Space within each status; but all would be renderings of a fundamental spiritual reality of Time-Space. In fact, when we go behind physical space, we become aware of an extension on which all this movement is based and this extension is spiritual and not material; it is Self or Spirit containing all action of its own Energy. This origin or basic reality of Space begins to become apparent when we draw back from the physical: for then we become aware of a subjective Space-extension in which mind itself lives and moves and which is other than physical Space-Time, and yet there is an interpenetration; for our mind can move in its own space in such a way as to effectuate a movement also in space of Matter or act upon something distant in space of Matter. In a still deeper condition of consciousness we are aware of a pure spiritual Space; in this awareness Time may no longer seem to exist, because all movement ceases, or, if there is a movement or happening, it can take place independent of any observable Time sequence.

If we go behind Time by a similar inward motion, drawing back from the physical and seeing it without being involved in it, we discover that Time observation and Time movement are relative, but Time itself is real and eternal. Time observation depends not only on the measures used, but on the consciousness and the position of the observer: moreover, each state of consciousness has a different time relation; Time in Mind consciousness and Mind Space has not the same sense and measure of its movements as in physical Space; it moves there quickly or slowly according to the state of the consciousness. Each state of consciousness has its own Time and yet there can be relations of Time between them; and when we go behind the physical surface, we find several different Time statuses and Time movements co-existent in the same consciousness. This is evident in dream Time where a long sequence of happenings can occur in a period which corresponds to a second or a few seconds of physical Time. There is then a certain relation between different Time statuses but no ascertainable correspondence of measure. It would seem as if Time had no objective reality, but depends on whatever conditions may be established by action of consciousness in its relation to status and motion of being: Time would seem to be purely subjective. But, in fact, Space also would appear by the mutual relation of Mind-Space and Matter-Space to be subjective; in other words, both are the original spiritual extension, but it is rendered by mind in its purity into a subjective mind-field and by sense-mind into an objective field of sense-perception. Subjectivity and objectivity are only two sides of one consciousness, and the cardinal fact is that any given Time or Space or any given Time-Space as a whole is a status of being in which there is a movement of the consciousness and force of the being, a movement that creates or manifests events and happenings, it is the relation of the consciousness that sees and the force that formulates the happenings, a relation inherent in the status, which determines the sense of Time and creates our awareness of Time-movement, Time-relation, Time-measure. In its fundamental truth the original status of Time behind all its variations is nothing else than the eternity of the Eternal, just as the fundamental truth of Space, the original sense of its reality, is the infinity of the Infinite.

The Being can have three different states of its consciousness with regard to its own eternity. The first is that in which there is the immobile status of the Self in its essential existence, self-absorbed or self-conscious, but in either case without development of consciousness in movement or happening; this is what we distinguish as its timeless eternity. The second is its whole-consciousness of the successive relations of all things belonging to a destined or an actually proceeding manifestation, in which what we call past, present and future stand together as if in a map or settled or very much as an artist or painter or architect might hold design all the detail of his work viewed as a whole, intended or reviewed in his mind or arranged in a plan for execution; this is the stable status or simultaneous integrality of Time. This seeing of Time is not at all part of our normal awareness of events as they happen, though our view of the past, because it is already known and can be regarded in the whole, may put on something of this character; but we know that this consciousness exists because it is possible in an exceptional state to enter into it and see things from the viewpoint of this simultaneity of Time-vision. The third status is that of a processive movement of Consciousness-Force and its successive working out of what has been seen by it in the static vision of the Eternal; this is the Time movement. But it is in one and the same Eternity that this triple status exists and the movement takes place; there are not really two eternities, one an eternity of status, another an eternity of movement, but there are different statuses or positions taken by Consciousness with regard to the one Eternity. For it can see the whole Time development from outside or from above the movement; it can take a stable position within the movement and see the before and the after in a fixed, determined or destined succession; or it can take instead a mobile position in the movement, itself move with it from moment to moment and see all that has happened receding back into the past and all that has to happen coming towards it from the future; or else it may concentrate on the moment it occupies and see nothing but what is in that moment and immediately around or behind it. All these positions can be taken by the being of the Infinite in a simultaneous vision or experience. It can see Time from above and inside Time, exceeding it and not within it; it can see the Timeless develop the Time-movement without ceasing to be timeless, it can embrace the whole movement in a static and a dynamic vision and put out at the same time something of itself into the moment-vision. This simultaneity may seem to the finite consciousness tied to the moment-vision a magic of the Infinite, a magic of Maya; to its own way of perception which needs to limit, to envisage one status only at a time in order to harmonise, it would give a sense of confused and inconsistent unreality. But to an infinite consciousness such an integral simultaneity of vision and experience would be perfectly logical and consistent; all could be elements of a whole-vision capable of being closely related together in a harmonious arrangement, a multiplicity of view bringing out the unity of the thing seen, a diverse presentation of concomitant aspects of the One Reality.

If there can this simultaneous multiplicity of self-presentation of one Reality, we see that there is no impossibility in the co-existence of a Timeless Eternal and a Time Eternity. It would be the same Eternity viewed by a dual self-awareness and there could be no opposition between them; it would be a correlation of two powers of the self-awareness of the infinite and eternal Reality, -- a power of status and non-manifestation, a power of self-effecting action and movement and manifestation. Their simultaneity, however contradictory and difficult to reconcile it might seem to our finite surface seeing, would be intrinsic and normal to the Maya or eternal self-knowledge and all-knowledge of Brahman, the eternal and infinite knowledge and wisdom-power of the Ishwara, the consciousness-force of the self-existent Sachchidananda.[1]

---

[1] Sri Aurobindo: *The Life Divine, Centenary Edition*, Volume 18, pp. 360-64

TOWARDS APPLIED PHILOSOPHY

Among all intellectual disciplines, Philosophy is intrinsically concerned with the search of essential significance, which impels uncovering of layers of facts, physical and psychological, and determination of the distinction between appearance and reality. It also provides an impetus to the quest of comprehensiveness as also of the ultimate reality that may exist, in the light of which relationships are understood and evaluated. And if we examine the dimension of significance, we shall find that there is in it an underlying sense of perception of the object and of the idea that signifies the object. Philosophical thinking is an expression of an inherent nisus that can be satisfied only if all that is there is cognised in a dispassionate search of a comprehensive and, if need be, a transcendental sweep, resulting in a meaningful state of completeness.

Mere vision of truth, even comprehensive vision of truth, may be an object of science, but the unique dimension of Philosophy is the search for meaning, which discloses what may be called deliberate reason that raises us up in suggesting not to accept things as they are but to inquire into why they are what they are and whether they could be or ought to be other than what they are. A complete philosophical argument involves this quintessential element.

If Philosophy is a critical search, if it is a search which is free from all presuppositions, it is because there is in the deliberate or critical reason an inherent freedom that seeks to rise above the subjection to the presentation of facts as they are. If Philosophy is a search for comprehensiveness and even of transcendence, it is because there is in the intellectual operation of the Reason an inherent sense that all that is presented to us is not enough and that much more is needed for the purpose of understanding the given data. It is this inherent quest that lifts Philosophy above the realm of science and gives to Philosophy a pre-eminent position among all the intellectual disciplines.

If this account is true, it follows that a true study of Philosophy should end, not in a mere spinning of abstractions, but in a state of satisfaction in which all that is presented stands in the context of comprehensiveness and in a grasp of their essential significance and meaning.

However, since Philosophy is an intellectual activity, the satisfaction that it provides is ideative in character, which reflects the possession of meaning in an ideative form, similar to the satisfaction of an artist in the perception and creation of a form that reflects the intended meaning, in a vehicle that represents colour, line, mass and proportion, or very similar to music in which the meaning is captured in the form of a sound in a vehicle marked by pitch, volume and rhythm. Idea is really a Form, as Plato conceived it and as Vishwamitra much earlier described it as something so transparent that it cannot be called either clad or unclad (*avasana anagnah*). But precisely because the purest idea is still a form, it does not give that utter satisfaction which our integral nature demands and which can come through experience, contact, activity and identity. For this reason, even the highest and the purest philosophical perception or comprehension needs to be complemented by such movements of consciousness that are fulfilled in corresponding currents of concrete experience and through the methods of application. Applications in conduct, action and direct contact and identity of the object of which idea is a mere form. In other words, purest Philosophy pushes itself towards Applied Philosophy so as to arrive at concrete possession of the object of thought in a state of being and becoming. This is what lies behind the Indian approach to philosophy when it is coupled with Yoga. To use Indian terms Samkhya and Yoga accompany each other.

II

It is not necessary that philosophical inquiry must end in a discovery of meaning; a Philosophy may even come to the conclusion that there is no such thing as meaning; but even such a Philosophy can be designated as philosophy only if it has attempted to exercise the sense of meaning in its fullness and arrived at its own conclusion after having exhausted its search for meaning. And even such a philosophy pushes itself for a corresponding satisfaction in an Applied Philosophy that advocates conduct of life based on the denial of meaning. It prescribes the cultivation of qualities or states of mind and experience that would result from the philosophical denial of meaning. This is very well illustrated in the Essay written by Bertrand Russell, "*A Freeman's Worship*" where he describes briefly his philosophy of meaninglessness and application of that philosophy in the conduct of life. For the sake of brevity, we may only quote the last paragraph of that article:

Brief and powerless is Man's life; on him and all his race the slow, sure doom falls pitiless and dark. Blind to good and evil, reckless of destruction, omnipotent matter rolls on its relentless way; for Man, condemned today to lose his dearest, tomorrow himself to pass through the gate of darkness, it remains only to cherish, ere yet the blow falls, the lofty thoughts that ennoble his little day; disdaining the coward terrors of the slave of Fate, to worship at the shrine that his own hands have built; undismayed by the empire of chance, to preserve a mind free from the wanton tyranny that rules his outward life; proudly defiant of the irresistible forces that tolerate, for a moment, his knowledge and his condemnation, to sustain alone, a weary but unyielding Atlas, the world that his own ideals have fashioned despite the trampling march of unconscious power.

We may draw a conclusion that a study of a Philosophy leads logically to the development of corresponding Applied Philosophy.

III

It may be noted that a number of systems of philosophy have developed in the East, which were accompanied by systems of applications. At first, as we see it in India, there was a period of spiritual development, but as in the Upanishads, the method was at first an intuitive seeing and an inspired expression, but afterwards there was developed a critical method, a firm system of dialectics, a logical organisation. The later philosophies were intellectual account or a logical justification of what had been found by inner realisation; or they provided themselves with a mental ground or a systematised Yogic method for realisation and experience. In the West, the syncretic tendency of consciousness was replaced by the analytic and separative mentality at an early stage; the spiritual urge and the intellectual reason parted company almost at the outset; Philosophy took from the first a turn towards a purely intellectual and ratiocinative explanation of things, even though there were systems like the Pythagorean, Stoic and Epicurean, which were dynamic not only for thought but for conduct of life and developed a discipline, an effort at inner perfection of being. A little later, this reached a higher spiritual plane of knowledge in later Christian or Neo-pagan thought-structures where the East and the West met together. But later on, the intellectualisation became complete and the connection of Philosophy with life and its energies or spirit and its dynamism was either cut or confined to the little that the metaphysical idea can impress on life and action by an abstract and secondary influence.

In recent times, however, there has come about a cleavage between Philosophy and Applied Philosophy to such an extent that reaction has started which emphasises the importance of studies in Applied Philosophy, and a number of subjects are developing today such as Ethics, Applied Ethics, Applied Philosophy of Law, Applied Philosophy of Medicine, Applied Philosophy of Management, -- in brief Applied Philosophy of Life.

It is against this background that we need to present to ourselves a fresh line of development, in which we can recover also the earlier Indian balance between Philosophy and Applied Philosophy.

IV

It is being increasingly recognised at present that the development of science, which is today holding the central stage of the field of knowledge, should be supplemented by enormous development of human goodness. Bertrand Russell, in his study of science and its impact on society, has pointed out that there are two ancient evils that science, unwisely used, may intensify: they are tyranny and war. He has, therefore, declared, in this context, the need for compassion and pursuit of values of higher order. In his words:

> There are certain things that our age needs, and certain things that it should avoid. It needs compassion and a wish that mankind should be happy; it needs a desire for knowledge and the determination to eschew pleasant myths; it needs above all courageous hope and impulse to creativeness. The things that it must avoid are cruelty, envy, greed, competitiveness, search for irrational subjective certainty, and what Freudians called the death wish...The root of the matter is very simple and old fashioned thing...The thing I mean – please forgive me for mentioning it – is love, Christian love or compassion. If you feel this, you have a motive for existence, a guide in action, a reason for courage, an imperative necessity for intellectual necessity.

It is being underlined that science and technology are human activities, and no human activity has a right to claim such an autonomy that it can indulge in its exclusive pursuit without considering the question of the necessity of promoting universal solidarity, unity and integrity. It is being acknowledged that a scientist, a technologist, is a human being and he has to bear the responsibility that every human being has to bear towards the universal good. In other words, it is recognised that science cannot afford to be value- neutral; it has to build a bridge between the realm of knowledge and the realm of values. And this is one of the gates by which science and technology can enter into the domain of Ethics, Applied Philosophy and Spirituality.

At one time, it was fashionable to explain the universe in terms of material and mechanical determinism. Recent advances have weakened the rigid hold of this determinism. For the theory of mechanistic necessity by itself does not elucidate indeterminacy and the free play of the endless unaccountable variations which occur in the evolutionary process. Recourse is sometimes made to a paradoxical concept of self-organising dynamic Chance. But even then, the assumption of an original unconscious energy at work leads us to incredible and inexplicable conclusion. It is also obvious that the theory, which attempts to suggest that anything can happen by chance, has no obligatory force, for chance and obligatory force are self-contradictory. In any case, the fact is that the mind has emerged in the evolutionary process, and this could be more than a chance, since mind betrays the quality of order and sense of unity, which are alien to the very idea of chance.

Again, the emergence of the theme of consciousness in the context of the recent advances of core sciences has momentous consequences for a new turning point in the history of knowledge and research. Again, the outposts of scientific knowledge come more and more to be set on the borders that divide the material from the immaterial; similarly, the highest achievements of practical science are those which tend to simplify and reduce to the vanishing-point the machinery by which the greater effects are produced. It is also increasingly acknowledged that materialism can be maintained only by ignoring or explaining away the vast field of evidence and experience which contradicts it. The arbitrariness of the materialistic premise is also being admitted in disguised or explicit form. At one time, it was confidently asserted that the physical senses are the sole means of knowledge and that reason, therefore, cannot escape beyond their domain. But today it is being acknowledged more and more widely that physical senses cannot give any disproof of anything that may be lying beyond their domain. In other words, it is admitted that physical senses cannot find any justification for the universal sweep contained in the orthodox premises of materialism.

It is true that materialism is still lingering in subtle forms. While matter is no more placed as the ultimate reality, there have emerged formidable methodologies of analysis or empiricism which do away with any conception of ultimate reality, thus preventing the formulation of any possible theory of Spirit as an alternative to crumbling theory of materialism. At the same time, the climate has greatly changed. Science has become less rigid, and it is unable to reject *a priori* any claim of supra-physical experience.

In the field of Biology, while the Darwinian Theory of Evolution by random chance, natural selection, struggle for existence and survival of the fittest is still surviving, powerful trends have emerged to challenge it through theories such as those of Vitalism of Bergson , Emergent Evolution of Alexander, Holism of Smutts, Ingressive Idealism of Whitehead, and Spiritual Evolution of Teillard De Chardin. In India, Sri Aurobindo's theory of Supramental Evolution is a formidable answer to Darwinism and to materialism in general.

A major difficulty lies in the insistence laid by the physical sciences on the application of their methods on all sciences, even when subject matters are not physical in character. The scientific method is so conceived that no evidence could be accepted of a fact unless it is objective and physical in character; even if the fact apparently be supra-physical, this method refuses to accept it as such unless it is totally inexplicable by any other imaginable hypothesis or conceivable conjecture. But it should be evident that this demand for physical valid proof of the supra-physical is irrational and illogical. For the method of knowledge should be appropriate to the object of knowledge. If the nature of the object is itself supra-physical, it would be unreasonable to demand that it should be physical and should be scrutinisable by means of physical senses.

On the other hand, the great science of Yoga, which has been developed for thousands of years in India as Applied Philosophy, has begun to command increasing recognition. Yoga has developed various kinds of evidence of the existence of other planes of beings and communication with them. They include objectification of the outer sense, subtle-sense contacts, mind contacts, life contacts, contacts through the subliminal in special states of consciousness existing beyond our ordinary range. It is normally argued that subjective experience or subtle-sense images can easily be deceptive, since we have no recognised method or standards of verification. It is, however, being gradually understood that the validity in any field must be scrutinised according to the laws operating in that domain. It is also being argued that in any field of experience, error is possible, and error is not the prerogative only of the inner subjective or occult parts of us. Even where physical and objective methods are employed, it is admitted, there is room for errors. Mere liability to error cannot be a reason for shutting out a large and important domain of experience. As in the physical science, so in the supra-physical sciences, it has a reason for scrutinising it and finding out in it its own true standards and its characteristically appropriate and valid means of verification. It is also observed that the very basis of our objective experience is our subjective being; hence it is not probable that only its physical objectivism are true and the rest unreliable. It is finally urged that the supra-physical consciousness, when rightly interrogated, is a witness to truth and its testimony is confirmed again and again even in the physical and objective field; that testimony can not, then, be disregarded when it calls our attention to things within us or to things that belong to planes or world of supra-physical experiences.

It is gradually coming to be recognised that consciousness is the great underlying fact, the universal witness for whom the world is a field. To that witness, the worlds and objects appeal for their reality and for the one world or the many, for the physical equally with the supra physical, we have no other evidence that they exist.

In the development of the Western thought, two contemporary movements have brought out forcefully the significance of consciousness and subjective experience, namely, Phenomenology and Existentialism. Even though they are still circumscribed within a narrow field of subjective experience, the question is whether there is or there can be a science of supra-physical data. While this search is gaining ground, the world seems to be preparing to return from the present period of scepticism to Applied Philosophy of Yoga, its assured methods resulting from the principles, powers and processes that govern experiences and realisation of the highest possible object of knowledge. It is also being recognised that the methods of Yoga have something of the same relation to the customary psychological working of man as has the scientific handling of the natural force of electricity or of steam to the normal operation of steam and electricity. And they, too, are formed upon knowledge developed and confirmed by regular experiment, practical analysis and constant results.

All these new data and contentions need to be studied, and the more they are acknowledged, the more will be relevance of the study of Yoga as Applied Philosophy.

V

There are growing today certain pressing concerns which impel practical studies and applications of knowledge, particularly that knowledge which is accessible to Philosophy.

(1)

Today humanity is gripped by three pulls and counter-pulls and the resultant situation is so difficult that nothing short of change in human consciousness can lift up humanity from its crisis. On the one hand, there is a downward gravitation; on the other hand, there is a pull towards horizontal development, and there is still a higher pull of vertical ascension.

The downward gravitational pull has many features that are related to the hugeness of the structures and super-structures of economic, industrial, social and political life. These structures and super-structures are being sustained by continuous scientific discoveries and inventions and technological devices and gadgets, -- all of which contribute to the efficiency of the system. All these structures tend to sub-serve certain intellectual goals, but also more and more increasingly those goals which enhance pragmatism, success in competition and gratification of sensual pleasures. The fabric of life that is getting woven yields more and more through impersonalisation, mechanisation, and even dehumanisation. Even the higher and the highest pursuits of life are getting pulled down under the weight of the hurry and fury of forces that tempt and weaken human will. The subconscious and the unconscious are finding in this situation increasing avenues of invasion, and the forces of reason are being greatly defeated by those of unreason. This gravitational pull is that of the infra-rational and to fight against it so as to retain humanism requires a gigantic effort.

Fortunately, the gigantic effort is not entirely missing. While scientific discoveries and inventions tend to be utilised in their applications largely by the infra-rational, science itself is a rational endeavour, and its impulse to know and to know as comprehensively as possible stands out in the contemporary scenario as an angel which can provide lofty wings to humanity to fly into higher and higher domains of efforts and achievements. There is also a widespread inquiry, -- multiple inquiry and critical inquiry, -- which is pushing humanity to develop philosophy and ethics as also stringent notions of justice and equity. There are also growing visions and experiments with the shining ideals of liberty, equality and fraternity, -- and even though they are being hampered by the forces of economic barbarism, they still provide a push of higher struggle. In these domains, humanity can fulfil its humanism, and numerous paths are constantly opening up to invite humanity to become more and more humane, more and more rational, and more and more ethical.

It is in this context that several lines of applied ethics are being studied and promoted.

This network of ideas and forces constitutes the peak of the cultural effort of today. The intellectual, the ethical and the aesthetic aspirations of humanity are combined here to pull humanity from its downward gravitation and erect a durable civilisation that can continue to spread over larger and larger areas of the world. It perceives quite clearly that even science, if it is not guided by values, can be dangerous and can injure the future of humanity. It is greatly concerned with humanism, it is international in its sweep, and it has given a decisive turn to the ideal of human unity.

(2)

Psychological studies have begun to reveal to us the strangeness and complexity of the components and powers of human personality. It has now become clear that the human being has many parts and planes and that each one of them has its own thrust of development, and these thrusts are far from being homogenous or harmonious with one another. The physical being is often in conflict with the vital pursuits, and when the vital ambitions and attractions impose upon the physical body their own burden, the physical often revolts or collapses. The demands of physical health are often in clash with the demands of the vital being. Again, the demands of the vital being are in conflict with the demands of the mind when it wants to pursue the purity of thought and knowledge and the purity of its ideals. Often the vital being tends to make the mental being the advocate of its desires and ambitions by means of rationalisation. At the same time, the pure pursuits of the mind succeed some times in obliging the vital being to make sacrifices, but the resultant condition is often that of disequilibrium.

Still, again, the triangular disposition of the mind in its pursuit of rationality, ethicality and aesthetics is itself a complex of battle and disequilibrium. The pursuit of the truth through the channel of rationality is often encumbered or even contradicted by the pursuits of the good and the beautiful through channels of the moral and aesthetic sense. Even in the field of the pursuits of the truth, there are conflicts between scientific truth and the philosophical truth, and even when a choice is made in favour of one or the other, some kind of disequilibrium still remains. Similarly, in the field of ethical pursuit, the demands of love and justice often collide with each other, the good of the individual often collides with the good of the society, and the standards of conduct have among themselves continually sessions of disagreement. In the field of aesthetics, we are aware of the relativity of aesthetic standards and aesthetic judgements, and we are also aware of aesthetic personalities actuated by perceptions, imaginations and inspirations that often collide with scientific and philosophical truth as also with demands of the ethical good. It is true that a certain stage, one does perceive that truth is beauty and beauty is truth, but we are also aware how beauty looks askance at the good and the truth, and *vice versa*. It is true that the highest developments of Reason can bring about some kind of truce among the conflicting demands of various parts of the being, but this does not amount to integration.

This is not all. The conflicts that we see between the conscious parts are nothing as compared to the conflicts that arise between the conscious and the subconscious or unconscious. How feeble is the rational, ethical, and aesthetic complex of the human being when it gets attacked by the subconscious and unconscious forces has become more and more evident when we examine the modern life in its conditions of anxiety and stress. Some of the acute psychologists have even felt that there are only two powerful subconscious impulses, those of Eros and Thanatos, the desire to love and desire to kill; and not only are both of them in conflict with each other, but both of them are in conflict with the pursuit of rationality, morality and aesthetics in their purest and highest flights. They have even warned or predicted that humanity cannot sustain its upward movement and must ultimately decline and succumb to the forces of the unconscious Unreason.

Again, when the three ideals of the social Reason, -- liberty, equality and fraternity, -- are attempted to be established in collective life, these three are found to be in conflict with each other and defeated by the powers of Unreason. When liberty wins, equality gets dethroned; when equality is attempted to be raised up, liberty gets strangulated; and fraternity does not get even a chance of getting into any programme of action.

These reflections turn us to inquire as to whether there is any other still higher uplifting force by means of which humanity can successfully be uplifted from the tentacles of the subconscious and the unconscious.

It is here that studies in Applied Philosophy can provide expertise to help and counsel.

We find that there has been in the history of the world a persistent recognition and experience of a higher light and both in the East and in the West there have been luminous examples of those who have provided evidence of the presence and powers of the superconscious, which far exceed the capacities of the reason in dealing with the subconscious or the unconscious. In our own country, there appears to be a kind of specialisation, which has resulted in the opening up of hundreds of ways by which one can enter into the portals of the superconscient. Right from the Vedic times, of which we have existing records, up to the present day, we have a large bulk of data to show that the superconscient light or knowledge is not a matter of subjective error or hallucination but a matter of repeatable, verifiable and abiding experience as also of a continuously developing tradition. The Veda clearly spoke of three oceans, of the ocean of the inconscient, the ocean of the conscient, and the ocean of the superconscient. They spoke of the battle between the forces of these three oceans and even of the triumph of the superconscient over the conscient and the inconscient. The tradition of Vedic knowledge has continued right up to the present day and in our times, Sri Aurobindo has made radical experiments for the total transformation of the Inconscient by the process of the Supermind, the highest cosmic power of the Superconscient.

It is again affirmed that the superconscient is at work just as the subconscious or unconscious is at work, whether we may be aware of it or not. And it is further affirmed that in many critical conditions through which humanity has passed in history, the uplifting pull of the superconscient has played a decisive role.

(3)

The pursuit of the superconscient has been, as stated above, a perennial theme both in the East and the West. This pursuit has taken three principal forms, and we need to derive from them the most valuable lessons, which are relevant to the creation of a new road of education. These three forms are those of religion, philosophy and Yogic science. Our concern will be, not with any specific formula, nor with their conflicts, nor, again, with outer details of practices. Our concern will be to consider mainly the theme of the conquest of the subconscient and the inconscient by higher powers of rationality, ethicality, aesthetic sensibility and the superconscient pursuits of the Truth, Beauty and Goodness.

The conflict of religions, each one of which claims to have discovered the superconscient knowledge and light as also the methods by which that knowledge and light can be attained or contacted, is one of the chief obstacles that needs to be crossed. Fortunately, humanity has made considerable progress during the last hundred years, particularly since Swami Vivekananda declared that everyone needs his or her own religion, since each one has his or her own specific road of specific method of contact with the superconscient knowledge. Adherents of different religions have begun to understand with greater and greater sympathy the main points of agreement and disagreement, and even the claims to the possession of exclusive truths have become tampered with greater flexibility, mutual respect and not only tolerance but even an effort to absorb new insights, experiences and realisations. If this new trend is supported by a fresh appraisal of religions without dogmatism, further progress can be achieved. Instead of excluding each other, religions need to come together and arrive at a synthesis of universal knowledge to which each higher religion can make a significant contribution.

Each one of the universal religions possesses a precious treasure of knowledge; many aspects of this treasure are common, and certain distinguishing aspects can serve as enrichment, which can be shared by all. All religions stress the need to abolish egoism and eliminate desires that obstruct the attainment of purity and unity with the higher levels of knowledge and power. All religions live in a spirit of sacredness and holiness; all religions prescribe concentration on the highest that is accessible to our consciousness; all religions affirm the possibility of transcending our normal psychological limitations and of experience of higher faculties of intuition, revelation and inspiration. Even in respect of the contents of superconscient knowledge, where there are wide disagreements, a greater understanding can be instituted, so that following the method of repeatability, verifiability and expandability of experiences, their contents of knowledge can be properly ascertained and synthesised.

Philosophy, too, is a quest to arrive at the knowledge of the essential reality or realities, their relationships with the world and with the individual human being. But as distinguished from religion, where methods consist of faith or acceptance of belief or doctrine, and practice or rituals, ceremonies and prescribed acts, -- ethical and religious, -- both in context of the individual progress and social living, the methods of philosophy consist of a critical and logical inquiry and rational judgements based upon the criteria of consistency and comprehensiveness. Philosophical pursuits can be very useful in arriving at a comparative idea of the contents of the superconscient knowledge as also in obtaining intellectual assessment in terms of ontology, epistemology, cosmology and axiology coupled with critical self-evaluation of philosophical knowledge in contrast to knowledge obtained through direct experience in revelation or inspiration. Philosophical pursuit will also enable impartial seekers to arrive at non-dogmatic knowledge in intellectual language and in intellectual concepts, and may even prepare the human mind to seek and practise methods by which the knowledge gained by philosophy can be verified by direct and abiding experience.

Yogic science is also a pursuit of the superconscient knowledge, and its distinction is that it is experiential and experimental in character, and it is the methodised effort at arriving at direct experience by the contact and union with the universal and transcendental realities which, as in any science, can be arrived at without any dogmatic assumptions or even without recourse to rituals and prescribed acts based on any religious creed or dogma. Even a sceptic, an agnostic, an atheist and non-believer can practise Yogic methods and arrive at an impartial perception and experience of the truths of the superconscient knowledge.

It is true that Yogic knowledge is central for a genuine pursuit of the supra-rational truth, beauty and goodness, but still the religious and philosophical pursuits can, whenever and wherever needed, also help, and this help can be of great value. It is also true that there has been a strong tendency in religion, philosophy and Yoga to pursue the supra-rational in such an exclusive manner that claims of pragmatic life and material existence are ignored or even denied. There is too much emphasis on the supra-terrestrial, supra-cosmic, acosmic, so that the cosmic and terrestrial concerns are subordinated or neglected, even rejected. Since our aim will be to utilise superconscient knowledge in the conquest of the inconscient, we have to assign a central importance to those pursuits of the supra-conscient and supra-rational which deal with the cosmic and terrestrial, right up to our material life and its subconscious and unconscious recesses. In this context, our aim should be to give the right place and justification to that tendency in materialism which affirms matter, discovers secrets of knowledge pertaining to matter and affirms the legitimate and right claims of matter in the totality of existence as also to the utilities which material knowledge has provided to humanity and is still continuing to provide so that they can sub-serve along with similar utilities of the knowledge of Life, Mind, and other higher domains, those ends which are to be fulfilled through the conquest of the super-conscient over the inconscient.

It is in the context of the above three needs and also to promote studies in the contemporary crisis and find remedies and their applications that the studies in Applied Philosophy need to be instituted and pursued.

VI

Applied Philosophy is often confined to the study of Ethics and Applied Ethics, but there is a need to enlarge the scope in the light of the following considerations:

We are all aware of the moral theories of hedonism, hedonistic utilitarianism, ideal utilitarianism, intuitionism, and other higher formulations of ethical and spiritual norms. They are all presented as universal doctrines intended to be prescribed uniformly for all people, but if we take human individual and human collectivity to be evolutionary in character, and if we take elements of the complexity of human nature in an ascending order rising from the infra-rational to the rational and from the rational to the supra-rational, we may be able to gain insights into an evolutionary mode of reconciling conflicting morals and ideals.

From this point of view, there are four main standards of human conduct that make an ascending scale. The first is the personal need, preference and desire; the second is the law and good of the collectivity; the third is an ideal ethic, the last is the highest and divine ideal and law of the nature. Standard of conduct, which is prescribed by psychological and ethical but egoistic hedonism, falls into the first category; its argument is that because every individual psychologically seeks satisfaction of his personal need for pleasure, -- because everyone psychologically prefers pleasures to pain and because every individual seeks the satisfaction of personal desire for pleasure, every individual ought to seek one's own pleasure. Students of philosophy and ethics are familiar with this argument and its criticism, such as whether each human being necessarily seeks pleasure or some other things also, and if pleasure alone, whether there are different kinds of pleasures, some inferior and others that are superior. They are also familiar with the naturalistic fallacy that is committed when it argued that because pleasure is desired, pleasure is desirable.

If we examine the history of ethical thought, we find that egoistic ethical hedonism came, in due course, to be defended in the name of altruism and, eventually, run over by universal ethical hedonism that embodied the force of collectivistic ideals. This moral law advocated, in effect, the search for maximum pleasure for maximum number of people. To use the terms of Indian philosophy, the demands of *vyashti* and *samashti* came to be pressed forward against the claims of *ahambhava*. The existence of the collectivistic law external to the individual suggests a power other than that of personal egoism and induces or compels the individual to moderate his average demands, to discipline his irrational and often violent movements and even to lose himself some times in a larger and less personal egoism. And yet, the collectivistic morality or idealism is found to be incapable of arriving at any satisfactory solutions. Consequently, claims of society and claims of the individual continue to confront one another. There is a demand of the group that the individual should subordinate himself more or less completely or even lose his independent existence in the community. On the other hand, the ideal and absolute solution from the individual's standpoint would be a society that existed not for itself, but for the good of the individual and his fulfilment, for the greater and more perfect life of all its members. An ideal society of either kind does not exist anywhere, and in actuality, the society somehow attempts to work out some kind of a compromise, which some times gives an upper hand to the claims of individuals and some times to the claims of collectivity. In the end, the complexity of the problem increases and multiplies its issues. A need is felt to call in a new principle, and humanity begins to climb to a level of the pure mind, where the life of personal need, preference and desire begins to be touched by a greater and elevated light, and the aesthetic, intellectual and emotional desires begin to preponderate over the demands of the physical and the vital nature.

At this higher level, search for pleasure, egoistic or universal, gives way to a search for higher ideals like knowledge and character. Hedonistic utilitarianism begins to be over passed by what has come to be called ideal utilitarianism, which in the history of Western ethics was formulated to advocate the combined fulfilment of three ideals of character, knowledge and happiness. But even this ethical theory could not sufficiently be defended within the formula of utilitarianism, because while the utilitarian judges an action by its consequences, it was found that things like knowledge and character are ends in themselves and can not be judged in terms of their consequences. This forced the ethical thinker to develop a search for the realm of ends, which are intrinsic and which are valuable in themselves.

In India, there was an early discovery of dharma, of duty, of values of righteousness, and of action that had to be performed with a sense of equanimity as far as its consequences are concerned. In the West, in the philosophy of Conscience and Intuitionism, similar ideas were put forward, and they came to a culminating point in the ethical doctrine of Kant, which enjoined duty for its own sake and attempted to give a standard of action that had to be judged not by its consequences but by its own intrinsic value.

At that new higher level, the primacy of universal values came to the forefront and began to influence the new equations between the individual and the collectivity. The question came to be asked as to what was the real nature of the individual, and Kant's own answer was that the true individual was capable of liberating himself from the clamour of desires into a realm of ends in themselves. Kant even went one step farther and declared that the individual himself should be looked upon not merely as a means but as an end in himself. In other words, it was affirmed that while individualism is valid, the individual in its true nature is not an egocentric entity subject to appetites and desires, but an entity capable of uplifting himself to a state of intrinsic and universal values.

Consequently, it came to be advocated that the needs and desires of individuals are to be surpassed in obedience to the moral law, and even the social law has no claims upon him if it is opposed to his sense of right and denied by Conscience or by the categorical imperative. In regard to the conflict between the individual and the society, the solution that the moralist presented was that the individual shall cherish no desires and claims that are not consistent with love, truth and justice, and that the collectivity shall hold all things cheap, even its safety and its most pressing interests, in comparison with truth, justice, humanity and the highest good of the people.

The moralist's ideal of the categorical imperative is basically individualistic, and when his ideals are applied to the society, the inadequacies of these ideals come to light. For justice often demands what love abhors. Man's absolute justice easily turns out to be in practice a sovereign injustice; for his mind, one-sided and rigid in its construction, puts forward a one-sided partial and rigorous scheme or figure and claims for its totality and absoluteness and an application that ignores the subtler truth of things and the plasticity of life.

The fact is that the categorical imperative of ideal law does not signify the end of human search of the truth that harmonises and delivers. We discover that the moral nature of the human being is not the last and the highest component; there is, in us, it will be found, a divine being that is spiritual and supramental. In that component of our complex nature, it is claimed, is the integrating power; in it the truths of the individual and the collectivity coalesce; there we discover, we are told, that the individual and the collectivity are not what they appear to be in the lower or infra rational parts of our being. Individual is not, it is discovered, fundamentally egoistic in nature; ego is only a temporary construction, but behind it there is the unegoistic centre of universality and universality finds its concentrated centre of fullness in the individual.

Beyond the moral law are spiritual ideals. These ideals are not limited to moral data but embrace the totality of our being and totality of existence. The true divine law is not fully represented in exclusive formations of the mind or even in religious creeds that collide with other religious creeds. That is the reason why exclusive religions, even when proclaimed to be universal, have come to be combated by other exclusive religions with similar claims; and no social harmony can be achieved in that state of conflict.

The true spiritual and supramental consciousness takes into account the truth of all that is manifesting in this imperfect but evolving world and supports each truth in its proper place and harmonises it with all the rest. This seems to be the ideal of *lokasangrah* (solidarity of the people) of which Sri Krishna speaks in his message to Arjuna. The true universality and unity resolve lower discords into a victorious harmony and point to the ideal of the creation of what may be called a spiritualised society, where love would be absolute and equality would be consistent with hierarchy and perfect in difference. In that society, absolute justice would be secured by the spontaneous action of the being in harmony with the truth of things and the truths of oneself and others and, therefore, sure of true and right results. In that society, the quarrel between the individual and the collectivity or the disastrous struggle between one community and another would not exist, since the cosmic consciousness imbedded in the embodied beings would assure a harmonious diversity in oneness.

The study of Applied Philosophy will need, therefore, to include the study of the relationship between the ethical and the spiritual and the resolution of ethical dilemmas in the light of higher spiritual knowledge.

VII

The course in Applied Philosophy would underline the study of those uplifting forces which have provided to humanity the basic impetus to rise to higher and higher levels of culture and would thus stimulate students to practise in their own life the lessons of human culture.

Illumination, Heroism and Harmony can easily be discerned as the powers of the sublimation of human nature and the root cause of humanity's upward march. It can also be seen that human aspiration, right from early stages when humanity began to cultivate awakened thought, has manifested itself in the divination of Godhead, impulse towards perfection, the search after pure Truth and unmixed Bliss, and sense of a secret Immortality. This aspiration, when analysed in fullness, can be said to be the urge to know, possess and be the divine being in an animal and egoistic consciousness, to convert our twilight or obscure physical mentality into the plenary supramental illumination, to build peace and a self-existent bliss where there is only stress of a transitory satisfaction besieged by physical pain and emotional suffering, to establish an infinite freedom in a world which presents itself as a group of mechanical necessities, to discover and realise the immortal life in a body subjected to death and constant mutation.

It is true that this aspiration is contradicted and denied by the ordinary material intellect, which takes its present organisation of consciousness for the limit of its possibility. But if we ask as to why there exists this opposition between realised fact and the ideal of the human aspiration, we shall find that this opposition is a part of Nature's profoundest method, and the greater the apparent disorder of the materials offered, the stronger is the spur to arrive at a more subtle and puissant order. The entire evolutionary movement can be seen from this point of view where life has been greatly harmonised with matter, and mind has also been similarly harmonised with life. It would, therefore, be seen that the upward impulse of man towards the accordance of yet higher opposite not only rational in itself, but the only logical completion of a rule and an effort that seems to be a fundamental method of Nature and the very sense of our universal strivings.

Applied Philosophy can institute a study of this subject and also exploration of methods by which the upward aspiration of humanity can be fulfilled.

VIII

Applied Philosophy can also be considered as a part of value-oriented education at the tertiary level.

It is often argued that while value-oriented education is important at the elementary and secondary levels of education, it is not required at the tertiary level. It has been urged that values can be taught or caught when children are young, and when they are grown up they have already a formed character, and education in character development at a higher level is therefore unnecessary. But this argument misses the point that it is only at the tertiary level that one can institute a critical examination of the concept of values and how values can be inculcated in the personality. In fact a critical examination of values is by itself an important part of value-oriented education. Values, which are simply transmitted without examination, can only result in some kind of dogmatism or even indoctrination. Therefore, value-oriented education is absolutely essential at the tertiary level.

Considering, therefore, the importance of value-oriented education, one can think of its inclusion in the course of Applied Philosophy.

Firstly, place could be given to a critical examination of the questions of the aim of human life.

Study of the aim of human life can be viewed under four headings:

1. The supra-cosmic aim of life;
2. The supra-terrestrial aim of life;
3. Cosmic-terrestrial aim of life; and
4. Integral aim of life.

Secondly, one could discuss the question of relativity and subjectivity of values and how values have changed from time to time and from country to country. In this connection, one can introduce the question of definition of values and distinction between moral and spiritual values, as also values related to aesthetic and emotional life and values of intellectual and physical culture. Ideals of Liberty, Equality, Fraternity could also be studied at this stage.

The study of values in relation to the psychology of development of human personality could also be important, and it could be suggested that the following ideas, which are essential for the development of personality, could be a subject matter of a detailed study, namely:

1. Ego, memory and self; Indian and Western views;
2. Planes and parts of the being;

3. Inconscient, subconscient, physical, vital, rational, aesthetic, ethical, psychic, spiritual, supramental and transcendental.

Next, there could be a discussion on the multiple personalities in man and conflicts within man and how these conflicts can be resolved by harmonisation of personality. The question of free will and determinism can also be discussed in this connection.

There are also other aspects of personality which need to be studied in this connection. These relate to multi-dimensional personality, balanced personality and personality of equanimity. There is also in India a concept of fourfold personality of Wisdom, Power, Harmony and Skill.

One part of the important concept of value, which should be examined at the higher level, is that of the relationship between science and values. Here one could study he nature of the scientific thinking and pursuit of the value of Truth through science. There is also the contention that just as there is science which deals with the knowledge of the outer universe, even so there is a science which relates to the domain of inner universe. Both these sciences need to be harmonised.

At present, there is a new subject which is coming up in the forefront, and that is the theme of consciousness. This subject should be introduced with a special emphasis on the relationship between body and mind, and also the study of the body and mind as the science of yoga looks upon them. This subject can also be studied in the context of evolution, and it can be argued that evolution does not stop merely at the evolution of man and that there is a possibility of mutation of species.

What is called philosophy of religion could also be a part of the curriculum at the tertiary level. It is here that certain features of universal religions could be studied with the methods of comparative studies. Particularly, we may emphasise the study of Hinduism, Confucianism, Taoism, Zoroastrianism, Buddhism, Jainism, Judaism, Christianity, Islam and Sikhism. Along with these religions, there should be a detailed study of the lives of great personalities associated with these religions, or various systems of yoga such as Rama, Krishna, Buddha, Mahavira, Zoroaster, Moses, Jesus Christ, Prophet Mohammed, Guru Nanak, Sri Ramakrishna, Swami Vivekananda and Sri Aurobindo.

What is called psychology of religion and spirituality could also be studied at least at the elementary level, and here the emphasis could be on the study of psychology of worship and prayer, psychology of action without desire, psychology of concentration including that of meditation and contemplation. Yoga and psychology of spiritual experiences could also be included such as those of liberation from ego, cosmic consciousness, transcendental consciousness and spiritual transformation and perfection.

Along with the subject of science and values, one could also have in this programme the study of art and values, and in this connection, the followings questions could be discussed:

1. What is art?
2. How is art viewed in India and the West?
3. Six limbs of Indian art: Rupa Bheda, Pramaana, Bhava, Lavanya, Sadrishya, Varnikabhanga.
4. Art and the pursuit of the value of Beauty in relation to poetry, music, painting, architecture,

dance and drama. Important illustrations on these themes could also be provided.

Another important subject which could be proposed is that of environment and values, and the following themes can be discussed:

1. The present trend towards depletion of environment and likely consequences which would be injurious to the species on the earth, including human species. In this connection, various attitudes towards environment which are present in Indian culture and ancient culture could also be emphasised.
2. The subject of harmony with Nature and love of vegetable and animal kingdom also could be stressed.

Finally, special studies should be made for physical culture and its values. This study should include the concept of health, strength, agility, grace and beauty. One could also introduce here the concept of ideal sportsman and sportswoman, and one could explain the specific contribution that can be made for the promotion of values of physical culture through gymnastics, athletics, aquatics, martial arts and games.

A programme for value-oriented education at the tertiary level should also include a special study of Indian culture and Indian system of values. It should also include the study of Indian religion and spirituality, Indian ethics and Indian concept of *dharma*, Indian literature, Indian art, Indian architecture, and Indian polity.

It may be suggested that these programmes can be spread over three years of courses.

IX

In the light of the foregoing, it may be said that the aim of the curriculum for the Applied Philosophy should be:

- ❖ To prepare young men and women to understand philosophical problems, as expounded by Indian and Western philosophers;
- ❖ To underline the necessity and justification of applying philosophical visions of the ultimate reality or realities and meaning of life in day-to-day problems of contemporary times;
- ❖ To develop in themselves integration of personality which would enable them to confront the problems of practical life with a sympathetic understanding, equanimity and ability to deal with them effectively;
- ❖ To be able to counsel and guide people in different vocations and thus play the role of leadership; and
- ❖ To promote value-orientation in various fields of creative and practical activities and profession.

The following tentative programme should be suggested for a three-year undergraduate course for Applied Philosophy:

First Year:

- ❖ Problems of Philosophy and Applied Philosophy;
- ❖ History of Applied Philosophy: Indian and Western;
- ❖ Practical lessons of human culture;
- ❖ Applied moral and social philosophy;

Second Year:

- ❖ Applied Philosophy of value-oriented education;

- Philosophy and Psychology of religion, science and yoga;
- Philosophy and practice of intellectual, aesthetic and practical skills.
- Applied Philosophy of nation-building and world unity.

Third Year:

- Applied Philosophy of law and economics;
- Applied Philosophy of integral health;
- Applied Philosophy of technology and management;
- Applied Psychology of spiritual liberation and perfection.

A good deal of research work would be needed to mature our thinking on the proposed subject of Applied Philosophy, and a greater effort will be needed to identify and prepare the required teaching-learning material.

What is suggested in these objects is merely to stimulate thought and co-operation of all who would like to be associated with the development of Applied Philosophy in our country.

YOGA, RELIGION AND MORALITY

While stressing the imperative need of Yogic education and of a radical change in the aims, methods and structure of education in the light of Yoga, it is necessary to point out that by Yoga — which is only one of the systems of Yoga — and that Yoga does not mean either religion or morality.

Yoga is not a body of beliefs, dogmas or revelations which are to be believed in without verification. Yoga is an advancing Science, with its spirit of research, with its methods of experimentation and methods of verification and advance of knowledge.

The knowledge that Yoga delivers at a certain stage is surpassable by a further research and experimentation; the spirit that Yoga demands is that of an absolute impartiality and a complete freedom from all prejudgments and preconceptions; its zeal is the zeal for the Truth and Truth alone; its criterion of Truth is verifiability in abiding experience, and even, finally, a physical change and transformation.

In all the above respects, Yoga is quite distinct from Morality and Religion.

Morality is a part of the ordinary life. The ordinary life consists of seeking satisfaction and the development of the body, life and mind without any reference to their original source or self. Morality is that part of the ordinary life which seeks to regulate and guide the various physical, vital, mental or rational thought or by some intuitive insight obtained at the level of the highest practical or pure Reason. But the standards of conduct erected by moral consciousness, even the so-called universal principles of the categorical imperative, cannot be determined with certainty, and these in the present application by a bewildered and imperfect humanity come easily to be conflicting principles. Justice often demands what love abhors, and in fact man's absolute justice easily turns out to be in practice a sovereign injustice. Morality is always in a state of disequilibrium.

Religion is an endeavour of man to turn away from the earth towards the Divine; but this seeking is still of the mind or of the lower ignorant consciousness, as yet without knowledge and led by the dogmatic tenets and rules of sect or creed which claims to have found the way out of the bounds of the earth-consciousness into some beatific Beyond. The religious life may be a first approach to yoga, but it is not indispensable. Religion is very often only a revolving about in a round of rites, ceremonies and practices or set ideas and forms without any issue.

Sometimes, the absoluteness of the moral values is sought to be derived from some religious sanction. Thus religions have attempted to erect a system and declare God's law through the mouth of the Avatar or Prophet. Such systems have proved more dynamic and powerful than the dry ethical idea. But quite often these systems conflict with what reason supports or they are so ingrained in certain religious dogmas that they cannot have any appeal to those who do not accept those dogmas, and, besides, there is too a conflict among the dogmas. Or, else, they are so rigidly framed that they prove unworkable and are, therefore, rejected by Nature. Or, sometimes, they are turned into a system of compromises and become obsolete in the march of Time.

The truth is that neither morality nor religion represents the highest status of man's consciousness. They may prepare, but they are only stations on an evolutionary journey. Both of them are a seeking. Morality is a seeking for a guiding principle of conduct; but this seeking is mental, and, when it goes beyond that, it no more remains morality. Religion is a seeking for the Divine, but the method of seeking is one of dogma, ritual, and ceremony, and an involvement in a fabric of moral, social and cultural institutions all determined and permeated wholly or partly by the dogmatic tenets and rules of the sect or creed. It is an ignorant and a mental way of seeking. When it goes beyond, and liberates itself from dogma, ritual and ceremony and rules, it ceases to be religion in the strict sense of the word. Beyond morality, beyond religion, is the path of Yoga.

Yoga proceeds directly by a change of consciousness, a change from the ordinary consciousness, ignorant and separated from its true self and from God, to a greater consciousness in which one finds one's true being and comes first into a direct and living contact by experience and then into a union with the Divine. For the yogin, this change of consciousness is the one thing he seeks and nothing else matters, no belief, no dogma, no rituals, no ceremonies.

Both morality and religion in their deepest core touch Yoga or spirituality, and both may prepare the change of consciousness; but the element of Yoga does not constitute the differentia by which we can define morality or religion. Yoga not only aims at the total change of consciousness, but even its method is that of a gradual and increasing change of consciousness by an entry into a domain higher than the body-life-mind complex. In other words, Yoga is an exploration of consciousness through consciousness.

In the yogic consciousness and in the knowledge and the effectivity that it delivers, there is the fulfilment of the highest element that morality and religion in their deepest core seek for but fail to realise. Yoga replaces the moral law by a progressive law of self-perfection spontaneously expressing itself through the individual nature. No more in this operation is the imposition of a rule or an imperative on the individual nature; the spiritual law that Yoga presents respects the individual nature, modifies it and perfects it, and in this sense it is unique for each individual and can be known and made operative only by a change of consciousness and by an entry into the real self. In its progressive movement, it may, if necessary, permit a short or a long period of governance by a moral law, but always as a provisional device and ever looking for going beyond into a plane of a spontaneous expression of the Right and the Good. To the yogic consciousness, moral virtue is not valuable in itself, but as an expression of a complex of certain qualities which are for the time being necessary and useful for a given individual in an upward journey. Again, for the yogic consciousness, what is commonly called a vice has, too, behind it, a complex of certain qualities which have some utility in the economy of Nature, and can therefore be converted by placing them in their right place, into a complement to what lies in the consciousness behind the commonly called virtues.

Yoga is not confined merely to the aspect of conduct; the conduct dealt with by morality is only a minor aspect of the totality of works, inner no less than outer. Yogic consciousness includes all these works and strives by the method of a progressive change of consciousness for the perfect expression of all the aspects of the works and in this striving it realises also the unity of works with the highest knowledge and deepest Love.

Religion too is an attempt to include all aspects of works and to arrive at some sort of unity of works with knowledge and love; but once again, its method is mechanical, mental, moral and dogmatic and, instead of arriving at a comprehension of all the values, it ends only in a system of compromises. The progressive law of yogic development may permit, if necessary, a short or a long period of governance of the individual or of the race by religion, but only as a provisional device: what it always makes for is a passage beyond into the plane of a comprehensive consciousness where the distinctive religious methods disappear or cease to have any fundamental or useful meaning. To the yogic consciousness, religion is not valuable as a form, but only in so far as it may aid the too ignorant consciousness of man to turn towards something that is deeper and higher and, even there, it stresses the necessity for every man to have his own distinctive religion. And again, for the yogic consciousness, what is commonly called agnosticism, scepticism, atheism, positivism or free thinking, has behind it a concern and a demand for a direct knowledge, which, if rightly understood, recognised, respected and fulfilled, would become a powerful complement to what lies in consciousness behind the commonly accepted religious qualities of faith and unquestioning acceptance of dogmatic teachings and injunctions. But as we speak today of the need of yogic education, it is felt that this is because the time of religionism is now overpassed, and what is now demanded is a direct development of yogic consciousness without any resort to any compromises that result from yielding to the methods of religion.

Yoga looks always behind the form to the essence and to the living consciousness; and in doing so, it brings to the surface that which lies behind, and its action is therefore of a new creation. Yoga transcends the forms and methods of morality and religion and creates and recreates its own living and progressively perfecting forms. As Sri Aurobindo wrote in one of his letters: "Yoga takes the stand that it is only by a change of consciousness that the true basis of life can be discovered; from within outward is indeed the rule. But within does not mean some quarter inch behind the surface. One must go deep and find the soul, the self, the Divine Reality within us and only then can life become a true expression of what we can be instead of a blind and always repeated confused blur of the inadequate and imperfect thing we were. The choice is between remaining in the old jumble and groping about in the hope of stumbling on some discovery or standing back and seeking the Light within till we discover and can build the Godhead within and without us."

Yogic methods are distinctive and must not be confused with either morality or religion. A mere learning about Yoga is not Yoga, and even the most catholic book cannot be a substitute for the direct yogic practice of an inner change of consciousness by which one can perceive and realise the inner and higher Self and transform the workings of the outer instruments of Nature. Nor can Yoga be practiced in a casual way or only as a part-time preoccupation. Yoga, to be properly practiced, must be taken as a sovereign and central occupation and must govern and permeate every aspect of life and every pursuit of knowledge and activity.

An education that aims at leading the students to the great portals of the infinitude of Knowledge, Action and Love, and of self-perfection which result from a disciplined yogic effort, must be as radical and uncompromising as Yoga itself.

It is recognised that to realise such a radical education is extremely difficult; but it is equally necessary to recognise that if we are serious about the solution of our educational problems, there is no other way.

SPIRITUALITY, SCIENCE AND TECHNOLOGY

One of the central issue of today is that of the uses and misuses of Science and Technology, of Science and Values, of Science and Spirituality, -- in brief, the issue of what Sri Aurobindo has called the denial of the materialist and the refusal of the ascetic.

Fortunately, it can be said that humanity has over passed the stage of naïve materialism, which was based on the vicious circular argument that physical senses are the only means of knowledge, since this very statement cannot be established by means of physical senses. No more are we like the uninstructed stranger who on witnessing the operation of the steam engine insists that it is the piston that produces the steam and has no patience to inquire that the reality might be that it is the steam that propels the piston. A new climate of patient and undogmatic inquiry is now being created where scientists are beginning to study the phenomenon of consciousness with fresh eyes that might detect that it is not the brain that generates consciousness but that it is the other way round. The latest trends are knocking the doors of the primacy of consciousness.

A major difficulty involved in a possible dialogue between science and spirituality lies in the insistence laid by the long-established habit of physical sciences on the application of their methods on all sciences, even when the subject matter is not physical in character. But it should be evident that the demand for physical proof of supra-physical fact is irrational and illogical. For the method of knowledge should be appropriate to the object of knowledge. We have to note that the occult, psychic and spiritual sciences have developed various kinds of evidence of the existence of other planes of being and communication with them. They include objectivisation of the outer sense, subtle-contact, mind-contact, life-contact, and contacts through the subliminal in special states of consciousness exceeding our ordinary range. We should note that in any field of experience, error is possible; error is not the prerogative of the inner subjective or occult part of us. Even when the physical and objective methods are employed, there is room for error. A mere liability to error cannot be a reason for shutting out a large and important domain of experience. As in the physical sciences, so in the supra-physical sciences, it is a reason for scrutinising it and finding out in its true standards and its characteristics appropriate and valid means of verification. It is also important to observe that the very basis of our objective experience is our subjective being; hence, it is not probable that only the physical objectifications are true and the rest unreliable. The supra-physical consciousness, when rightly interrogated is a witness to truth and its testimony is confirmed again and again even in the physical and objective field; that testimony cannot, then, be disregarded when it calls our attention to things within us, or to things that belong to planes or worlds of a supra-physical experience.

As Sri Aurobindo points out, "Consciousness is the great underlying fact, the universal witness for whom the world is a field, the senses instruments. To that witness the worlds and their objects appeal for their reality and for the one world or the many, for the physical equally with the supra-physical, we have no other evidence that they exist."

The question is whether there is or there can be a science of supra-physical data, the scientific character of which is as great as that of sciences of the physical data. Often we seem to be hesitant to answer this question, and often our claim for spirituality and its validity is sought to be authenticated on the basis of a few examples of intuition, inspiration, or random but radical experiences of the soul and the spirit. It does not occur to us that Indian culture has developed over millennia a multisided science through the pursuits of those faculties, which lie above the ranges of physical sciences and rational intelligence. This science is what Swami Vivekananda called science par excellence; this is the Science of Yoga, developed and matured by Rishis and yogins of the Veda and the Upanishads and still further perfected in unbroken chain throughout the history of India right up to our own times.

This Yoga has been looked upon as practical psychology and yogic methods have something of the same relation to the customary psychological workings of man as has the scientific handling of the natural force of electricity or steam to the normal operations of electricity or steam. And they, too, are formed upon a knowledge developed and confirmed by regular experiment, practical analysis and constant result. In yoga, again, the object is an assured method of personal discovery or living repetition and possession of past discovery and a working out of all the things found.

Spirituality is not a matter merely of sporadic or of occasional experiences but a matter of vast and authentic possession of knowledge of all that lies beyond limitations of the human mind as also positions of effective power of realisation and action. It is on the basis of this science that we can bridge the gulf that seems to exist between sciences and spirituality. It is on the basis of the yogic knowledge that we can confidently hope to seek enlargement of physical sciences, and also to develop the required power of transformation of human limitations, human passions, human ignorance, and all the facilities which are found in the human nature.

Again, if philosophy has to play its legitimate role, it has to deal with the field of spiritual experiences and spiritual realities on the basis that is integral. For the varieties of spiritual experiences can easily pose the baffling problem of conflict amongst them. Fortunately, in the spiritual experiences recorded in the Veda and the Upanishads, we have already the statements of supra-mental and integral experience. Sri Aruobindo has shown, in our own times, the profundity of the ancient synthesis of the Vedic Yoga and the Upanishadic Yoga, on the basis of which his own Integral Yoga is founded, even though it has built new methodologies for purposes of a new objective in order that the supra-mental knowledge can be harnessed for purposes of the highest collective welfare and for the mutation of the human species which would result in the development of a new humanity or super-humanity.

YOGA, SCIENCE, RELIGION AND PHILOSOPHY

We may begin with a preliminary elucidation of the three terms, science, religion and philosophy. Science may be defined as a quest of knowledge, which lays a special emphasis on detailed processes in order to arrive at utmost precision, and the distinguishing methods of this quest are those of impartial observation, experimentation by working on falsifiable hypothesis, verification in the light of crucial instances and establishment of conclusions which are repeatable and which are also modifiable in the light of advancing quest.

Religion may also be looked upon as quest of knowledge, but the object is to relate the human beings with something that lies beyond the realms of Matter, Life and Mind, and the distinguishing features of the methods are those of practice of beliefs, dogmas, rituals, ceremonies, prescribed acts and pursuits of social, ethical, and other institutional norms.

Philosophy is also a quest of knowledge, but it concentrates on the ultimate or intrinsic processes and substances so as to arrive at the most general and universal features of the universe as a whole and even of that that may transcend into what may be conceived as the original source of the Universe and Man. The distinguishing features of the methods of philosophy are those of: (i) impartial and critical questioning of beliefs (religious or otherwise), conclusions (scientific or otherwise), and speculations among all of the fundamentals of enquiry; and (ii) application of logical vigour in relating all fundamental processes of the world and underlying assumptions of thought and knowledge in an attempt to arrive at the most indubitable universal and essential conclusions, which may, even though not be verifiable, may yet be found to be rationally incorrigible.

Philosophy is often described as "No Man's Land", since it falls outside the domain of science and religion – the two domains to which the entire humanity is related in one way or the other. Philosophy is something like science and something like religion, but it belongs to neither. It is like science a critical inquiry, an impartial inquiry, and an inquiry that follows the vigour of logic. It is unlike science, because its attempt is to scale the highest heights of the study of the ultimate substance. Its main concern is with essence, not so much with processes or demands of processes in their minute precision. Unlike science, philosophy is satisfied with mere intellectual incorrigibility, even when verification in experience is provided for in regard to its conclusions. As a result, philosophy can freely examine critically the contentions and conclusions of science and there could develop also an elaborate philosophy of science. Philosophical inquiry can even anticipate scientific discoveries; it can even provide guidelines or chalk out possible lines of inquiry for science. The conclusions of philosophy need not necessarily coincide with the conclusions of science; and yet the future developments of science may eventually come to substantiate the conclusions of philosophy. In the intermediate stages, therefore, there could be conflicts between philosophy and science, but since both are critical in their approach, these conflicts do not take serious proportions as has happened in regard to conflicts between science and religion. In recent times, however, science has influenced the entire domain of knowledge to such an extent that certain tendencies of scientific thought have come to refuse the validity and justification of philosophy, or else, it has tended to provide only a subordinate role to philosophy and allowed it to exist only as a handmaid of science. But whatever be the temporary phases or relationship between science and philosophy, the best way to establish a harmonious relationship between the two would be to allow philosophy its own unique position, its own special methods, and respect its conclusions and even utilise them as helpful guidelines for pursuits of science. At the same time, philosophy should admit that although its own methods or Pure Reason may arrive at rationally incorrigible conclusions, it should accept with humility the truth behind the assertion that what is intellectually incorrigible need not be scientifically or even ultimately conclusive, particularly when its conclusions collide with higher levels of experience which lie beyond the level of Reason.

In India, there has been a tradition that philosophical conclusions, however convincing they be intellectually, must also be shown to be confirmed by the deliverance of spiritual experiences. Therefore, except for the materialistic school of Charvaka, all systems of Indian philosophy provide for a special room where philosophical conclusions are shown to be supported by spiritual experience either as they are obtained directly or as they are obtained through the records of Shruti. On account of this reason, as also on account of the fact that philosophy did not attempt to prescribe to science its own conclusions and respected the experiential and experimental character of science and its conclusions, there was hardly any conflict between science and philosophy. In the West, the conflict between science and philosophy has, in recent times, come into some kind of sharpness, and philosophy has also come to be increasingly discredited. This is mainly because certain tendencies in pure philosophy came to be a battleground of conflicting philosophical positions, each claiming some kind of incorrigibility and yet not admitting that the quarrel could probably be settled by verification in experience. It may also be added that there have arisen trends in philosophy in recent times which are themselves anti-rational or anti-philosophical and which plead for the supremacy of science or for the supremacy of deeper claims of experience in existentialism or in the philosophy of Will as against Reason as illustrated in trends of pragmatism or in trends of the revolutionary trends for Action.

Philosophy, science and theology have some kind of relationship, which needs to be brought out. Theology is normally connected with a specific religion and it attempts to defend the basic doctrines of that religion in terms of rationality. Theology consists of speculations on all matters, which constitute the subject matter of philosophy. But its tendency is, even though critical, ultimately supportive of the doctrines of a particular religion. Theology tend to support and defend dogma and develops a theory of Reason and Revelation and advocates supremacy of Revelation, even though that revelation has assumed the form of unquestionable dogma. Philosophy, on the other hand, appeals to human reason, and even when it develops a theory of Reason and Revelation, and even of the superiority of revelation, it refuses the authority of dogma, whether that of tradition or that of revelation. If it accepts the superiority of Revelation to Reason, it accepts it only on the basis of repeatable experience, which would verify the contents of revelation.

Science aims at and provides *definite* knowledge; dogma which claims to be unquestionable and yet which claims definite knowledge belongs to theology. Philosophy is a field of all the questions of deepest interest to speculative mind, which science cannot answer, or which science as yet within its present limits has not been able to answer. These questions relate to ontology and cosmology; but philosophy also raises the questions that relate to axiology and discusses the questions of purpose, goal and normative standards that should govern the quest of the *summum bonum*. Even the questions such as that of the distinction between knowledge and wisdom, for which no answer can be found in the laboratory, are dealt with by philosophy.

Science and philosophy have tended to oppose religion and theology, and this conflict arises from the sharpness with which theology or religion is defined as necessarily tied up with dogmatic belief. Historically, it is true that, in the West, science and religion have clashed with each other, and this clash rests on the claim that science is rational, empirical and progressive, while religion is supra-rational or anti-rational, dogmatic and conservative. It is also a fact that science and scientists came to be persecuted in the West, particularly at the commencement of Renaissance, by the Church. Even now, that conflict has not ceased, though scientists are no more persecuted by the authorities who uphold any dogmatic belief.

Evidently, science and religion must remain in perpetual conflict, if religion continues to uphold unquestionable dogma as the source of the knowledge of the truth and science continues to uphold that rationality and empiricism are the only sources of the knowledge of truth. This conflict is further complicated by the fact that although science provides definitive knowledge and science tells us what we can know, the disconcerting fact is that what we can know is little and what we cannot know by science relates to many things of great importance. The modern trends in knowledge have confirmed that axiological questions which science can never attempt to investigate or answer are indispensable if the right direction of human journey is to be determined and guided on the ground of definitive and ascertainable knowledge. If science cannot answer these questions, humanity must turn irresistibly to that which claims to answer these questions or to discover new means of knowledge by which these questions can be answered.

Sometimes, a compromise is effected. It is contented that in matters of the empirical world, rationality and science must be resorted to, but in respect of axiological questions, religion must be resorted to, even though religion may be anti-rational or supra-rational or dogmatic. But this compromise has been found to be unsatisfactory because compromise seems to be opposed to the inexorable demands of the quest of knowledge. It has been contended that it is not good either to forget the questions that ontology and axiology ask, or to persuade ourselves with the religionists that we have found indubitable answers to them. In the same line of argument, it is, therefore, advocated that the best thing is to teach people how to live without certainty, and yet without being paralysed. But even this counsel does not eventually succeed. There is, therefore, a legitimate pressure to re-examine the interrelationship between science, philosophy and religion and to consider whether all of them can be refashioned in such a way that the conflict among them can be resolved.

Fortunately, there are new trends in all these new fields, which need to be welcomed. The world "religion" has come to be redefined in some quarters. A distinction is being made between religion and religionism, where the latter connotes dogmatic assertion of a particular religion or religious creed and the former connotes the quintessential nature of religion that is common among all religions which emphasises living contact or experience of the individual in his or her encounter with the totality of the universe or that which lies beyond the universe. Swami Vivekananda, for example, constantly spoke of religion as experiential in character and contended that religion is a matter of experience, a matter of knowledge and a matter of verifiable and repeatable knowledge. He even expounded at length, systems of Yoga and declared that Yoga is veritably a science par excellence – a science relating to those domains, which modern science leaves out of its purview. Dr. Rabindranath Tagore also spoke of Religion of Man, which also seeks to underline the experiential aspect of religion. Religion of humanism is another aspect, which has developed in recent times, which wants to install man and his holistic search of knowledge and fulfilment as the central concern. Sri Aurobindo has spoken of spiritual religion of humanity as the hope of the future, a religion that is non-dogmatic, that is entirely removed from religionism and devoted to the Yogic pursuit of knowledge and action in their integrality.

There is also a powerful trend in recent times to bring about a resolution in the conflict among religions because this conflict hurts even those who want to follow religion but are placed in a sceptical mood when different religions give conflicting answers to the deepest questions regarding the meaning and value of life. Here, again, attempts are made to develop attitudes of equal respect to all religions or to discover common elements of all religions that present to humanity a path of axiological development, which might be free from the disabling conflicts among religions. As idealists many have tended to adopt this trend; but exclusivism of religious beliefs is so strong that it is doubtful whether and on what lines religions can come together. And even if they come together, the question will be whether this unity or synthesis or harmony of religions will be reconcilable with science. The question is also gaining importance as to whether philosophy will be able to play any important role, and, if so, whether while playing this role, philosophical standpoints of today will need to undergo a major change.

It seems fortunate that in the present web of emerging trends in science, philosophy and religion, Yoga has emerged; for Yoga has specific characteristics which bring it closest to science, philosophy and religion and has yet the potentiality of going beyond all of them so as to provide to humanity a new mode of knowledge whereby world-knowledge, soul-knowledge and God-knowledge can all be integrated.

The methods of Yoga can be pursued without recourse to any dogma, and they require the same rigour as science insists, namely, observation, experimentation, and verification by repeatable experience. Yoga can be looked upon as the experiential basis for philosophical speculations and conclusions, and if rightly used, Yoga can be a bridge between philosophy and science.

But how far these tasks can be accomplished will depend upon one central issue. Modern science has so far tended to concentrate on the knowledge of Matter or on life and mind as embodied in Matter. It has also tended to develop those methods, which have proved successful in studies where empirical observation and measurement are feasible. It is evident that the domains with which philosophy, religion and Yoga deal with centrally transcend Matter or the boundaries of embodied life and mind; the question is whether science would consent to extend its inquiry into these new domains, and if so, with what methods. The present scientific methods insist on empirical verification, measurement and objectivity; the question is whether science would consent to develop new methods where the domains of inquiry themselves are supra physical, which escape the boundaries of empiricism, measurability and physical objectivism. Indeed, it seems rational to admit that to insist on physical proofs of what is claimed to be supra-physical is illegitimate. But are there, it may be asked, appropriate methods of investigating the supra-physical which can give guarantee against subjective bias, subjective interference and lapse into incorrigible erroneous beliefs? Yoga claims that it has developed methods, which can deal with the supra-physical as rigorously and as objectively as modern science deals with physical phenomena. Yoga claims that its methods can deal both with the physical and supra-physical, and, if needed and encouraged it could develop an integral science of both the physical and supra-physical and their interrelationship.

This is where we stand today in regard to the issues that are confronting the contemporary scientists, philosophers and advocates of religions and Yoga. In the spirit of inquiry, all the emerging trends need to be taken into account, and one could repeat the fundamental spirit of science which is to explore knowledge and to reject all the dogmas, even though some dogmas might have come to be built in the minds of scientists in regard to science itself.

YOGA AND KNOWLEDGE

*K*nowledge may be regarded as the most fundamental aim of Yoga. Even Hathayoga, which utilises the body as its instrument and aims at its perfection, lays down that the enjoyment of knowledge of our liberated being which brings us into unity or union with the Supreme, is its consummation. A complete mastery of the body and the life and a free and effective use of them established upon a purification of their workings serves as a basis for the more important matter of the psychical and spiritual effects to which that base can be turned. At this stage, Hathayoga takes its stand on the connection between the body and the mind and the spirit and between the gross and the subtle body, and it comes into the line with Rajayoga. A point is then reached at which a transition from the one to the other can be made. And Rajayoga, with its psycho-physical science taking account of the psychical or mental body of which the physical is a sort of reproduction in gross form, aims at the awakening of the Kundalini, the Supreme energy, lying coiled up and slumbering like a snake in the lowest chakra, ganglionic centre, in the *muladhara*, so that it may rise upward breaking open each lotus as it ascends until it meets the Purusha in *brahmarandhra*, with the aid of various stages of concentration, in a deep samadhi of union marked with knowledge. In Karmayoga, works fulfil themselves in knowledge; all totality of works, says the Gita, finds its rounded culmination in Knowledge, *sarvam* *karmākhilaṁ jñāne parisamāpyate.*[1] In Bhaktiyoga, where love is fulfilled, it brings Knowledge, and the completer the Knowledge, the richer the possibility of love. "By Bhakti", says Lord Sri Krishna in the Gita, "shall a man know Me in all my extent and greatness and as I am in the principles of my being, and when he has known Me in the principles of my being, then he enters into Me."[2] In Jnanayoga, the attainment of the highest and integral Knowledge is obviously its ultimate aim.

Validity of Yogic Knowledge

The knowledge that yoga affirms is a self-revelation in consciousness where subjectivity and objectivity are discovered to be not independent realities, but as interdependent; they are the Being, through consciousness, looking at itself as subject on the object and the same Being offering itself to its own consciousness as object to subject. There is, indeed, a view which concedes no substantive reality to anything which exists only in the consciousness, or to anything to which the inner consciousness or sense bears testimony but which the outer physical senses do not provide with a ground or do not substantiate. But the outer senses can bear a reliable evidence only when they refer their version of the object to the consciousness and that consciousness gives a significance to their report, adds to its externality its own internal intuitive interpretation and justifies it by a reasoned adherence; for the evidence of the senses is always by itself imperfect, not altogether reliable and certainly not final, because it is incomplete and constantly subject to error. Actually, we are obliged to argue that we have no means of knowing the objective universe except

---

[1] Gita, 4.33
[2] Ibid., 11.54

by our subjective consciousness of which the physical senses themselves are instruments; as the world appears not only to that but in that, so it is to us. If we deny reality to the evidence of this universal witness for subjective or for supraphysical objectivities, there is no sufficient reason to concede reality to its evidence for physical objectivities; if the inner or the supraphysical objects of consciousness are unreal, the objective physical universe has also every chance of being unreal.

It is true that in each case understanding, discrimination, verification are necessary; but the subjective and the supraphysical must have another method of verification than that which we apply successfully to the physical and external objective. Subjective experience cannot be referred to the evidence of the external senses; it has its own standards of seeing and its inner method of verification; so also supraphysical realities by their very nature cannot be referred to the judgment of the physical or the sense-mind except when they project themselves into the physical, and even then that judgment is often incompetent or subject to caution; they can only be verified by other senses and by a method of scrutiny and affirmation which is applicable to their own reality, their own nature.

It may be admitted that all reality, all experience must, to be held as true, be capable of verification by a same or similar experience. In fact, yoga affirms that all human beings can have a spiritual experience and follow it out and verify it in themselves. But just as not every untrained mind can follow the mathematics of relativity or other difficult truths or the physical world such as those of the fourth dimension or judge the validity either of their result or their process, even so, the truth of the yogic knowledge can be followed and verified only when the required capacity is acquired by training and methodical practice.

Integral Knowledge

The knowledge that yoga affirms is a knowledge of the truth of all sides of existence both separately and in the relation of each to all and the relation of all to the truth of the Spirit. "That being known all will be known", such is the conclusion of the Upanishadic inquiry. The Isha Upanishad insists on the unity and reality of all the manifestations of the Absolute; it refuses to confine truth to any one aspect. It declares that Brahman is the stable and the mobile, the internal and the external, all that is near and all that is far whether spirituality or in the extension of Time and Space; it is the Being and all becomings, the Pure and Silent who is without feature or action and the Seer and Thinker who organises the world and its objects; it is the One who becomes all that we are sensible of in the universe, the Immanent and that in which he takes up his dwelling. The Upanishad affirms the perfect and the liberating Knowledge to be that which excludes neither the Self nor its creation; the liberated spirit sees all these as becomings of the Self-existent in an internal vision and by a consciousness which perceives the universe within itself instead of looking it out on it, like the limited and egoistic mind, as a thing other than itself. To live in the cosmic Ignorance is a blindness; but to confine oneself in an exclusive Absolutism of knowledge is also a blindness; to know Brahman as at once and together the Knowledge and the Ignorance, to attain to the supreme status at once by the Becoming and Non-Becoming, to relate together realisation of the transcendent and the Cosmic Self, to achieve foundation in the supramundane and a self-aware manifestation in the mundane, is the integral knowledge; that is the possession of immortality. It is this whole consciousness with its complete knowledge that builds the foundation of the Life Divine and makes its attainment possible.

Elementary Methods and Techniques for Integral Knowledge

The starting-point of the method and techniques that Yoga has developed and perfected to attain to the status of integral knowledge is the purification of our faculty of understanding, *buddhi*.

Buddhi is the true reason of human beings which is not subservient to the senses, to desire or to the blind force of habit, but works in its own right for mastery and for knowledge. It at once perceives, judges and discriminates. Normally, it is mixed with the lower half-animal action; in its purity, it should stand back from the object and observe it disinterestedly, put it in its right place in the whole by comparison, contrast, analogy, reason from its rightly observed data by deduction, induction, inference and holding all its gains in memory and in supplementing them by a chastened and rightly-guided imagination, view all in the light of a trained and disciplined judgment.

- ❖ The first cause of impurity in the understanding is the intervention of desire in the thinking functions. When the vital and emotional desires interfere with the pure Will to know, thought becomes subservient to them, pursues ends other than those proper to itself and its perceptions are clogged and deranged. For purifying understanding, one must lift it beyond the seat of desire and emotion.

- ❖ Secondly, the vital parts and the emotions themselves should be purified; they must be trained to rid themselves of craving and attachment.

* Thirdly, the heart must be liberated from subjection to false emotions of fear, wrath, hatred and lust. The tranquillisation and mastery (*shama* and *dama*) is most important for the immunity of the understanding from ignorance and perversion.

* Fourthly, the power of understanding should be freed from the illusion of the senses and the intervention of the sense-mind in thought-functions. For true knowledge comes by the examination of the truths of the world-force and by the examination of the principles of things which the senses mistranslate to us. The sense-mind must be stilled and taught to leave the function of thought to the mind that judges and understands.

* Fifthly, understanding should be liberated from partiality and attachment to its own preferred ideas and opinions and its tendency to ignore the truth in other ideas and opinions. Cultivation of an entire intellectual rectitude and perfection of mental disinterestedness are the radical means of purifying understanding.

The result of this purification of understanding provide to it the capacity of true and complete a perception of the truths of the Self and the Universe.

But for pure yogic knowledge something more is necessary.

First, intellect has to be trained to recognise the faculties of the intuitive mind. This intuitive mind is also sometimes called a higher *buddhi*, which is not understanding through concepts but which consists of vision; it is not understanding but rather an "over-standing" in knowledge. It does not seek knowledge and attain it in subjection to the data it observes but possesses already the truth and brings it out in the terms of revelatory and intuitional thought. Our ordinary human mind usually gets nearest to this power of over-standing when there is a great stress of thought and the intellect electrified by constant discharges from behind the veil and there occurs a resultant imperfect action of illumined finding. Again, usually, when one attempts to go beyond this imperfect action, and succeeds in some sort of in-streaming of the intuition and inspired faculty of knowledge, it is found that the action of intuition and inspiration in us is imperfect as well as intermittent in action. Intuition and inspiration are immediately seized upon by the intellectual understanding and dissipated or broken up so as to fit in with our imperfect intellectual knowledge or by the heart and remoulded to suit our blind or half-blind emotional longings and preferences. Therefore, secondly, there has to be a great tranquillity of the intellectual activity so that there is a clear recognition of the true intuition as distinguished from the false and a look upward without impatience and mixtures which begin to invade. Frequency of this kind of movement and the development of great stillness of the mind will create the necessary condition for the knowledge of the Self, of the Brahman.

Thirdly, turning of our consciousness inward for psychological self-observation and analysis is a great and effective instrument. It is only in ourselves that we can observe and know the process of Self in its becoming and follow the process by which it draws back into Self-being. Therefore, the ancient counsel "Know thy self" will always stand as the first word that directs us towards true knowledge. But mere psychological self-knowledge is not enough. Fourthly, therefore, there are further levels of developments until one arrives at what is known as the state of "realisation", which is making real to ourselves and in our selves of the Self, the transcendence and universe Divine and it is the subsequent impossibility of viewing modes of being except in the light of that Self and in their true aspect as its flux of becoming under the psychological and physical conditions of our world-existence.

Three Movements leading up to Realisation

According to the yogic science, this realisation consists of three successive movements, internal vision, complete internal experience and identity.

- ❖ Internal vision or *drishti* is the direct perception of psychical things and of the Self. To being with, we may hold firmly the conception of the Self derived from teachers or from luminous teachings. We may fix it by an entire and exclusive concentration; we may thus use the triple operation of Jnanayoga, *shravana, manana, nidhidhyasana*. It is only when after long and persistent concentration that the veil of the mind is rent or swept aside, and a flood of light breaks over the awakened mentality, and conception gives place to a knowledge – vision in which the Self is as present, real, concrete, as physical object to physical eye that we possess in knowledge.

  This experience must become more frequent till it is constant.

- ❖ In due course, there are other internal experiences so that the vision of the Self is completed by experiences of it in all our members. All this knowledge

Yoga and Knowledge

and experience are primary means of arriving at and of possessing identity.

❖ One not only sees the Self or God, one even embraces Him and become that Reality. The Ishopanishad describes the great experience culminating in identity in the following terms:

यस्तु सर्वाणि भूतान्यात्मन्येवानुपश्यति ।
सर्वभूतेषु चात्मानं ततो न विजुगुप्सते । ।
यस्मिन्सर्वाणि भूतान्यात्मैवाभूद्विजानतः ।
तत्र को मोहः कः शोक एकत्वमनुपश्यतः । ।[3]

But he who sees everywhere the Self in all existences and all existences in the Self, shrinks not thereafter from anything. He in whom it is the Self-being that has become all existences that are Becomings, for he has the perfect knowledge, how shall he be deluded, whence shall he have grief who sees everywhere oneness?

With this culmination in identity, one is able to live in the supreme Vedantic knowledge, "He am I" (सोऽहमस्मि).

Such is the foundational knowledge that Yoga promises, and from this foundational knowledge, several practical capacities of knowledge and will can be developed which should lift us from what Sri Aurobindo calls seven-fold ignorance to seven-fold integral knowledge. The result for practical life would be elimination of ignorance in our thought will, sensations, actions, and prevention from returning wrong or imperfect responses to the questionings of the world, liberation from wandering in a maze of

---

[3] Isha Upanishad, 6,7.

errors and desires, strivings and failures, pain and pleasure, sin and stumbling. Our crooked road of blind groping and changing goal is turned into a sunlit path.

Yoga and Science

Yoga has been rightly looked upon as practical psychology, and yogic methods have something of the same relation to the customary psychological workings of man as has the scientific handling of the natural forces of electricity or steam to the normal operations of steam and of electricity. And they, too, are formed upon a know-ledge developed and confirmed by regular experiments, practical analysis and constant results. Yoga depends upon the perception and experience that our inner elements, combinations, functions, forces can be separated or dissolved, can be new-combined and set to novel and formerly impossible workings or can be transformed or resolved into a new general synthesis by fixed internal processes. Yoga is an attempt to realise psychological and physical perfection of our being by devising self-conscious means and willed arrangement of activities and by ever-increasing expression of inner capacities in a persistent and guided effort to unite our being with the Divine Reality and Divine Nature. Indeed, Yoga is a science, which deals with ranges of the psychical and spiritual being and even discovers greater secrets of physical, psycho-physical and other higher realities and worlds. As in all true sciences, the object is an assured method of personal discovery or living repetition and possession of past discovery and a working out all the things found. There is also in it a high intention to hold the truth, the light found in our inner power or being and turn it to a power of being our psychic self, our spirit, our self of knowledge and will, our self of love and joy, our self of life and action.

YOGA, CONSCIOUSNESS AND HUMAN FULFILMENT

I

Man has been in search of himself through the ages, and yet, he remains a mystery. But among all the elements of his mystery, the most conspicuous is the phenomenon of his consciousness. What is, after all, consciousness? In this immense universe of Matter, which is or which appears to be unconscious, how does this consciousness emerge? Is consciousness entirely alien to Matter? Are they in any way related to each other? Is that relation merely external? Or is it internal? Again, is consciousness identical with what we mean by Mind? Or, is Mind itself a certain degree or kind of consciousness? And, as we begin to examine closely our own being, we are baffled by the interaction between the body and the mind, between the *unconscious* and the *conscious*. And still further, as we fathom into the possibilities of the extension of consciousness, the immensities and heights of the planes and levels of our being overwhelm us. We begin to ask, `What is man's beginning and what is his end?' Indeed, the mystery of Man seems essentially to be the mystery of consciousness.

Philosophers and psychologists have attempted to pierce through this mystery, and we have before us several speculations, hypotheses, conclusions, several claims, dogmas, faiths, and several doubts, disbeliefs and denials. To the seeker of knowledge, to the scientists of the unknown, to the worshippers of light, all these are of immense value as a great aid to the quest, and as we recapitulate in a synoptic view what is of utmost value of the past search, we feel that a central study of this subject is not only most fascinating, but something that is indispensable to the further immediate steps of humanity's progress.

In the Cartesian psychology, a sharp and radical division is made between mind and body; the two are regarded as separate substances and it is thought that the interaction between them is impossible. And yet, the facts of the connection between body and mind are so compelling that Descartes was obliged to assume the connection between the two through the pineal gland. But the pineal gland is, after all, physical, and thus, in effect, the original assumption of the impossibility of the interaction between body and mind is contradicted.

In the East, in the Samkhya Psychology, the mind and body are both grouped together, both considered as the results of *Prakriti*, which is fundamentally a material principle. Both mind, (that is, *manas, buddhi, chitta* and *ahamkara*) and body are physical, unconscious, *jada*. The phenomenon of consciousness is explained by supposing an independent principle of *Purusha* whose very nature is that of conscious luminosity and inactivity. Once again, we have a trenchant opposition between consciousness and the products of the physical principles. But once again, still, we find the Samkhya assuming a connection between them which is not fortuitous, but of signal significance. And, in spite of this connection, it still remains mysterious as to how the unconscious principle assumes, even though apparently, the consciousness that belongs only to *Purusha*. The phenomenon of consciousness remains a mystery in the Samkhya.

One begins to wonder if the supposed opposition between body and mind or consciousness is not a myth. It may be that the body is fundamentally of the nature of the mind or the mind is really material in nature. In the modern behaviourism, it is supposed that there is no such thing as consciousness, that all the so-called mental or conscious phenomena of perception, emotion, thought, imagination, can be explained in terms of the simple formula of SR or of SCR (Stimulus and Response or Stimulus and Conditioned Reflexes). But when we come to examine this psychological theory, we find that it fails completely to explain the core of our conscious experience, namely the phenomenon of *understanding*. Understanding is indeed not behaviour, and even though it can manifest through behaviour, it cannot entirely do so. Behaviour may manifest understanding but it cannot explain it. Besides, when we come to examine facts now brought forward by the psychical research, psychoanalysis and allied schools, we begin to wonder if the body is not a form of consciousness, having its own dumb or unconscious will, thought, and feelings. The difference between the conscious and the unconscious seems to be simply a matter of degree.

This is, however, still a matter of speculation, perhaps a workable hypothesis. But when we come to study the modern schools of psychology, their apex-ideas of *polarities of conflicting drives, dream analysis, personality styles, integration,* and the rest, in the light of Indian knowledge that has been gained through the ages by a rigorous process of research, experimentation, and verification, we feel that we are in possession of scientific data which far exceed the tentative and inadequate data of modern psychology and that these data when recognised, studied and re-established, would revolutionise our concept of consciousness and open the doors of new applications of the powers of consciousness in the fields of physiology, health, medicine, cybernetics, epistemology, mental sciences, education – in the very science and technology of evolution on the earth.

These data belong to Yoga, which has been regarded primarily as a Science of Consciousness, the science of Psychology, *par excellence*. One of the most striking ideas that Yoga puts forward is that no observation can be impartial or objective so long as there are modifications in the consciousness that observes. Even the so-called scientific observations of the scientists would not merit the title of objectivity in the realm of yoga, unless the scientist is free from the *chittavritti*, modifications of the stuff of his consciousness. There is, according to Yoga, a state of consciousness, the state of pure witness, the *sakshin*, without any ripple whatsoever, free from all partiality or narrowness, which alone can comprehend the objective fact objectively, without any personal bias, without any relativity. This is the phenomenon of the pure subject observing the object as it is, in itself.

It is important to note that the Science of Yoga admits as its data only those observations which qualify this rigorous test of objectivity.

It is in this context that we may note that the Vedic and Upanishadic Yoga regard the whole gamut of our existence to be a manifestation of a single conscious principle. Mind and body are not basically different from each other. Not only that, they also point to the phenomena which cannot ordinarily be covered under what we mean by the word *Mind*. Indeed in all schools of yoga, we have a distinction between consciousness and mind, in the sense that consciousness is a large complex of awareness, while mind is only a limited or a selected overt portion of that awareness. In the view of the comprehensive system of Yoga, Consciousness has a range which rises above our ordinary mind, and it has a range below it which may properly be termed as subconscient. Body, too, has or is itself a formation of consciousness, most of whose operations are subconscious. Mind itself is an intermediate status of consciousness. For it is recognised that behind our ordinary mental consciousness, there is the subliminal consciousness, and above the mind, there are ranges of the superconscious.

In modern times, the phenomena of the subliminal consciousness are being studied (although not fully or even adequately) by the Psychical Research – the phenomena of extrasensory perception, such as telepathy, telekinesis, foreknowledge and allied or cognate operations. But in India, there are schools which specialised in the study of this range of consciousness. And, in the system of the Tantra, we have a remarkable body of the application of the knowledge of the subliminal or occult consciousness.

The subliminal has to be distinguished from the subconscious. The subconscious is the consciousness which is emerging from a condition of the sleep of consciousness; it is a consciousness in the process of waking but which does not wake up, although it is active and operative and produces effects upon the conscious life and its movements. It covers what Freud calls the *Id*, and also what Jung calls the *Individual and Collective Unconscious*. It is the region in which our suppressed desires and wishes find their resort and from where they surge up during our dreams or during our physical and mental illness. It is the abode of the roots of habits, and it is the cause of repetitions of the thoughts, feelings and emotions which we have consciously rejected. It is, in short, a lair of dark and dumb surges of consciousness.

The subliminal, on the contrary, is a field of what are called the inner sheaths or *koshas*. There is, according to the Yogic knowledge, a sheath of the subtle physical behind our gross body. Similarly, behind the complex of our desires, emotions and superficial or deep-seated longings and attractions and repulsions, in short, what we may call the superficial vital being, there is the inner vital which is the source of our larger and wider action which is the cause of our frequent or rare outbursts of exhibition of superhuman strength and power. There is also behind our groping and labouring mental operations of perceptions, observation, imagination, ratiocination and pragmatic cunning and invention, an inner mental consciousness full of large and vast symptoms of ideas and images, clearly and systematically organised. The subliminal consciousness is what is popularly called the occult consciousness, the consciousness that is manifest in the phenomena of clairvoyance, telepathy, foreknowledge and cognate phenomena.

It has been affirmed that dreams are built not merely by the subconscious, but also by the subliminal consciousness. And, just as the subconscious has its own symbolism, the subliminal, too, has its own symbolism, a notation of its own language. As explained by Sri Aurobindo:

> If the subliminal... comes to the front in our dream consciousness, there is sometimes an activity of our subliminal intelligence, -- dream becomes a series of thoughts, often strangely or vividly figured, problems are solved which our waking consciousness could not solve, warnings, premonitions, indications of the future, veridical dreams replace the normal subconscious incoherence. There can come also a structure of symbol-images, some of a

mental character, some of a vital nature: the former are precise in their figures, clear in their significance; the latter are often complex and baffling to our waking consciousness, but if we can seize the clue they reveal their own sense and peculiar system of coherence. Finally, there can come to us the records of happenings seen or experienced by us on other planes of our own being or of universal being into which we enter: these have sometimes, like the symbolic dreams, a strong bearing on our own inner and outer life or the life of others, reveal elements of our or their mental being and life – being or disclose influences on them of which our waking self is totally ignorant; but sometimes they have no such bearing and are purely records of other organised systems of consciousness independent of our physical existence...[1]

There is a misconception regarding Yoga in which Yoga is exclusively identified with occultism or with the powers and so-called miracles that can take place when the subliminal consciousness operates effectively or visibly in the physical. The true yogins have repeatedly denounced this misconception and affirmed that the central occupation of Yoga is the inmost discovery of the soul and of the levels and powers of consciousness that lie behind or above the mind.

The subliminal is vast, large, powerful and organised but it is still remote from what Yoga terms as knowledge, *vidyā*. Knowledge is a perception or realisation of one Self

---

[1] Sri Aurobindo: *The Life Divine*, Centenary Edition, Volume 18, pp.424-25

in all, while in ignorance, *avidyā*, there is a false idea of the multiplicity as self-existent or of the individual as however vast and potent, is still shot through and through with this ignorance.

The science of Yoga, therefore, in its understanding of Consciousness, insists on the distinction between the subliminal on the one hand, and the psychic and the superconscious, on the other.

Of the soul, of the psychic consciousness, and of the superconscious, there are, in Yoga, numerous descriptions; among the Sufis, among the Christian mystics, among the Lamas, there are parallels in their descriptions, and in the Indian Yoga itself there are various classifications of the states of consciousness that pertain to these domains. The release from the ego, the realisation of the Self, of the Cosmic Consciousness, of the Transcendental Consciousness, -- these are among the most fundamental. Nirvāṇa and Advaita, Vishishtadvaita and Dvaita, Purusha and Prakriti, Brahman and Maya, Ishwara and Shakti and hundred other similar concepts have behind them the experiences and realisations which are of central significance to Yoga. And pertaining to each experience and each state of consciousness there are numerous powers of action, and at various levels of being they have varying degrees of effectivity. All these have been explored, experimented with, verified, and we have in Yoga a rich, complex, subtle and authentic body of knowledge. Yoga further affirms that it is not a closed book, but an ever-developing field of research. And in modern India, we have not only a recovery of the past knowledge, but as in Sri Aurobindo, new discoveries, new applications of the knowledge, new achievements, new proposals for further realisations. The concepts of the descent of the supermind on the earth, of the Gnostic Being, of the Divine Body are some of the results of the recent yogic research.

It may be noted that the science of Yoga not only provides us with the knowledge of the various states and levels of consciousness, but it gives us also the practical methods of verifying them by a fresh achievement in our own being. And these methods again are numerous, and pertaining to each method, there are steps and stages, and for each of them there are appropriate states and powers of consciousness. These, too, have been studied, experimented with and known with authenticity of verifiable repeated and repeatable experience. Even the minute vibrations of consciousness have been noted and described with precision; fine distinctions have been stressed; subtle variations of the methods and processes, whether of Raja Yoga or Hatha Yoga or Karma Yoga or Jñana Yoga, of Bhakti Yoga or of Tantra have been studied in detail. All in all, we have a vast and opulent treasure of the knowledge of consciousness in Yoga.

Consciousness is intrinsically related to personality. For personality is a pattern of qualities, and qualities are the vibrations of the consciousness of the being. The secret of personality and of the development of personality lies therefore in the nature and powers of consciousness. Yoga, in dealing with consciousness, necessarily deals with personality and yoga provides knowledge as to what constitutes personality. Yoga has, for instance, behind the concept of personality, significant concepts of the *real person, free person, witness person* and *supreme person*. And Yoga provides also a methodology of the development of the *person* that is conveyed by these concepts to its fullness in its integrality.

It is significant that in the new waves of research and experimentation in education, there is an increasing stress on the development of personality. The recent reports of the UNESCO for instance, endeavours to stress the very theme and aims of education in their very titles *Learning to be*, and *Learning: Treasure Within* and they explain that the integral development of personality is the content of *Learning to be* and other processes and aims of learning.

If this is the importance that is to be laid in our education on the development of personality, it is clear that consciousness and personality as understood in Yoga have an immediate relevance. To put forth, therefore, the Yogic idea of integral personality based upon its profound concepts of consciousness is an urgent need.

That consciousness of Man is greatly influenced by the *unconscious* has largely come to be accepted all over the world, and modern medicine has accorded a place to psychiatry in the treatment of certain diseases. The concept of mental health and its relation to various elements of consciousness has also come to be accepted. But if, as Yoga affirms, there are not only the subconscious and the conscious, but even the subliminal and the superconscious and if the laws of these in relation to cure and health are studied, there could occur a revolutionary change not only in the practice of psychiatry or of mental health, but even in our approach to medicine itself. It may have a result even on the knowledge of our body, its functioning, its possibilities and its future.

One of the important problems that still remains unsolved is that of Death. What is Death? Is death inevitable? Is it merely a habit? Or is it something inbuilt in the very structure of the body? And has this structure anything to do with our consciousness? And can this structure be changed by a revolutionary change in consciousness as is sometimes conceived by Yoga? And, in that case, can death be eliminated by Yoga? And what would this mean in terms of processes and methods that would be involved in the elimination of death? Would it mean a complete change of the human body, its need of blood circulation, food and oxygen? Recent research in Yoga has raised all these important problems not merely as matters of fascinating curiosity or in pursuit of some ambition to conquer death and enjoy the round circle of life perpetually, but as something so relevant to understand Man himself, his place in the evolutionary process, his function as a species.

It is being increasingly realised that the problems that Man confronts are the result of the consciousness in which he dwells. And it is undeniable that the problems that Man faces today are so complex, so critical, and so global as they have never been in his history. Has this situation not to do centrally with the consciousness of Man? And, if we are keen to resolve this situation, is it not necessary to study deeply man's consciousness, its relation to his problems and to find a solution to these problems in terms of a radical change of his consciousness? And in that case, shall we not find Yoga, which is not only a science of Consciousness, but also a technology of the change of consciousness, to be indispensable in the further progression of Man?

Man and his crisis, man and his limitations, man and his death, man and his evolutionary future, man as a species preparing a new species – all these seem to be related to each other, and they all seem to point to the mystery of man's consciousness. Yoga as a science of Consciousness promises to hold the key to this mystery and in the critical urgency of the human situation, we feel impelled to knock the doors of Yoga in the hope that these portals will open and show us the way. Or if the way is still not ready with all its past and present achievements, we shall march with Yoga to build it.

It has been said that Yoga was for long kept secret for a select few, but the time has come now to generalise it in humanity. Indeed, the pressure of our crisis leads us to feel that even we of ordinary humanity must turn to Yoga.

II

History of Indian culture may significantly be described as the history of the theme of Consciousness, and its supreme achievement has been the development of the science of Consciousness and practical application of that science. This entire science is the science of Yoga. Right from the times of the Veda up to the present day, we find extraordinary explorations of consciousness. Vedic Rishis attained, as the Vedas testify, loftiest domains and powers of consciousness. And the Yoga that we find in the Veda is the synthesis of Yoga. For this reason, Veda is known as the Book of Knowledge (*jñana kānda*), Book of Works (*karma kānda*), and Book of Prayers (*Upāsanā kānda*). Describing the attainment of these Vedic Rishis, Sri Aurobindo states as follows:

> They may not have yoked the lightning to their chariots, nor weighed sun and star, nor materialised all the destructive forces in Nature to aid them in massacre and domination, but they had measured and fathomed all the heavens and earths within us, they had cast their plummet into the inconscient and the subconscient and the superconscient; they

had read the riddle of death and found the secret of immortality; they had sought for and discovered the One and known and worshipped Him in the glories of His light and purity and wisdom and power.[2]

Ishopanishad describes the loftiest experiences of consciousness, where the individual, universal and the transcendental unite in the following verses:

> But he who sees everywhere the Self in all existences and all existences in the Self, shrinks not thereafter from aught.
>
> He in whom it is the Self-Being that has become all existences that are Becomings, for he has the perfect knowledge, how shall he be deluded, whence shall he have grief who sees everywhere oneness? [3]

Describing the journey of Yoga of *Ayasya*, the Rigveda speaks of the seven-headed Thought by which the lost sun of Truth is recovered. Again, it is this yogic journey that ends in the discovery of the fourth world, *turiyam svid*, the world of the supermind spoken of in the Veda as the world of the Truth, Right and Vast, -- *satyam, ritam,*

---

[2] Sri Aurobindo: *The Secret of the Veda*, Centenary Edition, Volume 10, page 439

[3] यस्तु सर्वाणि भूतान्यात्मन्येवानुपश्यति ।
सर्वभूतेषु चात्मानं ततो न विजुगुप्सते । ।6। ।
यस्मिन्सर्वाणि भूतान्यात्मैवाभूद्विजानतः ।
तत्र को मोहः कः शोक एकत्वमनुपश्यतः । ।7। । **Isha Upanishad, 6,7**

brihat. Describing the process of Yoga in its essential characteristic, the Rigveda states:

> They held the truth, they enriched its thought; then indeed, aspiring souls (aryah), they, holding it in thought, bore it diffused in all their being.[4]

We also find in the Veda a description of the culminating experience of immortality in the following words:

> They who entered into all things that bear right fruit formed a path towards the immortality; earth stood wide for them by the greatness and by the Great Ones, the mother Aditi with her sons came (or, manifested herself) for the upholding.[5]

In one of the most illuminating passage of the Ishopanishad, we have a brief description of the passage of the yogic process from where the face of the Truth is covered to the point where the supreme light and knowledge are realised:

> The face of Truth is covered with a brilliant golden lid; that do thou remove, O Fosterer, for the law of the Truth for sight.
>
> O Fosterer, O sole Seer, O Ordainer, O illumining Sun, O power of the Father of creatures, marshal thy rays, draw together thy

---

[4] दधन् ऋतम् धनयन् अस्य धीतिम्।
आद् इद् अर्यो दिधिश्वो विभृत्राः। । Rigveda, I.71.3

[5] आ ये विश्वा स्वपत्यानि तस्थुः कृण्वानासो अमृतत्वाय गातुम्।
महना महद्भिः पृथ्वी वि तस्थे माता पुत्रैः अदितिः धायसे वेः।। **Rigveda, I.72.9**

light; the Lustre which is thy most blessed form of all, that in Thee I behold. The Purusha there and there, He am I."[6]

It is significant that the yogic process which began with the Veda, culminated in the first cycle of knowledge in the Upanishads, which are called Vedanta, giving us the indication as to how and when the true soul of India was born. The description that we find in a few pages of the Upanishads restore for us the picture of that extraordinary stir and movement of spiritual inquiry and passion for the highest knowledge. It is in these Vedas and Upanishads that we find not only the sufficient fountainhead of Indian philosophy and religion, but of all Indian art, poetry and literature. It is there that we find the soul, the temperament, and the ideal mind which later ripened into what we now call Indian genius of spirituality, intellectuality, askesis and vitality.

The development of the science of Yoga can be seen in a new stage of synthesis when we come to the Bhagavadgita. The Bhagavadgita, which is known as the Yoga Shastra, provides us profound secrets of knowledge and application of knowledge by means of which human consciousness can be transformed into Divine consciousness. The first secret, *guhyam rahasyam*, is to find out how the field of circumstances in which one is placed can be apprehended or comprehended and mastered. This secret is the knowledge of the distinction between the field of circumstances and the knower of the field, *kshetra* and

---

[6] हिरण्मयेन पात्रेण सत्यस्यापिहितं मुखम्।
तत् त्वं पूषन्नपावृणु सत्यधर्माय दृष्टये।।15।।
पूषन्नेकर्षे यम सूर्य प्राजापत्य व्यूह रश्मीन् समूह।
तेजो यत् ते रुपं कल्याणतमं तत्ते पश्यामि योऽसावसौ पुरुषः सोऽहमस्मि।।16।।

Isha Upanishad, 15,16

kshetrajña. There is behind and above the field of circumstances the secret consciousness that can be experienced as a silent witness, *purusha* or as a transcendental immobility, *Brahman* or as the controlling and ruling giver of sanction and master, *anumanta* and *ishwara*. One of these experiences or all of them together can provide a sure basis of freedom from the tangles of the problems that the field of circumstances and the battle of life present to us by means of an interplay of the three *gunas* of Nature, *sattwa*, *rajas*, and *tamas*. But at this level of experience, although there is here freedom *from* action and its problems, one does not yet have the key to the freedom *of* action, freedom *in* action and freedom to disentangle the knots from the problems and their gripping difficulties. For that we need to have a deeper secret, *guhyataram rahasyam*, the secret of the origin of Nature in a higher Nature, the origin of *aparā prakriti* in the *parā prakriti*, where is also to be found the origin of multiple individualities which are the centres of the Supreme Self, *Purushottama*, who at once reconciles and synthesises the status of *Purusha*, *Brahman* and *Ishwara*. And the knowledge of this higher Nature not only liberates us from the tangle of Nature, but gives us also the capacity to harmonise various threads of Nature which would even allow the transmission of the dynamic and creative action that would resolve the knots and problems of all our activities of life. This is the knowledge by which the cognitive, affective and conative powers of our psychology can be perfected, and synthesis of *karmayoga*, *jñanayoga* and *bhaktiyoga* can be effected. But there is still a culmination of this deeper secret; there is still the deepest secret, *guhyatamam rahasyam*. This secret is that of the possibility of the transmutation of lower nature by higher nature, of the attainment of *sadharmyam*, where human law of action is substituted by the divine law of action. And the secret method is to move at a stage where all that one is or one has is reposed unconditionally in the hands and in the being of the Supreme, as a result of which all that flows through the individuality is the incorruptible breath of the Supreme which unites the Truth, Beauty and Goodness and constantly creates conditions suitable for the unity and harmony of the people, *lokasangraha*.

The subsequent history of Yoga is an account of specialised schools of Yoga, each one of which is distinguished by a specific goal, a specific instrument of human psychology that is utilised for its perfection, and a specific purpose of concentration. These systems of Yoga provided intensive fields of experimentation, each one realising in greater subtlety of realisation as also enrichment of the common goal of Yoga. In a later development in the Yoga of Tantra, we find another basis of a synthesis in which the aspect of *shakti* is prominently utilised for the attainment of a large and integral realisation of the Supreme Reality. In our own times, we find Sri Rama Krishna Paramhamsa providing us a synthesis of Yoga by his colossal spiritual capacity, and in the words of Sri Aurobindo:

> ...first driving straight to the divine realisation, taking, as it were, the kingdom of heaven by violence, and then seizing upon one Yogic method after another and extracting the substance out of it with an incredible rapidity, always to return to the heart of the whole matter, the realisation and possession of God by the power of love, by the extension of inborn spirituality into various experience and

by the spontaneous play of an intuitive knowledge.[7]

We have also in the works of Swami Vivekananda inspiring accounts of various systems of Yoga in large catholic and synthetic terms. In Sri Aurobindo, we have still a new synthesis which is effected by negating the forms and outsides of the yogic disciplines and seizing rather on some central principle, common to all which includes and utilises in the right place and proportion their particular principle, and some central dynamic force which is the common secret of the divergent methods and capable of organising a natural selection and combination of their varied energies and different utilities. Describing this process of synthesis and its aim, Sri Aurobindo states:

> The lower Nature, that which we know and are and must remain so long as the faith in us is not changed, acts through limitation and division, is of the nature of Ignorance and culminates in the life of the ego; but the higher Nature, that to which we aspire, acts by unification and transcendence of limitation, is of the nature of Knowledge and culminates in the life divine. The passage from the lower to the higher is the aim of Yoga; and this passage may effect itself by the rejection of the lower and escape into the higher, -- the ordinary viewpoint, -- or by the transformation of the lower and its elevation to the higher Nature. It is this, rather, that must be the aim of an integral Yoga.

---

[7] Sri Aurobindo: *The Synthesis of Yoga,* Centenary Edition, Volume 20, page 36

... The whole life is the Yoga of Nature. The Yoga that we seek must also be an integral action of Nature, and the whole difference between the Yogin and the natural man will be this, that the Yogin seeks to substitute in himself for the integral action of the lower Nature working in and by ego and division the integral action of the higher Nature working in and by God and unity. If indeed our aim be only an escape from the world to God, synthesis is unnecessary and a waste of time; for then our sole practical aim must be to find out one path out of the thousand that lead to God, one shortest possible of short cuts, and not to linger exploring different paths that end in the same goal. But if our aim be a transformation of our integral being into the terms of God-existence, it is then that a synthesis becomes necessary. [8]

III

The secret of Yoga lies in the understanding of what is technically called in the Indian systems, the study of ignorance, *avidyā*. This concept is difficult to grasp, but the essential characteristic is marked by exclusive concentration of consciousness on a limited field and identification of the being or *purusha* with that limited field, which is an expression of *prakriti* or Nature, the executive force of threefold *gunas* – *sattwa, rajas* and *tamas* intertwined with the sense of ego. This ignorance as analysed by Sri Aurobindo, is sevenfold: original ignorance, cosmic ignorance, egoistic ignorance, temporal ignorance, consti-

---

[8] Sri Aurobindo: *The Synthesis of Yoga,* Centenary Edition, Volume 20, pp. 39-40

tutional ignorance and practical ignorance. If this ignorance is to be removed, the means should consist of reversing the exclusive concentration of consciousness. Essentiality of the process of Yoga lies in effecting this reversal. All the various methods of Yoga are basically methods by which our outward consciousness is reversed in such a way that inner consciousness, and inmost consciousness and loftiest consciousness become the object of our consciousness. Sri Aurobindo speaks of sevenfold knowledge in which one can approach the Absolute as the source of all circumstances and relations, possess the world in ourselves in utmost wideness and in a conscient dependence in its source, and by so taking it up raises and realises the absolute values that converge in the Absolute.

IV

As we approach the philosophy and practice of Yoga, we find that there are two things that cannot be doubted. There is, first, the experience of our individual entity as an observer who observes, experiences, acts and reacts. There is, second, a field of circumstances in which the individual finds in himself or herself and in which he or she works, learns and struggles to arrive at mastery. Arrival at this mastery, individual and collective, may be considered to be the realisation of human fulfilment.

The history of the world may be regarded as an account of the human aspiration towards human fulfilment. It manifests itself in the drive towards knowledge, possession, and enlargement into a vast and universal and transcendental being so as to grow out of the animal and egoistic consciousness. This aspiration strives to convert our twilight or obscure physical mentality into the plenary supra-mental illumination, to build peace in self-existent bliss where there is only a stress of transitory satisfaction besieged by physical pain and emotional suffering. This aspiration strives to establish an infinite freedom in a world which presents itself as a group of mechanical necessities. It also strives to discover and realise the immortal life in a body subjected to death and constant mutation.

If this aspiration is to be fulfilled, there does not seem to be another way excepting the way of the Yoga, and this way, as latest researches in Yoga indicate, is the way of the synthesis of Yoga, which aims at total freedom of each individual in his or her method of approach and which aims at integral development of personality and integral self-perfection by the expression of the potentialities latent in the being and the union of the human individual with the universal and transcendent Existence which we see partially expressed in the human being and cosmos.

Yoga, then indeed, stands out as a subject of great contemporary relevance. This relevance arises from the acute crisis through which humankind is passing today. This crisis has arisen, it seems, from the fact that, while on the one hand, it does not seem unlikely that we may succeed in creating a system of life, practically covering the whole globe, which can provide to human beings means and materials to satisfy hedonistic, selfish and egoistic wants on such a scale that, for quite a long indefinite period, humankind might remain chained to circles of lower life marked by hunger and satisfaction, strife and success, and perils of small and great disasters, and yet, on the other hand, the upward human aspiration to build individual and collective life on the basis of mutuality and harmony, of peace and concord, and ever-increasing perfectibility of our highest potentialities must continue to struggle without any sound promise of its eventual fulfilment. In other words, while there is an upward endeavour to break the vicious circle of our present vitalism or economic barbarism, this very endeavour has come to be partly discouraged by the scientist by his demand to provide physical proof of the supra-physical and partly blocked by the religionist by his refusal to look beyond dogma and the revealed word of the past, and has thus come to be rendered unequal to the required tasks.

The vicious circle can be broken only if our upward endeavour can get unmixed positive support from science and only if the moral and spiritual foundations can be strengthened and made increasingly unshakable.

This is the real issue.

It has been contended that all true knowledge belongs to science and can be acquired only by scientific methods. Morality, it is argued, is a matter of emotional responses which are themselves relative and carry no authenticity of knowledge in their contents or in their foundations. As far as spirituality is concerned, it is argued that its claims in regard to its insights, intuitions, revelations and other allied operations of knowledge are at the best occasional flashes, somewhat like conjectures which may sometime hit the truth but which escape from any systematic scrutiny by means of criteria that can confidently be applied in any impartial search of validity of knowledge. It is, therefore, concluded that spirituality is a field of light and shadow where it is difficult to distinguish what really is light and what really is shadow.

Now it is true that morality is a field of relativities and that if its claims of knowledge of the good and the right are to have some secure foundation, it can find these foundations only in a field which is higher than morality, namely, the field of spirituality. But if spirituality itself is a field of uncertainties besieged by doubtful lights and shadows, we are thrown back into the vicious circle of vitalism which cannot be broken.

But is it true that spirituality is a field of uncertainties, of occasional flashes of light and of doubtful intuitions and revelations? It is here that the claims of Yoga need to be taken into account. For Yoga claims to be, among many other things, a methodised quest of spiritual and eventually of integral knowledge which is found to have succeeded in arriving at certain stable states of consciousness and of plenary illumination and knowledge of truths which can be verified both objectively and in personal experience by means of criteria which can be considered to be as sound as in any inquiry relating to validity of knowledge. In other words, Yoga claims to be a scientific discipline through which authentic knowledge can be gained in regard to any object, particularly, universal or transcendental, on which its methods are applied systematically and repeatedly.

It can at once be seen that if these claims of Yoga are valid, then we shall be able to have through Yogic methods that knowledge which can possibly break the vicious circle of the crisis of the present day and deliver us into new possibilities of a better humanity and a better world.

The next question, therefore, before us is whether the claims of Yoga are truly valid and whether they can be found to be sustainable. It has been contended that Yoga has discovered and perfected certain specific methods by application of which human consciousness can be so revolutionised that the ordinary functioning of the human body, human heart, and human mind can be united with superior faculties of knowledge and action, and ultimately the human being can become permanently united with the universal and transcendental states of consciousness and knowledge. It has been further contended that the Yogic science possesses assured data of the knowledge of methods and their processes of application as also of their corresponding results. It has even further been contended that the efficacy of these methods and their results can be verified by everybody who is prepared to undergo the necessary preparation and training, and that the results obtained by others can be confirmed through one's own personal experience and can be utilised for producing relevant consequences and results. Finally, it is added that there is a long history of the development of this science of Yoga, and as in the case of the history of development of any science, one can trace a credible account of the old methods and old knowledge, of how they have gradually grown and developed by methods of confirmation, modifications and fresh developments resulting from new experiments and fresh acquisitions of knowledge. It is, therefore, concluded that Yoga provides a sound basis of a vast field of knowledge which can even now be studied and reacquired by the present humanity, and that without any need of falling into any trap of dogmatism, blind belief, superstition or even of half-knowledge and half-blindness, we can come to tap those resources of knowledge which can provide us the required guidance for the building up of a world illumined by ever-progressive knowledge and inspired by universal love.

These contentions and the conclusions to which they lead are so important that they deserve to be heard and noted with utmost seriousness, and they also deserve to be studied in full depth with all the required objectivity and even microscopic scruple so that whatever gates of knowledge that Yoga can open up before us are entered into, and we are enabled to ensure that no possibility or avenue of knowledge that we require to break the present crisis has been ignored or allowed to remain under clouds of our dogmatic refusal to inquire and to learn.

This is where we stand today, and in the situation in which we find ourselves today demands on our part a serious inquiry and study of the entire theme of Yoga and Consciousness. Our study will show that the supreme gift of India to itself and to the world is the knowledge of Yoga and the practice of Yoga, for Yoga is a discipline that can give us the true basis for the hope of arriving at a true individual and collective fulfilment.

BONDAGE, LIBERATION AND PERFECTION

I

One of the greatest contributions of the Indian science of *Yoga* is that of the discovery of the state of the human soul's bondage, and that of the fashioning of the various methods which would ensure liberation and its other consequences relating to perfection.

Every human being is required to deal with a given environment and a certain set of circumstances, and at a certain stage, a conscious feeling begins to grow that there is something in the human personality which needs to be distinguished from the environment and circumstances in an effort either to escape from the burden of life and its responsibilities or to refashion the inner psychological complexities of the being so as to control, master and perfect the outer life and the world. This feeling is, in the beginning, evanescent or temporary; but in due course, it grows, under various pressures of experience, and one begins to suspect one's ignorance and one's state of bondage, accompanied with a growing aspiration to remove ignorance and to attain to liberation and perfection.

It has been rightly observed that a special characteristic of ignorance is that it does not suspect itself. To discover that one is ignorant is itself a sign of a certain growth of knowledge. It is only at that stage that one begins to ask some of the deepest questions about the riddle of the world and the intricacies of varieties of relationships in which one is entangled in one's commerce with the outer world.

At a farther stage, one is led to inquire into the questions as to whether sorrow and suffering, disabilities and death, dualities and incapacities can truly and effectively be removed altogether. The question, "What am I?" assumes then a great prominence, and one is led to the quest of the most Ultimate or of Something in which all afflictions and incapacities can be extinguished permanently.

A special feature of Indian philosophy is that it measures its own relevance in terms of the answers it provides to existential questions relating to bondage and the quest for liberation. And, while the Indian philosophical inquiry is pure, impartial and thorough-going, the ultimate test that it imposes upon itself is not merely that of logical consistency and comprehensiveness but also of its ability to show the way to liberation from delusion and sorrow and even to a total collective welfare by attainment of states and powers of perfection.

II

All Yogic disciplines maintain that the state of bondage is marked by an identification of the experiencing consciousness with the instruments and objects that constitute for the experiencing consciousness its world of experience. Different systems of *Yoga* use different terms for the experiencing consciousness and for the experienced world. According to one system, the experiencing consciousness is called Purusha and the experienced world is called Prakriti, and it is maintained that the identification of Purusha with Prakriti constitutes the state of bondage;

according to another system, the individual soul, which is called Jiva, when identified with the mind, is said to be in the state of bondage. According to a third system, the individual soul or jiva is nothing but a temporary conglomeration of perceptions and impressions, which by repetitive actions creates an apparent sense of self or ego-sense, which identifies itself with the experienced world, which, in turn, is also a conglomeration of perceptions and impressions; there is yet another view according to which the individual soul, which is in some way dependent on the supreme Reality, and which, when instead of dwelling in that Reality, identifies itself with the instruments of experience and objects of the experienced world, gets into the state of bondage.

Among these and similar views, what is commonly emphasised is that there are two elements in the psychology of bondage, which are central experiences of bondage. These are: desires and ego-sense. All systems of Yoga are fundamentally different ways by which desire and ego-sense can be eliminated. Again, all yogic systems agree that the state of liberation is attained when desire and ego-sense are annihilated or extinguished.

All yogic systems consider the state of bondage to be the result of Ignorance, which causes the confusion between the real and the unreal, superimposition of the unreal on the real, or superimposition of the not-self on the self, or else perception of fleeting impressions which are extinguishable but are not yet extinguished. The question as to how ignorance can be removed, has been answered differently by different systems of Yoga, although they have some common elements.

According to *Raja Yoga*, ignorance can be eliminated by means of cessation of modifications path of consciousness as a result of disciplined pursuit of an eight-fold path consisting of processes of purification, self-control and concentration leading up to *Samadhi* in which the mind is completely stilled. According to *Jnana Yoga*, the intellect should be so trained that it can distinguish between the unreal and the real, and with the help of the intellectual conviction of this distinction, one should follow up a line of concentration, so that one disassociates from identification with the unreal and arrives at identification with the Real. According to *Bhakti Yoga*, the individual needs to turn the entire complex of the emotional being in spirit of worship, adoration, service and love for the supreme Reality; and, by constant in-dwelling in the supreme Reality or rather in the supreme Person, one gets disassociated from everything else with which one was earlier identified. According to *Karma Yoga*, the discipline consists of a gradual elimination of desire and egoism, - which are normally intertwined strongly with action, - by means of a gradual process in which one disassociates oneself from the fruits of action and later on disassociates oneself from the sense of doership of action, and finally one becomes a mere vehicle of action proceeding from the Supreme Reality. In the Yogic system of *Jainism*, the discipline consists of disassociating *Jiva* from matter by means of gradual or rapid exhaustion of action, *karma*, with the help of various practices that underline rigorous practice of truthfulness, non-violence, continence, non-covetousness and burning away of all attachments to possession. In the Yoga of *Buddhism*, the process of yoga consists of the eightfold path, namely, right beliefs, right aspirations, right speech, right conduct, right mode of livelihood, right effort, right mindedness and right rapture. There are also many other systems of *yoga* which emphasise disciplines of the body, or of life-force and mind or else they combine various systems of *yoga* in some kind of synthesis. There are, of course, claims and counter-claims, in regard to the superiority of one system over the other, but, as stated above, they all agree that the state of liberation is impossible without the elimination of desire and ego-sense.

III

The state of the liberated soul has been variously described. But there are two important characteristics of this state which are commonly to be found among these descriptions. First, the state of liberation is a state of recovery, -- recovery of a state which was always in a state of freedom. It is said that it is the state of the *Purusha* or *Brahman* which is for ever free. Secondly, it is a state beyond the mind-consciousness, which could be defined as consciousness that is discursive, successive, and centred on apprehensive as opposed to a comprehensive point of view. If this state of liberation is that of consciousness or knowledge or bliss or all of them together, they are other than what they are at the mental level. It is fundamentally a state of stillness or peace that transcends the state of understanding or of resignation or surrender, or of all of them together, and if there is any movement or dynamism or action it's a movement of the soul's relationship of unity and harmony of all things in transcendence or with the transcendental and universal Reality or Being. In that state of freedom, the soul may merge into the infinite of Being or choose to dwell in union with the Supreme Being, and in that case, at the fall of the body, all connection with Nature or *Prakriti* is cut off without any possibility of return. However, as long as the bodily life continues, the psychology of a liberated soul is so poised that the inner freedom is not lost even when outer activities of *Prakriti* of the body, life and mind, continue by the momentum of the past. At the same time, even in the outer Prakriti, the root of desire and egoism are annihilated, and the activities of the gunas, as understood in the terminology of *Samkhya*, are harmonised in such a way that the *sattwa* predominates and *rajas* and *tamas* are subordinated, and all the three gunas reflect or carry out, in spite of their inherent limitations, something of the state of the liberated soul.

Among the numerous experiences which have been described in respect of the state of liberation, there are three experiences which are frequently mentioned, and each one of them appears to the experiencer to be so overwhelming that it excludes the other two, or even if admitted, they appear to be sublated.

The first of these experiences is that of the soul as *Purusha* in a state of silent witness that stands unaffected by the determinations which were earlier imposed upon it by the power and action of *Prakriti*. The second experience is that of an overwhelming awakening to Reality when the thought is stilled, when the mind withdraws from its constructions, and when one passes into a pure Selfhood void of all sense of individuality, empty of all cosmic contents. If the spiritualised mind then looks at the individual and cosmos, they appear to it to be an illusion, a scheme of names and figures and movements falsely imposed on the sole reality of the Self-Existent, or even the sense of Self becomes inadequate, both knowledge and ignorance disappear into sheer consciousness and consciousness is plunged into a trance of pure superconscient existence. Or even existence ends by becoming too limiting a name for that which abides solely for ever; there is only a timeless Eternal, a spaceless Infinite, the utterness of the Absolute, a nameless peace and overwhelming single objectless Ecstasy. The third experience is that of the omnipresent Divine Person, Lord of a real Universe and the Lord of the supreme *Shakti*, of which the individual soul is a centre without circumference or a portion or a child that lives by mutuality with all and in utter ecstasy of union with the Lord and His *Shakti*.

There is also, it is claimed, an experience where all the above three experiences are transcended into something that can be described as *Shunya*, the Nihil, which is also sometimes described as the Permanent. Again, there is an affirmation of a supramental and integral experience in which all these experiences are held simultaneously and where the Supreme is realised, as in the *Gita*, as *Purushottama* in his Absoluteness and Integrality uniting within Himself both the *kshara* and *akshara purusha*, the static and the dynamic *purusha*. This experience answers to the great pronouncements of the Upanishads where the supreme is described at once as *Brahman* or *Atman*, *Purusha* and *Ishwar*.

As the Ishopanishad declares:

> That moves and That moves not; That is far and same is near, That is within all this and That also is outside all this.
>
> But he who sees everywhere the Self in all existences and all existences in the Self shrinks not thereafter from aught.
>
> He in whom it is the Self-Being that has become all existences that are Becomings, for he has the perfect knowledge, how shall he be deluded, whence shall he have grief who sees everywhere oneness. (5,6,7)

IV

There appears to be in the Indian tradition a distinction between liberation and perfection, although these two terms are often understood to be interchangeable. Nonetheless, when we study the *Vedic* and *Upanishadic* concept of immortality, *Gita's* concept of *sadharmya* in connection with the perfection of *Karmayoga*, and the *Tantric* view of *siddhis* including those of mental, vital and physical being, we are obliged to bring out the full value of the idea of perfection as distinguished from that of liberation.

The *Vedic Yoga* may be looked upon as an earliest synthesis of the psychological being of man in its highest flights and widest rangings of divine knowledge, power, joy, life and glory with the cosmic existence of the gods, pursued behind the symbols of the material universe into those superior planes which are hidden from the physical sense of the material mentality. The crown of this synthesis was in the experience of the *Vedic Rishis* something divine, transcendent and blissful in whose unity the increasing soul of man and the eternal divine fullness of the cosmic godheads meet perfectly and fulfil themselves. This experience culminates in the ascent to the plane of Truth-consciousness (*rita-chit*) and its descent into the lower planes of the mental, vital and physical consciousness in the human body up to a point where the physical consciousness becomes so vast that the truth-consciousness can dwell in it. The *Vedic Rishis* have called that state to be the state of immortality. *Parashara* speaks of the path which leads to immortality in the following words: *"They who entered into all things that bear ripe fruit formed a path towards immortality; earth stood wide for them by the greatness and by the*

Great Ones, the Mother Aditi with her sons came (or manifested herself) for the upholdings."[1]

Commenting on this, Sri Aurobindo states:

> That is to say, the physical being visited by the greatness of the infinite planes above and by the power of the great godheads who reigned on those planes breaks its limit, opens out to the Light and is upheld in its new wideness by the infinite Consciousness, Mother Aditi and her sons, the divine Power of the supreme Deva. This is the Vedic immortality.[2]

The *Upanishads* also speak of immortality, and as we study these great books of the profound masters of the spiritual knowledge, we find that, starting from the crowning experiences of liberation and perfection of the *Vedic* seers, they arrive at a high and profound synthesis of spiritual knowledge; they draw together into a great harmony all that had been seen and experienced by the inspired and liberated knowers of the Eternal throughout a great and fruitful period of spiritual seeking.

The *Gita* starts from the synthesis of the *Upanishads* and, on that basis, builds another harmony of the three great means and powers, love, knowledge and works, through which the soul of man can directly approach and cast itself into the eternal. It even goes farther and through its injunction to surrender totally to the Divine, it opens up the door by which the spirit can take up the individual

---

[1] ā ye viśvā svapatyāni tasthuh krnavānāso amṛtatvāya gātum.
   mahnā mahadbhih prithvi vi tasthe mātā putrair aditih
   dhāyase veh.
[2] Sri Aurobindo: *The Secret of the Veda*, pp. 191-192

into the universal Power of higher Nature, *Para Prakriti*. In effect, this would be the method by which the concept of *salokyamukti* and *sayujyamukti* is further extended into *sadharmyamukti*, the liberation and perfection of the lower nature of life, body and mind by infusion into it of the divine nature, the *Para Prakriti* – which is evidently the divine *Aditi* of the *Veda*. The *Tantric Yoga* has developed methods for a richer spiritual conquest that would enable the seeker to embrace the whole of Life in his divine scope as the cosmic Play of the Divine. In other words, it grasps that idea of the divine perfectibility of man, which was possessed by the *Vedic Rishis*.

V

In the *Integral Yoga* of Sri Aurobindo a new dimension is added to conceptions of bondage, liberation and perfection. It founds itself on a conception of the spiritual being as an omnipresent existence, the fullness of which comes not essentially by a transcendence to other words or a cosmic self-extinction, but by a growth out of what we now are phenomenally into the consciousness of the omnipresent reality which we always are in the essence of our being. To open oneself to the supracosmic Divine is an essential condition of the integral perfection; but to unite oneself with the universal Divine is another essential condition. Here the *Integral Yoga* coincides with the *Yoga* of knowledge, works, and devotion. Since human life is accepted as a self-expression of the realised Divine in man, the *Integral Yoga* insists on action of the entire divine nature in life. It is here that by a new effort of research and development of new *Yogic* methods, as also by bringing all the relevant materials from the synthetic *yogas* of the *Vedas, Upanishads, Bhagvadgita* and *Tantra*, that the aim of the supramental manifestation on earth is sought to be realised.

Sri Aurobindo equates the Vedic *"truth-consciousness"* with the supermind, with the *Gita's* concept of *paraprakriti* and with the supreme *Shakti of Tantra,* and builds up a path to the ascent to the supermind and of the descent of the supermind right up to the mental, vital and physical parts of the being, the climax of which is reached when the supermind is made to permeate the cells of the body so that the perfection which is attained would result in the transmutation of the human species for the evolution of a new species on the earth.

Three elements, - a union with the supreme divine, unity with the universal Self, and a supramental life – action from this transcendent origin and through this universality, but still with the individual as the soul-channel and natural instrument, -- constitute the essence of the integral divine perfection of the human being. In the *Integral Yoga,* what is called *moksha* or liberation from the ego and the will of desire is an essential step, but this liberation is enriched by the synthesis of knowledge, devotion, and action, and one is prepared for development of perfection of the instruments of *prakriti. Mukti,* and in this case *jivanmukti,* liberation from Nature in a quiescent bliss of the supreme is the first form of release. A farther liberation from Nature into a divine quality and spiritual power of world experience fills the supreme calm with supreme kinetic nature, which can be termed as a state of integral liberation, becomes the true foundation of farther consequences which constitute the six-fold perfection.

The first element of perfection is that of perfect equality and perfect action of equality.

The second element of perfection is attained by raising all the active parts of the human nature to that of higher condition of working pitch of the power and capacity on which they become capable of being divinised into true instruments of the free, perfect, spiritual and divine action. This would mean the perfection of the powers and capacities of the mind, the vital and the physical. This would also imply the perfect dynamic force of the temperament, character and inmost soul-nature, which would result in what Sri Aurobindo calls the perfection of the fourfold personality, the personality of knowledge, of strength, of harmony and love and of skill and service. This movement is further strengthened by calling in the divine Power or *Shakti* to replace the limited human energy so that it may be shaped into the image of and filled with the force of a greater infinite energy.

The third element of perfection is, according *Sri Aurobindo*, the evolution of the mental into the supramental gnostic being which would progressively take up all the terms of intelligence, will, sense-mind, heart, the vital and sensational being and translate them by a luminous and harmonising conversion into a unity of the truth, power and delight of a living existence.

The next element of perfection is that of the gnostic perfection in the physical body.

And the fifth element is arrived at when this perfection is pushed to its highest conclusion which, according to *Sri Aurobindo*, brings in spiritualising and illuminations of the whole physical consciousness and divinising of the law of the body.

The sixth element is that of the perfect action and enjoyment of being on the supramental gnostic basis. And this integrality of perfection cannot remain confined to the individual, but would extend progressively to the collective divine life on the earth. In the words of Sri Aurobindo:

> The divinising of the normal material life of man and of his great secular attempt of mental and moral self-culture in the individual and the race by this integralisation of a widely perfect spiritual existence would thus be the crown alike of our individual and of our common effort.

VI

The treasure of knowledge that India possesses in its science of yoga is, it may be said, of direct relevance to the contemporary crisis through which humanity is passing today. Not only an increasing number of individuals in the world are finding themselves in the grip of dilemmas, which have become impossible of solution through any of the ordinary known means at the disposal of humanity, but even the collective life of humanity has reached such an acute stage of mechanisation, standardisation and unbearable structuralisation that the ideals of progress which have been put forward, - the ideals of liberty, equality and fraternity, - can never be realised, - even though it is clear that they must be realised, by means of methods or trends which are being currently pursued. It may be argued that the Yogic knowledge is too difficult, and it would be impossible for humanity to accept it. But when we examine in full the maladies of the contemporary humanity, it would be idle or even misleading to suggest that any lesser remedy is likely to work. It is best to propose to humanity what is known to us to be the best, however difficult it may be.

PHILOSOPHY OF INDIAN PEDAGOGY

I

Presuppositions of Pedagogy

All systems of pedagogy, Eastern or Western, have certain presuppositions which are derived from a larger canvas of human experience. These presuppositions include the following:

❖ Human growth takes place by means of a natural process, supported or aided by certain deliberate processes and methods;

❖ Human growth implies increasing self-consciousness, development of skills and faculties, and the capacities required to meet the challenges of life and of the cultural context in which one is required to meet the demands of the individual and collective life;

❖ At a deeper level, human growth is aided by the development of arts, sciences, and technologies that enable the individual and collectivity to build up bridges between the past and the future through accumulation of experience and transmission of valuable lessons of that experience to the growing generations;

❖ Increasing effectivity of educational process depends on the degree to which natural processes of growth and deliberate processes of growth are blended harmoniously; and

❖ Deliberate processes that are employed for aiding human growth require to be constantly subtilised so that the processes of growth attain increasing acceleration at an optimum level, which may differ from individual to individual and from collectivity to collectivity.

Pedagogy and Aim of Life

The greatest educationists, who have played important roles in fashioning educational systems have, in their quest to develop ideal processes and structures of education, have found it necessary to understand the real meaning and aim of life, the real meaning and aim of culture, and the real meaning and aim of the highest human welfare; and it is in this context that educationists have differed among themselves, and different systems of pedagogy owe their differences to the differences that have developed in this regard.

Not long ago, education was merely a mechanical forcing of the child's nature into arbitrary groves of training and knowledge in which his subjectivity was the last thing considered, and his family upbringing was a constant repression and compulsory shaping of his habits, his thoughts, his character into the mould fixed for them by conventional ideas or individual interests and the ideals of teachers and parents. Even today, the behaviourist pedagogy prescribes principles and methods of teaching that aim at development of behaviour rather than the development of inner being and inner personality of the learner. Even today, even where behaviouristic pedagogy is not preponderate, importance is attached to the external and mechanical means of imparting information and of the development of skills that are required to fulfil the demands of certain specific jobs or occupations. It is sometimes admitted that apart from skills, taste also should be developed, a certain sense of culture also should be promoted, and a certain sense of value should also be stimulated. But all this is still sought to be managed within the narrow formula of mechanical and external systems of methodologies. At the root of this methodology is a certain view of the aim of life. According to this view, life is a struggle in which one is obliged to adjust with the present system of inequalities and competition, and a system in which one is required to find a place within a narrow range of situations of life where one can earn one's livelihood and sustain a small family and its responsibilities.

This view also prescribes the need to learn and practise some kind of prudent economics, so that one can save for a rainy day, and one can lead a certain length of life so as to merit a tolerable amount of pension, in the process of enjoying which, one can wait for a smooth transition to the grave. The aim of life, according to this view, is to live, to perform duties appropriate to one's own station of life, to struggle through competition, to enjoy possible comforts and to enjoy some kind of security and learn a few lessons of life which teach prudence and tolerable human existence.

New Ideas of Pedagogy

Fortunately, new ideas of pedagogy are marching forward, and behind these ideas we can discern a new vision of the aim of life and a new vision of a world order that demands building of defences of peace in the minds and hearts of people and new attitudes required for living together through cooperation and through the processes of mutuality and interdependence. Thanks to the pioneering educational philosophers like Rousseau, Montessori, Pestalozzi, Bertrand Russell, Paulo Freire, and Piaget, it is now being increasingly recognised that education must be a bringing out of the child's own intellectual and moral capacities to their highest possible extent and must be based on the psychology of the child- nature. There is also a glimmering of the realisation that each human being is a self-developing soul and that the business of both parent and teacher is to enable and to help the child to educate himself, to develop his own intellectual, moral, aesthetic and practical capacities and to grow freely as an organic being, not to be kneaded and pressured into form like an inert plastic material. It is this glimmer of the realisation that we find in the two momentous Reports of UNESCO: "*Learning To Be*" and "*Learning: Treasure Within*". The message of these two Reports is to develop a new pedagogy that is to be centred on learning to learn, learning to know, learning to do, learning to live together, and learning to be.

New Pedagogy and Ancient Indian Pedagogy

This new pedagogy impels a further realisation of the potentialities of the child and its soul, a realisation that was explicitly stated in the writings of the nationalist leaders who inspired and led the movement of national education in India, such as those of Dayananda Saraswati, Swami Vivekananda, Mahatma Gandhi, Rabindranath Tagore and Sri Aurobindo. These writings gave a clear expression of the deeper self and the real psychic entity within. They pointed out that, if we ever give it a chance to come forward, and still more if we call it into the foreground as "*the leader of the march set in front*", will itself take up most of the business of education out of our hands and develop the capacity of the psychological being towards the realisation of its potentialities of which our present mechanistic view of life and mind and external routine methods of dealing with them prevent us from having any experience of forming any conception.

The resultant new educational methods which were experimented upon were a kind of recovery of the methods of ancient pedagogy and knowledge that sought to express through spiritual and social symbolism. In this light, we seem to understand better the educational system which was envisaged by the Upanishads in India and it is in that light that we can understand properly what we can call distinctly Indian pedagogy. And while recovering it and expressing it in the context of the latest philosophies of education and the modern march of knowledge, we may be able to give to India of today a new pedagogy which would be rooted in the ancient soul of India and yet ever progressive soul of India which has the capacity to express itself in new forms appropriate to the needs of the contemporary culture of India and of the world.

II

Formulation of Indian Pedagogy

The meaning of the symbolism in which the ancient knowledge of human life, of man and of the universe was expressed is practically lost to us, and if we are to profit from the recovery of that knowledge, a very great effort will be needed. Fortunately, a great effort has been made during the last two centuries, and we have today a considerable understanding of the truths of the Veda and the Upanishads, of the recovered sense of Buddhism and also of the secrets of the knowledge of the soul that was expressed in the ancient Jaina texts. And we can say with confidence that the ancient Indian records of knowledge manifest profound knowledge of the deepest secrets of existence, of the meaning and aim of life, and of the secrets of the growth of the human soul towards true inner freedom and true inner and outer mastery that can lead to fulfilment of the human race.

The composers of these records of knowledge had measured and fathomed the heights and depths of our being, they had cast their plummet into the inconscient, and the subconscient and the superconscient; they had read the riddle of death and found the secret of immortality. The system of education which they founded had thus a vast basis of experience and a fund of verifiable knowledge.

The ancient Indian pedagogy has still not been ascertained in clear terms, and much research would be required before we can formulate it adequately. A few pages in the Upanishads give us the indication of teachers and the methods of their teaching; they also give us an idea of the stir of the quest which inspired young seekers in their inquiry and in their enthusiasm; in the Taittiriya Upanishad, in particular, we have a more direct indication of the ancient scheme of education; and in the Upanishads like the Isha and Kena, we have profound statements of the art and science of life as also of the distinction between ignorance and knowledge, -- *avidyā* and *vidyā*. Upanishads also speak of *aparā* and *parā vidyā* – the lower knowledge and the higher knowledge, of different states of consciousness and their interrelationship. In the subsequent writings in Indian literature, we have further glimpses of the systems of education that flourished in ancient times and in the later periods. From all these accounts, we can gather an idea of the knowledge that was practised of the truths, principles, powers and processes that govern the human growth and development towards the liberating excellence and mastery. We can also formulate the process of interaction between the teacher and the pupil, as also an idea of the art to accelerate the progression of development.

Call of the Word and Awakening

A basic foundation of Indian pedagogy is the perception that there is in the heart of every thinking and living being a growing bud of knowledge and perfection that can open swiftly or gradually, particularly when the right Word is heard. Ordinarily, the Word from without, from a living teacher is needed as an aid in the self-unfolding. The hearing of the right Word, *shravana*, is followed by reflection and meditation, *manana* and *nidhidhyasana*. The Indian pedagogy allowed the processes of questioning and free inquiry, but it also insisted on continuing questioning with increasing emphasis on gathering experience and on awakening to crowning discovery of truths. It was also underlined that the true knowledge is arrived at by living in one's own soul beyond written word. In the ultimate analysis, this pedagogy encouraged liberation from any binding influence of a text by emphasising that pursuit of knowledge and pursuit of excellence is a free pursuit of the sense of wonder and mystery that is infinite in character. An absolute liberty of experience is the condition for the attainment of a true self-knowledge and world-knowledge.

Indian pedagogy recognised that beyond written texts, the great teacher of life is life itself, and totality of life is to be embraced if one has to gain integral knowledge and integral realisation. It also recognised that each individual has his own unique method of experiencing life and it provided to each individual a free adaptability in the manner and type of the individual acceptance of the object of knowledge that one encounters in the experience of life. The Indian pedagogy also laid down the outcome of past experience as a help to future realisation; and the accumulated experience of the past was laid before the seeker as an aid to accelerate the pace of progression. The rest depended on the personal effort of the pupil and the uplifting power of the teacher. A great stress was laid on the cultivation of the quality of the aspiration in the mind and heart of the pupils. The entire process of learning was marked by a living message to the human soul that it has to rise from the egoistic state of consciousness absorbed in the outward appearances and attractions of things to higher states in which the true knowledge can grow, a knowledge that can constantly expand the individual mould and transform it. The pupil was constantly advised to develop the intensity of quest, the power of the aspiration of the heart, the force of the will, the concentration of the mind, the perseverance and determination of the applied energy.

Upliftment of Pupils Aspiration: Role of the Teacher

Aspiration of the pupil needs to be uplifted, and the upliftment of the aspiration is the basic function of the teacher. The Indian pedagogy recognises three instruments of the teacher: *instruction, example,* and *influence.* Instruction was not limited merely to verbal discourse; it utilised the methods of conversation and dialogue; it included the methods of providing hints and suggestions, presenting riddles and puzzles, and it provided instructions to find, discover and invent; it also involved imparting of skills to the pupils by direct dealing with materials or by accompanying in the journey towards mastery. More important than instruction was in the Indian pedagogy the living example of the teacher. This example was not merely of the external behaviour of the teacher but that of inner integrity and inner mastery in regard to knowledge and character. More important than example was the living influence of the teacher. Influence is not the outward authority of the teacher, but the power of his contact, of his presence, of the nearness of his soul to the soul of another, infusing into it, even though in silence that which he possesses. Indian pedagogy did not encourage the teacher to arrogate to himself the sense of superiority in a humanly vain and self-exalting spirit. The teacher was looked upon as a man helping his students, a child leading children, a light kindling other lights, an awakened soul awakening souls, at the highest a channel, a representative of the higher truth and realisation.

Method of Indian Pedagogy: Towards Fourfold Integral Personality

The method of Indian pedagogy did not consist of any fixed and mechanical framework. The teacher's system was a natural organisation of the highest processes and movements of which the nature is capable. Every student, it was assumed, has in him or her certain combination of faculties and powers, a combination in the process of formation, with some tendencies predominant and central, others peripheral and even transient. The task of the teacher was to recognise in each student the four basic powers, their present status in the process of formation and in their interrelationship. These powers related to the pursuit of knowledge, pursuit of courage and heroism, pursuit of emotional upliftment and mutuality and interdependence in relationships; and pursuit of skills and their applications. The resultant aim was the development of integral personality that blended as perfectly as possible a harmony of four personalities of knowledge, power, harmony and skilful service. This pedagogy aimed at providing sunshine for the flowering of the inner soul of each individual, and it perceived and applied the truth that the secret of each one's profession lies in his or her personality. The skill of the teacher lay in his deep understanding of the nature of the pupil and in guiding the development of that nature so that it can flower into a fully bloomed lotus. The teacher was expected not to be offended by the ignorant reactions of the pupils. He was expected to have the entire love of the mother and the entire patience of the teacher. The good teacher, according to Indian pedagogy, used error in order to arrive at truth, suffering in order to arrive at bliss, imperfection in order to arrive at perfection. The good teacher sought to awaken much more than to instruct, and he aimed at the growth of the faculties and the experiences by a natural process and free expansion. He gave a method as an aid, not as an imperative formula or a fixed routine. He guarded against the turning of the means into a limitation, against the mechanisation of the process. The good teacher, again, was not expected to impose himself or his opinion on the passive acceptance of the receptive mind; he threw in what is productive and sowed as a seed which would grow under the divine fostering within.

The basic guideline of the Indian pedagogy is that nothing can be taught to the mind which is not already concealed as a potential knowledge in the unfolding soul of the individual. All perfection of which the power of personality is capable is only a realising of the eternal perfection of the spirit within him. In a deeper sense, all becoming is an unfolding. To be is the secret; to be is self-attainment, and self-knowledge and an increasing consciousness are the means in the process.

All education is a deliberate process by which what can ordinarily be attained over a certain period of time can be attained more and more rapidly at an optimum rate of acceleration. The secret of this acceleration in Indian pedagogy is the secret of the process of concentration. And

Philosophy of Indian Pedagogy

the first step in concentration is the process by which consciousness can be drawn more and more inward, *antarmukha*. By inward gaze of consciousness with increasing concentration and by the progressive discovery of the inner soul, knowledge can be commanded more and more readily, more and more creatively, more and more harmoniously.

Indian pedagogy recognises immense importance of Time in the process of development; for in all things there is a cycle of their action and a period of efflorescence. The secret of mastery over time-movement is a harmonious blending of patience and an effort by means of which increasing power is developed for instantaneous achievement. If the students and teachers learn the art of carrying out activities as quickly as possible and yet as perfectly as possible, optimum acceleration and the right speed of progression will be achieved. All progress will be marked by a happy process of joy and continuous and increasing movement towards perfection.

III

Aparā Vidyā and Parā Vidyā
(Lower Knowledge and Higher Knowledge)

An important distinction has been drawn in the Indian pedagogy between two kinds of knowledge, -- lower knowledge and higher knowledge, -- *aparā* and *parā vidyā*.[1] Science, art, philosophy, ethics, psychology, the

---

[1] शौनको ह वै महाशालोऽङ्गिरसं विधिवदुपसन्नः पप्रच्छ। कस्मिन्नु भगवो विज्ञाते सर्वमिदं विज्ञातं भवति। तस्मै स होवाच ः द्वे विद्ये वेदितव्ये इति ह स्म यद् ब्रह्मविदो वदन्ति परा चैवापरा च। तत्रापरा ऋग्वेदो यजुर्वेदः सामवेदोऽथर्ववेदः शिक्षा कल्पो व्याकरणं निरुक्तं छन्दो ज्योतिषमिति। अथ परा यया तदक्षरमधिगम्यते ' यत्तदद्रेश्यमग्राह्यमगोत्रमवर्णमचक्षुःश्रोत्रं तदपाणिपादम् नित्यं विभुं सर्वगतं सुसूक्ष्मं तदव्ययं यद्भूतयोनिं परिपश्यन्ति धीराः। Mundaka Upanishad I.3-6

knowledge of man and his past, action itself are means by which we arrive at the knowledge of the becomings of the world, of the multiplicity and of the appearances. That knowledge is lower knowledge.[2] But as we go deeper and deeper, a completer view and experience develop, and each of the lines of growth brings us face to face with knowledge of the ultimate Reality. That knowledge is *Parā vidyā*. We begin to grow in the sense of comprehensiveness and in the sense of universal harmony and progressive equilibrium of the manifestation of the underlying perfection. The more we begin to understand and experience the underlying unity, the more we perceive the key of multiplicity in unity, the more we surpass the limitations of the lower knowledge and the more we enter

---

Śaunka, a man of reputation, approached seer Aṅgiras duly prepared for learning from him, and asked: *"What, Sir, is that thing by knowing which all this whatever becomes automatically known."*

Aṅgiras replied: *"There are two sorts of vidyas which knowers of the Ultimate Reality call as the higher and the lower. The lower is the learning of the Rigveda, Yajurveda, Sāmaveda, Atharvaveda, education in phonetics, science of sacrifice, grammar, science of derivation, chandas and astronomy.*

The higher vidyā, on the other hand, is that by means of which is understood the Immortal which can neither be seen nor caught hold of, which is beyond the range of caste and class, which has neither eyes, nor ears nor even hands and feet. He is rather eternal, all-embracing, all-pervading, absolutely subtle and imperishable. Him the wise realise as the source of the entire creation."

[2] The Upanishad declares that even the records of the highest knowledge, the Rigveda, Yajurveda, Samaveda and Atharvaveda are components of the lower knowledge aparā vidyā, since they are not themselves the direct experience of the Self and of the eternal that is beyond all becomings.

into the portals of the higher knowledge. The more we are occupied with multiplicity and different domains of knowledge, the more we remain entrenched in *aparā vidyā*; the more we overcome our bondage to appearances and multiplicity, the more we transcend into the knowledge of the imperishable and ineffable, the more we become liberated into the realm of *parā vidyā*. Knowledge attained by senses and even the knowledge that remains confined to intellectual processes, even the highest stores of information keep us confined to lower knowledge. The more we cross the borders of sense-knowledge and intellectual knowledge, the more we grow inward, the more we discover the inner self and inner unity through inner vision and inner intuitive concreteness of experiences that lead us into the secrets of higher knowledge.

Aparā vidyā is a kind of knowledge which seeks to understand the apparent phenomena of existence externally, by an approach from outside, through the senses and the intellect. That gives us the lower knowledge, the knowledge of the apparent world. *Parā vidyā* is the knowledge which seeks to know the truth of existence from within, in its source of reality, by processes of intuition, inspiration, revelation and inmost and profoundest realisation. Both are two sides of one's seeking. *Avidyā* is the knowledge of multiplicity, and *vidyā* is the knowledge of unity and oneness. When knowledge of multiplicity is pursued by excluding the knowledge of unity and oneness, we remain in the field of darkness; if we pursue unity and oneness and exclude the knowledge of multiplicity, then also there is some kind of incompleteness, inadequacy, and as one Upanishad declares, one is led into even greater darkness.[3] Both *vidyā* and *avidyā*, the knowledge of

---

[3] *Ishopanishad,* verse 9

multiplicity and the knowledge of unity are to be synthesised.

Indian pedagogy does not exclude the pursuit of the knowledge of multiplicity or the pursuit of knowledge through senses and intellect; but it also insists on the pursuit of knowledge of unity and oneness, and it insists on the pursuit of that knowledge through the development of the faculties of intuition and concrete realisation. The knowledge of unity and multiplicity, and the knowledge as grounded in unity is the ideal that Indian pedagogy puts forward in its total scheme of knowledge.

Jñāna: Illumination through Intuition of the Self

There is another important word that is often used in Indian pedagogy, and that word is *jñāna*. This word is used in the sense of a supreme self-knowledge. To understand this properly, we have to make a distinction between knowledge and object of knowledge. Knowledge is the light by which the object of knowledge is lit, is perceived, is realised. When the object of knowledge is our true being or our true self, there is a special phenomenon of growth into our true being; it is not information about our true being, it is our inner enlargement by which the limitations of our egoistic consciousness are annulled, and there is the realisation of wideness, universality, and even transcendence; there is self-possession, there is self-knowledge. Knowledge *about* the self is *aparā vidyā*; knowledge that unveils the self, the knowledge that makes self revealed is *parā vidyā*. And Indian pedagogy has this distinct feature that the aim of its entire programme of education is to nourish the growth of the light by which we grow into our true being.

Knowledge and Information

There is, no doubt, the light of the senses and the light of the intellect; and through this light, too, the corresponding objects of knowledge, the corresponding multiplicity, become more and more known; but this knowledge increasees our information and our intellectual riches regarding becomings, but not of the being. This is the character of the scientific or psychological or philosophical or ethical or aesthetic or worldly and practical knowledge. This informative knowledge helps us also to grow but in the realm of becoming and not of the being. If the highest learning is learning to be, then the appropriate method is the development, not of the light of senses or the light of the intellect, but of the light of profounder and higher faculties of intuition, revelation and inspiration as also of automatic discrimination between the real and the unreal, and between the real and the appearance. Indian pedagogy also recognises that sense knowledge and intellectual knowledge can be used as aids to arrive at self-knowledge. In that case, scientific knowledge can be used to get through the veil of processes and phenomena and see the one Reality behind which explains them all. Psychological knowledge can be used as an aid to know ourselves and to distinguish the lower from the higher, so that we can renounce the lower and we can enter and grow into the higher. Philosophical knowledge can be used as an aid when we turn it as a light upon the essential principles of existence so as to discover and live in that which is eternal. We can use ethical knowledge as an aid when through that knowledge we can distinguish the wrong from the right, and distinguish the evil from the good, and we put away the wrong and the evil and rise above into the pure innocence of the divine Nature. We can use the aesthetic knowledge as an aid so that we can discover by it the beauty of the universal and the transcendental, the beauty of the ineffable and of the formless that manifests through the mystery and wonder of the form. We can use the knowledge of the world as an aid when we see through it the way of the glory of the higher being and consciousness, and learn how that being deals with movements and affairs of the world, and we can use that knowledge for the service of the highest in man. Even then, they are merely aids. According to Indian pedagogy, the real knowledge is that which is intuitive and supramental, of which the mind gets various kinds of reflections.

Jñāna from Within

According to the Indian pedagogy, we come to the true self-knowledge, we get first intimation of it from the men of knowledge who have *seen*, not those who merely by the intellect know its essential truths. The actuality of that knowledge comes from within ourselves; that knowledge grows within ourselves, and grows on as one goes on increasing in the state of equality, *samvatvam*, in self-control, in commitment and vision of the highest reality and the highest aim of life. It is when one grows in the realm of values that the light of self-knowledge grows. In fact, it is this pedagogical truth that renders the truly Indian system of education inherently value-oriented. For it is through value-oriented consciousness that the inner light grows, and that light manifests in our dynamic nature as a state of equality that enables us to rise above the turmoil of our nature and makes us seated high above where the world can be seen as to a spectator and the world can be dealt with a mastery that is not deflected by partialities and preferences. In the Indian pedagogy, to know oneself is to be liberated from the limitations of the turmoil of our nature; that is why we have the dictum – *sā vidyā yā vimuktaye* – that is the true knowledge which leads us to liberation, liberation from the bondage to nature and to its limitations. Self-knowledge is the seat of wisdom, and Indian psychology regards it as self-existent, intuitive, self-experiencing, and self-revealing. We arrive at it more and more readily when we conquer and control our mind and senses, so that we become more and more free from subjection to their delusions. In the process, the mind and senses become pure reflecting vehicles. In the final analysis, education becomes a process of *yoga* when we are enabled to fix our inner conscious being on the truth of that supreme reality in which all exists, so that it may display in us its luminous self-existence or that which transcends the limitations of description in terms of existence.

Jñāna, Vidyā, Parā Vidyā

The words, *Jñāna*, *Vidyā* and *Parā Vidyā* are normally used interchangeably; but they seem to have, in certain contexts, special connotation and point of emphasis. Thus, the word *Jñāna* is often used when our primary concern of emphasis is related to the state of illumination obtained through the faculty of intuition. The word *Vidyā* is often used when our primary concern of emphasis is related to unity and oneness of the object of knowledge. The phrase *Parā Vidyā* is often used when our primary concern of emphasis is related to the context of various kinds and systems or branches of knowledge. From the pedagogical point of view, what is important to note is that Indian pedagogy has developepd the methods and facilities to develop the faculty of intuition, in contrast to the methods and facilities to develop sense-experience and intellectual ratiocination, the methods and facilities to nurture the sense and experience of unity and oneness, -- in contrast to the methods and facilities to nurture the sense and experience of multiplicity, and the methods and facilities for the growth of the sense and experience of transcendence of limitation inherent in varieties of systems of knowledge so as to arrive at the imperishable and ineffable, -- in contrast to the sense and experience of all that can be sublated. Pedagogically, again, Indian experiments in education have striven to bridge and harmonise lines of growth of sense-experience, rationality and intuitive powers of the soul and spirit, of the experience of the multiplicity and of the various domains of knowledge and transcendences as also comprehensive methods of synthesis.

IV

Indian Pedagogy and Indian Quest of Knowledge

Indian pedagogy and Indian quest of knowledge, experience and realisation stimulated and influenced each other throughout the ages. Indian quest passed through three main stages before the period of exhaustion of the life-force overcame the process of development of the integrality of Indian culture. The first stage of the Indian quest was that of the efflorescence of the intuitive knowledge; next, the age of intuitive knowledge gave place to the age of rational knowledge, during which metaphysical philosophy reached great heights of subtlety and excellence, during the third stage, metaphysical philosophy gave way to experimental science. This process which seems to be a descent, is really a circle of progress. For in each case, the lower faculty is compelled to take up as much as it can assimilate of what the higher had already given and to attempt to re-establish it by its own methods. By the attempt it is itself enlarged in its scope and arrives eventually at a more supple and a more ample self-accommodation to the higher faculties. Without this succession and attempt at separate assimilation, we should be obliged to remain under the exclusive domination of a part of our nature, while the rest remained either depressed and unduly subjected or suppressed in its field and therefore poor in its development. With this succession and separate attempt, the balance is righted; a more complete harmony of our parts of knowledge is prepared.

The development of Indian culture and the transmission of that culture from generation to generation played a major part in Indian pedagogy. Indian culture had reached over millennia great heights, not only in the fields of spiritual and philosophic domains, but also in the fields of science, technology, aesthetics and sociology, polity and other fields of life, pragmatism and administration and conquest. Spirituality is indeed the master-key of the Indian mind, and spiritual genius of Indian culture had moulded Indian pedagogy right from the beginning. India's first period of the known history was luminous with the discovery of the Spirit. Her second period, completed the discovery of the *dharma*. Her third elaborated into detail the first simpler formulation of the *shastra*; but none was exclusive, the three elements were always present. An ingrained and dominant spirituality, inexhaustible vital creativeness and gust of life, and a powerful, penetrating and scrupulous intelligence combined with the rational, ethical, and aesthetic mind, -- these three created the harmony of a great part of the unbroken history of Indian culture. If India's spiritual disciplines, philosophies and her long list of great spiritual personalities, thinkers, founders, saints are her greatest glory, they are by no means her sole-glories. It is now proved that India had gone farther than any other country before the modern era in the field of science, and even Europe owes the beginning of her physical science to India as much as to Greece, although not directly but through the medium of the Arabs. Specially in mathematics, astronomy and chemistry, the chief elements of ancient science, India discovered and formulated much and well anticipated by force of reasoning and experiments some of the scientific ideas and discoveries which Europe first arrived at much later, but was able to base more firmly by her new and completer method. India was well equipped in surgery and her system of medicine survives to this day and has still its value. The mere mass of intellectual periods extending from the period of Ashoka well into the Mohammedan epoch is something truly prodigious. There is no historical parallel of such an intellectual labour and activity before the invention of printing and the facilities of modern science. All this colossal literature was not confined to philosophy and theology, religion and yoga but extended into the fields of logic and rhetoric and grammar and linguistics, poetry and drama, astronomy, mathematics, various sciences and medicine. This intellectual literature embraced all life, politics and society, various arts from painting to dancing, and even such practical minutiae as the breeding and training of horses and elephants, each of which had its *shastra* and its art, its apparatus of technical terms, its copious literature. For three thousand years at least, India created abundantly and incessantly. This creativity was many-sided and led to the development of republic, kingdoms and empires, philosophies and cosmogonies and sciences and creeds and arts and poems and all kinds of monuments, palaces, temples and public works, communities and societies and religious orders, laws and codes and rituals, physical sciences, psychic sciences, systems of yoga, systems of politics and administration, arts spiritual, arts worldly, trades, industries and fine arts. This vast canvas of Indian culture continued to be transmitted from one age to another, and this process of transmission contributed greatly to the development of Indian pedagogy. We must confess that a good deal of research is required to ascertain more precisely and accurately the methods which were employed by Indian pedagogy to keep the Indian frontiers of knowledge constantly expanding and constantly transmitted. And this research is important because, as in no other country, India still requires to transmit the cultural heritage of an unbroken history of many-sided development that goes back to more than three or four thousand years. When this research matures, we shall be able to enlarge, alter and even revolutionise our present methods of teaching and learning and renew our pedagogy for greater tasks that lie ahead of us.

Macaulayan System of Education

From the thirteenth century or fourteenth century onwards, however, the Indian quest became weary and it reached a point of disastrous decline when the British arrived on the scene and disturbed totally our indigenous system of education and imposed on us an unfamiliar pedagogy. Macaulayan system of education grew, and it has become so hardened that in spite of great efforts at the recovery of Indian pedagogy, we find it extremely difficult to develop and establish in our country the real soul of the Indian pedagogy and its new and progressive forms.

This is the stage where we find ourselves today, groping in bewilderment and thwarted in our efforts by the rigidity of the system and the load it has accumulated of obstruction and mechanisation.

In fact, the problem is very serious, and a good deal of research is required before we can find the right direction and the right remedies to the maladies of our present system of education. As a part of this research, we have to recognise that the greatness of the Indian system of education, during the periods when it proved to be more fruitful in producing great and multisided systems of knowledge, in developing profound and inspiring systems of conduct and character building, in creating economic, social, political and stable systems of civilisation, stability and prosperity, and in providing unfailing heroism and power of triumph in various directions, as also in creating inspiring multisided forms of art, literature and other aesthetic and pulsating activities, we shall find that there were the following elements which were dynamically operative.

Chief Elements of Indian Pedagogy

❖ Firstly, and centrally, there was what may be called a comprehensive science of living. This science was a result of a long and detailed experimentation with the truths of life, mind and spirit as also with the truths of the relationship between Matter and Spirit. This science of living was that of self-knowledge and self-control. This science provided the basic ground for the art of life which aimed at development of value-oriented integral personality.

The science was also based on the knowledge of the physical world as also of the worlds of life and mind. This knowledge embraced the knowledge of what was called the fourth world, the world of Right and the Truth, the world of *ritam* and *satyam*. This knowledge was also based on the discovery of what was called "*the golden immortal, who is seated within the cave of the inner heart*". Finally, this knowledge had profound basis in the study of righteousness and of the secrets of self-mastery and of the conditions in which peace of the inner being can be perpetually held in the body, life and mind. The *Tattiriya* Upanishad gives us, in brief, the quintessence of this science and art of living in brief but instructive terms.

❖ Secondly, there was a great emphasis on the study of the secrets of Speech, which provided powerful grounding in the study of languages.

❖ Thirdly, there was a harmonious blending in the courses of studies in the spiritual knowledge, philosophical knowledge, and scientific knowledge. In the harmony of the blending, the scientific spirit did not conflict with the philosophic spirit and the philosophic spirit was recognised as a prelude to the training by which intuitive spiritual knowledge can be gained and mastered.

❖ Fourthly, physical education was widespread, and the development of health and the strength of the body were constantly nourished and developed under the illuminating dictum that body is verily the instrument of the achievement and realisation of the highest ideals. (*shariram ādyam khalu dharma sādhanam*).

❖ Fifthly, a number of specialised studies were developed and imparted. Starting with grammar, prosody and astronomy, the field covered science and art of healing and longevity (*ayurveda*), science and art of aesthetic creativity such as drama, music and dance (*gandharva shastra*), science and art of warfare (*dhanurveda*), and science and art of prosperity, constructive and well-established infrastructure of civilisational stability (*arthaveda, vastu shastra*, etc.).

There was an emphasis on a comprehensive understanding of various domains of knowledge, their interrelationship, and the methods by which unified knowledge can be gained.

❖ Sixthly, there was an emphasis on specialisation against the background of general holism and unity of knowledge as also against the background of sixty-four arts [4]; and

---

[4] **Sixty-four Arts mentioned by Vatsyayana in his Kamasutra:** 1. Singing; 2. Playing on musical instruments; 3. Dancing; 4. Union of dancing, singing, and playing instrumental music; 5. Writing and drawing; 6. Tattooing; 7. Arraying and adoring an idol with rice and flowers; 8. Spreading and arranging beds or couches of flowers, or flowers upon the ground; 9. Colouring the teeth, garments, hair, nails and bodies, i.e. staining, dyeing, colouring and painting the same; 10. Fixing stained glass into a floor; 11. The art of making beds, and spreading out carpets and cushions for reclining; 12. Playing on musical glasses filled with water; 13. Storing and accumulating water in aqueducts, cisterns and reservoirs; 14. Picture making, trimming and decorating; 15. Stringing of rosaries, necklaces, garlands and wreaths; 16. Binding of turbans and chaplets and making crests and top-knots of flowers; 17. Scenic representations, stage playing; 18. Art of making ear ornaments; 19. Art of preparing perfumes and odours; 20. Proper disposition of jewels and decorations, and adornment in dress; 21. Magic or sorcery; 22. Quickness of hand or manual skill; 23. Culinary art, i.e. cooking and cookery; 24. Making lemonades, sherbets, acidulated drinks, and spirituous extracts with proper flavour and colour; 25. Tailor's work and sewing; 26. Making parrots, flowers, tufts, tassels, bunches, bosses, knobs, etc., out of yarn or thread; 27. Solution of riddles, enigmas, covert speeches, verbal puzzles and enigmatical questions; 28. A game, which consisted in repeating verses, and as one person finished, another person had to commence at once, repeating another verse, beginning with the same letter with which the last speaker's verse ended, whoever failed to repeat was considered to have lost, and to be subject to pay a forfeit or stake of some kind; 29. The art of mimicry or imitation; 30. Reading, including chanting and intoning; 31. Study of sentences difficult to pronounce. It is played as a game chiefly by women and children and consists of a difficult sentence being given, and when repeated quickly, the words are often transposed or badly pronounced; 32. Practice with sword, single stick, quarter staff and bow and arrow; 33. Drawing inferences, reasoning or inferring; 34. Carpentry, or the work of a carpenter; 35. Architecture, or the art of building;

Philosophy of Indian Pedagogy

❖ Seventhly, a constant emphasis was laid on the study of human psychology, human history, and classical literature with a deliberate effort to provide education of the inner soul through poetry, art, and music, -- all set in the atmosphere of the harmony between the human and physical nature that up-

---

36. Knowledge about gold and silver coins, and jewels and gems; 37. Chemistry and mineralogy; 38. Colour jewels, gems and beads; 39. Knowledge of mines and quarries; 40. Gardening; knowledge of treating the diseases of trees and plants, of nourishing them, and determining their ages; 41. Art of cock fighting, quail fighting and ram fighting; 42. Art of teaching parrots and starlings to speak; 43. Art of applying perfumed ointments to the body, and of dressing the hair with unguents and perfumes and braiding it; 44. The art of understanding writing in cipher, and the writing of words in a peculiar way; 45. The art of speaking by changing the forms of words. It is of various kinds. Some speak by changing the beginning and end of words, others by adding unnecessary letters between every syllable of a word, and so on; 46. Knowledge of language and of the vernacular dialects; 47. Art of making flower carriages; 48. Art of framing mystical diagrams, of addressing spells and charms, and binding armlets; 49. Mental exercises, such as completing stanzas or verses on receiving a part of them; or supplying one, two or three lines when the remaining lines are given indiscriminately from different verses, so as to make the whole an entire verse with regard to its meaning; or arranging the words of a consonants, or leaving them out altogether; or putting into verse or prose sentences represented by signs or symbols. There are many other such exercises; 50. Composing poems; 51. Knowledge of dictionaries and vocabularies; 52. Knowledge of ways of changing and disguising the appearance of persons; 53. Knowledge of the art of changing the appearance of things, such as making cotton to appear as silk, coarse and common things to appear as fine and good; 54. Various ways of gambling; 55. Art of obtaining possession of the property of others by means of mantras or incantations; 56. Skill in youthful sports; 57. Knowledge of the rules of society, and of how to pay respect and compliments to others; 58. Knowledge of the art of war, of arms, of armies, etc.; 59. Knowledge of gymnastics; 60. Art of knowing the character of a man from his features; 61. Knowledge of scanning or constructing verses; 62. Arithmetical recreations; 63. Making artificial flowers; 64. Making figures and images in clay.

lifted the aspiration of the individual to attain states of universality, oneness and transcendence.

Maladies due to Macaulayan System

We need to revisit of these elements that gave distinctness to Indian pedagogy, and we need to give to our country a scheme of education that would be appropriate to the soul of Indian pedagogy and which at the same time would be relevant to the progressive demands of today and tomorrow. While doing so, we shall need to diagnose more properly maladies that have been created by the Macaulayan system of education in India. Macaulay has succeeded in demolishing the Indian art and science of living, it has succeeded in creating in our mind the inability to recovery of that special kind of scientific spirit that was sustained by high intellectual and philosophical culture and by the aspiration and power of climbing the peaks of higher levels of spiritual consciousness; and by knocking off Sanskrit from the mainstream of education, we have been robbed of the power to recover our true cultural heritage and of our power of assimilation, creativity and synthesis. Macaulayan system has enfeebled us physically, vitally, mentally and spiritually. It has omitted from our educational programme those arts and sciences which can make our body strong and healthy, which can make our vital being heroic and courageous, and our mental being subtle, complex and comprehensive Philosophy, which was for long a part of the cultural education in our country, accessible even to the rustic, has been flung aside to such remoteness that even highly trained scientific and other professionals reamin strangers to this noble pursuit which fostered love of wisdom. It has also omitted from our scheme of education those venues through which great quests of knowledge and effectivity can be stimulated. Our educational heights and horizons have been narrowed down to the study of English and to the study of other subjects, namely, mathematics, science, history and miscellaneous pursuits of other natural and human sciences. Astronomy, which was the great achievement of Indian scientific spirit, has been so eclipsed that our students and teachers remain blissfully ignorant of the vastness and wonder of the universe. Neglect of astronomy has also resulted in our inadequacy to appreciate the root-importance of the study of mathematics and physical sciences. History is being taught within a narrow compass, and we fail to give to our students a true account of the human adventure and human thrill to explore and conquer vast stretches of psychological space and time. Poetry, Music and Art, which constitute the perfect education of the human soul, has no place in our educational curriculum, except at the peripheral boundaries. We have come to believe that to be educated is to be educated basically in five subjects prescribed in the Macaulayan scheme of education and that all that falls outside that limited scheme can be neglected altogether or can be prescribed to be cultivated during leisure hours, which are hardly available under the present circumstances of our daily life. We need to give to our self a new scheme of education.

Need to Develop a New Programme of Educational Research

This is where we stand today, and we need to explore, in greater detail, truths of Indian pedagogy and we need to initiate a new programme of educational research. New models need to be rapidly developed, and for that process, various workshops need to be organised continuously and effectively.

Nothing that is presented here is more than tentative and nothing presented here is more than indicative of the need to explore and to undertake new programmes of relevant research. Our aim should be to create for our country a new system of national education, rooted in the fundamentals of Indian pedagogy, which, when properly explored, will be found capable of providing to us today new and progressive forms that would respond to the highest needs of humanity's goals of integral fulfilment.

PHILOSOPHY OF SPIRITUAL EDUCATION

Why do we need Spiritual Education? What does it really mean? Is it practicable? And what reforms could we propose in our educational system so as to have the right place for spiritual education in it?

All these are important and difficult questions, and within the short time available, we can only touch upon them very briefly and inadequately.

We need spiritual education, firstly, because we want a true national system of education. Education, in order to be national, must reflect that basic urge, which is distinctive of our national history, which is the real genius of our country, which accounts for the amazing continuity of our long and complex history, and which continues to burn even in our decline and darkest periods and serves as the saving light. Veritably, it can be said that what distinguishes Indian cultural history from any other cultural history, is its genius for spirituality and profusion of spiritual developments and great treasures of spiritual knowledge and experience. If we are to search for our cultural identity, — and do we not see the upsurge for cultural identity everywhere in the world today, even when there is an unprecedented demand for internationality, universal citizenship, and oneness of humanity? – We can say that the first task of India is to understand what may be called Indian spirituality, its synthetic tendency, its catholicity, and its power to rejuvenate springs of culture and irrigate the paths of perfection of intellectuality, vitality of heroism and vitality and capacity to build strong physical foundations in various domains of life. In this context, our need for spiritual education stands out as an article of supreme importance.

But this is not all.

We need spiritual education not only in India but everywhere because it is becoming increasingly clear that the present crisis through which humanity is passing today can be effectively met only if the entire humanity knocks the doors of spirituality, for that alone seems to hold out the promise of the power that can deliver us. This is evident from the way in which the West is turning to the East. This is also evident from the counsels of some of the greatest historians of our times, who have pointed to India and Indian spirituality for the cure of the decline and fall of the Western civilisation that is built upon the vital and pragmatic drives and intellect as the sole and highest governor of social building.

And when the West is turning to India for some spiritual light, what is it that will enable us to respond? The best way by which we can prepare ourselves to give the right response is to build up the sound edifices of a robust system of education with due place assigned to spiritual education.

Thirdly, with the growing stress on the creation of a classless society or a society that aims at equality and equity, freedom and brotherhood, there is an increasing stress on every individual to participate as fully as possible in the activities of the totality of the society. As a result, individuals are required to expand their horizons, develop multiple interests and responsibilities and equip themselves with the capacities and powers that can be chiselled only by the development of an integral personality. Hence, there has been unprecedented emphasis in our times on integral education for the complete human being. The complete human being is not a sum of its parts, each one put in juxtaposition of the other. Each part of our personality, physical, vital, mental, rational, aesthetic, ethical and spiritual, — has its constitutional relationship with the other and it has to be discovered and, instead of juxtaposition, there has to be integration. And what is the integrating point in a personality is a matter today of psychological investigations. It is easy to admit the Indian psychological contention that nothing can integrate the physical and the vital as the mental, *manomaya pranashariraneta*, to use the expression of the Taittiriya Upanishad; — but considering that the conflict in the mind itself of its rational, aesthetic and ethical elements as also the conflict between the Reason and the Unreason are becoming acute, we need to turn to still higher levels of integration and admit still higher principles, — principles of spiritual consciousness, which are supramental in character, — *vijñānamaya* and *ānandamaya*, — to use again the terms of Taittiriya Upanishad. And this underlines, by implication, the theme of spiritual education as the overarching domain of integral education.

Fortunately, we have a good fund of spiritual knowledge in the roots of our cultural history, if only we make the effort to recover it. We have also been continuously developing spiritual experimentation and renewing it right up to the present day. And the significant fact is that in our renascent India, our greatest experiments in education were inspired by the ideals of spiritual education.

II

But let us ask the central question: "What is spiritual education? And what are the real issues pertaining to spiritual education as far as its nature and methodologies are concerned?" There is here a great deal of inadequacy of inquiry, and a good deal of confusion. In the first place, spiritual education tends to be confused with the unexamined concept of "religious education". And it is argued that because religious education is constitutionally not allowed to be promoted by the State funds, even spiritual education, which is more or less religious education, has to be exiled from the portals of education in our country.

As against this, it must be stressed that there is a clear distinction between spiritual education and religious education. It may be said that the distinguishing feature of a religion is a doctrine or a belief or a dogma. Every religion has its distinctive doctrine, "prescribed acts", its rituals, ceremonies, social and religious institutions. On the other hand, what is distinctive of spirituality is its stress on the psychological contention that there is a vast domain of states of consciousness, which are beyond and deeper than mental consciousness and beyond and deeper than the realm of doctrines, beliefs or dogmas. Spirituality can be developed by Yogic methodised effort that is scientific in character, since it can be practiced without any prior belief, and the conclusions or results of that effort can be repeated, verified and expanded by questioning, correction, revision, enlargement, deepening, and heightening. Secondly, another distinctive feature of spirituality is its spontaneous attitude and effortless and abiding stability of consciousness that is marked by universality, silent concentration and contemplation, which is free from the fever of desires, clamours of egoism and prejudices of partiality and attachment. These states of consciousness, these attitudes and these abiding experiences are not states of opinions and beliefs; nor are they tied up with one or the other dogma, and they depend upon no rituals or ceremonies or social or religious institutions. Thirdly, various states of spiritual consciousness tend to constitute four psychological traits of personality, which are commonly found universally among all who have gone beyond mental consciousness or who stand on the borderlines of the mental and spiritual consciousness. These psychological traits are connected with those powers of the Spirit, which flower as the sage, as the hero, as a saint and as a servant. And integral spiritual education would aim at the integral personality that combines and synthesises the sage, the hero, the saint and the servant, —the kind of personality that is illustrated so remarkably in the personality of Sri Krishna, who had, as the Gita testifies, both essential knowledge and comprehensive knowledge that marks the culmination of sagehood; he was dynamic and heroic, since he battled from early boyhood and throughout his life for the upholding of justice and unity of people; and he was full of divine love, which has been sung as an immortal theme of harmonious unity, duality and multiplicity; and he readily agreed to serve with consummate skill as the charioteer of his friend and disciple, Arjuna.

III

Underlying the sage is the drive for knowledge, which does not rest merely on the questioning and opinion-making, but which strives for the discovery of the truth and certainty of the truth as also the certainty of comprehensive truth. Orientation towards truthfulness and indefatigable labour and arrival of mastery to live in truthfulness and to gain deeper and deeper knowledge in regard to any subject matter by means of concentration and contemplation, —this entire process, this orientation and this mastery is what may be rightly termed as a process of spiritual education. To arrive at sagehood, to arrive at that quietude and tranquillity and calm and silence and peace in which knowledge can grow spontaneously, — this may be regarded as one of the aims of spiritual education.

Another power of the spirit develops into what may properly be called spiritual heroism. Whereas the sagehood is the culmination of the powers of knowledge, the state of spiritual heroism is a result of the development of the powers of Will. It is often argued that spiritual consciousness encourages withdrawal from action and it leads to world-negation and to the belief in meaninglessness of world and life. It is true that the states of silence and peace point to world-transcendence, since there is something like going beyond all the dynamism of action. But it is not inevitable that world-transcendence must necessarily mean world-negation. Psychologically, knowledge always stands to be superior to Will, but knowledge can also inspire such dynamism of action that Will can never possess, unless it gets rooted in knowledge and gets issued from knowledge. What is the secret, we might ask, of the tremendous potency of action of Buddha that made him the greatest personality that ever walked on the earth? It was his utter silence, a silence that was not blank but that was filled with will and compassion. What is the secret of Christ of going up to the gallows so as to bleed on the cross and manifest that great heroism, which battles for the truth and sacrifices everything for the sake of the entire humanity and prays that his prosecutors be pardoned for they knew not what they were doing? It was that power of the Will, which was rooted in knowledge and in peace that "passeth understanding".

Spiritual heroism involves the practice of the Yogic method of arriving at perfection of action, the path of *Karmayoga*, just as the path to sagehood is the path of knowledge, *jnanayoga*. The methodised effort here involves a great psychological change brought about by three stages, first, of the control and abolition of desire for fruits of action, second, of the control and abolition of the sense of egoistic doership of action, and third, of the mastery that arises from the discovery and the operation of the impersonal and universal will without any hindrance from our subjective egoism or preferences.

The third power of the spirit flowers in sainthood. The state of consciousness that constitutes sainthood is marked by universal goodwill, sympathy and friendliness and harmony that extends to the totality of interrelationships. The methodised yogic effort here involves, first, the awakening of our inmost being that is capable of intense sympathy, compassion, spiritual love and harmony, secondly, of concentration and contemplation of internal communion with the subjective and the objective forces of unity and diversity, and thirdly, of internal union with the highest possible source or sources of love, joy and beauty. Sainthood consists of effortless inspiration to be engaged in works of friendliness, charity and service inspired by compassion.

The fourth power of the Spirit grows into universal spiritual servanthood, which is reached by the combination of the yogic processes that are required for spiritual heroism and sainthood, but it has also a special mode, which insists on the development of *skill*s that are required from the highest level to the lowest level of activity as also the sense of obedience to all that is considered to be issuing from the highest Knowledge, Will and Love. The true servant-hood is scrupulous both in regard to the development and employment of all the skills that are required to accomplish the minutest demands of work; it is this consciousness which is ever vigilant and has spontaneous readiness to execute what is demanded from above; it omits nothing that is to be done, and when the work is done, nothing is found forgotten. To arrive at the state of spiritual servant-hood is the highest glory of spiritual effort and spiritual education.

It will be seen that in attaining various states of spiritual consciousness and various traits or aspects of spiritual personality, various psychological processes, and their scientific handling of materials of Knowledge, Will and Emotion are adequate, and the aid of dogmas, rituals, ceremonies is not indispensable. Thus spiritual education can be so conceived and designed as to be free from those methods and practices, which are uniquely related to religious education.

IV

At the same time, spiritual education need not be averse to what can be called the spiritual core of religions, —the core, which transcends the limitations of doctrines, dogmas, rituals and ceremonies or prescribed acts or specific rules connected with social and other institutions rooted in religious doctrines. Religious education can be distinguished from education about religions, and spiritual education is quite consistent with the study of various doctrines and institutions connected with different religions, biographies of religious founders, a comparative study of religions, sources of their conflict and means and methods by which these conflicts can be resolved. This study should, however, be guided by a wide and strict philosophical discipline, which demands impartiality, rational scrutiny and detailed understanding of the relationship between reason and revelation, reason and dogma, and reason and spiritual means of knowledge such as intuition, inspiration, and discrimination.

Spiritual education will admit those elements of studies in ethics and practice of ethical values, which are not tied down to any particular religion and its exclusive claims. The aid that can be received from ethical education, which deals with purification of the powers of knowledge, will and emotion must be fully welcomed in the programmes of spiritual education. All ethics is fundamentally a process of self-control, and spiritual education will admit all processes of self-control, which are related to self-knowledge and to the development of sage-hood, spiritual heroism, sainthood and spiritual servant-hood. The programme of spiritual education will also encourage the philosophical study of standards of conduct that have developed at various stages of human history and will aim at establishing the clarity of the concepts of Freewill *versus* determinism, of goodwill, of the categorical imperative and others in the attempt to understand how this clarity is a great aid in the practice of ethical values, virtues and austerities that aim at purification, strengthening of will-power and transcending those limitations that lead to the conflict between the rational, ethical and aesthetic.

Spiritual education will have no quarrel with all that is rational and all that is scientific. The insistence on the pursuit of truth that is inherent in rational and scientific education must be welcomed in the processes and methods of spiritual education. True spiritual education will aim at the harmonisation of spiritual knowledge, philosophical knowledge and scientific knowledge; in the ultimate analysis, all knowledge tends to be one or holistic, and liberating oneself from the rigidities of the dogmatic assumptions that hinder the true processes of knowledge, one can arrive at a spontaneous harmony among all studies and practices, which aim at the discovery and practice of impartial search for the truth and a comprehensive truth. Spiritual education will never prohibit but always insist on philosophy and science, their methods, and scrupulous adherence to their specific criteria and to critical and self-critical inquiry into these criteria.

There are three great domains of aesthetics, — music, art and poetry, — which are normally encouraged and promoted among young people. If they are rightly interwoven in our educational system, they can constitute powerful means of spiritual education. In fact, art comes very close to spirituality because both art and spirituality insist on depth of experience. In art, experience of an object leads to the formation of images, and the artist employs various techniques for giving expressions to these images in forms of beauty. Intensity of experience, vision of the truth and its images and harmonious forms of expression so that the substance and style correspond to each other as intensely as possible, — these are the elements of all art. And music and painting and poetry —these three forms of art, when combined together, can become perfect education of the soul. In poetry, the instrument is the rhythmic word, in painting it is the colour and proportion and charm, and in music it is the melody and harmony of sounds. Colour, sound and word are extremely close to the Spirit, and that is the reason why the spiritual sage easily becomes a poet, and the spiritual saint easily becomes a poet-singer and a musician and every spiritual seeker becomes an artist of life and expresses his art of life in various other arts through which harmonious forms of joy and beauty can be expressed. In an ideal system of education, art will be used for spiritual education and spiritual education will be used for promoting artistic expression. Essence of all art is the discovery and expression of *rasa*, and one of the definitions of the Spirit is that it is *rasa* (*raso vai sah*).

Spiritual education will also take great care to train and purify the vital impulses, vital drives, vital emotions, vital desires, vital attractions and longings and vital activities of acquisition, possession, influence and enjoyment. Spiritual education will not kill the dynamism of the vital, but will employ the methods of illumination, love, harmonisation and heroism so that the potency of the vital can act effectively and victoriously. The vital will be purified, trained and perfected, so that the dynamic traits of human personality get their proper treatment of transformation. It will be realised that all that is heroic and noble, great and powerful but which is still raw or unripe or mixed will be purified but not discouraged, will be heightened and perfected but not blunted or impoverished. Spiritual education will not aim at weakness but at strength, not at escape from action but at mastery of action.

Just as mental and vital education can form part of spiritual education, even so, physical education, too, can be so conceived and practiced that it forms part of spiritual education. First is the question of attitude towards the body. There are those who consider the body to be the tomb of the spirit, but the right understanding of the body will show that the body is the indispensable instrument of the practice of every ideal. *Shariram adyam khalu dharmasādhanam* – this is how the Sanskrit adage lays down. Secondly, the values of physical education are perfectly harmonious with the totality of values of vital, mental and spiritual education. One great value of physical education is that of health, and it is very well known that good health of the body is indispensable for the integral health of the entire being. Yogic methods of pranayama and *āsanas* clearly indicate how the physical and spiritual are interrelated, and in India we have elaborate science of the relationship between the gross body and the subtle body as also of the centres or charkas of subtle body, the opening of which is essential for the fullness or perfection of the body, life and mind as also of spiritual realisation and manifestation. The recent discoveries of the powers that lie embedded in the organic cell of the body are amazing, and it has been found that the spiritual and supramental powers, when captured by the cells of the body, can effect even the mutation of the human body. It is with this high aim that the possibilities of physical education that our educational system should provide full facilities for the perfection of the human body. For that perfection can be a vehicle of the highest possible spiritual manifestation.

It may be remarked that spiritual states of consciousness can be obtained only when the capacities of the body, life and mind are first maximised and purified, and these capacities can again be perfected when the powers of spiritual states of consciousness can, by their descent, penetrate into them and spiritualise them. The total programme of spiritual education is, therefore, a very long one, and it should be undertaken as a life-long programme. But for that very reason, it can suitably commence as early as possible. An appropriate programme needs to be chalked out.

V

Three principles characterise the programme of spiritual education, which necessarily includes education of the body, life and mind. First, there is insistence on the pursuit of truth, — truth as it is and not as one would like it to be; and this pursuit demands a high degree of rigor and scrupulous care, which discourages hasty arrival at conclusions, exaggerations of claims, and disregard for patient processes, which are required for verification. Particularly, in matters connected with the development of higher faculties, one needs to learn how to avoid wishful thinking and clouding of clarity and sincerity. Haphazard experiences and sporadic experimentations with truth lead to disbalancement and avoidable pitfalls into error and misjudgement. In all scientific inquiries, these difficulties present themselves, and where spiritual education enters into the field, one has to be more scientific than the current sciences demand of the scientist; for current sciences deal with objective facts, whereas spiritual processes involve both objective and subjective facts. This is the reason why spiritual education should constantly be surcharged with relentless patience, perseverance and unfailing discrimination between appearance and reality, as also between darkness, confusion and light. *Asato ma sadgamaya, tamaso ma jyotirgamaya, mrityor ma amritam gamaya* – these three great aspirations should pervade the atmosphere of educational processes as they did in the Upanishadic times.

The second characteristic follows from the first, and that is the cultivation of the spirit of harmony between the teacher and the pupil, between educational administrators and all the partners of education. Spiritual education demands right attitudes among teachers and pupils. Spiritual education is totally child-centred, and this child-centredness is so great that the teachers should expect to interweave their own outer and internal progress with the outer and internal progress of the children entrusted to their care. The teachers have always to be ready to uplift children's enthusiasm to inquire, to question and to explore and experiment in regard to various processes of learning; teachers cannot afford to be taskmasters and create revolt in the minds and hearts of the children; teachers have to realise that they have no external authority, and the only authority that they have issues from their intense care to develop their own purity and their own increasing expansion and mastery over knowledge; the relationship between teachers and pupils should reflect the interrelationship between inspirations from teachers and aspirations from pupils. Only on that basis harmonious teaching-learning processes can be assured. In the ultimate analysis, teachers will have to be themselves children leading other children.

Harmony depends upon goodwill from oneself and goodwill from others. Among teachers themselves, there has to be the reign of mutuality of goodwill; and similarly, educational administrators have to realise that if there is one place where administrators are real servants and not masters, it is in the field of education; and an educational administrator has to promote educational aims and ideals, and this can be done only where there is a good deal of consultation and absence of arbitrary decision-making. Administrators have to ensure that all support that is needed for a smooth functioning of the educational processes will be forthcoming, and they will act as promoters of goodwill among the parents of children, management, pupils and teachers.

All this demands *tapasyā*, an austerity that aims at friendliness, right types of exchange and mutuality, co-operation and an inner sense of fraternity.

The third characteristic is that of liberty. If there is one field where freedom must rule without any abridgement, it is in the flowering of the spiritual consciousness; spiritual development cannot be brought about by compulsion; all that is desirable should be voluntarily accepted or voluntarily self-imposed. It is for the teachers to create such conducive conditions that all that is desirable comes to be valued among pupils as also in the general atmosphere. Even if something is to be compulsory, under certain circumstances, that compulsion fades away as soon as possible, and it becomes interwoven in the process of self-discipline. Problems of conflict between liberty and discipline often arise, but the solutions depend upon how discipline is enforced, not by external means, but by internal adhesion on the part of all the concerned. Discipline is best when it is self-discipline and when it is the child of freedom. It is only when the child comes to accept a process of discipline that the teacher has the right to demand from the child unwavering adherence to discipline, whenever there is deviation from discipline out of unjustifiable relaxation or idleness or a whim of momentary defiance or negligence. No education and much less spiritual education can be perfected without discipline, just as even in the functioning of the physical body, every part and every organ has to function with the perfect sense of discipline and co-ordination. In the very atmosphere of the educational process, there must be an overriding sense of self-imposed discipline and it must be the responsibility of everyone to adhere to what is accepted as a part of discipline. Absence of compulsion, minimum of rules and overriding self-discipline coupled with a freedom of choice given to every individual to pursue his or her own lines of inquiry, pace of progress and direction of progress, — a combination of these elements would lead to the resolution of problems that are bound to arise when the entire education process is to vibrate with freedom, joy, creativity and happiness that comes from constant progress.

It is mistakenly thought that spiritual education should be pursued, if at all, only at advanced levels of education. Actually, a study of child's psychology indicates that children are, in many ways, budding angels; with their innocence, unpretentious sincerity, ready obedience and their sense of trust and confidence in all those who can deal with them with love and encouragement, children are often morally and spiritually superior to the adults. A number of children respond splendidly to truth, beauty and goodness, and if they receive the right encouragement in the right manner, the formation of the character can greatly be imprinted with orientation towards these great values. These values are imbibed by children, not so much by lectures as by encouragement that they receive from their teachers and parents. A good story, — long or short, — if told at the right moment can make a tremendous impact, which cannot be wiped out throughout the entire life, and it continues to inspire the right action even in times of crisis and under heavy pressures of temptations.

VI

Three remarks may, however, be made which relate to the question as to how spiritual education can be introduced in our present system of education and what reforms in the present system would be necessary, if we are to make spiritual education an effective instrument of the aims that we have in view, — particularly in regard to turning our system into a genuine system, as an instrument of enhancing the global effort to meet the challenges of the contemporary crisis, and as an aid to the fulfillment of the idea and practice of integral education.

❖ It may be recalled that all major Reports on education, Commissions and Committees have acknowledged and underlined the theme of value-education, and even of moral and spiritual education. Dr. Radhakrishnan had recommended a series of measures by which moral education can be a preparation for the spiritual education; he had also recommended the need to provide for study of different religions. He had stressed the importance of the spiritual state of silence and made recommendations as to how this state of consciousness can be promoted. The Kothari Commission Report had also emphasised the need to synthesise science and spirituality and even brought out the truth of the ancient Indian ideal, which spoke of true knowledge as that which leads to spiritual liberation, — *sa vidya ya vimuktaye*. Shri Prakasa Committee had given detailed recommendations in respect of moral and spiritual education. Value-education came to the forefront during the 70s and 80s, and there was also a report on imparting value-orientation to teachers' training programmes. The National Education Policy – 1986 had one full chapter on value education and had underlined the need to foster eternal values and values embedded in Indian culture through the entire educational programme in the country. The duties of citizens as laid down in the Constitution include the promotion of Indian heritage, which implies the study of Indian spirituality. With all these enabling factors, there should be no great difficulty to propose and implement spiritual education.

There are, however, those who maintain that the mind is the highest faculty of the human being; that the limitations of mental consciousness can never be broken, and that there is no such thing as spirituality or that there are no spiritual states of consciousness. But this contention is now as outmoded as the contention that anybody unacquainted with modern developments of Physics may hold out that the atom is the last limit of unimaginable outburst of energy. There are also those who feel that spiritual education will foster communalism; but this is only a superstition. In reality, communalism can rightly be combated only if we can foster universality and unity, — which in the ultimate analysis can be accomplished through spiritual education. The greatest antidote to communalism, we might affirm, is spiritual education. There are, however, those who maintain that the ideals of spiritual education cannot be made practicable in our present system of education. Here, it may be acknowledged that since the present system of education was primarily designed to manufacture clerks, and since this system has changed only slightly since the advent of the British, and even after their departure, it is but natural that such a sublime theme as spiritual education may not find place in that so-called Indian system of Education.

❖ But – and this is the second remark – if we are to introduce spiritual education, three things will have to be undertaken: firstly, we have to change the present system of teachers' training so radically that every teacher under training receives education for integral development of personality, which will, by implication, include the overarching programme of spiritual education; (ii) the present lecture-oriented, book-oriented, syllabus-oriented, and examination-oriented system will have to be replaced by child-centred and youth-centred education that will employ dynamic methods of exploration, experimentation, practice of values and those processes, which will lead to the fostering of spiritual states of consciousness and powers; and (iii) we shall have to institute widespread education of parents and other partners of education so that the theme of spiritual education finds full support of the people.

None of these things is impracticable or impossible, but we cannot minimise the difficulties involved in these tasks. It must, however, be emphasised that because the tasks are difficult, we tend to find excuses to escape from these difficulties. But difficulties have to be overcome, and we must chalk out a programme of overcoming these difficulties and implement that programme with perseverance and without any depressing or cynical thought.

And this brings us to the third remark. Our state, whether in the country or in the world, presents us a powerful confrontation between the best possibilities and the worst possibilities; it is a battle being fought at a critical point, and if we do not act, we shall automatically be registering ourselves as members of the army of those who are working for the realisation of the worst possibilities; if, however, we make a choice and join the army of those who are working for the realisation of the best possibilities, we can be sure that we shall have done the right thing and that, irrespective of immediate results, we shall have enhanced the power of that force which is best for our country and the world. To work for spiritual education is to my mind, to join the army, however small it may be, that holds out the promise of the eventual fulfilment of humanity.

YOGA AND EDUCATION

I. The Meaning of Education and Yoga

There is at present a need to clarify the meaning and aim of Education, just as it is necessary to clarify the meaning and aim of Yoga. Yoga is often identified exclusively with Hatha Yoga and thus its true psycho-logical nature remains quite veiled. Similarly, Education is often identified with vocational training or with some kind of mental culture, but its fundamental nature of integral psychological process remains quite veiled.

"Yoga", as Swami Vivekananda has said, "may be regarded as a means of compressing one's evolution into a single life or a few months or even a few hours of bodily existence." And, Education too, when rightly understood, would mean a rapid psychological process towards perfection. Education is a search for knowledge, and it is a search for values. It is also an uncovering of the layers of faculties, cultivation of them and perfection of them. It is a process of the discovery of the self, and it aims at a true self-knowledge, which gives liberation from ego and imperfections. *Sa vidya ya vimuktaye.* Education is a search for that knowledge which would fulfil oneself individually and as a harmonious member of the universe. But this is also the meaning of Yoga. By Yoga, says Sri Aurobindo, "We mean ... a methodised effort towards self-perfection by the expression of the potentialities latent in the being and a union of the human individual with the universal and transcendent existence we see partially expressed in man and in the cosmos."

In the right view of Yoga and of Education, we find, Education and Yoga are one and identical process.

II
The need for Research in Yoga for Purposes of New Education

In our own times, there is a crisis in the field of knowledge. With the advancement of Science, there has come about an accelerated process of accumulation of knowledge of Facts and also the manipulation of Facts. But it has also come to be realised that Science cannot give the knowledge of Values. And yet, it is increasingly felt that the knowledge of Values is even more important than the knowledge of Facts. How then to attain the knowledge of Values?

Moreover, mere knowledge of Values is not sufficient. In Education, we would like to develop those methods by which values would spontaneously grow and manifest among those who are being educated. What are then the best methods by which students can be so trained as to enable them to embody the highest Values?

Yoga is the answer to these questions. Yoga gives the knowledge of Values and the methods of embodying Values. But it should be stressed that Yoga is neither religion, nor morality, nor philosophy. Its attitude and method are entirely scientific. Yoga aims at a direct contact, verifiable experience and union with the Supreme Value.

It is noteworthy that the logic of modern experiments in educational methodology seems to point to the need of a yogic orientation in education. The ideas of individual differentiation, the stress on multiple methods of teaching for different categories of students, recognition of the phenomena of genius, insistence on the development of the latent faculties of the child, emphasis on creativity and on an integral development of personality, and an ardent attempt at implementing the idea of freedom and that of consulting the child in his own development – these have created a new atmosphere perfectly ready for a plunge in the direction where the truths of Yoga will be found increasingly relevant.

But in the past, Yoga has largely been and more particularly so in the middle past, life-negating. On the other hand, modern education is science-based; and in science and technology, there is the affirmation of Life and of Life in Matter. Science-based education is thus life-affirming education. If, therefore, Yoga is to be relevant to modern education, it will have to cease to be life-negating. A life-affirming Yoga is a necessity, and a research in this Yoga is centrally relevant to the solution of the modern problems of education.

It is also important to note that Education Commission Report have directed that education in India should be science-based and yet in coherence with the spiritual values. Indeed, if this recommendation is to be implemented, the research in Yoga which reconciles Spirit and Matter is indispensable.

Indeed, there has been a good deal of research in Yoga since a number of decades in the wake of the Renaissance in India, and a good deal of experimentation has been attempted to relate this research to the problems of education. It is in the light of this research and experimentation that we can make a few suggestions that would be useful in arriving at a new yogic basis of education and the way in which Yoga can permeate the entire spirit of education and even in the actual processes of education.

III
New Education in the Light of Recent Research in Yoga

Yoga and yogic research affirm that there are principles and means by which there can be achieved a greater perfection of the body, life and mind than can ordinarily be conceived or imagined. It is also affirmed that there are great hidden faculties and powers which can be awakened by a methodised effort. Finally, there is a supreme affirmation that there are great psychological superconscient states and powers which are central to the creative and integral perfection of personality.

But a mere learning about Yoga is not Yoga, and even the most catholic book on Yoga cannot be a substitute for the direct yogic practice. Nor can Yoga be practised in a casual way or only as a part-time preoccupation. Yoga to bc properly practised must be taken up as a sovereign and central occupation and it must govern and permeate every aspect of life and its activity. Yogic research affirms that there is no aspect of life or knowledge which cannot be dealt with by Yoga and that therefore there is no need to make a gulf between Yoga and Life, between yogic knowledge and mundane knowledge.

All disciplines of knowledge can in this view be made the vehicles of yogic knowledge. In the words of Sri Aurobindo:

> The Yogin's aim in the sciences that make for knowledge should be to discover and understand the workings of the Divine Consci-

ousness-Puissance in man and creatures and things and forces, her creative significances, her execution of mysteries, the symbols in which she arranges the manifestation. The Yogin's aim in the practical sciences, whether mental and physical or occult and psychic, should be to enter into the ways of the Divine and his processes, to know the materials and means for the work given to us so that we may use that knowledge for a conscious and faultless expression of the spirit's mastery, joy and self-fulfilment. The Yogin's aim in the Arts should not be a mere aesthetic, mental or vital gratification, but, seeing the Divine everywhere, worshipping it with a revelation of the meaning of its works, to express that One Divine in gods and men and creatures and objects. The theory that sees an intimate connection between religious aspiration and the truest Art is in essence right; but we must substitute for the mixed and doubtful religious motive a spiritual aspiration, vision, interpreting experience. For the wider and more comprehensive the seeing, the more it contains in itself the sense of the hidden Divine in humanity and in all things and rises beyond a superficial religiosity into the spiritual life, the more luminous, flexible, deep and powerful will the Art be that springs from the high motive.

In the light of life-affirming Yoga, life is meaningful, and life itself could be so organised as to serve as a natural means of education. Also, a complete yogic education is a life-long process, and yet, in so far as it truly gives a meaning to the life-development, it must determine the entire process of the education of the child and the youth. The secret of this life-long education is a constant aspiration for progress and perfection, a thirst for progress, and a zeal, *utsāha*, for self-perfection should govern the rhythm and law of self-development. To progress constantly is to remain young perpetually, and constant progress comes by perpetual education.

To limit the hours of education during the day and during the year, to organise education on the idea of finishing it one day, to bifurcate education in curricular and extra-curricular courses, to regard studies as work and games as a mere play and pastime, to give exclusive value to reading, writing, reasoning and eloquence and to regard all else as secondary or a mere decoration, -- these tendencies are inimical to the conception of all life as education, and all education as Yoga.

Yoga is essentially a creative process of the flowering of personality, and yogic research gives us the secret of the perfection and integration of personality. In recent times, a stress is being laid on education for an all-round personality. There has come about a recognition that there are in us various personalities, conflicting personalities, and thus conflicting potentialities of our profession. It has been pointed out that this entire domain of the secrets of the growth of personality has remained ignored, and the consequences are that most of us possess smothered personalities, and most often we are engaged in the work that has no correspondence with our real genius, with our inner delight of existence. Most of us live in deep suffering, alienated from ourselves. It is this inner suffering that causes ageing, and even in our youth we feel so often old and worn out. These are indeed excellent ideas and they will have a valuable place in the New Education. But yogic research takes us to a still deeper perception. It fathoms into the secret of the true person behind all personalities and discovers there the real power of healing our conflicts and integrating the fullness of all personalities. This is a deep and precious Wisdom, the true self-knowledge of self-perfection, which reveals that the secret of perpetual youth is not a mere progression, but a deeper *art* of progression, namely, the constant harmonisation of our outer work and circumstances with the inner needs of the manifestation of the powers of the real Person seated deep within us.

It is this secret of eternal youth that will be the inner soul of the New Education.

The deepest yogic research affirms that:

There is a Supreme Reality that is constantly at work; it does not impose itself upon us, but manifests more and more effectively as we aspire to know it and to work for its manifestation.

It is this aspiration that must be lit in the temple of our hearts; and if it is lit and continues to burn, then, we are assured, we shall arrive.

A thousand-rayed sun of solid mass of knowledge illuminating, by an incessant downpour of its sheer lustre, the universal skies and the hidden and distant secrets of Matter, a most potent drive of energy and action, and an irresistible bursting forth of love, joy and marvellous forms of beauty – these are the new ideals which result from the recent yogic research, and which, if accepted, would infuse a new spirit in education.

IV
A Syllabus of Yoga

If all life is education, and if all education is Yoga, how shall we make and propose a programme of the study and practice of Yoga?

In a sense, there cannot be a formal syllabus of Yoga, which is a highly creative process, and which is to be the central and all-permeating thread of all processes of education right from the earliest stages.

And yet, Yoga is a Shastra, a Science, and it is possible to study it and practise it with all the rigour and discipline of a scientist.

The recent research in yogic education promises to give us some help in formulating, not a rigid or flexible programme of Yoga, but certain broad hints so as to guide the entire educational process on yogic lines as well as to provide for a specialised study of Yoga.

What is attempted below is only in the form of a tentative formulation – a very brief one.

The following practical hints that result from the application of yogic methods of psychological development are suggested:

- ❖ It may first be noted that a good many children are under the influence of the inner psychic presence which shows itself very distinctly at times in their spontaneous reactions and even in their words. All spontaneous turning to love, truth, beauty, knowledge, nobility, heroism is a sure sign of the psychic influence.

❖ To recognise these reactions and to encourage them wisely and with a psychic feeling would be the first indispensable step.

❖ The best qualities to develop in children are:
>   Sincerity
>   Honesty
>   Straightforwardness
>   Cheerfulness
>   Courage
>   Disinterestedness
>   Patience
>   Endurance
>   Perseverance
>   Peace
>   Calm
>   Self-control
>   Self-mastery
>   Truth
>   Harmony
>   Liberty

❖ These qualities are taught infinitely better by example than by speeches.

❖ The undesirable impulses and habits should not be treated harshly. The child should not be scolded. Particularly, care should be take-n not to rebuke a child for a fault which one commits oneself. Children are very keen and clear-sighted observers; they soon find out the educator's weaknesses and note them without pity.

❖ When a child makes a mistake, one must see that he confesses it to the teacher or the guardian spontaneously and frankly; and when he has confessed it he should be made to understand with kindness and affection what was wrong in the movement and that he should not repeat it. A fault confessed must be forgiven.

* The child should be encouraged to think of wrong impulses not as sins or offences but as symptoms of a curable disease alterable by a steady and a sustained effort of the will – falsehood being rejected and replaced by truth, fear by courage, selfishness by sacrifice and renunciation, malice by love.

* A great care should be taken to see that unformed virtues are not rejected as faults. The wildness and recklessness of many young natures are only the overflowing of an excessive strength, greatness and nobility. They should be purified, not discouraged.

* An affection that is firm yet gentle sees clearly, and a sufficiently practical knowledge will create bonds of trust that are indispensable for the educator to make the education of a child effective.

* When a child asks a question, he should not be answered by saying that it is stupid or foolish, or that the answer will not be understood by him. Curiosity cannot be postponed, and an effort must be made to answer questions truthfully and in such a way as to make the answer comprehensible to his mental capacity.

* The teacher should ensure that the child gradually begins to be aware of the psychological centre of his being, the psychic being, the seat within of the highest truth of our existence.

- With this growing awareness, the child should be taught to concentrate on this presence and make it more and more a living fact.

- The child should be taught that whenever there is an inner uneasiness, he should not pass it off and try to forget it, but should attend to it, and try to find out by an inner observation the cause of the uneasiness, so that it can be removed by inner or other methods.

- It should be emphasised that if one has a sincere and steady aspiration, a persistent and dynamic will, one is sure to meet in one way or another, externally by study and instruction, internally by concentration, revelation or experience, the help one needs to reach the goal. Only one thing is absolutely indispensable; the will to discover and realise. This discovery and this realisation should be the primary occupation of the being, the pearl of great price which one should acquire at any cost. Whatever one does, whatever one's occupation and activity, the will to find the truth of one's being and to unite with it must always be living, always present behind all one does, all that one thinks, all that one experiences.

All the above suggestions are to be implemented from day to day under various circumstances and in the context of living problems of the growth of children.

The role of the teacher is to put the child upon the right road to his own perfection and encourage him to follow it, watching, suggesting, helping, but not imposing or interfering. The best method of suggestion is by personal example, daily conversation and books read from day to day.

These books should contain, for the younger student, the lofty examples of the past, given not as moral lessons but as things of supreme human interest, and for the older student, great thoughts of great souls, passage of literature, which set fire to the highest emotions and prompt the highest ideals and aspirations, records of history and biography which exemplify the living of those great thoughts, noble emotions and inspiring ideals.

Opportunities should be given to the students of embodying in actions the deeper and nobler impulses which rise within them.

An informal but profound study of the following questions would prove to be of immense value:

i. What is Action? How does it operate normally? Can Action be controlled and guided? How can one achieve the maximum effectivity and largest scope of action?

ii. To whom should I belong? What does it mean to belong to the Divine? How can one belong to the Divine?

iii. What is the purpose of the human body? What are the means by which the perfection of the body can be achieved?

iv. What are the highest means of Knowledge? The Upanishads declare that there is Something, which being known, everything is known. What is that Something? And how can that be known?

v. What is the nature of the Mind? How does it operate in (a) Scientific thinking, (b) Mathematical thinking, and (c) Philosophical thinking? How to transcend Thought?

vi. What is the nature of Yoga? What is the relation of Yoga with Psychology, Science, Philosophy, Religion, Occultism, Art, Music, Literature, Technology and Life?

vii. How can we arrive at an artistic and creative experience?
What is the essence of Music?
What is the essence of Art?
What is the essence of Literature?

viii. What is the indispensable utility of Technology in the human life and its perfection?

ix. What is the meaning of "Story"?
Is history an interesting and meaningful story?
Is there an aim in history?

x. What is my own specific role in the world-progress? How can I train myself to fulfil this role?

The above question can be studied in the context of the following and allied topics:
- ❖ The Human Aspiration
- ❖ The Methods of Knowledge
- ❖ Evolution
- ❖ What is Time?
- ❖ The Destiny of the Individual
- ❖ Infinity and Eternity
- ❖ Mind, Life and Matter

- In Search of the Soul
- Death and Conquest of Death
- Personal Effort
- The Meaning of Prayer
- The Supreme Teacher
- Varieties of Mystical Experience
- The Law of Sacrifice
- The Concept of *Lokasangraha*.
- What is Concentration? How to practise it?
- The Difference between Religion and Yoga
- Occultism – the Science of the Subliminal.
- What is Philosophy?
- Scientific Method
- Limitations of Science and Philosophy
- Is Mathematics Knowledge?
- Beauty of Nature
- Beauty of Poetry, Art, Music
- Six Limbs of Indian Art
- Yoga and Art
- The Secret Meaning of the Legends of the Veda
- Stories of the Upanishads and their Yogic Import
- Evolution and the idea of the Avatar
- The Great Greeks and Romans
- Augustus and World-Unity
- Puranas and Tantras
- The Bhakti Age of India
- Renaissance and Leonardo da Vinci
- Ideal of Liberty, Equality, Fraternity: A Call to Yoga in World-Action
- Ideal of Nationalism and Internationalism
- The Place of Yoga in India's Role for the New Future
- Has Man made Progress?
- What is the Meaning of Evolutionary Crisis of Man?
- The Role of Yoga for the Evolution of the Divine Superman.

Care should be taken to see that the above mentioned questions and topics do not get compressed within a rigid framework of a formal study and examination. These are all living questions and the only thing that can be done is to see that they arise spontaneously during the educational process, and the courses of study regarding them develop in an evolutionary way, developing with the inner growth of the students. It is best when these questions arise in the context of the living experiences of the students.

The handling of these questions and topics should be informal and the following methods can be suggested:

1. Each student should be free to choose the topics of the above study in accordance with his need of a deep inquiry;
2. Students should study these questions individually with a possibility of consultation with their teachers when needed;
3. To enable individual study, special worksheets on these questions should be prepared; these worksheets should be so designed that each student can study them individually at his own pace of progress;
4. Informal talks on these questions can be arranged, but they should not take the form of any moral or religious preaching; the temper of these studies should be scientific and profound;
5. There should be a room of Silence in every school and college, and students should be free to go to the Silence Room whenever they wish to have an inner reflection, meditation or quiet study;
6. Seminars on the above questions and topics should be held periodically in the schools and colleges and

the students and teachers should be encouraged to participate in them;
7. Debates too can be organised relating to these questions and topics, but an attempt should be made at the end of every debate to synthesise various points of view; an idea must develop that behind every point of view there is some truth, and we should grow into a comprehensive vision in which all truths can be reconciled and synthesised, and in which all conflicts of views can be transcended;
8. Artistic pictures and sculptural pieces relating to these questions and topics should be displayed prominently not only in schools and colleges, but everywhere in towns, villages, etc.;
9. Other media of communication should also be widely used for this purpose. In particular, films on these subjects should be produced and made easily available to students and teachers;
10. Informality in instruction, joy in learning, utter dedication and strictness in training, and widest comprehension in student-teacher relationship – these will, in brief govern the methods of learning.

There are aspects of the mental, vital and physical education which contribute to the yogic education.

They can be briefly mentioned:

(i) In its natural state the human mind is always limited in its vision, narrow in its understanding, rigid in its conceptions, and a certain effort is needed to enlarge it, make it supple and deep. Hence, it is very necessary to develop in the child the inclination and capacity to consider everything from as many points of view as possible. There is an exercise in this connection which gives greater suppleness and elevation to thought. It is as follows. A clearly formulated thesis is set; against it is opposed the antithesis, formulated with the same precision. Then by careful reflection the problem must be widened or transcended so that a synthesis is found which unites the two contraries in a larger, higher and more comprehensive idea.

Another exercise is to control the mind form judging things and people. For true knowledge belongs to a region much higher than that of the human mind, even beyond that of pure ideas. The mind has got to be made silent and attentive in order to receive knowledge from above and manifest it.

Still another exercise: whenever there is a disagreement on any matter, as a decision to take, or an action to accomplish, one must not stick to one's own conception or point of view. On the contrary, one must try to understand the other person's point of view, put oneself in his place and, instead of quarrelling or even fighting, find out a solution which can reasonably satisfy both parties; there is always one for men of goodwill.

A wide, subtle, rich, complex, attentive and quiet and silent mind is an asset not only for the discovery of the psychic and spiritual realities, but also for manifesting the psychic and spiritual truths and powers.

(ii)The vital being in us is the seat of impulses and desires, of enthusiasm and violence, of dynamic energy and desperate depression, of passions and revolt. The vital is a good worker, but most often it seeks its own satisfaction. If that is refused totally or even partially, it gets vexed, sulky and goes on strike.

An exercise at these moments is to remain quiet and refuse to act. For it is important to realise that at such times one does stupid things and in a few minutes can destroy or spoil what one has gained in months of regular effort, losing thus all the progress made.

Another exercise is to deal with the vital as one deals with a child in revolt, with patience and perseverance showing it the truth and light, endeavouring to convince it and awaken in it the goodwill which for a moment was veiled.

A wide, strong, calm but dynamic vital capable of right emotion, right decision, and right execution by force and energy, is an invaluable aid to the psychic and spiritual realisation.

(iii) The body by its nature is a docile and faithful instrument. But it is very often misused by the mind with its dogmas, its rigid and arbitrary principles, and by the vital with its passions, its excesses and dissipations. It is these which are the cause of bodily fatigue, exhaustion and disease. The body must therefore be free from the tyranny of the mind and of the vital; and this can be done by training the body to feel and sense the psychic presence within and to learn to obey its governance. The emphasis on the development of strength, suppleness, calm, quiet, poise, grace and beauty in physical education, whether done by Yogic Asanas or by other methods of physical culture, such as games and sports, or Japanese Judo and similar exercises, will ensure the contact of the body with the psychic centre and the body will learn to put forth at every minute the effort that is demanded of it, for it will have learnt to find rest in action, to replace through contact with universal forces the energies it spends consciously and usefully. By this sound and balanced life a new harmony will manifest in the body, reflecting the harmony of the regions which will give it the perfect proportions and the ideal beauty of form. It will then be in a constant process of transformation, and it will be possible for it to escape the necessity of disintegration and destruction.

At a certain stage of development, when the seeking of the student is found to be maturing, he can be directed more and more centrally to the inner heart of Yoga and yogic discoveries and experiences.

One of the great aids in the practice of Yoga is a knowledge of the Shastra of Yoga, the knowledge of the truths, principles, powers and processes that govern the yogic realisation and perfection.

An outline idea of the broad principles and stages of Yoga, which can be useful for any student who is generally interested in Yoga is suggested below:

> Psychology and Yoga as Applied Psychology
> Psychology of Nature, Psychology of Life
> Life and Yoga
> Systems of Yoga: Hatha Yoga, Rāja Yoga, Jñāna Yoga, Karma Yoga, Bhakti Yoga, Tantra Yoga, the Synthesis of Yoga
> Analysis of Personality;

Parts of the Being; Inconscient, sub-conscient, physical, vital, mental, subliminal, psychic, superconscient

- ❖ Ego, Memory, Self-consciousness, Concept of dynamic nature of Prakriti and static Purusha
- ❖ The Jivatman and Psychic Entity, Psychic Being and its character, growth, development, fulfilment
- ❖ Psychic and Spiritual personality

- ❖ Soul-Powers and Fourfold personality of Knowledge, Power, Love and Skill
- ❖ Integral Personality
- ❖ Fundamental Experiences of the Yogi
- ❖ Experiences of the Witness Self, Cosmic Consciousness, Silent Self, Nirvana, Personal Divine, Supramental Consciousness and Power
- ❖ Yoga in the Veda, Upanishads, the Bhagavadgita, the Yoga Sutra, Yoga and Yogic Research; New Paths of Yoga
- ❖ Yoga and Knowledge of Sciences and Arts,
- ❖ Yoga and Medical Sciences, Yoga and Technology
- ❖ Yoga, Religion and Morality, Yoga and Collective Life, Yoga and change in the world-conditions: the idea of Cosmic Yoga, Yoga and the New World of Truth, Harmony and Liberty

Books recommended:
   The Principal Upanishads
   Yoga Sutra
   Collected Works of Swami Vivekananda
   The Bhagavadgita
   The Synthesis of Yoga by Sri Aurobindo
   Collected Works of Nolini Kanta Gupta

In addition to the above, the following may be suggested for those who are more deeply interested in the study of Yoga, leading up to a specialisation in this study:

I. **Schools of Psychology:**
   Funtionalism, Structural-ism, Gestalt Psychology, Behaviourism, Psycho-analysis, Analytical Psychology, Hormic Psychology, Personalism, Social Psychology.

Psychology and Yoga: Indian Schools of Psychology and Yoga. Higher Reaches of Yoga and Psychological knowledge.

Detailed Study of the Systems of Yoga: Hatha Yoga, Rāja Yoga, Karma Yoga, Jñāna Yoga, Bhakti Yoga, Yoga of Tantra, Kundalini Yoga, Synthesis of Yoga.

Knowledge, Understanding, Concentration, Meditation, Contemplation, Purification, Renunciation, Yama, Niyama, Asana, Pranayama, Pratyahara, Dharana, Dhyana, Samadhi:Savikalpa and Nirvikalpa, Release from the identification with the Body, Heart, Mind and Ego, Realisation of Sachchidananda, Supermind

Self-consecration in Works, Gita's way of Self-surrender, The yogic meaning of Sacrifice, The ascending stages of Sacrifice, Standards of Moral Conduct and Spiritual Freedom, The Divine Work, Supermind and the Yoga of Divine Works

Emotions and Devotion, Aspiration and Prayer, The Divine Love and Grace, The Divine Personality. The Delight of the Divine Love, Ecstasy and Union with the Divine

Self-Perfection, Instruments of the Spirit and their purification, Psychology of Self-Perfection, Perfection of Personality by Yoga, Supermind, its descent and its action upon the earth, Supermind and Collective life, Divine life on the earth

II. **Yoga and Health:**
Psychology, Yoga and Health
Esoteric Causes of Illness and Yogic Remedies

Role of Hypnotism and allied Processes of Cure: Uses and Misuses
Dangers of Psychoanalysis, Radical Difference between Psychoanalysis and Yoga
Integral Education for Integral Health
Yogic Care of the Body
Higher States of Consciousness and their power over the body's functions

III. **Physical Transformation by the Methods of Integral Yoga:**
   i. What is Death?
   ii. The Structure of the Body and the Problems of the inevitability of Death
   iii. Causes of the Resistance of Matter
   iv. Possibilities of the Radical Change in the Structure of the Body and the elimination of the necessity of Death
   v. The concept of *Ichchhamrityu*
   vi. The possibility of a new stuff of Matter for a Transformed Body
   vii. Perfection of the Body
   viii. The Functions of the *Chakras* and their Mastery for the perfection of the Body
   ix. The Powers of the Supermind and their operation on the Physical for its transformation
   x. The Divine Body
   xi. Intermediary Bodies as a preparation for the Divine Body
   xii. Projection of the Divine Body (without the intervention of animal means)

IV. **Yoga and Evolution:**
   i. The Modern Theory of Evolution, Indian Theory of Evolution: Samkhya, Vedanta,

	Integral Theory, Psycholgoical basis of Evolution
ii.	The Origin of species from the standpoint of Yoga
iii.	Yoga as a means of Mutation of the Human Species
iv.	Evolution by means of Yogic Transformation: Psychic Transformation, Spiritual Transformation, Supramental Transformation
v.	Conditions of the advent of the Supramental Being

V. **Yoga and Collective Life:**
Collective Aspiration: Its Necessity for General Health and Perfection;
Formation of the Collective Aspiration at various Psychological levels;
The formation of the Group soul by yogic aspiration and methods: Its necessity and purpose;
Problems of Collective Life and Yogic Solutions
Transformation by Yoga and its rationale as a collective achievement for the earth-life.

VI. **Yoga and Education:**
Education and Life;
Life and Yoga;
Yoga and its distinction from Morality and Religion;
Yoga and the methods of learning: Learning by doing, learning by concentration, learning by purification, learning by creativity;
Yoga and the search for meaning and unity of Knowledge
Yoga and life-long education and perpetual youth;
Yoga and the mental education, vital education, physical education;

Yoga and development of latent faculties and powers;
Yoga and development of spiritual experiences;
Yoga and education for values;
Methods of education, content of education and structure of educational organisation in the light of Yoga;
Yoga and education for self-perfection.

A Special Note on Yoga and Physical Education

Although Yoga is not identical with physical culture or the system of Asanas and Pranayama, a perfection of physical culture is a part of the total perfection that is achieved by the Integral Yoga.

The perfection of the body is primarily a question of the application of consciousness and powers of consciousness on the functions of the body. Given this basic assumption, the different systems of physical culture, eastern or western, can be found to be useful aids. Kundalini's awakening which is supposed to be the result of the Indian system of Asanas, can also be achieved by the systems of western physical culture, including games and sports.

In India, physical education has been neglected almost completely and this neglect is one of the causes of the low morale of the people. It is, therefore, necessary to bring forth the value of physical education not only for the fitness of the body but also for the great contribution it makes for the intellectual, moral and yogic development of personality.

It has been found necessary by recent research in yogic education that students should develop a high sense of physical culture and a bodily need of daily physical exercise. Our programmes in schools and colleges should be so organised that everyday a student is able to devote at least one hour for physical education, either in the form of Yogic Asanas and allied exercises or in the form of gymnastics, athletics, aquatics or games.

There are many sports which help to form and necessitate the qualities of courage, hardihood, energetic action and initiative for skill, steadiness of will or rapid decision and action, the perception of what is to be done in an emergency and dexterity in doing it. Another invaluable result of these activities is the growth of the sporting spirit. That includes good humour and tolerance and consideration for all, a right attitude and friendliness to competitors and rivals, self-control and scrupulous observance of the laws of the games, fair play and avoidance of the use of foul means, an equal acceptance of victory or defeat without bad humour, resentment or ill-will towards successful competitors, loyal acceptance of the decisions of the appointed judge, umpire or referee. More important still is the custom of discipline, obedience, order, and habit of teamwork, which certain games necessitate.

In the words of Sri Aurobindo:

> If they (the above qualities) could be made more common not only in the life of the individual but in the national life and in the international where at the present day the opposite tendencies have become too rampant, existence in this troubled world of ours would be smoother and might open to a greater chance of concord and amity of which it stands very much in need. ... The nation

which possesses them in the highest degree is likely to be strongest for victory, success and greatness, but also for the contribution it can make towards the bringing about of unity and more harmonious world order towards which we look as our hope for humanity's future.

Physical culture is a matter of great yogic educational value. The physical body is the instrument for the final victory of the highest values on the earth. We need therefore to develop health, strength, plasticity, grace and numerous physical perfections so as to make the body fit for the service and manifestation of the highest ideals.

CONCEPT OF EDUCATION IN ANCIENT INDIAN TRADITION AND CULTURE : ITS CONTEMPORARY RELEVANCE

I

Introductory Questions

At the outset, let us ask the question as to why we need to explore the concept of education in the Ancient Indian Tradition, and why we want to ascertain the relevance of that concept to the present time. Justification for this exploration could arise if we ask a further question as to whether our present system of education is relevant to our own times, and if we are prepared to undertake a critique of the present system.

Do we need to change present system of Education?

There is a view that the present system of education is, after all, quite reasonable and what we need is to make it a little more sophisticated, much more polished, with some modifications here and there like vocationalisation and job-orientation, and what we further need is to ensure accountability of teachers and educational institutions. It has even been prominently asked, in defence of the present system, if we ourselves are not the products of that system and whether we are not, more or less, quite well-equipped to deal with our responsibilities.

There is, on the other hand, a more progressive view, which does not admit that we, the products of the system of education, are what we ought to be, that a better system could have made us better equipped, in terms of both personality and skills, and capable of meeting the demands and challenges of our times. The spectrum of this view is quite wide, and at one end, it advocates some major reforms, and at the other end, it advocates a number of radical reforms. In any case, this view argues that education must aim at the integral development of personality and that we need to have complete education for the complete human being. Analysing the concept of the integral development of personality, it pleads for the harmonisation of the physical, vital and mental personality. It also recognises that the mental personality itself requires harmonisation of the rational, the ethical and the aesthetic. Two further propositions are also added: first, that the personality develops best when the educational atmosphere provides to every student a good deal of freedom; -- freedom in pursuing inner inclinations, freedom in regulating pace of progress, and freedom in determining directions of education; and secondly, that education should be so child-centred that it not only puts the child in the centre of the classroom but also in the centre of the society itself.

Implications of these contentions are momentous. They require major changes in the attitudes of teachers, parents and educational administrators, even of the students themselves. They demand applications of new methodologies of education and transformations in the classroom situation, teaching-learning materials and in the established routine of the educational institutions; they also demand radical reviews of curricula, syllabi and the current examination system.

Closely connected with these demands, life-long education is also being underlined. Correspondingly, great expansion of non-formal education and open system of education is also being advocated. Finally, the concept of learning society is being increasingly proposed as the right setting for all the innovations and reforms of education.

Difficulties

The major difficulty in implementing these important proposals is threefold: (i) as noted above, these reforms call for great changes in the attitudes among all the partners of education and these changes are not at all easy or facile; (ii) they also imply difficulty structural changes, which need to be conceived, designed and implemented on a sustainable basis and there are no agencies that could accomplish these tasks; and (iii) they require not only major funding but also prudent planning, prioritisation and delicate balancing between the act of modifying or dismantling the old and that of creation of the new.

Need for bolder Reforms

It is in the context of this situation that serious and sincere educationists feel hesitant to make some further and bolder proposals, particularly in the context of the Indian system of education, -- the proposals which are indispensable and which can be postponed only on the peril of risking loss of cultural identity and even of crippling the very soul of India.

Let us examine this aspect in some detail.

We are all aware that the current Indian system of education was designed by the Britishers for their narrower purposes and for promoting in our country the Western view of India, -- her past and her period of decline or backwardness and the cure by which they thought

India could occupy some place among those countries, which could tolerably be described as "civilised". Unfortunately, what the Britishers designed has hardly been altered even after our attainment of Independence, and whatever changes have occurred can only be regarded as cosmetic in character. Worst of all, those institutions which had come up under the influence of the nationalist movement, came to be closed down or they were obliged to fall in line with the "normal" system of education, designed by the Britishers. And the financial allocations made to the education departments were distributed among the increasingly multiplying number of institutions belonging to the "normal" pattern. Free India's money was thus pumped more and more vigorously to spread in India on a vast scale that very system which the nationalist leaders had dreamt to demolish once Independence was won. This situation is continuing with increasing vigour, and unless we bestir ourselves vehemently to think afresh, and design afresh, one does not see how else we shall be able to redress the harm that we are inflicting on generations upon generations and to the cause of Indian renaissance.

Free India's Failure

It is noteworthy that the greatest representatives of the Indian renaissance, from Maharshi Dayananda Saraswati to Sri Aurobindo, had perceived in the ancient Indian system of education such an uplifting and inspiring model that they had all advocated for free India a national system of education rooted in the ancient Indian conception of education, which would, at the same time, cater to the ideals of internationalism and universality. They had all dreamt of free India where students would relive the presence and guidance of the wise and benign and courageous Rishis who had sown in the soil of India the seeds of perennial inspiration. They wanted to re-create sanctuaries of living souls who could be fostered by teachers who would, like Vashistha and Vishwamitra, Vamadeva and Bhardwaj, remain unfettered by dogma or any restraining force of limitation or obscurantism. They wanted perfect harmony between the human and the natural, between the individual and the universal, between the mundane and the supramundane. Their message was clear that the ancient Indian concept of education should not only be revisited by free India but should also be resurrected, renovated and perfected by the aid of all that is modern and useful, by all that is Indian and universal.

Let us do the needful

There is no point in crying over the fact that free India has so far failed in giving shape to the dreams and aspirations of these great pioneers. But is it not overdue that we try to understand them, get into the heart of the ancient Indian system of education, evaluate it in the light of the needs of today and tomorrow and design for our children something new that will give to them the best fruits of their heritage and also the best fruits of modern advancement?

II
Three characteristics of the Ancient Indian Concept of Education

If we study the Veda and the Upanishads, and the related literature from where we can get glimpses of the ancient Indian concept of education, we shall find that there were three special characteristics of that conception. The first characteristic stresses the fact that the educational process had resulted from the understanding of the fullness of life, its own methods of instruction and how these methods can be employed by teachers to secure acceleration of progress of students. The second characteristic is related to the astonishing fund of integral knowledge that could serve as the foundation of the contents of education. And the third emerges from the ancient pursuit of individual and collective perfectibility in the light of their laborious experiments related to the human potentialities.

Let us briefly elucidate them.

1. Educational and Life: Methods of Education; Role of Teachers and Students:

Education was conceived as something springing from life itself, and it was conceived as a part of the organisation of life and it was designed to relate education with life and its highest possible fulfilment.

It was observed that life itself is the great teacher of life, that life which is in its outer movement a series of shocks of meeting between individuals and circumstances, has in its inner heart a secret method of progression from untruth to truth, from darkness to light, and from death to immortality. It was further observed that this process of life can be systematically organised and methods can be built by which the intended progression can be accelerated. Accordingly, education came to conceived as a methodised organisation of life in which threads of progression are so woven that each individual can be aided to bring about judicious acceleration of the rate of his growth and development.

In this conception the home of the teacher represented the fabric of life in which educational process was subtly and methodically intertwined in such a way that all life was education and all educational activities throbbed with life-experience.

The home of the teacher, which came to be called the *ashrama* or *gurukula*, was centred on students, and each student received individual attention. The teacher looked upon his task as that of an observer, as a helper, as a guide, -- not as that of a taskmaster. He taught best, not so much through instruction, as through the example of his wisdom and character and through his personal and intimate contact with the soul of each student. He had no rigid or uniform methods; but he applied every possible method in a varying manner in regard to every student. For *Satyakama*, the teacher would apply the simple method of learning through the activities connected with grazing the cattle; for *Shvetaketu*, the teacher would apply the method of meaningful questioning and demonstration through apt examples; *Pippalada* asked his pupils to dwell for one year in holiness and faith and askesis before they could put their questions; and *Bhrigu* was asked by his father and the teacher, *Varun*, to concentrate himself in thought and discover the truth of Matter, of Life, of Mind, and of the Supermind and of the Bliss by successive and higher and higher meditations. Often the teacher communicated through silence so as to destroy the doubts in the minds of the pupils; the teacher taught students in groups but also individually; the teacher, in fact, utilised every incident of life for imparting knowledge and experience.

The student was looked upon as a seeker, not to be silenced by any dogmatic answers but to be uplifted in higher processes of thought, meditation and direct experience or realisation. In the educational process, student's enthusiasm, *utsaha*, was of utmost importance. *Svadhyaya* was the cornerstone of the learning process.

Nothing was imposed upon the student except the willing acceptance of the discipline. The pupil was the *brahmacharin,* devoted to self-control and askesis; *he* was asked to obey the command of the teacher, knowing very well that the teacher asked nothing arbitrary and only laid down the path by which self-perfection can be attained. The teacher was the Rishi who knew the inmost needs of the growth of the soul of the student, and he had the knowledge and power to place each student on the right road to perfection. It was left to the student to walk or run on that road, according to his ability, inclination and rate of progression.

The teacher and the pupil lived a joint life, a life of joint prayer, of joint endeavour, of joint conquest of knowledge. Just as the student sought the teacher, even so, the teacher, too, sought the student. As the teacher in the Taittiriya Upanishad announces: *"May the Brahmacharins come unto me. From here and there, may the Brahmacharins come unto me."*

An important element in the organisation of education was that of Time, *kāla*. The teacher knew that everything in life has a rhythm of germination and flowering, and every process of life has a rhythm of development, which can be measured in terms of time. The teacher, therefore, combined the methods that required patience with those that ensured perfection. He knew how the student can be enabled to arrive at progression, neither too quickly nor too slowly, but by slow building up of foundation and a rapid process of the blossoming of the faculties. Each student was, therefore, helped to obtain a judicious rate of progression and a judicious rate of acceleration.

The most important element in the educational process was the illumined condition of the teacher, -- his state of knowledge, his command over different domains of life, his ripe experience, his wisdom, his realisation.

This brings us the second characteristic of the ancient Indian concept of education.

2. Integral Knowledge: Importance of the Intellect; Exploration and Realisation of the Superconscient

As we study the Veda and Upanishad, we are struck by the profundity and loftiness of the knowledge that the Rishis had attained. The Veda and the Upanishads can rightly be regarded as the records of "integral knowledge" -- the synthesis of God-knowledge, self-knowledge and world-knowledge. The Rishis, the composers of these great compositions, had arrived at the secret methods of attaining deeper and higher states of consciousness; and they had formulated various forms of concentration, which served as the key to knowledge. They had discovered that what the world revealed to us in response to our seeking and questioning depended on the state of sincerity, of impartiality, of complete identity between the subject and the object of knowledge. Thus they knew the secret of intuition, revelation, inspiration and discrimination. But they knew very well also the knowledge by separative means of knowledge, knowledge that can be attained by senses, and the knowledge that can be obtained by reasoning and intellectual thought.

The famous *Gayatri* mantra of *Vishwamitra* singles out one faculty of the human being as of singular importance, without whose cultivation and concentration, the best or the highest cannot be attained. This is the faculty of *dhi*, the pure intellect. This mantra indicates that it is only when the intellect can be trained in the system of meditation and contemplation that the major step in the process of knowledge can be taken. This *Gayatri* mantra also indicates that *Vishwamitra* had discovered the highest domain of luminous knowledge, which is symbolised as *Savitri*. He had further discovered that intellect can be so trained that it can succeed in concentrating upon that higher Light. Finally, it indicates that the intellect can be properly directed when it joins itself with *Savitri*, with the most beautiful form of creative Light.

The Vedas and the Upanishads abound with thousands of statements and indications that the world can best be known when its source is known and only when its relationship with the individual is known, -- individuals who take it as a field of their experience, their enjoyment, their bondage and their liberation. The modern psychologist takes great pride in his discovery of the unconscious and the subconscious, but the *Rishi*, the Vedic teacher, had discovered even the inconscient, that which was wrapped darkly in the shroud of darkness. He had discovered also how the inconscient awakens and becomes the subconscient and how the subconscient and conscient are related to each other. He had also the assured knowledge of the deeper and deepest domains of consciousness that lie behind (not below) the outer layers of consciousness. He had also scaled the heights of the superconscient, and not stopping anywhere, he had declared that as one rises the ladder higher and higher, more and more becomes clear as to what still remains to be known. The Vedic Rishi declares his own state of knowledge where all darkness gets shattered and where his soul, like the falcon, liberates itself from the hundred chains of iron and soars above in the wide sky of consciousness in liberation, to the unmixed truth and to the unmixed bliss. The Vedic Rishi tells us of the secret of immortality and of the great path by which that secret can be attained by every human being.

The ancient Indian concept of education had its foundations in the Vedic and Upanishadic integral knowledge. Its aim was to transmit to the new generations this knowledge and to develop it further by means of fresh quest and experimentation.

3. Human Potentialities and Pursuit of Individual and Collective Perfectibility

The third characteristic of the ancient conception of education was its emphasis on harmonisation of different aspects of personality so that the physical being of the individual is made a strong base for sustaining the growth and perfection of the vital, mental, and higher aspects of personality. The *Taittiriya Upanishad* speaks of five sheaths in the human being, all of which need to be integrated, -- *annamaya*, the physical, *prāṇamaya*, the vital, *manomaya*, the mental, *vijñānamaya*, the supramental, and *ānandamaya*, the bliss that is conscious and self-existent. The Vedic and the Upanishadic Rishis had made a thorough study of the problem of integration and come to the conclusion that the mental being, *manomaya*, is the leader of the physical and the vital, -- *prāṇa sharira neta*, and that it is by developing the mental powers that the vital and the physical can be controlled and mastered, although the real and lasting integration can come about only when one develops higher degrees of consciousness which transcend the mental consciousness.

According to the ancient Indian psychology, the physical, the vital, and the mental can be uplifted to their higher perfection when the Spirit is made to manifest its four powers, the power of wisdom, the power of heroism, the power of harmony and the power of skill in works. The *Purusha Sukta* of the *Rigveda* makes it clear that these four powers are all spiritual in character and that it is when all of them are fully manifested that the deepest divinity can become operative in our dynamic life. At the same time, the concept of *swabhāva* and *swadharma* was developed on the basis, a full exposition of which we get in the *Bhagavadgita*. Each individual has, according to this system of knowledge, a predominant force which gives rise to a special tendency in the being, either of wisdom or of heroism or of harmony or of skill. This predominant tendency is what is called *swabhāva* and each individual needs to be given the freedom to develop on the line of one's own *swabhāva*. The Indian system of education made a special provision so that each *swabhāva* receives the necessary aid and framework of development as also the system of culture and the system of developing those qualities which can ultimately foster and nourish the totality of the personality. It was a later corruption of this great psychological principle of *swabhāva* that led to the development of caste system where *swabhāva* was the least to be considered and its inner truth was sacrificed in favour of the system of determination by birth and a system of privileges and handicaps – a parody of the ancient insights of profound psychology.

Nonetheless, the ancient system of education in India, in its peak period, produced amazing results in terms of development of faculties and capacities, and their integration, a supreme example of which is to be found in the personality of *Sri Krishna* who was at once a spiritual teacher, a heroic warrior, a great harmoniser, and skilful worker, who could excel in the task of a charioteer in the field of *Kurukshetra*. If we consider the spiritual history of India and also its history of dynamic activities that built up great edifices of mathematics and natural sciences, medical sciences, numberless philosophies, teeming *dharmashastras*, profusion of literature, art and architecture, and powerful administration and system of governance, we shall find that these great achievements were traceable to the ancient system of education. This system, though spiritual in character, did not reject the life on the earth but laid it down that the higher achievements are to be attained in the life of the earth, -- here itself, *iha eva.*

This system put forward the conception of *shreshtha*, and pointed out various qualities that we should expect in the ideal personality. This conception was emphasised because it was consciously recognised that people tend to follow the best and distribution of the best qualities among the people at large can be effected only by encouraging and fostering the best.[1]

In the heart of the *shreshtha,* these qualities blossomed: benevolence, love, compassion, altruism, long suffering, liberality, kindliness and patience; in his character, the qualities of courage, heroism, energy, loyalty, continence, truth, honour, justice, faith, obedience, and reverence. These qualities included also a fine modesty and yet noble pride, and power to govern and direct.

The *shreshtha* was required in his mind wisdom and intelligence and love of learning, openness to poetry, art, and beauty, and dedicated capacity and skill in works. In his inner life, he had the urge to seek after the highest and nourish the spiritual turn. In his social relations and conduct, he was strict in his observance of all social

---

[1] As Sri Krishna points out in the Gita:
यद्यदाचरति श्रेष्ठस्तत्तदेवेतरो जनः ।
स यत्प्रमाणं कुरुते लोकस्तदनुवर्तते ।।
Whatsoever a great man does, the same is done by others as well. Whatever standard he sets, the world follow the same. (Bhagavadgita 3.21)

responsibilities as father, son, husband, brother, kinsman, friend, ruler, master or servant, prince or warrior, or worker, kind or sage. *Shreshtha,* the best, was an ideal seeker of the spirit endowed with robust rationality, both spirit-wise and world-wise, nobility, and devotion to *dharma.* He was tolerant of life's difficulties and human weaknesses, but arduous and self-disciplined.

The ancient system of education at once indulged and controlled man's nature, it fitted him for his social role, it stamped on his mind the generous ideal of an accomplished humanity, refined, harmonious in all capacities and noble in all its endeavours; and above all, it placed before him the theory and practice of Yoga, the theory and practice of a higher change, and it familiarised him with the concept of a spiritual existence and encouraged in him hunger for the divine and infinite.

The scope of the ancient system of education was comprehensive; it rejected no discipline of knowledge, no means of expression, -- literary or artistic, -- no craft, and technology that could make for best utility of matter and substance. The Indian tradition speaks of sixty-four sciences and arts, and it catered to the education of women in such a liberal way that we still speak of great examples of *Lopāmudra, Gargi,* and *Maitreyi.* In the courses of study, apart from the study of the Veda, which was in itself a great science and art of living, emphasis was laid on comprehensive training of all that could equip each one for the role that was suitable to each individual on the lines of *swabhāva* and *swadharma.* Study of healthcare and *Ayurveda* was also an important part of the programme of study. In course of time, six *Vedangas* had developed as also four *Upavedas* and a number of other sciences and *shastras.* With the development of *Buddhism,* a different system of education developed

Concept of Education in Ancient Indian Tradition And Culture

which laid great emphasis on practices of asceticism, rules of *dharma* and studies of philosophy, medicine and other sciences. This had also effect on the orthodox system of education, and in due course of time, different systems of education developed. But the history of this development does not concern us here.

Image of the Ancient Indian System of Education

Of the ancient Indian system of education that flourished for a considerable period of time, we have in our mind an inspiring image as it is described in a few pages of the *Upanishads*. This image has been presented to us by *Sri Aurobindo* in the following words:

> The sages sitting in their groves ready to test and teach the comer, princes and learned Brahmins and great landed nobles going about in search of knowledge, the king's son in his chariot and the illegitimate son of the servant-girl, seeking any man who might carry in himself the thought of light and the word of revelation, the typical figures and personalities, Janaka and the subtle mind of Ajatashatru, Raikwa of the cart, Yajnavalkya militant for truth, calm and ironic, taking to himself with both hands without attachment worldly possessions and spiritual riches and casting at last all his wealth behind to wander forth as a houseless ascetic, Krishna son of Devaki who heard a single word of the Rishi Ghora and knew at once the Eternal, the Ashramas, the courts of kings who were also spiritual discoverers and thinkers, the great

sacrificial assemblies, where the sages met and compared their knowledge.[2]

III

Question of Relevance:

It is not possible to go into greater details and delineate a more precise and comprehensive description of the ancient Indian conception of education. But while considering the question of the relevance of this concept to the needs and demands of our own times, we should distinguish between the essence and outer forms in which that concept was made operative in the ancient times. It is evident that we have to concentrate on essence rather than on outer forms.

Ideal Teachers:

In the first place, it is not easy to find in our current times *Rishis* like *Vashishtha* and *Vishwamitra* and *Yajnavalkya* around whom the ancient system was built. But still, we can make use of the ideal and consider as to how that ideal can be brought nearer to actuality and what conditions of atmosphere, conception, vision, and equipment would be necessary to create among our teachers a new aspiration to embody in themselves those qualities and concerns which dominated the ideal teachers of that antiquity. It is not entirely impossible to build up a new system of teachers' training through which new roles of teachers can be visualised and imparted to the coming generations of teachers.

---

[2] Sri Aurobindo: *The Foundations of Indian Culture*, Centenary Edition, p.280.

That the task of the teacher is not primarily to teach but to observe the students and to guide them on the proper lines which are suitable to their potentialities, inclinations and capacities can be emphasised. That the teacher's instruments are not confined only to methods of instruction but include also the example of the inner character of the teacher and his capacity to enter into the depths of students' inner souls can also be stressed. That the teacher must concentrate and embody vast and true knowledge and continue to learn more and more can also be underlined. In any case, the country can take a major decision to create such conditions where the image of the ideal teacher is made vividly visible, so that we can have in the coming decades a growing number of teachers who can approximate in their qualities and in their character as also in their knowledge and skills to the ideal teacher of our ancient system.

This we should strive to do, not only to maintain our continuity of cultural development but also because the ancient Indian pedagogy was extremely sound, and India will stand to gain if that pedagogy can be brought back to life, and can be further enriched by applications of the results of various progressive educational experiments which have been conducted in India and in different part of the world during the last two centuries.

Child-centred Education; Integral Education on the lines of Swabhāva and Swadharma:

Modern emphasis on child-centred education is consonant with the care that was bestowed upon the child and the *brahmacharin* in the home of the teacher in our ancient system. And there is no doubt that the more will this emphasis be translated into practice, the more will our modern system begin to resemble our ancient system in spirit, although not in outer form.

Among the idea-forces which have powerfully emerged in the modern world and which will determine the future, there are two which will stand out for the universal acceptance. The first among these is the conception of the right of all individuals as members of the society to full life and the full development of which they are individually capable. No ideal will persist which will allow an arrangement by which certain classes of society should arrogate development and full social fruition to themselves while assigning a bare and barren function of service to others. And the second idea is that of individualism, which proclaims that the individual is not merely a social unit, that he is not merely a member of human pack, but he is something in himself, a soul, a being, who has to fulfil his own individual truth and law as well as his natural or assigned part in the truth and the law of collective existence. The individual thus demands freedom, space, initiative for his soul, for his nature, for his *swabhāva* and *swadharma*, to use the Indian terms. These two ideas together are bound to force the contemporary system of education to undergo such a radical change that the ideal of the integral development of personality is given highest importance and, considering that the concepts of integral personality are getting increasingly enriched under the stress of modern search of the inner soul, the ancient Indian concept of education, in which integration of human personality was sought to be effected by the fourfold powers of the soul will be found directly relevant and useful. It is increasingly recognised that the human beings of the present day are so acutely torn by the inherent conflicts between the rational, the ethical and the aesthetic that they are obliged to look for something else, something higher than the rational and the pragmatic, something spiritual and much more truly effective in solving the problems of life.

It is often contended that the Indian system of education had for long been instrumental in sustaining the pernicious caste system and therefore, in the new atmosphere where casteless and classless society is being envisaged, the Indian system will be found to be entirely irrelevant. But this is a misreading of Indian history, and it commits the error of attributing what happened at one stage during the period of decline to the entire long history of Indian education. There was in the early times of Indian history, a system of four *varnas*, but this system was quite different from its degenerated and distorted caricature that the later caste system represents. In any case, without going into disputes regarding the ancient *chaturvarnya* and the later caste system, two things can be safely stated that the individual develops best when he develops on the lines of inherent propensities, potentialities, capacities and predominant interests; and secondly, that the individual develops perfection only when all the potentialities are developed and integrated into a harmony. This is now being increasingly acknowledged in the modern educational psychology, and this was already acknowledged and practised to a greater or a lesser degree in the ancient system of education. The Indian educational theory and practice laid special emphasis on *swabhava* and *swadharma* and on the idea of fourfold personality which can be perfected by developing the individual soul, conceived not as an ego but as a harmonious entity which has its own uniqueness and which yet lives by mutuality and harmony with the totality. This theory and practice will be found most relevant to the task of rebuilding a new system of education.

Teacher Education:

It is also increasingly recognised that corresponding to the aim of the integral development of personality, the teacher also must have a personality that is very well developed and integrated. Our present system of teacher education is not only superficial but also mechanical and uninspiring. The time that we have allotted to the programme of teacher education, which practically comes to eight months, is hopelessly inadequate, and the wiser counsel that we are now hearing in our country is that we should institute an integrated course of teacher education, which can extend over to four to five years. This wise counsel seems destined to succeed, and we shall, therefore, be in a better position to design a comprehensive programme of teachers' education. In that design, all the valuable aspects of the ancient concepts of education and the ancient concept of the role of the teacher will find some kind of rebirth and renewal.

Environment:

It is often contended that one of the most salutary aspects of the ancient Indian system of education was the setting that was provided to the *Gurukula*, -- the setting of a forest, which was remote from the hustle and bustle of worldly life. It is, however, argued that this condition is hardly feasible in our times and this reduces the relevance of the ancient system. The argument has some force, although it must be stressed that a large number of universities which have come to be developed in India after independence have been provided with beautiful settings, but unfortunately, many of them have been ruined by human misuse. Many private schools also are being developed in our country in beautiful settings. In any case, it is true that with the development of modern media, the isolation which was sought for the educational institutions in ancient times has now become almost impossible. But these practical difficulties do not contradict the truth that the educational institution must be set up in such a beautiful environment that the harmony between human being and Nature can become a part of the organisation of life and, therefore, a powerful medium of education. If this truth is kept in view, it will serve a great purpose when our country will be required to build increasing number of educational institutions, even in remote villages and groups of hamlets. The importance of environment, of surroundings full of vegetation, flowers and fruits, can never be underestimated, and the fact that our ancient system of education had underlined this important aspect will remain a permanent contribution to the higher causes of civilisation.

Contemporary Crisis; Value-Education; Spiritual Education:

It is important to note that there is an increasing awareness both in India and the world that the contemporary crisis is fundamentally the crisis of the disbalancement, of an exaggerated development of the outer structures and organisations and means of physical and vital satisfactions, on the one hand, and the neglect of the ethical and spiritual dimensions of human life, on the other. One, therefore, hears of the crisis of character, crisis of values and crisis of spiritual evolution. Gripped as we are in this crisis, we are bound to look for the knowledge of ethics and spirituality, of values and of the knowledge that can bridge the gulf between the life of matter and the life of spirit. In the West, increasing number of leaders are now speaking of return to basics, and in India we have begun to conceive of programmes of value-education. This subject has not yet received the attention that it deserves, but there is no doubt that under the pressure of circumstances or of our enlightened foresight, when we shall explore this subject, we are bound to raise three important questions, helpful answers of which will largely be found in our ancient Indian conception of education.

Meaning of Values:

1. The first question will be related to the meaning of values, particularly when they are not to be restricted only to the domain of morality but will extend to the domain of aesthetics, rationality, and even to the domain of suprarationality. This question will become complex when we come to consider values of physical education, vital education, and mental education in the context of integral development of personality and of the perfectibility of the individual and the collectivity.

Science and Values:

2. The second question will be related to science and values, particularly when humanity is awaking to the necessity of directing scientific knowledge towards the goal of higher welfare of humanity. This question will again become complex when we examine the claim of scientific knowledge that knowledge by its very nature has to be scientific and that the knowledge of values is not strictly speaking knowledge. The question will be whether this claim is sustainable in view of the growing idea that knowledge is not a matter merely of inductive or deductive process of thought but that even instincts, desires, emotions, aspirations, faith and intuitions give clues to knowledge and are themselves imbued with knowledge. This will necessarily lead us to the question of harmonising positive knowledge with axiological knowledge and of developing an integral system of knowledge.

Values and Self-Knowledge:

3. The third question will be related to relationship between self-knowledge and pursuit of values, particularly when it is seen that pursuit of values demands increasing self-control and self-mastery, which in turn, are related to self-knowledge. For, as it was realised by the ancient Rishis, the Self cannot be known except through self-discipline, and self-discipline cannot become perfect without the true knowledge of the self. Again, this question will become complex when it is realised that self-knowledge is intimately related to world-knowledge and God-knowledge.

It will be seen that these questions will oblige us to converge upon the profound psychological, ethical and spiritual knowledge which was so central to the ancient India's conception of education.

Modern Knowledge; Physical, Supraphysical and Spiritual Knowledge:

We realise that modern knowledge is expanding at a tremendous rate of progression; in course of this rapid movement, materialism of yesterday is being increasingly overpassed. Philosophical inadequacy of materialism has become obvious when we see that the advanced materialists of today refrain from making any metaphysical propositions, including those regarding material-ism. The argument that science can deal only with matter is also being overpassed. The development of life sciences, psychological sciences and humanistic sciences has shown that what is important in science is the scientific method but not the unsustainable assumption that this method can be applied only in the domain of Matter. As a matter of fact, the boundaries between the physical and the supra-physical are being broken up quite rapidly, and as against the earlier assumption of materialism that only that is real which can be physically verified, it is clearly proved that the basic sub-atomic substratum of matter is physically invisible although real. Even in technological matters, dependence on material means alone is being increasingly substituted by inventions which reduce dependence on material means, such as in the case of wireless telegraphy.

Increasing importance of the Yogic Knowledge:

With these developments, we can see that the knowledge of the physical will gradually or rapidly begin, for its further development or completion, to knock at the doors of the supraphysical knowledge. And, in that context, the importance of the knowledge – physical and supraphysical – that constituted the contents of the ancient Indian system of education will come to be underlined.

And this will lead also to the study of Yoga as a science. As *Swami Vivekananda* had declared, Yoga is science *par excellence*, since it proceeds by the scientific method of observation, experimentation and verification, of repetition and of rectification as also of continuous expansion. And with the admission of the Yogic knowledge, it appears that the entire body of discoveries made by the Vedic and Upanishadic Rishis and by the subsequent numberless Yogic explorers will become the central focus of advancing research. Already some Western scientists are turning to the knowledge that Yoga can provide, and we can foresee that this movement is bound to move forward. And this will enhance the relevance of the heritage that we possess of the ancient Indian conception of knowledge and education.

Renewal of the old Spiritual Knowledge; Need for Developing New Knowledge:

This is not to say that all that we need today and tomorrow was already contained in the ancient system; although loftiest and central discoveries of the secrets of the Spirit were made in those ancient times, there is still much more to be done in the coming days. New knowledge of matter and new knowledge of spirit are likely to be the preoccupation of the seekers all over the world. It is also possible that the older synthesis of knowledge will be replaced by newer synthesis. But still old foundations will always be found to be not only relevant but of basic value.

As we visualise these future developments, we can see at once how they will affect our present day curricula and our entire present system of educational aims, educational methods and educational contents. Radical changes will be required; and we shall need to revisit the ancient Indian concept of education and derive from it valuable insights, which can guide us in the right direction, provided we also take care to embrace the latest results of the latest educational research and experimentation that has been conducted in India and elsewhere.

Upanishadic Secret of embracing unending Knowledge:

We have to realise that our present Indian curricula hardly provide to our students any adequate idea of the unbroken history of Indian culture, which extended in the past at least beyond five thousand years. If we are to give even a faint idea of this vast canvas of Indian culture, -- which incidentally, is indispensable if we want to sustain our cultural identity, -- and if we are to add, as we must, also the new and expanding horizons of knowledge, which are vastly developing, we shall be obliged to consider ways and means by which our entire system of curriculum-making and our system of educational methodology can undergo radical changes. We shall have to find a central answer to the question as to how to master knowledge when it is very vast and when it is expanding at an exponential rate. And shall we not be tempted to listen seriously to the Upanishadic declaration that there is a kind of knowledge having acquired which all can be known?

PHILOSOPHY OF VALUE-ORIENTED EDUCATION – I

The need for value-oriented education requires clarification.

Value-Oriented Education Inherent in the Concept of Education

There are at least three fundamental assumptions of the educational process:

a. There is, first, the pursuit of man to know himself and the Universe and to relate himself with the Universe as harmoniously as possible. This pursuit constitutes the very theme of human culture. And education derives its fundamental thrust from the cultural setting at a given point of time.

b. Secondly, there is a process of transmission of the accumulated results of the past to the growing generation so as to enable it to carry forward the cultural heritage and to build the gates and the paths of the future.

c. And thirdly, there is in the process of transmission, a deliberate attempt to accelerate as far as possible the process of human progress.

In its very nature, education is a normative endeavour. Being at once a product or instrument of culture, education tends to promote the highest aims of culture. Hence, education tends to be a process of training whereby individuals in the society are enabled to embody progressively those values, which we in our highest thought and aspiration come to regard as something most desirable. It is in this context that education encourages and fosters the arts and sciences as well as technologies whereby man and the Universe can be ideally interrelated. At the same time, the idea of human progress is built up, and education endeavours to discover and apply efficient means of the right rhythm of acceleration of individual and social progress as also of human progress in general.

Education is thus in its nature value-oriented.

Today's conditions necessitating value-oriented education.

The conditions through which human culture is passing today provide additional reasons fro value-oriented education:

- ❖ An increasing number of people of thought and action feel that humanity has been gripped by serious maladies and that these maladies are the result of our disequilibrium between the ideals that mankind is labouring to realise during the recent centuries and the disconcerting actualities which refuse obstinately to change. With the passing of every decade, humanity seems to feel more and more acutely that the realisation of its ideals has become imperative, while at the same time, it seems almost impossible to accomplish this realisation. It is, therefore, felt that humanity is passing through an acute crisis.

Philosophy of Value-Oriented Education - I

❖ A huge structure is being built up with an increasing insistence on efficiency needed for industrialised society, leaving practically no room for the growth of profounder wisdom which can rightly guide human progress in the critical times through which we are passing today.

❖ As never before, humanity is able to envisage several alternative possibilities of the imminent future. As never before, it is felt that human volition can play a decisive role in selecting, planning, designing and actualising these possibilities. As never before, humanity is convinced that the most desirable course for the human race is to strive with fixed determination for human unity, global peace and for the advancing of the three great ideals of progress, namely, liberty, equality and fraternity. As never before, there has been an increasing perception that the most effective means for achieving these desirable objectives is value-oriented education.

❖ This feeling is reinforced by the fact that while under the pressure of technological development, the world is shrinking and we are dreaming of the possibility of a planetary civilisation, for which we have not yet secured a corresponding psychological development, which could enable human consciousness to sustain such a planetary civilisation. On the contrary, there is a growing preponderance of those impulses, which can thrive only in ignorance, fragmentation, discord and violence.

❖ In India, there is a feeling that the country is sinking under the weight of problems such as those of terrorism, corruption, and plutocracy, and it is

403

realised that solutions need to be sought at a level that is far deeper than the level at which we are now thinking and acting and that special attention has to be paid to the promotion of values that can counteract the increasing destruction of the country and its culture. Against this background, both from the global point of view and from the Indian point of view, we need to develop and practice value-oriented education.

II

But what is the meaning of values?

- ❖ As understood in the context of educational philosophy, values refer to those desirable ideals and goals which are intrinsic in themselves and which, when achieved or attempted, evoke a deep sense of fulfilment to one or many or all parts of what we consider to be the highest elements of our nature.

- ❖ In a sense, the world "value" is basically indefinable, since it denotes a fundamental category and it is itself the highest genus of that category.

- ❖ There is a common understanding that truth, beauty and goodness (*satyam, shivam, sundaram*) can be conceived as the supreme values of life. They are intrinsic in character and they are ends-in-themselves. Even if there are wide differences as to what is meant by these three terms, there is an agreement that they are the most desirable ideals and mere orientation towards them inspires development of those states of our being and becoming in which we can hope to find some kind of ultimate fulfilment.

Philosophy of Value-Oriented Education - I

III
Basic Issues

❖ There is a view that values are relative and subjective in character. It is, therefore, argued that individuals should be left to themselves to determine their own value systems and that educational institutions should confine themselves only to those domains where objective knowledge is discernible or determinable.

❖ There is also a view that value systems stem from religious beliefs, and since these beliefs are dogmatic in character, they conflict with the demand of reason, and hence, they have no place in education, where one of the chief objectives is to cultivate among students the pursuit of rational and scientific temper.

❖ According to some educationists, values, even if they are determinable, cannot be taught and for this reason also, it is argued that there is no rationale to bring value-oriented education within the purview of schools and universities.

❖ On the other hand, there is a view that value systems have determined the orientation of civilisations, and these value systems should be emphasised in the educational system. It is also argued that there should be a rigorous inquiry into those values, which transcend relativity and subjectivity. It is also argued that many religions and moral systems advocate certain common values and that these common values, when identified, could be recommended for any education system in its value-oriented programme. It is also argued that there is a common agreement in the world in respect of rights and responsibilities, and many of them are even incorporated in constitutions and legal systems. All these are value-oriented and these values should constitute the core of value-oriented education.

- A recent and disturbing increase in the trend of drug addiction among youths tends to reiterate the necessity of education that promotes the values of self-control, discipline and right habits of thought and conduct among youth.

IV
The Question of the Relativity and Subjectivity of Values

If we examine the history of value systems, we find that there have developed several standards of conduct, which can be arranged in an ascending scale or ladder.

- The first is personal need, preference and desire. There is no doubt that the standards of conduct based on what the individual feels to be his own needs, whether these are constrictive or derived from desire or instinct or egoistic pressure, it is bound to be relative and subjective. The individual would then be the measure of all things, and what is good for one individual is good for him and what is good for another is good for that other. Might would be right; and there could be no place for any impartial or universal law of action. When man is primitive, historically or psychologically, he tends to be individualistic and egoistic and tends to create standards of action or conflict, which result in self-seeking and self-aggrandisement.

Philosophy of Value-Oriented Education - I

❖ But no individual can live in isolation, and no individual can be allowed by the very fact of his social existence, to impose upon others what an individual considers to be his good, based upon his personal need, preference or desire. Every social group tends to create its own standards of conduct and impose it upon its individual members.

❖ In erecting the group's standards, there are several strands of consideration. At the highest level of these strands is what may be called objective utilitarianism. According to it, an action is to be judged by the consequences it produces, and if the consequences are pleasant for the largest number in the society, then that action is judged to be better than any other action.

❖ There is also another form of objective utilitarianism, according to which an action is judged to be good not merely by reference to the pleasure that is produces but also by the degree to which it promotes both knowledge and character. According to this view, there is a hierarchy, and the value to be attached to knowledge is greater than the value to be attached to pleasure, and the value to be attached to character is greater than the value to be attached to knowledge. It maintains that an objective calculus can be created in every social group on the basis of these criteria and social law can be framed on the basis of this calculus.

❖ It is argued that objective utilitarianism forms a higher step in the ladder of evolution of value-systems, and that the standards and prescriptions it proposes cannot be termed to be as relative or subjective as those created merely by personal need, preference or desire.

❖ However, it is still subject to criticism in that it is not able to resolve the conflict between the social good and the individual good.

❖ A higher law of morality seems to prescribe what may be called intrinsic good or intrinsic right without reference to consequences. Indeed, at a higher level of development of civilisation and culture, we find a law of conduct emerging from the moral intention and will, and moral will is considered good because it is goodwill. Here goodwill is recognised to be goodwill intrinsically, merely by reference to intention and motive and not by reference to what issues in the form of actual action and its consequences.

❖ In one of the forms of this view, which can be termed as rationalistic and objective intuitionism, an objective criterion is attempted to be laid down by which the intrinsic rightness can be adjudged. It points out that an action can be adjudged to be right if it can be willed universally without self-contradiction.

❖ It is at this level of a value-system that we attain to the concept of absoluteness and objective of the good and the right, and we have the concept of love, justice, right reason, or of the categorical imperative.

❖ From a certain point of view, the answers given by rationalistic intuitionism, may meet the criticism that morality is relative and subjective. *Shastras of*

Dharmas have often been erected at higher levels of culture, and they have been thought to be objective and universally justified on the grounds of right reason.

❖ But we find that even in arriving at the standards of absolute love, absolute justice, absolute right reason, we are not able to resolve the state of disequilibrium. Right reason dispassionately considering facts of nature and human relations in search of satisfying norm or rule is unable to rest without modification either in the reign of absolute justice or in the reign of absolute love.

Man's absolute justice easily turns out in practice to be a sovereign injustice. Again, justice often demands what love abhors. It is, therefore, difficult to find an absolute and objective agreement where a given particular action can really be adjudged to be right, where love and justice can meet together in harmony and where absolute right reason can unalterably indicate in actual situations of life what is conceived to be absolute justice or absolute love.

❖ A distinction needs to be made between the human thrust towards the values of the right reason, absolute love and absolute justice, on the one hand, and various manifestations of this thrust in the form of certain specific and particular actions, on the other. While it is true that there can be differences of opinion as to whether certain specific actions are absolutely good – or not – and here relativity and subjectivity do enter – there is still no doubt that good will is independent of personal need, desire or preference; the judgement of goodness of goodwill is free from relativity or subjectivity. In other words, there is in the human consciousness the possibility of the development of goodwill that can be considered to be objectively good.

❖ This discussion has important consequences for value-education. If value-education proposes to prescribe any particular specific action or any particular value-system by any specific and preferred criteria, then the criticism against subjectivity and relativity in regard to the same would stand with considerable force. But if the proposal is to promote thrust and aspiration towards goodwill, then the case for value-education can be set on sound and strong footing.

❖ This would mean that it is preferable to propose value-oriented education rather than value-education. For value-education is likely to end up with prescription of do's and don'ts, and this prescription will have a weak ground. But if our aim is to provide in education, conditions for the promotion of the growth of aspiration towards goodwill and cultivation of goodwill, and if an attempt is to provide to each individual the inspiration and means to transcend his own limited needs and preferences and egoism, so that in his own personality, subjectivity is progressively attempted to be transcended, then such education can be defended both philosophically and pedagogically. Such education can be properly called value-oriented education.

❖ Value-oriented education should then be defined as a progressive and exploratory process of development, which promotes unconditional pursuit towards goodwill. This education leaves each individual free to determine the contents of the good and the right, provided they are motivated by goodwill.

- ❖ Not value-education but value-oriented education, not prescription but exploration – this is the conclusion to which we seem to arrive, when we consider the domain of values and its study and practice through processes of education.

V
Values Prescribed by Religions and Moral Systems

- ❖ In view of the above analysis, it appears that there is no need to labour unduly on preparing lists of values and to enter into controversies as to which values should be advocated, whether they should belong to one specific religion or the other, or of one particular moral system or the other, or of one particular culture or another. Value-oriented education is to be a process of development of goodwill, and its method would be that of an exploration of the realm of values, and, again, what is to be emphasised is to orient the students to the dimensions of values rather than to the prescription of do's and don'ts of any set of values. If properly explored, this would lead to the exploration of various other sets of values, so that each student would then be free to determine for himself or herself what values one should adopt as a result of a sincere exploration of the realm of values.

- ❖ Under the guidance of this general and overarching spirit of value-oriented education, we may take the Socratic view that Virtue is Unity and that no virtue can be fully practised unless in the course of practice, all virtues are embraced. There is no harm in preparing lists of virtues, and we may even contemplate hierarchy or relationships among virtues. But all this can be encouraged as a part of exploration, allowing every student to arrive at his or her own conclusions.

❖ Indeed, it is very useful to explore and compare one set of realms with other sets of values.

❖ In the process of exploration, it is certainly salutary to emphasise those values, which foster unity and harmony, integration and integrity of the nation and human unity and peace. Inevitably, those values, which have been laid down as binding under constitutional law as rights or duties will also come to be emphasised and cultivated as a part of citizenship. Also, in our own times, there are universal declarations of rights and responsibilities and these also have to be underlined and cultivated amongst students. In the process of education, however, examination of these values and even a critical examination has to be fostered and has to be considered as a part of the pursuit of value dimension.

VI
Integral Value-Oriented Education

❖ A very important concept that has become predominant in recent educational thought is that of integral education. At the international level, this concept came to be centrally highlighted by UNESCO through its famous report "Learning to Be", which laid down "that the aim of development is complete fulfilment of the human being, in all the richness of personality, complexity of form of expression and various commitments."

❖ It is increasingly realised that in the contemporary world, the humanist and the technologist are finding themselves in greater and greater need of each other and the scientist and the mystic are getting ready to embrace each other.

❖ It is being acknowledged that human personality is complex and that each major element of the personality needs to be integrated with the totality in a harmonious manner. In other words, the physical, the vital, the mental, the psychic and spiritual do not stand in juxtaposition, but they have among them a constitutional relationship. The physical and the vital can, to a great extent, be controlled and guided by the mental, and to a certain stage of development the mind can act as a leader. But the leadership of the mind is rather restricted and often fails and fails disastrously in controlling or leading the vital and the physical. Reason is opposed by Unreason, and conflict between the two, as seen today, is extremely grave. Moreover, as the rational, ethical, and aesthetic powers of the mind begin to develop, they begin to collide among themselves. It is, therefore, being recognised that the psychic and the spiritual powers of the human personality need to be brought forward so as to establish the true integration of all the powers of the being.

❖ In our present system of education, we are too occupied with mental development, and we give preponderant importance to those qualities, which are relevant to subject-oriented and examination-oriented systems. In contrast, the concept of integral education implies a simultaneous integrated process of the development of the qualities and values relevant to physical education, vital education, mental education, psychic and spiritual education.

❖ In the domain of physical education, the values that are implied are those of health, strength, plasticity, grace and beauty. In the domain of emotional education or vital education, the values that are pursued are those of illumination, heroism, and harmony. In the domain of the rational development, the values that are to be sought after are those of utmost impartiality, dispassionate search after truth, calm and silence and widest possible synthesis. The values pertaining to aesthetic development would be those of vision of beauty and creative joy of the deepest possible aesthetic experience and expression. Values that the moral being ought to seek are those of sincere goodwill and obedience to whatever one conceives to be the highest. In psychic education, the values to be sought after are those of the aim of life, the highest development of the individuality free from egoism and knowledge that guides the inmost and harmonious relationship between the individual and the cosmic, and fulfilment in the light of the supreme discoveries of the ultimate reality, whatever it may be. The values of the spiritual domain are those of highest unity and oneness and pursuit of perfection of all parts of the being and of instruments of personality.

❖ Integral value-oriented education is a matter of research, and the results of this research indicate the need to simultaneously develop knowledge, will, harmony and skill, and that this development should be for each individual a system of natural organisation of the highest processes and movements of which he or she is capable.

❖ It may be observed that integral value-oriented education could be pursued independently of any particular, moral or religious doctrine or any particular spiritual discipline. Whether one belongs to one religion or the other or to no religion, one can pursue this integral process through a process of exploration, even experimentally and experientially.

VII
Morality and Spirituality

❖ In any sound philosophy of value-oriented education, an effort should be made to arrive at clear conceptions of morality and spirituality, since both are distinct and yet related, and since both need to be distinguished from religion. Again, this matter is very important in the context of the Indian system of education, since the Indian Constitution clearly states that "No religious instruction shall be provided in educational institutions wholly maintained out of the State Funds", and that "No person attending any educational institution recognised by the State and receiving aid out of State Funds shall be required to take part in any religious instruction that may be imparted in such institutions or to attend any religious worship that may be conducted in such institutions or in premises attached thereto unless such person or, if such a person is a minor, his guardian has given his consent thereto."

- As far as the distinction between morality and spirituality is concerned, it may be said that much depends upon what we intend to include in our definition of the word "morality" or in the word "spirituality". In Indian thought, a distinction between morality and spirituality has been clearly made and we have two definite terms, *naitik* and *adhyatmik* each having its own specific and distinguishing connotation.

- The word "morality" connotes a pursuit of the control and mastery over impulses and desires under the guidance and supervening inspiration of a standard of conduct formulated by thought in consideration of man's station and duties in the society or in consideration of any discovered or prescribed intrinsic law of an idea. Morality is often conceived as a preparation of spirituality. Spirituality, on the other hand, begins when one seeks whatever one conceives to be the ultimate and the absolute for its own sake unconditionally and without any reservation whatsoever. Moreover, while morality is often limited to the domain of duties, spirituality is fundamentally a search of the knowledge that liberates (*sa vidyā ya vimuktaye*). As it is declared, true knowledge is not intellectual knowledge but spiritual knowledge.

- Both the moral and the spiritual are to be distinguished from what is called "religious" when we speak of religious instruction. Religion, which can be called *sampradaya* has the following distinguishing features:

Philosophy of Value-Oriented Education - I

1. Specific religious dogma regarding the nature of Reality, laid down in scripture or by traditional founder, prophet or incarnation;

2. Every specific religion has, as its essential ingredient, certain prescribed acts, rituals and ceremonies;

   A religious authority to which religious matters are referred and the decision of which is final.

3. Both moral and spiritual values can be practiced irrespective of whether one believes in one religion or another or whether one believes in no religion. Both morality and spirituality can be independent of the rituals or ceremonies and of any acts specifically prescribed by any particular religion. Furthermore, both of them are independent of any authority expect that of one's own free judgement and direct spiritual experience.

4. It is also useful to distinguish religion from what in India is called *dharma*. *Dharma* is not any religious creed or dogma nor a system of rituals, but a deeper law of the harmonious and interdependent growth of the deepest aspirations of the collectivity and of the individuals that constitute the collectivity. *Dharma* can be regarded as an ordered system of moral and spiritual values.

5. Spirituality proceeds directly by change of consciousness, change from the ordinary consciousness to a greater consciousness in which one finds one's true unegoistic being and comes first into direct and living contact and then into union with the Spirit. In spirituality, this change of conscious-

ness is the one thing that matters, nothing else. Spirituality not only aims at the total change of consciousness, but its method is that of a gradual and increasing change of consciousness. In other words, spirituality is an exploration of consciousness through a progressive change of consciousness.

6. In spiritual consciousness, and in the knowledge that it delivers, there is the fulfilment of the highest that morality and religion in their deepest core seek and succeed only when they cease to be limited within their specific boundaries. It replaces the moral law by a progressive law of self-perfection spontaneously expressing itself through the individual nature. In this operation, no more is the imposition of a rule or an imperative on the nature of an individual. The spiritual law respects the individual nature, modifies it and perfects it, and in this sense, it is unique for each individual and can be known and made operative only during the course of the change of consciousness. In its progressive movement, it may, if necessary, provide a sort of long period of governance by a moral law, but always as a provisional device and always looking for going beyond into a plane of spontaneous expression of the Right and the Good. To spiritual consciousness, moral virtue is not valuable in itself, but only as an expression of a complex of certain qualities, which are, for the time being, for the given individual, necessary and useful in an upward journey. For the spiritual consciousness, what is commonly called vice has, too, behind it a complex of certain qualities, which have a certain utility in the economy of Nature, and can, therefore, be converted by placing them in

Philosophy of Value-Oriented Education - I

their right place, as a complement to what lies in consciousness behind what are commonly called virtues.

7. Spirituality is not confined merely to the aspect of conduct; it includes all works and strives by the method of a progressive change of consciousness for the perfect harmonisation of all the aspects of works; and through this striving it realises also the unity of works with the highest Knowledge and the deepest Love.

8. For spiritual consciousness, that which is commonly called agnosticism, scepticism, atheism, positivism or free thinking has behind it a concern and a demand for a direct knowledge, which, when rightly understood, recognised, respected and fulfilled, becomes a powerful element of spirituality.

9. For spirituality always looks behind the form to the essence and to the living consciousness; and in doing so, it brings to the surface that which lies behind, and its action is therefore of a new creation. Spirituality transcends the forms and methods of morality and religion and recreates its own living and progressive forms.

10. In the words of Sri Aurobindo:

    Spirituality is in its essence an awakening to the inner reality of our being, to a spirit, self, soul, which is other than our mind, life and body, an inner aspiration to know, to feel, to be that, to enter into contact with the greater Reality beyond and pervading the universe which inhabits also our own being, to be in communion with It and union with It and a turning, a conversion, a transformation of our whole being as a result of the aspiration, the contact, the union, a growth or waking into a new becoming or new being, a new self, a new nature.

VIII
Values of Indian Culture

a. It is natural that Indian education underlines the importance of what can be called Indian values.

b. In Indian thought, a distinction has been made between the ego and the self. According to Indian thought, egoistic personality is ridden with self-contradiction and conflicts and true self is the integrating centre in which physical, vital, mental and other personalities are harmonised. Pursuit of self-realisation is held out in Indian educational thought as one of the supreme spiritual values.

c. There are, indeed, certain other values which are uniquely Indian, in the sense that even though these values may be commonly shared by India and other countries, they are pursued in India either with a certain special zeal and dedication or pursued with a certain speciality or completeness. For example, the value that we attach to the ideal of tolerance is something special in India. In fact, the word tolerance itself is not adequate to convey the intended meaning. In the ordinary idea of tolerance, there is still a feeling that our own preferred idea is somewhat superior to the other contending ideas. On the other hand, what is peculiarly Indian is the sentiment and the

Philosophy of Value-Oriented Education - I

recognition that various principal contending ideas are all equally legitimate ideas and that superiority lies not in holding one idea as some preferred idea but in trying to find such a synthesis that each idea finds its own highest fulfilment in it. What is uniquely Indian is that the value and ideal of synthesis has been pursued throughout the long history of Indian culture as the most desirable goal – and that too repeatedly and with very special insistence.

d. Along with the basic idea of synthesis, there is also the accompanying idea of unity, mutuality and oneness in diversity.

e. Similarly, what is meant by secularism in the Indian context is uniquely Indian. According to the Western idea, secularism means a tendency or a system of beliefs, which rejects all forms of religious faith or worship. It means something that pertains to the present world or to things, which are not spiritual or sacred. In the Indian context, however, secularism means comprehensiveness in which all religions receive equal protection, treatment and respect, and in which there is place for every one whether he belongs to one religion or another or to no religion. Again, Indian secularism encourages us to approach everything, whether material or spiritual, with a sense of sacredness. In Indian secularism, there is freedom for the propagation of each religion without hindrance or bar and there is also the freedom to promote and propagate synthesis of religions. At the same time, Indian secularism insists on the promotion of moral and spiritual values, which are common to all religions and to no religion as also on the promotion of a synthesis of science and spirituality. Secularism so defined and understood is, thus, a very special value that is uniquely Indian.

f. There are several other Indian values, which require a special mention and which should find their right place in our educational system. The sense of joy that is behind various festivals in India, which are shared by the people of the country is something, which can be understood only when one enters into the heart and soul of Indian culture. The Indian idea of the rhythm of life and the law of harmony, expressed by the word *Dharma* is also uniquely Indian. Again, the value that we attach to pursuit of knowledge, to the pursuit of purity, to the pursuit of wisdom is something unique, in the sense that these things are valued most and they are cherished most, and on the call of which we are inspired to renounce everything. We feel that all this and many other values, which are uniquely Indian should be encouraged and fostered.

g. It is noteworthy that the great Indian values, some of which we have mentioned above, became dynamically vibrant during the period of India's struggle for freedom. In fact, this period was marked by the rise of great men and women who embodied these values and enriched them. Again, it was during this period that these values guided and shaped great movements and events. Thus a study of our nationalist movement provides a perennial source of inspiration, and it should be a part of a programme of value-oriented education.

PHILOSOPHY OF VALUE-ORIENTED EDUCATION- II

We are passing through a critical stage of a battle between the best possibilities and the worst possibilities. At a time when forces of unity and harmony can triumph and science and technology can be used to abolish poverty and deprivation, precisely at that time, the forces of violence and gravitational pulls of impulses of the lower human nature are pressing forward on a global scale. Rationality, in which humanity has placed great trust for arriving at the fulfilment of its ideals of true knowledge and comprehensive knowledge, appears to be overtaken by the forces of Unreason. It has, therefore, become imperative to explore deeper and higher dimensions of human resources by means of which we can successfully work for the victory of the ideal dreams, which have inspired the onward march of civilisation.

It is in this context that the theme of education for character development has emerged with some imperative force. And our eyes have turned to the dimensions of values, the dimensions of will-power and the dimensions of cultural, ethical and spiritual potentialities. These dimensions have not yet been sufficiently explored, but we have begun to uncover what lies in our present framework that would meet our urgent need to uplift ourselves and the coming generations.

In India, our constitution has been wisely prefaced with the ideals of justice, liberty, equality and fraternity in its very Preamble. It has guaranteed certain basic fundamental rights and it has given a chapter on Directive Principles of the State Policy, which although not legally enforceable, embodies ideals and values, which are salutary for the progress of India on the lines which had come to be articulated and cherished during the Freedom Struggle.

In 1976, realising that apart from Rights, there is a need to emphasise responsibilities, obligations and duties of the citizens; Article 51 A was inserted to lay down certain fundamental duties. It is to that Article that we have recently turned our focal attention, with the hope that its operationalisation in the field of education would bring about a new climate of recovery of forces that can regenerate national ethos, unity and integrity.

Government of India did well, therefore, in appointing a high level committee, in July 1998, to operationalise suggestions to teach fundamental duties to the citizens of the country. This Committee was chaired by Mr. Justice J.S. Verma, the former Chief Justice of India, and it submitted its final Report to the Minister of Human Resource Development on 31st October, 1999.

The Verma Committee has done well to highlight the work which has been done by the International Interaction Council in drafting a Declaration of Human Responsibilities.

This Council had a preliminary meeting in Vienna, Austria in March 1996, April 1997, and the Plenary Session was held in Noordwijk, Netherlands, in June 1997. On 1st September 1997, the Inter-Action Council proposed a universal declaration of human responsibilities, just one year before the 50th anniversary of the Universal Declaration of

Philosophy of Value-Oriented Education - II

Human Rights adopted by the United Nations. A number of former prime ministers, former presidents, and leading personalities in the fields of thought and practical action have endorsed this draft of the Universal Declaration of Human Responsibilities. The basic point that has been made by the Universal Declaration of Human Responsibilities is that the concept of human obligations serves to balance the notions of freedom and responsibilities. Without a proper balance, unrestricted freedom is as dangerous as imposed social responsibilities. It declares, in effect, that if we have a right to life then we have the obligation to respect life; and if we have right to liberty, then we have the obligation to respect other peoples' liberty too. In other words, the golden rule of responsibility is that we do not do to others what we do not wish to be done to us; or that we should do unto others as we would have them to do unto us.

This draft declaration, which has now been submitted to the world community at large reaffirms that the time has come to talk about responsibilities, about obligations. It also shows that the action taken by the Government of India to set up a Committee of Teaching Fundamental Duties is timely and that while have talked for decades of value education, we have now to take decisive action in implementing the programmes of value education.

Let us recall that various commissions and committees of the Government of India have underlined the importance of value education and important recommendations have been made to distinguish morality and spirituality from religious creeds, so that imparting of moral and spiritual values does not come within the purview of the prohibition that is laid down in the Constitution to impart religious education in educational institutions that are financially supported by the Government. Dr.

Radhakrishnan had made a distinction between a religious education and education about religions and advocated that there is no constitutional disability in imparting education about religions in our educational system. The Sriprakasa Committee had advocated moral, emotional and cultural education as understood in their widest connotations. The Kothari Commissionr recommended value-education that is in coherence with the development of science and scientific temper. The National Education Policy, 1986, devoted one full section to value education.

Unfortunately, our curricula, by and large, have changed little or only marginally. The main difficulty has been that there has been a long drawn out debate on what values should be promoted and what place should be given to the study of religions, which are closely connected with value systems. In answer to this debate, there is one thing which is very clear, and that is the Fundamental Duties, which have been listed in the Constitution, which represents national consensus and which has some kind of binding force.

The Fundamental Duties include, first and foremost, the obligation on the part of the citizens to abide by the Constitution and to respect its ideals and institutions. In large terms, this would mean obligation to secure justice, liberty, equality and fraternity as also the values that are embedded in the Fundamental Rights and the Directive Principles of the State Policy. In declaring that these duties will include the obligation to cherish and follow the noble ideals which inspired our national struggle for freedom, we have a wide spectrum of values, spiritual, moral, economic, social and political. Again, in laying down the obligations to value and preservation of the rich heritage of our composite culture, the Constitution has stressed the wide range of values that have come to be cherished right from the times of the Veda to the present day, which has played a role toward assimilation and synthesis. Again, in laying down the duties to develop scientific temper, humanism and the spirit of inquiry and reform, the emphasis has been laid on the value of truth, knowledge and freedom from dogmatism and obscurantism – all that is valuable in modernism. In requiring everyone to protect and improve the natural environment and in renouncing practices that are derogatory to the dignity of women and in developing compassion for living creatures, some of the most pressing problems of contemporary times in the fields of environment and empowerment of women has been taken into account. Finally, by insisting on striving towards excellence in all the spheres of individual and collective activity, a great ideal has been stressed in respect of the perfectibility of the individual and the society and their harmonious relationships.

This is not an occasion to bring out the implications of these duties and salutary effects that the operationalisation of duties in the field of education could bring about. It must be said, however, that this operationalisation should be regarded as a good beginning in the right direction, although the highest goals of man-making education of which Swami Vivekananda spoke will imply a still greater effort and we should not lose sight of this higher goal and the need for still greater efforts.

There is a dimension of values, which transcends the dimension of duties. That dimension is the spontaneous perception and commitment to ends-in-themselves. If I love a friend only as a matter of duty, it is, in a sense, not as valuable as I do so out of my spontaneous appreciation and admiration for him and for his achievements and qualities. Love for my own country as a duty is inferior to the love of a patriot that arises spontaneously in his heart and soul, as he looks upon his country as the very source of his breath and life. Search for truth is an end in itself; search for goodness is an end itself, search for beauty is an end itself; and they have to be encouraged not as duties but as irresistible demands of our being as we begin to uncover deeper and higher depths of our Selves, which transcend the limitations of egoism.

Self-knowledge and self-control are the true foundations of value education. As Socrates had pointed out, virtue is knowledge, and it is when knowledge is rightly pursued, that pursuit of virtue attains its right place as a spontaneous action and it has lustre brighter than that obtains in performance of our duty.

These reflections have two important consequences in our formulations of value-education. Firstly, value-education does not merely remain a matter of do's and don'ts; it becomes a process of exploration, and it crosses the border of constraints that are felt in the performance of duties and leads us into a realm of freedom of which discipline for performance of duty is a happy product. Secondly, value education opens before us the gates of the harmony between truth, beauty and goodness, which impart to us the sources of true humanism and even our true godliness.

It is necessary to bring out, even though briefly, these important dimensions of value education, since it will hep us better to prepare our curriculum of value-education in its wider aspects, and also to prepare corresponding programmes of teacher-education.

The role of the teacher in education is irreplaceable, and unless the teachers' programmes or training are conceived in the light of the full implications of value-education, we shall not be able to equip the teachers with the right inspiration and with the required tools. If value-education has suffered so far, it is because teachers' training programmes fall short in many ways of an ideal system. We require to redesign programmes of teachers' education, both pre-service and in-service; in a certain sense, we need to overhaul our entire system of teacher-education, keeping in view that value education is absolutely imperative and unless a good teacher is himself value-oriented, we cannot fulfil the objectives of value education.

We have to realise that methods of value education have to be different from those, which are required in respect of many other subjects. The reason is that in value education what we need is not merely the cultivation of cognitive faculties but also affective and conative faculties. One cannot merely give lectures on value education and expect to fulfil the objectives. Just as swimming cannot be taught merely by lecturing, but by leading the learner to jump into the water and help him in the practical art of swimming in the midst of water, similarly, value education requires of the teacher the ability to inspire the students to enter into the waters of life-situations and give him practical abilities and art of practising values in concrete situations of life. In a sense, it may be said that value education is perhaps the most difficult domain among all domains of education.

Without going into details, it may be said that we need to undertake a three-pronged exercise in the teacher education programmes:

Firstly, our programmes must be so inspiring that teachers come to look upon the task of teaching as sacred;

Secondly, the curriculum of teachers' training programme should have the component of the theory of value-education, both in terms of the foundations of Fundamental Duties and of the values, which lie beyond the domain of duties; and it should have also a component of practical art of the practice of exploration of values in life-situations.

And thirdly, the duration that is normally assigned to teacher education programmes should be sufficiently enlarged. A most salutary combination would be to propose an integrated programme of teacher education of the duration of five years on the completion of class XII, leading to a qualification equivalent to post-graduation. That has also consequences for career development and other aspects relevant to the structure and framework of teaching profession. But this is an aspect, which needs to be looked into separately.

In any programme of education for character development, we need to ask three important questions. Firstly, we have to determine with greater precision what we mean by character and how the development of character can be stimulated and nourished through the processes of communication and information, cultivation of faculties, and the methods by which the states of consciousness, which express themselves in virtues can be stabilised. For character development is concerned with what may be called being or the central core of the individuality, which tends to grow into universality and sovereignty of transcendence. Indeed, the concepts of individuality, universality and transcendence can be communicated to some extent in the form of information which relates to the history of these concepts and how these concepts have been interpreted by different thinkers, scholars and practitioners and how they have been applied in life and in the development of civilisations and cultures. Indeed, this information can kindle the inner urge of the individual to grow inwardly and to fashion the processes of learning, which can properly be called the processes of learning to be. But still, the part played by communication of information in the development of character is only peripheral or of primary importance and not of chief importance.

A greater part is played in the character development by the development or cultivation of faculties and if we study numerous faculties that human personality comes to posses, we shall find that they relate to four main groups namely, (1) those which pertain to understanding, comprehension, synthesis, universality, knowledge and wisdom; (2) those that relate to will-power, fearlessness, courage, heroism, control, mastery, power and strength; (3) those that relate to imagination, sensibility, emotional refinement, harmony in relationships, friendship, co-operation, loyalty, allegiance, and unfailing love, and (4) those that pertain to skills of expressions, patience, perseverance, endurance, love for precision, and detailed execution of command, order, system and search for perfection. Unfortunately, in our curricular framework preponderant emphasis is laid upon communication of information, but no deliberate attempt is made to the task of stimulating the cultivation of faculties; and yet, if faculties develop among our students, they do so because faculties have an inborn stress in themselves to push forward their developments. But a more rational and careful curriculum should provide guidelines, occasions and exercises by which faculties can be cultivated consciously and systematically.

But of even greater importance in character development is the role-played by development of attitudes and states of consciousness. The depth of seriousness, which accompanies the process of search or quest will determine the quality of search or quest and its eventual success. And the states of seriousness result from the cultivation of sincerity. If we examine closely, we shall find that what we call virtues are basically manifestations of certain states of consciousness; it is virtues that constitute character; and the stability of character depends upon the stabilisation of those states of consciousness which constitute virtues. How to develop, therefore, virtuous states of consciousness and how to stabilize them should constitute a major constituent of education for character development?

Closely connected with this first set of questions is the second set of questions which relate to the aim of life. The moment we raise the question of aim of life, we begin to address ourselves to something that is central in our being, in our potentialities and in what we can become and can be fulfilled. No great character can be built where the aim of life remains a matter of doubt or tends to be neglected or retained for consideration or amusement in our hours of idleness or superficial leisure. Indeed, the theme of the aim of life should become a theme of exploration, and during the process of exploration one has to pass through periods of doubts, periods of long reflection, periods of experimentation and even of uncertainty. Educational process should provide both time and scope for this kind of exploration and every student should be provided with enough material in respect of this theme. Indeed, no prefixed aim of life should be proposed and no indoctrination or dogmatic assertions should be thrust upon the mind and heart of the student. But the educational process should allow each student a process of exploration, experimentation and reflection as a result of which a mature decision is arrived at as to what aim of life one should pursue. It will then be seen that the quality of life and the quality of character reflect the quality of aim of life that one determines to realise.

Finally, there is a third set of questions, which are also relevant to the development of character. These questions relate to the ways and means by which students become conscious of the methods of learning and methods by which character can be developed. In other words, character development has to become a conscious process, a deliberate process, voluntary process. Students have to become conscious of the psychological complexities and how the tangles of instincts, desires, emotions, will-force, powers of thought, and imagination and the powers of aesthetic, ethical and spiritual consciousness can be understood, disentangled and yet controlled, mastered and harmonised. This perhaps is the most important part of education for character development. Here we have to focus upon the process by which students can gradually become conscious of their inner being, of their potentialities, of their own character so that students can take upon themselves the task of fashioning and perfecting what is best in them.

PHILOSOPHY OF INDIANNESS

I

An attempt to capture in conceptual grasp the meaning and content of Indianness is to plunge ourselves into the depths of Indian history and to discern those characteristics that are unique to India and which bring us to the understanding of the genius, spirit and soul of India.

Geographically, India's boundaries have often been fluctuating, although the great land between the Himalayas and the Indian ocean gives us a sense of unity of our dwelling, the land of our parents and the land of our birth; it is our sacred soil that we cherish and for which we have a passion of belongingness. But at a deeper level, our inner body is the men and women who compose our nation, and we realise that even our physical geography is a pulsating living power of the national soul that has its own line of development, its own temperament, and its law of being and becoming. We see teeming millions of our nation at work and in an ever-continuing labour, greatly determined and determining environmental motives, a play of economic forces, and a gradual course of institutional evolution. We go deeper and witness those exceptional individuals whose lives and examples have moulded the national thought and character and shaped the course of events. At a still deeper level, we discover Mother India, Bhārat Mātā, protector and nourisher of her children, inspiring them and helping them in their battle and victory, and leading them to the gradual revelation of her intention and will for her children as also the children of other nations, working for herself and for the world in collaboration with the mother-souls of all the nations in a spirit of collaboration, mutuality and goodwill for the Supreme Good of all.

To understand India is to understand Mother India and to grasp and possess four of her essential powers that have been developing since ages, *viz.*, the power of spirituality, the power of intellectuality, the power of vitality, and the power of skills, -- skills of art and craft, and skills of emotional bonds and durable relationships, and skills of fruitful life and harmony.

II

We must not judge India and derive the concept of Indianness from any superficial study or from the study of India of its latest phase when it began to show signs of exhaustion after having sought and attained and worked and produced incessantly at least for preceding three thousand years. The period of decline has to be admitted, and we have to acknowledge that the decline reached a nadir of setting energy. But that period cannot give us basic clues to the real spirit and soul of India and its expressive power of life, its intellectuality and creativity.

The British rulers gave to us three words to describe what they understood to be the chief characteristic of India, namely, metaphysics, religion, and the sense of Maya or illusoriness of the world; and by metaphysics, they meant an abstract and clouded tract of thought; by religion, they meant a system of ceremonies and rituals; and by Maya, they meant dreaminess, unpracticality and inefficiency to deal with life. For a time, Indians submissively echoed their new Western teachers and masters and considered these three words to be the formula of Indianness. The British could hardly understand the spirit of Indian art and dismissed it as something primitive. Fortunately, Europe discovered in due course that Indian art had remarkable power and beauty. But in regard to other domains of life, the British imposed upon India the view that India could hardly be recognised as a civilised country, and, in their ignorance of the true account of Indian history, derided the Indian discovery of the Dharma, belittled the enormous developments of Indian systems of knowledge or Shastras, considered Indian sociology as an unintelligent basis of the rigid and oppressive caste system, and thought of India's political ability as of no significance other than that of series of quarrels resulting in failure to achieve the unity of the country. Their views were imprinted strongly on the subjects that they ruled, and even though much has been discovered by Indians themselves and others to contradict the earlier distorted opinion concerning India, and even though during the Freedom Struggle much was done to recover the sense of India's greatness, there is still unpardonable misunderstanding, among many Indians, of the real meaning of the Indian genius, obliging us to study deeply and formulate to ourselves in clearer terms what we ought to mean by Indianness.

If we study Indian history properly, we shall find that her first period was luminous with the discovery of the Spirit; her second completed the discovery of Dharma; her third period elaborated into detail the first simpler formulation of the Shastra; none was exclusive, the three elements were always present; into the fourth period India had, even while getting exhausted, a kind of rejuvenation with the birth of a number of Indian languages and new religions of Bhakti and submission to Divine Love and Will. We must examine these periods and arrive at our own impartial judgement of India's Indianness.

In broad terms, it can be stated that Indian spirit and Indian temperament have manifested themselves, broadly speaking, on five lines:

i. Integrality, assimilation, and synthesis, based on centrality of spirituality;

i. Development of exuberance of life and robust and meticulous intellectuality so as to support multisided inquiry and questioning, and experimentation of every major line of spirituality, thought, and life activity and tendency to its extreme acuteness, followed by a wide and catholic assimilation and quintessential crystallisation;

ii. Development of organisation of life on principle of decentralisation followed by the process towards unity that supports and encourages diversity;

iii. Highest worship for knowledge and wisdom, highest admiration for courage and heroism that involve self-sacrifice, and battle for the Right and Justice, intense appreciation for mutuality in relationship and artistic creativity and generous charity that aims at welfare of all; and

iv. Intense labour to manifest a detailed perfection and exuberance of joy of life, as also for system, organisation and restraint that secure equilibrium, balance and graduality of development.

III

The master-word of Indianness is spirituality, and this word has to be understood in its distinct clarity and fullness. For although the spiritual is associated with religion and morality and refinement of mental or aesthetic sensitivity, it still transcends them all and fulfils them all, and acts as a sovereign and liberating and integrating power. Although India developed a number of religions like a banyan tree and even gave place to religions that came from other countries, it still pointed to a distinct and higher power of spiritual development, which goes beyond belief or dogma and rituals and ceremonies and codes of conduct. It begins with experiential contact with reality or realities that lie above body, life and mind and supports union, growth or waking into a spirit, self, soul by the practices of inner aspiration to know, feel and to be, to enter into a greater Reality beyond and pervading the universe and to be into communion with It and union with It. It culminates not only into a turning and conversion but into a transformation of our whole being and our entire ordinary physical, vital and mental nature. So distinctive is this spirituality of India that its entire domain constitutes the field of experimentation and verifiable and repeatable experiences and realisations and a well-developed discipline that has been acknowledged increasingly as a Science of Yoga.

Long ago in the remote past, there arose a quest in a small nucleus of people, surrounded by a large population, still in the early conditions of life, in the subcontinent that came to be called Bhāratavarsha and much later India. This quest, which appears to have been extremely arduous and heroic, resulted in a momentous spiritual attainment and victory, the records of which have been called the Veda, the Book of Knowledge. The language of this book is highly symbolic, and even though its meaning is greatly veiled, it allows occasional transparency and even full revelation to those who are enlightened and illumined. During this quest, the leaders, who were called poets or Rishis, had made a number of discoveries, which were repeated and verified and internalised and even transmitted to the initiates, as a result of which there grew up what can be called a Tradition. The knowledge attained was fundamentally spiritual in character, even though it had also many other aspects connected with the knowledge of the physical universe and several other planes of existence, which are clearly described in these ancient records.

The Vedic seers also developed specific methods by which their fund of knowledge can be sustained, enriched and further developed. These methods, in due course, came to be known as Yogic methods, and the Veda can rightly be looked upon as the foundation of Yoga. However, as it often happens, spiritual knowledge and spiritual methods often get clouded and deteriorated into external ritualism, and this seems to have happened in regard to the Vedic knowledge, as can be seen from the Brahmana literature. Normally, under the excessive weight of ritualism and growing obscurity, the original knowledge would have been eclipsed almost totally, but in India there came about a period of a fresh movement of quest, and the Vedic knowledge was revisited in a constant recurrence of realisation, the records of which are known as Upanishads and they became a perennial reservoir from where numerous fountains sprang up and continue to be rising until today. As a result, the central characteristic of Indianness came to be firmly established, and spirituality can unhesitatingly be seen as the distinguishing speciality of the Indian soul and the defining differentia of Indianness.

The description of the quest that we find in the Upanishads is so living and vibrant that the scenes of the old world live before us and we seem to witness the sages sitting in their groves ready to test and teach the visitor; we witness also princes and learned Brahmins and even great landed nobles going about in search of knowledge, and we see how the soul of India was born and how the highest vistas of the knowledge of the Spirit came to be embodied and expressed in terms, less symbolic and much more accessible to philosophical thought. The Vedic and the Upanishadic spirituality has remained constantly alive in varied degrees, and the Upanishads have particularly been the sufficient fountainhead not only of Indian philosophy and religion, but of all Indian art, poetry and literature.

The Vedic and the Upanishadic quest was that of immortality and of the eternal Truth in its integrality, discoverable on the heights beyond the mind and in the planes described symbolically as those of higher light and highest light, *swar* and *surya* respectively. As a Rigvedic *rik* proclaims:

उद्वयं तमसस्परि स्वः पश्यन्त उत्तरम्।
देवं देवत्रा सूर्यमगन्म ज्योतिरुत्तमम्। *RV.I. 50.10*

> We perceived the higher light of Swar beyond the darkness, and we arrived at the highest light of the Sun.

And when the Vedic seers spoke of the attainment of immortality, they spoke of their victory while in the physical body. As Parashara points out:

आ ये विश्वा स्वपत्यानि तस्थुः।
कृण्वानासो अमृतत्वाय गातुम्।।
मह्ना महद्भिः पृथिवी वि तस्थे।
माता पुत्रैरदितिर्ध्यसे वेः।। *RV. I.72.9.*

The physical being visited by the greatness of the infinite planes above and by the power of the great godheads who reign on those planes breaks its limits, opens out to the Light and is upheld in its new wideness by the infinite Consciousness, mother Aditi, and her sons, the divine Powers the supreme Deva.[1]

It was the search of this victory that we find in the Kathopanishad when Naciketas asks of Yama to reveal to him the meaning of immortality and the method by which immortality can be won. And it is this immortality to which reference is made in the Brihadaranyka Upanishad in its famous prayer:

असतो मा सद्गमय।
तमसो मा ज्योतिर्गमय।
मृत्योर्मा अमृतम् गमय।। *Brihadaranyaka Upanishad I.3.28.*

Lead me from the unreal to the Real;
Lead me from darkness to Light;
Lead me from death to Immortality.

---

[1] Sri Aurobindo: *The Secret of the Veda*, Vol. 15, The Complete Works of Sri Aurobindo, 1998 Edition, pp.199-200.

Philosophy of Indianness

And the Vedic seers have laid down that immortality cannot be won except by Truth – Truth that is all-comprehensive and capable of manifestation without disintegration. It is this realisation that led to the powerful formulation of the Mundaka Upanishad: सत्यमेव जयते (It is truth that conquers), and it is significant that these potent words have now become the motto inscribed in the emblem of free India.

Let us first note the fact that the loftiest spiritual experiences are found recorded in the Vedic Samhitas, and it can be said that the spirituality of the Veda and the Upanishads was already synthetic and integral. An exclusive spirituality emphasises and remains confined only to one state of spiritual consciousness, -- such as that of eternal Silence or of eternal Joy, or of dynamic Power, to either divine Personality or to divine Impersonality. It emphasises only one method of approach, such as that of works, knowledge or devotion. But we do not find this kind of exclusiveness in the Veda and in the Upanishads like the Isha, or Kena or Katha or Taittiriya. The fullness of spiritual life is perceived in the great pronouncement of the Vedic and the Upanishadic Rishis: तेन त्यक्तेन भुञ्जीथाः (by having renounced thou shouldst enjoy) is one of the formulas of the integral spiritual life; and there are several others in the Ishopanishad itself, such as those relating to the Reality that is at once moving and unmoving, that relating to the synthesis of Ignorance and Knowledge, and that relating to birth and non-birth (सम्भूति and असम्भूति). We do not find here the rejection and meaninglessness of life and the world but rather the secret of transcending the limitations of the world and yet embracing with mastery the life and works in the world. The idea that the world and its activities must be renounced was a later development, when India made an experiment of sounding each line of spiritual experience to its farthest point, and chose to look from that farthest point at existence, so as to see what Truth or power it could give. That was the part of the heroic adventure of the Indian spirituality that manifested the spirit of experimentation and even a risky experimentation. There have been from this point of view the birth and growth of a number of exclusive spiritual pursuits, but underlying them there has been the spirit of synthesis and assimilation. It is remarkable that after the period of decline, when India is rising once again, we find among the leaders of the renascent spiritual India a definitive turn, with a greater richness and fullness, to a new integrality, such as what we find in Sri Ramakrishna and Sri Aurobindo. We have now in our own times the development of spirituality that found itself on the special emphasis on synthesis and dynamic manifestation of the Spirit in life on the earth.

In a larger perspective of the history of the Indian spirituality, we can derive three important lessons that characterise true Indianness; firstly, that spirituality does not flourish on earth in the void; secondly, that spirituality and exuberance of life and robust intellectuality are not opposed to each other, but are rather complementary to each other; and thirdly, that spiritual tendency does not imply inefficiency or incapability to deal with life successfully and fruitfully, but, on the contrary, it can provide the highest basis for perfection of life on the earth.

It has, indeed, been argued that too much religion ruined India, because India made whole life religion or religion the whole life. This is a complete misreading; it is true that India did fall in its period of exhaustion, and it did fail for a certain period of time; but if we study the period of this fall and failure, we shall find that it was because the public life became most irreligious, egoistic, self-seeking, and materialistic that India fell and had to pass through a painful period of slavery and deprivation. But once again, when India rose in the 19th and 20th centuries, the most leading power of reawakening has come from the impulse of dynamic spirituality and a synthetic spirituality.

IV

To speak only of Indian spirituality is an incomplete and misleading description of Indianness. For before the period of exhaustion, for at least three thousand years, India created abundantly and incessantly, lavishly, with an inexhaustible many-sidedness; it built republics, kingdoms and empires; it constructed philosophies and cosmogonies; it developed sciences and arts and poems; it raised all kinds of monuments, palaces and temples and public works; it organised communities and societies and religious orders, laws and codes and rituals; developed and systematised physical sciences, psychic sciences, systems of Yoga, systems of politics and administration, arts spiritual, arts worldly, trades, industries and fine crafts. We are struck with India's stupendous vitality, her inexhaustible power of life and joy of life, her prolific creativeness.

We have to remember, too, that India expanded even outside its borders; its ships crossed the oceans and the superfluous surplus of its wealth brimmed over Judea and Egypt and Rome. India's colonies spread Indian arts, and epics, and creeds in the Archipelago; Indian religions conquered China and Japan and spread westwards as far as Palestine and Alexandria. In the ancient architecture, sculpture and art, India laboured to fill every rift with ore, occupy every inch with plenty. This was because of the necessity of India's super-abundance of life, of the teeming of the infinite of the Indian soul.

Intellectuality is also an essential part of Indianness. This intellectuality is strong and at once austere and rich, robust and minute, powerful and delicate, massive in principle and curious in detail. It has been rightly said that India has been pre-eminently the land of the Dharma and the Shastra. India laboured to discover the inner truth and law of each human or cosmic activity, its Dharma, and it went father to apply it and cast it into elaborate form and detailed law of arrangement and rule of life. There appears to be no historical parallel for such an intellectual labour as we find during the period from Ashoka well into the Mohammedan epoch. Prior to the invention of printing and facilities of modern science, India produced colossal literature, which certainly dealt with philosophy and theology, and religion and yoga; but it also dealt with logic and rhetoric and grammar and linguistics; it dealt with poetry and drama; it produced works on medicine and astronomy and other sciences; in the fields of arts, the literature spanned from painting to dancing, of the 64 accomplishments, and all that was known and could be useful to life and interesting to the mind. There is also literature available to us of that period that deals with such practical minutiae as the breeding and training of horses and elephants, each of which had its shastra with its art, its apparatus of technical terms and its copious literature. India's intellectuality can be seen to have been marked by insatiable curiosity, the desire of life to know itself in every detail, and at the same time by a spirit of organisation and scrupulous order, the desire of the mind to tread through life with a harmonised knowledge and in the right rhythm and measure. Indian mind was powerful, penetrating and scrupulously intelligent, -- combined of the rational, ethical, and aesthetic mind at a height of intensity.

As noted earlier, India has a tendency to pursue most opposite extremes to their highest point of climax, but this never resulted in disorder. Even its most hedonistic period offers nothing that at all resembles the unbridled corruption which have a similar tendency that was once produced in Europe. The reason is that the Indian mind is not only spiritual and ethical but intellectual and artistic, and both the rule of the intellect and the rhythm of art are hostile to the spirit of chaos. In every extreme, the Indian spirit seeks for a law in that extreme and its rule, measure and structure in its application. In the ultimate analysis, the Indian mind returns always towards some fusion of the knowledge it has gained and to a resulting harmony and balance in action and in institution. The Greeks had also arrived at balance and rhythm, but they arrived at it by self-imitation; India arrived at balance and rhythm by its sense of intellectual, aesthetic and ethical order and the synthetic impulse of its mind and life.

V

We stand today at a very important juncture of our history. We have already been able to recover ourselves to some extent, but we still need to understand our inmost soul and its need to express itself in the light of its own law of self-development. India has since ages erected the ideal of universal brotherhood, and this is the moment when the issue of unity of the world has come to the forefront. It can be said that India can make the most important contribution to the growth and development of internationalism, unity of religions and spiritual disciplines, to the creation of a world union which can emphasise the freedom of each nation and the principle of decentralisation. Realising India's Indianness, India can fulfil its Indiannesss by embracing the totality of humanity and by regaining her true position among the nations in their world-wide unity.

Sri Aurobindo, speaking of the new awakening and the new impulses of the Indian Renaissance, has placed before us three tasks that India must undertake and fulfil. Let me conclude with the statement of these three tasks in Sri Aurobindo's own words:

> The recovery of the old spiritual knowledge and experience in all its splendour, depth and fullness is its first, most essential work; the flowing of this spirituality into new forms of philosophy, literature, art, science and critical knowledge is the second; an original dealing with modern problems in the light of Indian spirit and the endeavour to formulate a greater synthesis of a spiritualised society is the third and most difficult. Its success on these three lines will be the measure of its help to the future of humanity.[2]

---

[2] Sri Aurobindo: *The Foundations of Indian Culture*, Vol. 14, p. 409, Centenary Edition

INDIAN IDENTITY AND CULTURAL CONTINUITY

*T*he history of India is so long and complex and the continuity of Indian culture so enigmatic and astonishing that it is difficult to bring out in a brief compass those quintessential elements which distinguish India's identity and the real secret of her continuity through millennia. To many, who are not acquainted with Indian modes of life and thought feel so baffled that they might even declare that there is no such thing that one can trace from the confusing multiplicity and variety any single central thread by means of which Indianness can be understood or defined. To them, India still seems to be somewhat primitive which places together polytheism, monotheism, monism and nihilism, or else allows itself to be a field of battle between various conflicting philosophies, sharply criticising each other, and yet forgetful of the differences and compromising with a curious sense of tolerance, or to allow itself to be a perplexing scenario of endless castes and classes, lumping them all together in a framework that is neither capitalistic nor socialistic and yet sharing virtues of neither but vices of both. To them, it seems strange and inexplicable as to how India has managed to survive through vicissitudes of tides and ebbs and how, in recent history in which the degeneration became extremely marked, she has been able to rise with some kind of rapidity and even surprising boldness in a mood that can challenge the great, rationalistic, scientific, progressive and well-structured modernity of the West.

But all this enigma can be more easily cleared up if we can go back to the Vedas and try to understand that these records of ancient people contain not only wisdom but also quest of knowledge that had borne fruits in the form of great discoveries of the psychological being and had even attained lofty levels of perfection. For the Vedic seers were discoverers and they had discovered not only the triple world of matter, life and mind but, as the Aṅgirasa's legend tells us, they had even opened the gates of the fourth world *turiyam svid* and found there the key to divine perfection. They had discovered oneness and multiplicity and found the wideness in which varieties of experience can find their culmination in a rich harmony and unity.

What we call Indianness was shaped by the Vedic quest, and this quest arrived at an affirmation that:

1) beyond the body, life and mind, there is a spirit, -- vast, universal and transcendental which can be attained and realised and in realising which one finds oneself liberated in peace and delight that cannot be diminished or annihilated; and

2) that this realisation can come, -- not by neglecting body, life and mind, but only when these powers or at least some of them are greatly developed, cultivated, sharpened and perfected.

The Vedic quest also provided another element of Indianness, and that is its insistence on *ṛta*, the law of life and the law of development of individual and of the collectivity, a law which is, in a sense, eternal or the *sanātana*, and which is yet so supple that for each stage of life, each epoch of time, each nation, each collectivity and each individual it provides its own specific rhythms that govern their specific and unique development of life. This is what has come to be developed in due course as "*sanātana dharma, yuga dharma, rāshtra dharma, kula dharma*", and even *swādharma*. The profundity and depth of the concept of dharma, which is not religion, but which is a complex principle of guidance that can lead individuals and collectivities from lower levels to higher levels, and which in reaching culminations widens itself into freedom to the infinity of the spirit.

Another element that the Vedic quest provided to the Indian identity was that what is important in the human quest is not specific doctrine or thought-formulation but the search for or an orientation towards the highest which can be experienced, realised, and verified, repeated and made permanent. This is what explains how the Indian consciousness can permit various thought-formulations and philosophies and religions and yet maintain the spirit of mutual understanding, synthesis and even comprehensiveness in which contraries can meet and confess to each other their uniqueness, limitations and needs for all and the totality.

Finally, a further great element of Indianness was the highest aspirations that insisted on reaching social, political, economic and collective perfection that can be measured in terms of togetherness of people, upliftment of all, and widest embrace of the universal brotherhood. We still hear the last hymn of the Rigveda, *samgacchadwam samvadadhvam* and we feel unfailingly that this call of the Veda defines best the Indian identity.

It is remarkable that these essential elements of Indianness have inspired the complex structure of Indian religion and spirituality, Indian philosophy and ethics, Indian sociology and polity, Indian art and literature, -- indeed, every aspect of Indian life. In every field of culture great and noble ideals have been erected, and even the practical applications have been quite effective, and even when there have been failures and periods of decline, there have been sudden revivals and creations of new institutions and forms which have not hurt the fundamental continuity.

Indian psychology is profound and its receptivity of external influences has been so sympathetic that by some kind of alchemy of identification the best of the foreign has been received and assimilated. The secret of India's continuity can be traced to the original reservoirs of ancient wisdom, to renew itself, to advance further and create novelties that are not entirely novel.

India is today at a critical stage where external influences are rushing from various directions with great speed, attractiveness and power. It is even feared that these influences might penetrate so victoriously that they might succeed in wiping out Indianness of India and may bring about a rupture in the continuity of its culture. Some, indeed, believe that India will be greatly profited if these influences succeed, since India will be renewed, it will become modernised and will be able to sit with pride in the company of the modern and developed countries.

But those who understand the depth and the truth of India cannot feel reconciled that this attitude, -- particularly, when the progressive and developed countries of the world themselves are increasingly experiencing in their life the strangulating effects of uncontrollable mechanisation, depersonalisation and dehumanisation and are now looking for the liberating wisdom and knowledge which India possesses in its depth, even though in its outer life, it is, in many ways, in a state of degeneration and agony.

We have, therefore, to look at this problem very closely so as to dwell upon this very important subject of Indianness and cultural continuity of India.

Let us, first of all, emphasise the fact that as we look deeply into the new consciousness that is fundamentally vibrating among the children and the youth, is manifesting itself through flashes of their amazing talents, genius and dexterity, we find that there is a sound basis to feel confident that the present stage of degeneration in our country can be reversed and remedied. We have, however, to stress that we have to create conditions under which that new consciousness is allowed to be liberated from the clutches of ignorance and imprisoning modes of social structures and uninspiring ideals that are constantly being bombarded on the minds of the youths. Let us also admit that while recovering the ancient wisdom, we must stress the need for new creation. What has been golden in India's past is so refashioned and chiselled that it can bear the burden of a new quest and a new accomplishment.

The country needs a new polity and a new economy, but not imitative of foreign polity and foreign economy; for our goal will be to uphold *all* and serve and glorify *all* the millions of souls of our country. The secret of this upliftment of *all* is not visible in any current political or economic philosophy or practice. We have to realise that there is something precious in our own national genius that can absorb all that was precious in India's antiquity and in the western modernity and yet develop something fresh and new. We need to develop new philosophies and new forms of critical knowledge; but we do not need to imitate western philosophy and western criticism; we can assimilate all of them, but we have to go still farther, and that can come only when we understand the essential soul of ourselves. Let us at the same time declare that not everything that is foreign is necessarily injurious. The western ideals of progress, -- those of liberty, equality and fraternity, -- if received rightly and assimilated properly, can ensure the rejuvenation of our individual and collective life. The west can teach us secrets of modern science, and if we can learn these lessons rightly but in accordance with Indian spirit, we can recover and even refashion our own national intellectual, moral, and spiritual resources and capacity. The message of individual freedom, productivity and prosperity flowing upon us from the West, if received rightly, can help us in developing among us not only the most needed work ethos but also enable us to apply the secrets of the Yoga of works and stimulate a new Yogic research which may lead us out of the bewildering egoistic dynamics of life that has brought us to a great crisis.

Let us, however, not be overwhelmed by a number of those ideas that are coming upon us which imply some kind of economic barbarism. Let us not fall prey to the invasion of vulgar sensuality; and let us not ape those life styles, which are injurious to our body, mind and soul. Our own culture has a great deal to teach us in regard to sacredness of human relationships. India can tell us how stability and dynamism of life can be blended harmoniously; India can also counsel us that the spirit of sacrifice is much greater than the seeking of all that is merely pleasant. Long ago, we were told to chose *shreyas* rather than *preyas*, and this ancient prescription needs to be heard by us with great attention and earnestness. India had discovered long ago how to liberate ourselves from egoism and yet not lose but rather greaten our capacities for dynamic action. We need to receive that knowledge once again and make it active in the present difficult conditions of modern collective life. We do not need to worship selfish self-centredness and narrow competitiveness in self-assertion. India has been constantly teaching that the world is vast and that everybody has a place in it which one can have, if only takes pains to discover one's own capacities, inner nature and soul.

The task is great and difficult, but living in difficult days we have only to accept heavy and onerous responsibilities. Hence, we need not fear but aspire; for during the last hundred years and more much has been done and achieved, -- not by the so-called leaders of political and economic life, -- but by those who have had the courage to scale once again the ancient heights of the spirit and develop the vision that can look into the far distant future. By the aid of the heritage that we can receive from them, we can confidently move forward. We can reaffirm India's Indianness, we can change, even radically change, and yet we can maintain the cultural continuity without any disabling rupture.

Sri Aurobindo has given an inspiring message for the renascent of India in the following words:

> India of the ages is not dead nor has she spoken her last creative word; she lives and has still something to do for herself and the human peoples. And that which must seek now to awake is not an anglicised oriental people, docile pupil of the West and doomed to repeat the cycles of the occident's success and failure, but still the ancient immeasurable Shakti recovering her deepest self, lifting her head higher towards the supreme source of light and strength and turning to discover the

complete meaning and a vaster form of her Dharma.[1]

---

[1] Sri Aurobindo: *The Foundation of Indian Culture*, Volume 14, Centenary Edition, p. 381

INDIAN CULTURE: PAST, PRESENT AND FUTURE

The history of India would remain enigmatic, particularly, the remarkable phenomenon of the continuity of Indian culture through the millennia would remain a mystery, if we do not take into account the role that spirituality has played not only in determining the direction of her philosophical and cultural effort but also in replenishing the springs of creativity at every crucial hour in the long and often weary journey. It is true that spirituality has played a role in every civilisation and that no culture can claim a monopoly for spirituality. And yet, it can safely be affirmed that the unique greatness and continuity of Indian culture can be traced to her unparalleled experimentation, discovery and achievement in the vast field of spirituality.

Indian culture has recognised spirituality not only as the supreme occupation of Man but also as his all-integrating occupation. Similarly, the entire spectrum of Indian culture, -- its religion, ethics, philosophy, literature, art, architecture, dance, music, and even its polity and social and economic organisation, -- all these have been constantly influenced and moulded by the inspiring force of a multisided spirituality.

The distinctive character of Indian spirituality is its conscious and deliberate insistence on direct experience. It affirms that deep within the heart and high above the mind there is accessible to our consciousness a realm of truths, powers and ecstasies that we can, by methodised effort of Yoga,[1] realise in the direct experience, can even hold permanently, and express in varying degrees through our instruments the mind, life and body. This affirmation has conditioned the entire development of religion in India and has introduced in the body of religion the recognition that direct experience of the spirit is far superior to dogma, belief and ritualism, and that dogmatic religion can and must ultimately be surpassed by experiential spirituality.

Consequently, the history of Indian spirituality and religion shows a remarkable spirit of research, of an increasing subtlety, plasticity, sounding of depths, extension of seeking. There have been systems of specialisation and also conflicting claims and counterclaims, but the supervening tendency has been to combine, assimilate, harmonise and synthesise. In the past, there have been at least four great stages of synthesis, represented by the Vedas, the Upanishads, the Gita and the Tantra. And, in modern times, we are passing through the fifth stage, represented by a new synthesis, which is in the making.

It is impossible to describe Indian spirituality and religion by any exclusive label. Even in its advanced forms, it cannot be described as monotheism or monism or pantheism or nihilism or transcendentalism, although each

---

[1] Yoga is a comprehensive system of concentration, passive and dynamic, leading to a living contact, union and identity with realities or Reality underlying the universe, with appropriate consequences in our nature and action, individual and cosmic. In recent times, Yoga is often misrepresented to be identical with Hathayoga, a system of physical and subtle exercises, which is only a specialisation, and a dispensable one, of the real and comprehensive system.

one of these is present in it in some subtle or pronounced way. Even the spiritual truths behind the primitive forms such as those of animism, spiritism, fetishism and totemism have been allowed to play a role in its complex totality, although their external forms have been discouraged and are not valid or applicable to those who lead an inner mental and spiritual life. It is this complexity that bewilders the foreign student when he tries to define Indian spirituality and religion in terms and under criteria that are not born of the Indian experiment. But things become easier once it is grasped that the fundamental point of reference is not the outward form of a given belief and practice but the spirit behind and the justifying spiritual experience.

Indian scriptures and records abound with the statements and descriptions of varieties of spiritual experience. But there are three central spiritual experiences in terms of which all these varieties can be readily understood. The first is that of the individual in a state of complete detachment from all movement, dynamism and activity. In this state, the individual finds himself in an utter passivity and inactivity, but also of a complete luminosity and discrimination between himself as an eternal witness (*sākshin*), free from the sense of ego and the activities of Nature in the universe. This experience is the basis of the *Sāmkhya* philosophy. The second experience is that of the eternal and infinite Reality above Space and Time in which all that we call individuality and universality are completely silenced and sublated, and the experiencing consciousness discovers itself to be That Reality (*tat sat*), one, without the second (*ekam eva advitiyam*), entirely silent and immobile, the Pure Being, so ineffable that even to describe it as Being is to violate its sheer transcendence. This experience has given rise to the philosophy of Advaita (non-dualism), in particular that only the

Brahman is real, and the world is an illusion. The third experience is that in which the individual and cosmos are found to be free expressions of the Supreme Reality (*Purushottama*) which, although above Space and Time, determines Space and Time and all activities through various intermediary expressions of itself. This experience and some variations of it form the basis of various theistic philosophies of India. These theistic philosophies are those of qualified monism (*vishishtadvaita* philosophy), integral monism (*poornadvaita*) and dualistic philosophy (*dvaita* philosophy). Each of these experiences, when permanently established, gives liberation (*moksha*), and it is this which has in India been regarded as a high consummation of man's destiny upon earth. But, more importantly, the ancient ideal as given by the Vedas, Upanishads and the Gita, was to achieve an integrality of all these experiences, to combine utter Silence with effective Action, to be liberated from ego and yet at the same time to be a free living centre (*jivanmukta*) of luminous action that would aid the progressive unity of mankind (*lokasangraha*).

This integral ideal was to be realised in its integrality not only by a few exceptional individuals but also by an increasing number of people, groups, collectivities, even on massive scale, through a long and conscious preparation and training. This great and difficult task was pursued with an increasing unfolding of its aim through the ages, and it has passed through two main stages, while a third has taken initial steps and promises to be the destiny of India's future.

Indian Culture: Past, Present and Future

The early Vedic was the first stage; the Purano-Tantric was the second stage.² In the former, an attempt was made to approach the mass-mind through the physical mind of man and make it familiar with the Godhead in the universe through the symbol of the sacrificial fire (*yajña*). In the latter, deeper approaches of man's inner mind and life to the Divine in the universe were attempted through the development of great religious movements, philosophies,³ many-sided epic literature (particularly Ramayana and Mahabharata), systems of Puranas and Tantras,⁴ and even through art and science. An enlarged secular turn was given, and this was balanced by deepening of the intensities of psycho-religious experience. New tendencies and mystic forms of disciplines attempted to seize not only the soul and the intellect, but the emotions, the senses, the vital and the aesthetic nature of man and turn them

---

² The date of the Vedic age is controversial, but according to a conservative hypothesis, its origins are dated 2000 B.C. The Purano-Tantric age can be regarded to have extended from 600 B.C. to 800 A.D.

³ Particularly, the six systems, Nyāya, Vaisheshika, Sāmkhya, Pūrva Mimamsa and Uttara Mimamsa and their numerous interpretations and commentaries. These six systems are Vedic systems of philosophy. There developed also Buddhism and Jainism and their numerous philosophical systems which did not accept the authority of the Vedas. Similarly, Cārvāka philosophy, the philosophy of materialism, which also developed during this period, was entirely anti-Vedic.

⁴ There are 18 Puranas. Each Purana has five parts: (1) Creation of the World, (2) Destruction and recreation of the world, (3) Reigns and periods of Manus, (4) Genealogy of Gods, and (5) Dynasties of solar and lunar kings.

Tantras are called Agamas. We do not know the exact number of Agamas, but it is estimated that there are 64 of them.

into stuff of the spiritual life. But this great effort and achievement covered all the time between the Vedic age and the decline of Buddhism. Vaishnavism and Shaivism flourished during this period, and although there were during this period conflicts of religions and claims of superiority of one system of religion or Yoga over other systems of religion or Yoga, there was fundamentally a large Catholicism and a spirit of assimilation and even of synthesis. Christianity came to India early in the first century A.D. and there came also several other influences, all of which were welcomed and given a place in the large and developing field of the Indian Religion. All this rich growth gave rise to a further development through the third stage. But it was arrested as it synchronised with a period of general exhaustion, and, in the eighteenth century, which can be regarded as the period of dense obscurity, the work that had begun seemed almost lost.

The aim of this third stage was to approach not only the inner mind and life of man, but to approach his whole mental, psychical and physical living, his totality of being and activity, and to turn it into a first beginning of at least a generalised spiritual life. Philosophers and saints such as Sri Chaitanya (1485-1533) and others of 15th and 16th centuries belong to this stage. There was also during this period a remarkable attempt to combine Vedanta and Islam or of establishing lasting communal harmony. In particular, the work of Guru Nanak (1469-1538) and of the subsequent Sikh Khalsa movement was astonishingly original and novel. The speciality of this third stage was an intense outburst and fresh creativity, not a revivalism, but based upon a deep assimilation of the past, a new effort and a new formulation. But the time was not yet ripe, and India had to pass through a period of an eclipse, almost total and disastrous.

Happily, the 19th century witnessed a great awakening and a new spiritual impulse pregnant with a power to fulfil the mission of the work that had started in the third stage. Great and flaming pioneers appeared, Raja Rammohun Roy (1772-1833), Dayananda Saraswati (1824 -1883), Sri Ramakrishna (1836-1886), Swami Vivekananda (1862 -1902), -- to name just a few of them, -- and through their work the entire country was electrified not only spiritually but even socially and politically. India became renascent, and there began to develop a capacity for a new synthesis, not only of the threads of Indian culture but also of world culture. Nationalism came to be proclaimed as the new spirituality and this nationalism was right from the beginning international in its spirit and sweep. Not an escape from life, but acceptance of life, integration of life and transformation of life by an integral spirituality – this ideal came to be felt and expressed in various ways and through various activities of the renascent India.

Gradually, it has become evident that this new movement has to do not merely with India but fundamentally with the essential problem of Man and his future evolution. It is becoming clearer that Man is a field of interaction between Matter and Spirit, that this interaction has reached a point of criticality, and that this criticality demands a new knowledge, an integral knowledge of Matter and Spirit.

This is the task which Free India has begun to perceive as central to her real fulfilment. It is significant that we have in India a most comprehensive statement of this task in the luminous writings of Sri Aurobindo (1872-1950), who has been described by Romain Rolland as "the completest synthesis of the East and the West." Sri Aurobindo has declared that man is a transitional being, that his destiny is to be the spiritual superman, and that the present hour is the hour of his evolutionary crisis in which his entire life, his very body, must undergo an integral spiritual transformation, not indeed by an escape into some far-off heaven, but here, in this physical earth itself, by a victorious union of Spirit and Matter. This, he has declared, is not an issue of an individual but of collectivity, not an issue of Indian spirituality and culture, but of the entire world's upward aspiration and fulfilment.

It must be noted that in this task of universal importance, India, the East, has received from the West a collaboration of incalculable magnitude and value. For it is from France that The Mother (Madame Mira Alfassa [1878-1973]) came to Sri Aurobindo and made India her permanent home in order to collaborate with him and to fulfil this task of integral transformation. The work that she has done is not yet sufficiently known, but as we study the great account of Her work in "Mother's Agenda", we find in her the highest heights that Indian spirituality has reached, and we feel that the near future is bound to show the revolutionary effects of her work for humanity, for its lasting unity and harmony, and for its transmutation into super-humanity.

Indeed, the renascent spirituality of India opens up new vistas of experience and research. It transcends the boundaries of dogma and exclusive claims of Truth. It is not opposed to any religion, but points to a way to a synthesis and integrality of spiritual experience in the light of which the truth behind each religion is understood and permitted to grow to its fullness and to meet in harmony with all the others. The important thing is to turn the human mentality, vitality and physicality to the realm of spiritual experiences and to transform the human mould by an ever-widening light of the Spirit. In this perception, even scepticism, agnosticism and atheism have a meaning and value as an indispensable stage for a certain line of mental development. But here, too, the dogma and denial behind the doubt and atheism have to be surpassed, and whether by rigorous methods of philosophy and science or by a deeper plunge into deeper experiences, a way can be opened to transcend the dogmatic refusal to seek and to discover. It is in this direction that we seem to reach a point where a fruitful synthesis of science and spirituality can be effectuated.

The renascent spirituality is all-embracing and is deeply committed to undertake all activities of human life and to transform them. It has begun to influence literature and art and music, education and physical culture. Even social and economic and political fields are being taken up, not indeed to cast them once again into some rigid formula of a religious dogma but rather to liberate them and to inundate them with a spiritual light and motive and to restructure them by a gradual evolution so that they may breathe widely and freely the progressive harmonies of Liberty, Equality and Fraternity. Thus is it that the old forms of society, casteism and all the rest, are being broken and there is a fresh search for new forms, plastic and flexible, to permit the highest possible perfectibility of the individual and the collectivity to blossom spontaneously and perpetually. In the ultimate analysis, it is through such a vast and potent change in the social milieu that the total man can be uplifted to his next stage of evolutionary mutation.

It is in this context that India needs to view the various social and political upheavals of the recent times. These upheavals have their own genesis in so far as that nature wants the human being to resolve by finding out deeper resources which have hitherto been ignored and ill-explored. Contemporary humanity has reached a point where two conflicting ideals have to be harmonised, the ideal of individual perfection and the ideal of collective perfection. This conflict has presented itself throughout the history both of India and the rest of the world from time to time and different answers have been given at different epochs according to the needs and circumstances and possibilities of circumstances. In early times, the individual was subordinated to the collectivity; in due course of time, the individual began to gain some freedom against the demands of the collectivity; but it is only in recent times, particularly after the European Renaissance, that individualism has gained a great predominance; but even then, with the rise of collectivistic philosophy, the ideal of individual perfection had to suffer a great setback. With the collapse of the Communist regime in USSR, however, the pendulum has swung back again in favour of individualism. In India, the balance between the ideal of the perfection of the individual and the perfection of the collectivity was sought to be achieved by means of a profound sociological and psychological understanding of human development. A great stress was laid on the needs of the welfare of the collectivity, and the individual was required to subordinate himself through the system of duties towards the members of the family or of the joint family, to the guild and to the community, the state and the country, and even the humanity at large and to universal dharma. At the same time, the demands of individual perfection were sought to be met by erecting the ideal of the *Shreshtha* or of the *Arya*; facility for integral education for all those aimed at perfection were amply provided for, and the system provided for the realisation of the individual's perfection, if he qualified himself for it by undertaking the life of renunciation, *sanyasa*. However, in due course, the system of these obligations broke down, and the subordination of the individual to collectivity became more and more prominent. During the last thousand years, various invasions, battles and the subjugation of the country under the heavy hand of foreign rulers crippled not only the ideal of individual perfection but even that of collective perfection. The weakening of the ideal of the individual and the collective perfection became severest under the British rule, and it is only recently that there has been some beginning, after the attainment of independence, of an uneasy and uncertain groping to gain freedom for the individual and collectivity. But, again, under the choice that India made for the road of socialism or socialistic pattern of society, the individual came to be subordinated, and in spite of the recent orientations towards liberalisation, it is difficult to say how this liberalisation will go beyond the economic sphere so that the real purposes of the ideal of individual perfection and the ideal of collective perfection can come to their own and affirm themselves powerfully. In the West, too, where individual freedom which flourished under the ideals of liberty, equality and fraternity, which were pronounced powerfully by the French Revolution, came under a great constraint because of the powerful rise of Nazism and Communism, and even though the latter have now fallen to a great extent, and the ideal of individual freedom has come to be reaffirmed, it is mostly being advocated in the economic field, and that, too, in the services of the system that is being sought to be perfected for the life of standardisation, mechanisation and of a comfortable search and satisfaction of appetites for pleasure and egoistic domination.

What is happening in the West is bound to have a great impact upon India, and the central problem of India is whether India wants to become a province of western culture and whether, even while assimilating the best that the West has to offer, it can find from great resources of culture which are available in its heritage, a new solution of the harmony of the individual perfection and the collective perfection, and whether it can give that solution as a gift to the world which also needs it, and which will suffer if that solution is not made available to it.

But while dealing with this problem, India will have to resolve four important questions, namely, those related to (1) the conflict of religions, (2) the conflict of religion and science, (3) the conflict between science and philosophy, and (4) the conflict between asceticism and materialism.

It is evident that the conflict of religions cannot be resolved at the level of dogmas. For dogmas are themselves unquestionable, and if the unquestionables are in conflict, there can be no issue and no answer. It is only if we go behind the dogmas, as Indian religion has always attempted to do, in search of the living experience which are at the core of various religions, that there can be a hope of the resolution of the conflict. Not, therefore, the synthesis of religions, but the synthesis of spiritual experiences seems to be the answer. It is significant that in modern India, we have today – as fully exemplified in Sri Aurobindo – a puissant and irresistible drive towards the synthesis of spiritual experiences.

The conflict of religions and science can be resolved only if science expands itself into an inquiry of the 'invisible' actuality, and if religion enlarges itself and transforms itself into an impartial open search of the verifiable and repeatable spiritual experience. Here, again, there are signs in modern India which promise a new orientation initiated by scientists like Jagadish Chandra Bose. This orientation, however, needs to be pursued much more rigorously than has been done during the last several decades. We have achieved much in the field of science, but we have still not related science to spirituality, and we have not yet seen how science itself can be enriched by the knowledge that spirituality can deliver.

The conflict between science and philosophy has grown in the modern intellectual world and the credentials of philosophy have been severely questioned. The modern Indian philosopher, sympathetic to the Indian philosophical traditions, attempts to reconstruct the Indian philosophy in the light of the modern trends of philosophical and scientific thought, but he finds himself in the grip of a most acute conflict and difficulty. There has, however, been one special element in Indian philosophy which promises to be a great aid in a possible resolution of the difficulty. For Indian philosophy has not really been merely speculative. This is not to say that speculation has been absent. There is, we might say, even a profusion of it; the pure reason has been at full play and has been allowed to arrive at its own independent conclusions, and it can even be said that Indian metaphysics has been as powerful as any metaphysical systems in the world. But, still, Indian philosophy has been primarily a *darshan*, a vision based upon spiritual experience and channelised into a metaphysical system by means of intellectual processes of reasoning. Even when intellectual speculations have been free both in regard to the premises and conclusions, still the conclusions have never been accepted as authentic unless they have been found verifiable in spiritual experience or confirmed by the records of spiritual experience, *shruti*. In other words, Indian philosophy has always recognised the claim of experience to be superior to that of mere intellectual reasoning, and it is interesting to note that the entire trend of modern inquiry seems to turn back to the primacy and superiority of experience over mere speculation and 'fictions' of reasoning. It is then in the recovery of this Indianness of

Indian philosophy that the future conflict of science and philosophy may be resolved in India, and this might probably benefit the entire movement of the world-thought.

But the conflict between asceticism and materialism will still remain to be resolved. And this is perhaps the most difficult issue concerning modern India in its search of the new future. It is true that the economic, social and political necessities of our modern life have imposed the necessity of a robust dynamism which is remote from the tenets of asceticism, but still the spirit of asceticism has been so deeply ingrained since the last two thousand years that at every turn we feel confronted with the ideas of the illusoriness of the world and of the escape of life as the very meaning of life. The present Indian scene is, therefore, divided and torn between the invasion of materialism and the persistent whisper and call of the gospel of the renunciation of world and life. This conflict can be resolved only if it is discovered that Spirit is not the negation of Matter, but that Matter itself is an expression of the Spirit, and that Spirit is unfolding itself gradually in Matter so that there would be a total spiritual transformation of material life, here itself, *ih eva*, in this earthly Earth. There is no need to renounce Matter in order to embrace the Spirit. Indeed, all life is an evolving expression of the Spirit, and therefore, a truly spiritual culture embraces all life and transforms it into spiritual terms. A spiritual manifestation in the physical life would be the only possible and acceptable solution to this conflict between asceticism and materialism. And it is in this direction that India needs to move forward and fashion itself for the new future and for the new role that it has to play in the comity of nations.

If we are to ask ourselves what specific things we should do, we may refer to a brief statement of Sri Aurobindo in which three important tasks have been identified. He has said:

> The recovery of the old spiritual knowledge and experience in all its splendour, depth and fullness is its first, most essential work; the flowing of this spirituality into new forms of philosophy, literature, art, science and critical knowledge is the second; an original dealing with modern problems in the light of Indian spirit and the endeavour to formulate a greater synthesis of a spiritualised society is the third and most difficult. Its success on these three lines will be the measure of its help to the future of humanity.[5]

Let us hope that we shall become aware of the implications of these tasks and rededicate ourselves in carrying them out in the service of Mother India.

---

[5] Sri Aurobindo: *The Foundation of Indian Culture*, Volume 14, Centenary Edition, p.409

PHILOSOPHY OF INDIAN ART

I

From various accounts which have evidential value, it is clear that India pursued the quest of the knowledge and the experience of reality through a multiple and even integral approach. The basic quest of India was to discover the causes of disintegration and to find effective remedies by which disintegration can be prevented. In positive terms, this was the quest for immortality, and the ancient literature gives us convincing proof of this quest as also of the victory that was attained. We also find accounts of the processes by which this victory was attained. In this process the major role was played by a difficult psychological discipline in which thought power, will power, and affective power were so elevated and perfected that higher realms of comprehensive knowledge and power were discovered and possessed. Truth, Right, and Vast – *satyam, ritam, brihat* – these three words con-stituted the formula of the process and the victory. This process was so comprehensive that every gate of inquiry was required to be opened up and explored. And it is for this reason that the basic science of this quest, namely the science of Yoga, included pursuit of Dharma, Darshan, Shastra as also Kalā. Hence, the range of cultural activities of India centred on the quest of spiritual truth but it also promoted quest through science, philosophy, art and several other means. Intense spirituality, robust scientific and philosophical intellectuality and powerful literature, poetry, art and inexhaustible vitality have marked the essential characteristics of Indian culture.

If our educational system is to reflect these characteristics of our culture, we must have full provision for pursuit of all these aspects, so that our students can be recipients of our true Indian heritage.

Just as science is a quest of truth, just as philosophy is a quest of truth, even so art, too, is a quest of truth. But each one of them has its own specific method which distinguishes it from all others. The chief characteristics of scientific method are that of observation, experimentation and verification as also expansion by progressive inquiry. The essence of philosophical method is exploration of the realm of ideas, of eternity and infinity, of essence of universality and individuality, and a comprehensive approach to grasp the totality and reality not merely through speculation but particularly through investigation of the significance and meaning of the totality of experience, so that what is thought is also attempted to be realised and experienced and utilised for the enhancement of the fulfilment of life. Art is also characterised by a quest, but its chief characteristic is to fathom the depths of experience of an object or a field until the depths of experience begin to vibrate with images appropriate to the object of experience. This fathoming of the depths of experience reveals the truth of the object but it also inspires formulations that can express themselves variously so as to give us special techniques and cannons of art forms such as painting, sculpture, architecture, music, poetry and others. Art is a voyage of discovery and expression, a voyage inspired and marked by joy, love and beauty, a voyage that brings us closest to the inner recesses of consciousness and unites in its expression the inner and the outer in such a way that the formulations lead the artist and the viewer or the hearer to something that is within us in order to hear the inaudible, to see the invisible and to seize the unseizeable.

This is the boon of art, and the bounty of this boon we should be able to shower on all the seekers, particularly students and teachers of all ages.

Considering that our present system of education has no place or only peripheral place for art education, it is imperative that we explore the philosophy of art, the philosophy of Indian art in particular, and the values that art education can furnish in the process of a total development of personality.

II

There are certain essential elements that are the distinguishing features of art and art experience. There is, first, intuition of the artist, -- intuition that marks the awakening in an experience that unites the self of the artist and the object on which the artist concentrates. This experience may be at various levels, ranging from a contact to a penetration leading up to an identity. Again, this experience is marked by a sincerity which is intensified at deeper and deeper levels. The result of the experience is the discovery of the truths of the object and the discovery of the beauty of the object. This beauty vibrates in the consciousness in a state of joy, in a state of feeling, in a state of *rasa* of creation and some kind of inevitability of the expression of form through a technique that is appropriate to the given form of art. Form and technique are interrelated and they demand each other in their road towards perfection. At a given stage of expression and creativity, they assume great importance, and the great masterpieces of art embody these elements and determine their excellence.

There is, we might say, mystery, miracle and magic of form, and the joy of the artist, the creativeness of the artist is in the discovery and expression of this mystery, miracle and magic. The artist arrives in the great stress of experience at the origin of the form, where the form seems to emerge from the womb of the formless, from the reality that is ineffable, which is yet no monotone and which is not devoid of potency, but is capable of power, and of multiple formations of significant symbolism. Art is thus essentially a journey to the secret where the unseizeable is seized, where significant forms are discovered and expressed. The subtlest experience of art consists in arriving at the subtlety of the relationship between the form and the formless, the finite and the infinite, the qualified and the unqualified, the conditioned and the unconditioned. But this subtlety has degrees, and there are ways and manners, and there are levels at which this subtlety is grasped and expressed. The differences of manners and levels lie at the root of differences among art traditions, different habits of creation and different modes of appreciation. In one of the traditions, the artist gets his intuition of a suggestion from an appearance in life and nature, and even when it starts from something deeper, he relates it at once to an external support. Often this results in a colourable imitation of life and nature. In another tradition, the artist begins with the intuition or contact or experience at deeper levels, something that is true of the Indian or Chinese or Japanese tradition, and these starting points make a difference in the creativity of forms and in the emphasis that one lays in expressing the inner and the truer, the inner being or the inner form of the object.

Every artistic creation has an object and a field of the intuitive vision or of the depth of experience; every artistic creation has a method of working out the vision or experience or suggestions of vision or experience; and every artistic creation is marked by the vibration of the vision or experience into the mode of its rendering by the external form and technique, and every artistic creation has behind it something holistic, both in its composition and its appeal, in the manner in which the creation is rendered to the human mind and how it is related to the centre of the being to which the artistic work is intended to appeal.

If we now ask the question as to what distinguishes Indian art, and what is the central philosophy of Indian art as we can gather it from the rich and long course of history through which that art has been sustained through several millennia, we shall find that it is a self-conscious endeavour in which aesthetic experience and aesthetic creativity as also beauty, joy and love were discovered at the loftiest and deepest recesses of the deeper soul in its expansion towards universality and infinity. The spirit, motive and aim of Indian art is to render the sense of infinity, and the sense of cosmocity through symbolic forms, forms that are subtle, forms which are symbolic and forms which are distinctive and which may correspond, in varying degrees, to the external forms which nature has fashioned in its own creative and artistic play. In the following lines, Sri Aurobindo brings out briefly but precisely the theory of ancient Indian art at its greatest.

> Its highest business is to disclose something of the Self, the Infinite, the Divine to the regard of the soul, the Self through its expressions, the Infinite through its living finite symbols, the Divine through his powers. Or the Godheads are to be revealed, luminously interpreted or in some way suggested to the soul's understanding or to its devotion or at the very least to a spiritually or religiously aesthetic emotion. When this hieratic art comes down from these altitudes to the intermediate worlds

behind ours, to the lesser godheads or genii, it still caries into them some power or some hint from above. And when it comes quite down to the material world and the life of man and the things of external Nature, it does not altogether get rid of the greater vision, the hieratic stamp, the spiritual seeing, and in most good work – except in moments of relaxation and a humorous or vivid play with the obvious – there is always something more in which the seeing presentation of life floats as in an immaterial atmosphere. Life is seen in the self or in some suggestion of the infinite or of something beyond or there is at least a touch and influence of these which helps to shape the presentation. It is not that all Indian work realises this ideal; there is plenty no doubt that falls short, is lowered, ineffective or even debased, but it is the best and the most characteristic influence and execution which gives its tone to an art and by which we must judge.[1]

Indian architecture, particularly Indian sacred architecture, in its inmost reality is an altar raised to the Divine Self, a House of Cosmic Spirit, an appeal and inspiration to the Infinite. Symbolism is the main characteristic of Indian architecture, and this is true even of the Indo-Muslim architecture, where the Indian mind has taken in much from the Arab and the Persian imagination. As Sri Aurobindo points out in regard to the Taj Mahal:

---

[1] Sri Aurobindo: *The Foundations of Indian Culture*, Centenary Edition, Volume 14, p.208

> The Taj is not merely a sensuous reminiscence of an imperial amour or a fairy enchantment hewn from the moon's lucent quarries, but the eternal dream of a love that survives death.[2]

Indian sculpture, particularly the more ancient sculptural art, springs from spiritual realisation, and what it creates and expresses at its greatest is the spirit in form, the soul in body, this or that living soul-power in the Divine or the human, the universal and the cosmic individualised suggestion but not lost in individuality. Its aim is not to express the ideal physical or emotional beauty, but the utmost spiritual beauty or the significance of which the human form is capable. Soul-realisation is its method and soul realisation must be the way of our response and understanding. The statute of a king or a saint is not merely meant to give the idea of a king or a saint or to portray some dramatic action or to be a character portrait in a scene, but to embody rather a soul-state or experience or deeper soul-quality. This is what we find in the great Buddhas or the Natrajas. The figure of the Buddha expresses the infinite in a finite image, embodies the illimitable calm of Nirvana in human form envisaged. The Kālasamhāra Shiva expresses the majesty, pure calm and forceful control, dignity, and kingship of existence. The pose of the figure visibly incarnates that whole spirit of the cosmic Shiva. Again, the cosmic dance of Shiva expresses the cosmic movement and delight, and the posture of every limb is made to bring out the realm and significance, the rapturous intensity and fullness of the movement.

The art of painting in later India covers a long period of more than two thousand years. Long before the Christian

---

[2] Ibid., p. 224

Era began, we find the theory of the art well founded from previous times, where six essential elements, *shadanga*, were recognised and enumerated. Historically, reference in ancient literature also indicates a widespread practice and appreciation of the art of painting by both men and women of the cultural classes. Even the later Rajput work continues the spirit and depth of the interpretation of spirituality, religion, culture and life of the Indian people.

The six essential elements described in the Indian shastra of Indian painting can be considered to be something that is common in painting everywhere. But the Indian shastra gives us the evidence of self-consciousness of the Indian painting that was presented since early times. The six limbs of Indain art refer, first, to the distinction of forms, *rupa-bheda*; secondly, to proportion, arrangement of line and mass, design, harmony, perspective, *pramāna*; thirdly, to the emotion or aesthetic feeling expressed by the form, *bhāva*; fourthly, for seeking for beauty and charm for the satisfaction of the aesthetic spirit, *lāvaṇya;* fifthly, to the truth of the form and its suggestion, *sadrishya*; sixthly, to the turn, combination, harmony of colours, *varnikabhanga*. The distinctive character of Indian art, however, emerges from the turn given to each of the constituents of *shadanga*.

III

Let us try to understand this distinctive character of the Indian art of painting. *Rupabheda* in the Indian art is faithfully observed. But here there is no attempt at an exact naturalistic fidelity to the physical appearance; the objects are not reproduced in the image of the outward shapes of the world in which we live. Indeed, there is vividness, naturalness, reality, but it is more than a physical reality. We do not turn to Indian painting in order to study the science of anatomy. We turn to study the reality of the soul, to experience a vivid naturalness of psychic truth. We turn to it to perceive the convincing spirit of the form to which the soul bears witness. What is repeated is the truth of the essence of the form, the reproduction of the subtle embodiment which is the basis of the physical embodiment, the purer and finer subtle body of an object which expresses its own essential nature, *swabhāva*. This is brought out very clearly in the paintings of Ajanta and of Bagh and other frescos. We find here the pure and strong outline and suppression of what would blur and dilute the intense significance of the line. The whole essential human being is present in the human figure but what is brought out is the divinity that has taken this garb of the spirit, which is visible to the eye. We find the ideal psychical figure in its charm and beauty. The line is filled in by a disposition of pure masses, design and colour and wave-flow of the body. What is expressed is the one spiritual emotion, feeling, suggestion which the artist intends to convey. Particularly, hands are used in a miraculously subtle and meaningful way so that the psychic suggestion is expressed, and the face and the eyes are expressed psychically and the same expression is supplemented by the expression of the hands. We find in the Indian painting the law of significant line and suppression of distracting detail even when it is applied to the animal forms, buildings, trees, objects. There is an inspired harmony of conception, method and expression. Even colour is used as a means for spiritual and psychic intention. There is a union of greatness and moving grace and this continues even in the Rajput paintings, although the vividness and suggestiveness of the line are bolder and more decisive. Form in the Indian paintings emerges from the deeper source of the soul and the spirit rather than from the external and physical nature.

Pramāṇa, proportion, harmony and perspective follow the same inner law of formulation of the inner form, of the inner atmosphere, of the inner dimensions. *Bhāva* in Indian painting is the expression of the universal spiritual essence of the emotion modified by the essential soul-type that is presented in the image. Complexity of the dramatic insistence is avoided, and so much stress is only laid on character in the individual feeling as to give the variation without diminishing the unity of the fundamental emotion. Emotion is transmitted directly from the spirit to our own spirit, but in later art, a greater stress is laid on the psychic thought and feeling which are thrown outward in movement; but still the soul-motive is constitutive of the whole atmosphere. This is true even where the subject is not spiritual or religious but secular. *Lāvaṇya* in Indian painting is again a charm and beauty of that which is subtle, of that which is psychic and spiritual. Physical beauty is not the only beauty in the world; this truth is vividly illustrated in the Indian painting. The deeper we travel in the heart and thought, in the soul and in the spirit, the deeper we travel from the form to the formless, and from the individual to the universal, the greater is the aesthesis, the greater is the charm, the greater is the harmony, the greater is the beauty and the underlying *rasa* of the experience of art. *Sadrishya*, *varnikabhaṅga* and *rupabheda* are all correlated to each other, and what is to be appreciated is not only the technique or the fervour of the deeper and of psychic feeling. What is to be appreciated is the intent served by the technique, the psychic significance of line and colour and the whole purpose of the artist.

I should like to present a citation from Sri Aurobindo in order to illustrate how we should look at an Indian painting and how its real spirit is to be grasped. Sri Aurobindo has given us an analysis of the adoration group of the mother and the child before the Buddha, which according to Sri Aurobindo is one of the most profound, tender and noble of the Ajanta paintings.

> That which it deepens to is the turning of the soul of humanity in love to the benignant and calm Ineffable which has made itself sensible and human to us in the universal compassion of the Buddha, and the motive of the soul-moment the painting interprets is the dedication of the awakening mind of the child, the coming of younger humanity, to that in which already the soul of the mother had learned to find and fix its spiritual joy. The eyes, brows, lips, face, poise of the head of the woman are filled with this spiritual emotion which is a continued memory and possession of the psychical release, the steady settled calm of the heart's experience filled with an ineffable tenderness, the familiar depths which are yet moved with the wonder and always farther appeal of something that is infinite, the body and other limbs are grave masses of this emotion and in their poise a basic embodiment of it, while the hands prolong it in the dedicative putting forward of her child to meet the Eternal. This contact of the human and eternal is repeated in the smaller figure with a subtly and strongly indicated variation, the glad and childlike smile of awakening which promises but not yet possesses the depths that are to come, the hands disposed to receive and keep, the body in its looser curves and waves harmonising with that significance. The two have forgotten themselves and seem almost to forget and confound each other in

that which they adore and contemplate, and yet the dedicating hands unite mother and child in the common act and feeling by their simultaneous gesture of maternal possession and spiritual giving. The two figures have at each point the same rhythm, but with a significant difference. The simplicity in the greatness and power, the fullness of expression gained by reserve and suppression and concentration which we find here is the perfect method of the classical art of India. And by this perfection Buddhist art became not merely an illustration of the religion and an expression of its thought and its religious feeling, history and legend, but a revealing interpretation of the spiritual sense of Buddhism and its profounder meaning to the soul of India.[3]

IV

Art opens the gates of our consciousness to the depths of truth and beauty; it imparts to our consciousness the sense and experience of joy and love and adoration and uplifts us into realms of purity, restraint, balance and equilibrium. And if truth is beauty and beauty is goodness, art is a great builder of character. If we wish to overcome excesses of desires and passions, if we wish to refine our roughness and indecency in action and manner, and if at the same we wish to overcome excesses of soulless ceremony and formalism, of privation and dryness of temperament, and if we wish to attain the golden mean where the true virtue resides, we must enthrone art education in our system in its fullness.

---

[3] Ibid., pp.250-51

Science of living and art of living can best be cultivated in the brain and in the heart and in our entire being through art education. Indeed, art through art education can bring our students nearer to the experience of *rasa* that constantly flows in all aspects of life and in all circumstances. At the highest level, pursuit of beauty is the pursuit of *ānanda*, and *ānanda* is a source of *akhanda rasa*, undifferentiated and unabridged delight and delightfulness in things. We can prepare a road to this goal by the pursuit of poetry, music and art at lower levels at first and gradually at higher and higher levels of experience and contemplation. Even in the training of the intellectual faculty, art can play a great role. Subtlety is the soul of art, and art education makes the mind also in its movement subtle and delicate. Art is suggestive, and the intellect that is habituated to the appreciation of art is quick to catch suggestions; the intellect that has been refined by the experience of art can easily be led to master not only the surface reality and appearances but also that which leads to ever-fresh widening and subtlising of knowledge. For art opens a door into the deeper secrets of inner nature which the instrument of science cannot measure. Above all, art takes us beyond reaches of thought and morality and takes us deeper into spiritual truths and into the joy and God in the world as also the beauty and desirableness of the manifestation of divine force and energy in phenomenal creation. Indian art, particularly, provides a ready means through which body, heart and mind can be brought into touch with the Spirit. That is the reason why, if the Indian system of education is to become truly Indian, Indian art and its great heritage should be brought into the very life of our students and teachers.

It is not necessary that every student should be trained to become an artist. But it is necessary that every student should be given facilities to develop his or her artistic faculty and to train his or her taste and also to refine his or her sense of beauty and the insight of form and colour. It is also necessary that those who create should be habituated to produce higher forms of art. Our endeavour should be such that the nation is habituated to accept the beautiful in preference to the ugly, the noble in preference to the vulgar, the fine in preference to the crude, the harmonious in preference to the gaudy. In the words of Sri Aurobindo:

> A nation surrounded daily by the beautiful, noble, fine and harmonious becomes that which it is habituated to contemplate and realises the fullness of the expanding Spirit in itself.[4]

---

[4] Sri Aurobindo: *National Value of Art*, Centenary Edition, Volume 17, p. 251

TOWARDS UNIVERSAL FRATERNITY

I

If there is one central theme in human history, it is that of universal solidarity. None is alone in the world, except that psychologically one may feel lonely in the darkness of night, even when stars twinkle and invite for company. The whole world is our friend and our helper, only we know not that there is an underlying unity in the whole universe, and this unity never leaves us even if we, in our egoism, try to separate our-selves in a vain attempt to feel self-existence and independence from our relationships, whether with the world or with the transcendental, which are always present. The entire history of humanity can be regarded as a struggle between human egoism which builds up divisions against the overpowering forces of unity.

The individual and the universe have an intimate and mutual relationship, and this relationship is inalienable, even when the individual combats with the universe by building up the walls of division, of ego and of separateness. It is by means of the universe that the individual is impelled to realise himself. But this universalisation does not mean the annulment of the individual; for the, universal also individual realises itself for manifesting itself in its totality. That is why the individual universalises and the universal individualises and both have some kind of mutuality, which can be realised only when the limiting egoism is abolished. It is this large truth that is translated in the human endeavour to arrive at universal solidarity, which yet retains the individuality of the constituent groups, nations and individuals. And this is governed by a law of simultaneous unity and diversity, — diversity manifesting unity and unity manifesting diversity.

There is, however, a limiting factor — the factor of the operation of ignorance, which creates the law of conflict and the law of struggle. According to this law, every individual finds himself or herself in a long march through the night, surrounded by foes, tortured by weariness and pain, towards the goal that few can hope to reach, and where none may tarry long. In modern times, Darwin has formulated in Biology the law of evolution, and its formula is that of struggle for existence and survival of the fittest. Bertrand Russell, describing the law of struggle in another context, points out:

> One by one, as they march, our comrades vanish from our sight, seized by the silent orders of omnipotent Death. Very brief is the time in which we can help them, in which their happiness or misery is decided... Brief and powerless is Man's life; on him and all his race is raised the slow, sure doom falls pitiless and dark. Blind to good and evil, reckless of destruction, omnipotent matter rolls on its relentless way...[1]

Bertrand Russell represents the materialist or neutralist view of the law of struggle. But even the opposite view, the spiritual view of the universe, cannot be blind to the law of struggle which operates in the world under the

---

[1] Bertrand Russell: *Freeeman's Worship and Other Essays*, Unwin Paper Back, 1976, p.19

compulsion of cosmic ignorance. Therefore, the old Upanishads described this law in the formula which is uncompromising and thoroughgoing, namely, "the eater eating is eaten". And Sri Aurobindo describes it in the following words: *"War and destruction are not only a universal principle of our life here in its purely material aspect, but also of our mental and moral existence. It is self-evident that in the actual life of man intellectual, social, political, moral we can make no real step forward without a struggle, a battle between what exists and lives and what seeks to exist and live and between all that stand behind either."*[2]

The materialist, even when he aims at the realisation of ideals, falls ultimately into an abyss of the darkness of Matter. On the other hand, the spiritual seeker, even when he attains peace, unity and oneness, cannot abrogate the law of struggle which is so pervasive and so compelling. In other words, none, the materialist nor the spiritualist, can wish away the fact of struggle, of division, of conflict and even of destruction. The only way by which this law can be overcome is to conquer the fact of ignorance and ultimately to eliminate it from the life of the individual and ultimately from the life of the collectivity. And there is no other way than that of spiritual contemplation; and even spiritual contemplation has to be matured in spiritual realisation. And considering that even when a few individuals live in spiritual realisation, the world continues to live in struggle and destruction, in strife and pain, we are obliged to conclude that even the individual spiritual realisation is not enough. We have to contemplate collective self-realisation. In any case, if unity is to be realised, if unity is to actualised, it seems that it

---

[2] Sri Aurobindo: *Essays on the Gita*, Centenary Edition, Volume 13, pp.40 -- 41

can only be done by the abolition of the root cause of division and conflict. This means that abolition of ignorance; and the abolition of ignorance is fundamentally a spiritual issue.

II

We are living today at once in the best of times and in the worst of times. Ours is the best time because at no time in the world history, men and women have aspired for human unity as ardently and as comprehensively as today. The fact that the combined will of the people of the world has produced the agency of United Nations to prevent war, to maintain peace and to subserve the goal of universal solidarity, is a concrete proof of the fact that we are living at a very propitious moment. And yet, we find humanity gravitating downward, in spite of tremendous scientific advances, — or else because of these very advances, which have provided ready means to gratify and multiply material pleasures, — into a state of arrestation from where higher aspiration can easily be exiled. We are threatened by the possibility of nuclear bombardment at the hand of some capricious will and of collapse of the environmental protection; we are threatened by the spread of diseases, which destroy the principle of life itself; we are threatened by the possibility of misuse of biological engineering, which can create monsters or anti-human species, perhaps much worse than dinosaurs; we are threatened by the acute accumulation of inertia, on the one hand, and uncontrolled passions of competition and search for the gratification of undying hunger, on the other. This is the proof that we are living today in the worst of times. This battle between the best and the worst can be triumphantly settled in favour of the best if three wise counsels prevail:

1. That humanity rises in maturity so as to make the right use of scientific discoveries and inventions in order that they are not utilised in the service of the lower impulses but for raising the heights of cultural life;

2. That the nations of the world cooperate with each other in assuring environmental protection and raising the standard of life even of the least developed countries; and

3. That human beings become global in their consciousness so as to generate genuine goodwill and a sense of universal brotherhood.

It is fortunate that in the advanced thought of the world, these three things are being advocated, but the voice of this advocacy is rather shrill and it is hardly heard by those who matter. The real difficulty is that these three things demand a radical change in human nature, and humanity does not seem to be prepared to respond to the demands of this change.

In 1967, U Thant the then Secretary-General of the United Nations Organisation had stated the need for this change. He had declared:

> That a fraction of the amounts that are going to be spent in 1967 on arms could finance economic, social, national and world programmes to an extent so far unimaginable is a notion within the grasp of the man in the street. Men, if they unite, are now capable of foreseeing and, to a certain point, determining the future of human development. This, however, is possible if we stop fearing and harassing one another and if together we accept, welcome and prepare the changes that

> must inevitably take place. If this means a change in human nature, well, it is high time we worked for it; what must surely change is certain political attitudes and habits man has.

It will be evident that the issue is spiritual; the issue is that of spiritual contemplation; the issue is of spiritual action.

III

Let us dwell on this point in a different context. The aim of universal solidarity has come up in the forefront of human idealism today; but we are not able to understand the real significance of this turn; we have not yet grasped the necessity of this solidarity, on the one hand, and its dangers, on the other. Its necessity is still being conceived in terms of the drive towards economic centralisation, legislative and social uniformity and towards mechanisation even in matters of human management and control of human affairs. It is still not being recognised that the social and political unity of humankind is not necessarily propitious, and its necessity lies in the fact that humanity can fulfil its higher dreams for freedom and brotherhood only if the sense of oneness, the sense of mutuality and harmony can prevail.

As Sri Aurobindo has warned us:

> It must be remembered that greater social or political unity is not necessarily a boon in itself; it is only worth pursuing in so far as it provides a means and a framework for a

better, richer, more happy and puissant individual and collective life.³

Let us take the example of the Roman Empire; for it provides a historical illustration of an organisation of unity which transcended the limits of the nation, and its advantages and disadvantages are there perfectly typified. The advantages of unity that mere forged by that great Empire were its admirable organisation, peace, widespread security, order and material well being. But the disadvantages arose from its tendency to centralise, to impose uniformity, and, as a result, the individual, the city, the region had to sacrifice their independent life and they became mechanical parts of a machine. The organisation was great and admirable, but the individual dwindled and life lost its colour, richness, variety, freedom and victorious impulse towards creation. Eventually, therefore, the Roman Empire declined and failed; the huge mechanism of centralisation and uniformity brought about the smallness and feebleness of the individual; mechanisation prevailed, and the Empire lost even its great conservative vitality and died of an increasing stagnation.

From this example, we can conclude as to what is likely to happen if the push towards unity which has become prominent comes to be sustained only on the basis of uniformity, centralisation and mechanisation. We can foresee that after some first outburst of satisfied and joyous activities there would follow a long period of conservation; there would then come about an increasing stagnancy and ultimately decay. We must, therefore, underline that unity, which must come about, must be created under

---

³ Sri Aruobindo: *The Ideal of Human Unity*, Centenary Edition, Vol. 15, p.263

other conditions and with safeguards, which will keep the race intact in the roots of its vitality, richly diverse in its oneness. We must have unity, but we must also have decentralisation, diversity and richness of interchange. But this can happen only if humanity and not only leading powers but all the nations join together to create a World Union of free nations.

We have to realise the peril of the World-State as opposed to World Union; for if it comes about, the nation as we know it might disappear and strict unification would come to be imposed; a vast uniformity would come to rule; and a united humanity would result in a regulated socialisation. This must be avoided; we must ensure a vigorous life of free and united nations; we must ensure liberty, mobile variations that act upon each other, and united but differentiated life.

But the central difficulty of synthesising unity with freedom lies in the tendency that is created in favour of centrifugal forces, — forces that tend to assert so much of independence that it would become inimical to unity. And this, in turn, results in a reaction that favours a heavy hand of uniformity and mechanisation. What then, is the solution?

In clear terms, the solution lies in creating a new psychology that is able to sustain interrelationship between nations which does not allow freedom to lapse into egoism, sense of rivalry, sense of division. Freedom must be wedded to the sense of mutuality and interdependent sharing of the contributions that each nation would bring into the common pool of richness of culture. This necessarily implies an inner change. We come here to the issue of unlocking the spiritual light and force, which lies latent in all of us, and which alone can bring about the needed inner change.

IV

In recent times, two ideas have become prominent, and if they are rightly fostered by humanity, we can arrive at universal solidarity that is based upon freedom and mutuality. The first idea is that of internationalism and the second idea is that of the religion of humanity. But both these ideas will require to be more chiselled and much more forged than what they attempt to convey to us today. Mere internationalism may provide a sense of wideness and globality. But unless internationalism comes to acknowledge and practise not only the political ideas of liberty, equality, and fraternity, but also their psychological, ethical and spiritual implications, internationalism may run the risk of falling into the peril of the idea of the World-State. The cause of the world union of free nations would then come to be injured. Therefore, we have to integrate internationalism with the religion of humanity. But, again, religion of humanity must not be construed in the image of a dogmatic, ritualistic and institutional framework of any particular creed. Religion of humanity should be conceived in terms of spirituality that transcends the boundaries of institutional religion. Spirituality demands, not adherence to any credal belief, but a living sense of fraternity. It is only when fraternity generates mutual goodwill among human beings and among nations that we can avoid the downward gravitation of unity into uniformity. It is only on the basis of the real brotherhood that the ideals of liberty and equality can become united.

As Sri Aurobindo points out:

Yet is brotherhood the real key to the triple gospel of the idea of humanity. The union of liberty and equality can only be achieved by the power of human brotherhood and it cannot be founded on anything else. But brotherhood exists only in the soul and by the soul; it can exist by nothing else. For this brotherhood is not a matter either of physical kinship or of vital association or intellectual agreement. When the soul claims freedom, it is the freedom of its self-development, the self-development of the divine in man in all his being. When it claims equality, what it is claiming is that freedom equally for all and the recognition of the same soul, the same godhead in all human beings. When it strives for brotherhood, it is founding that equal freedom of self-development on a common aim, a common life, a unity of mind and feeling founded upon the recognition of this inner spiritual unity. These three things are in fact the nature of the soul; for freedom, equality, unity are the eternal attributes of the Spirit. It is the practical recognition of this truth, it is the awakening of the soul in man and the attempt to get him to live from his soul and not from his ego which is the inner meaning of religion, and it is that to which the religion of humanity also must arrive before it can fulfil itself in the life of the race.[4]

---

[4] Sri Aurobindo: *Social and Political Thought,* Centenary Edition, Vol. 15, pp.546.47

V

We have spoken of the spiritual issue and of the spiritual solution, but the question is as to what we should mean by the term "spirituality". We have already distinguished spirituality from religion and pointed out that spirituality is not something institutional, ritualistic, mechanical or ceremonial; it is not related to dogma or creed. In positive terms, spirituality is a matter of knowledge and light and of spontaneous action that proceeds from intimate sympathy and oneness. But often spirituality is conceived as something ascetic and something which has no relationship with the world and its activities. Spirituality is thus conceived as something negative and even abstract as far as the mundane life is concerned.

But this view is partial and even misleading. It has arisen from an exclusive concentration only on one phase of experience in human history, during which the world came to be seen as meaningless or purposeless. If we examine the history of Indian spirituality, we shall find that the ascetic tendency of spirituality was only as experiment in sounding the extreme consequences of one of the aspects of spirituality. But in order to understand the all-comprehensive meaning of spirituality, we have to note that in India, spirituality has not been content merely to conquer the peaks of the spiritual self-existent Reality but also gained firm footing on the physical earth. This is the reason why India was at least for three thousand years vibrant with stupendous vitality, inexhaustible power of life and joy of life, and almost unimaginable prolific creativeness. This spirituality was also the force of strong intellectuality. It can even be said that this intellectuality was so robust that there is no historical parallel to such an intellectual labour and activity before the invention of printing and the facilities of modern science.

Indian history shows that it is a great error to suppose that spirituality flourishes best in an impoverished soil with the life half-killed and the intellect discouraged and intimidated. The Indian spiritual tendency did not shoot upward only to the abstract, the hidden and intangible; it cast its rays downward and outward to embrace the multiplicity of thought and richness of life. This would show that it would be a mistake to consider spirituality as something irrelevant to the problems of the world. In fact, if there is any power that can cure the ills of life and of the world truly and satisfactorily, it is only the power of the spirit; for Spirit, as conceived in the Veda and Upanishads, is the source of the world, it is the soul of the world, it is the inner breath of the world. This is the reason why when we are considering the question of the solution of the problem of the universal solidarity or of human unity, we have suggested that if unity must not degenerate into uniformity, the only way is to emphasise the need for a spiritual change, a change which does not run away from the world, but a change that transforms the world with the power of knowledge of the inmost self.

It is remarkable that the spirituality of the Indian renaissance has proclaimed the message of dynamic spirituality. Whether it is Maharshi Dayananda Saraswati, Swami Vivekananda, or Swami Ramtirtha, they have laid stress on applying spiritual knowledge to the problems of the world; they have advocated the view that spirituality is not an escape but it is an affirmation of power and sovereignty, that spirituality is not a matter of running away to the Himalayas but of transforming human life even in the densest fields of complex activities. Sri Aurobindo has spoken of acceptance of life in order to transform it by the power of the spirit; he has even looked upon all life as Yoga.

In this context, what vision shall we put before ourselves in regard to the activities of life and their organisation if we are to prepare ourselves to make our own contribution to the aim of actualisation of human unity which, as we have argued here, can be truly salutary for the human race, only if dynamic spirituality is applied? As Sri Aurobindo has pointed out, even in the early stages of spiritualisation, the pioneering individuals and the society would make the revealing and finding of the divine Self for the human being the first aim of all activities, of education, of science, of ethics, of art, of economic and political structure. There would be an emphasis on embracing of the entire range of knowledge but the whole trend and aim would be to concentrate on the spirit as the object of discoveries, of self-development and self-finding, even while not neglecting efficiency and chiselled perfection. Physical and psychical sciences would be pursued not merely to gain the knowledge of the world and nature and to use them for material human ends but also to know the spirit in the world and the ways of the spirit in its masks and behind them. Ethics would be pursued not to establish a rule of action, supplementary to the social law but to develop the divine nature in the human being. Art would be pursued to reveal the Truth and Beauty of things visible and invisible in the forms or symbols and significant figures.

The new society would look upon every individual as a living soul, and each one would be given the help and the power so as to grow into self-perfection. This society would give to every individual not only the joy of work but also free leisure to grow inwardly, and lead a simple and beautiful life. Spirituality applied to social organisation would aim at realising the ideal law of social development. This ideal law would seek the harmony of the individual and the society. There is no better formulation of the ideal law of social development than that of Sri Aurobindo:

> Thus the law for the individual is to perfect his individuality by free development from within, but to respect and to aid and be aided by the same free development in others. His law is to harmonise his life with the life of the social aggregate and to pour himself out as a force for growth and perfection on humanity. The law for the community or nation is equally to perfect its corporate existence by a free development from within, aiding and taking full advantage of that of the individual, but to respect and to aid and be aided by the same free development of other communities and nations. Its law is to harmonise its life with that of the human aggregate and to pour itself out as a force for growth and perfection on humanity. The law for humanity is to pursue its upward evolution towards the finding and expression of the Divine in the type of mankind, taking full advantage of the free development and gains of all individuals and nations and groupings of men, to work towards the day when mankind may be really and not only ideally one divine family, but even then, when it has succeeded in unifying itself, to respect, aid and be aided by the free growth and activity of its individuals and constituent aggregates.[5]

---

[5] Sri Aurobindo: *Social and Political Thought*, Centenary Edition, Vol. 15, pp.63-64

VI

The path that lies before us is a difficult path; many might even consider it to be impracticable; many, even if they concede that it is practicable, might not pursue it, since it might seem to be a path that would take extremely long to arrive at success. But we have to consider the fact that humanity has irreversibly become global and the advantages of its globality can be rightly promoted and its disadvantages can be rightly avoided only if we can apply the truth of spiritual knowledge to the difficult issues of unity and freedom.

If this path is to be declared impracticable, we shall still need to make experiments on this path before we can scientifically declare it to be impracticable; similarly, to those who may refuse to walk on this path simply because success on that path would be so far off as not to be achievable in their own life time, we have to make an appeal by reminding ourselves that we do not live for ourselves, that we can only sow in our life true seeds of trees which can give fruits only to the coming generation.

At the same time, who can say that success would not come now? History teaches that unexpected events take place suddenly because of the past accumulation of the forces. We know of revolutions that have swept off the obstacles of the past within a relatively short period. We may also find, by means of detailed scrutiny of the revolutions of the past that behind them a spiritual revolution was already taking secret shape. It would not, therefore, seem unreasonable to predict that, considering the critical stage through which we are passing today where no solution that seems to be practicable will ultimately work, there would grow up an increasing number of individuals and even groups with a new urge and resolution to break a new path and to arrive at some fulfilling result rapidly rather than slowly. In any case, for those who see that spiritual solution is the only solution, the only course of action is to pursue that solution resolutely, irrespective whether we shall attain success in our own life time or whether the effort we make today will bear fruit later and benefit the posterity.

Let us then conclude that we have no reason to fear to aspire; we have no reason to feel discouraged in determining the spiritual course of action; we have no reason merely to stand and watch, — we have every reason to take the staff in our hand and set out for the journey.